STILL
PUMPED
FROM USING THE
MOUSE

A DILBERT® Book by Scott Adams

BXTREE

First published in the UK 1996 by Boxtree Limited,
Broadwall House, 21 Broadwall, London SE1 9PL.

First published in the USA 1996 by Andrews and McMeel,
4900 Main Street, Kansas City, Missouri 64112, USA

Copyright © 1996 United Feature Syndicate, Inc. All rights reserved.

DILBERT® is a registered trademark of United Feature Syndicate, Inc.
DOGBERT and DILBERT appear in the comic strip DILBERT®, distributed
by United Feature Syndicate, Inc.

10 9 8 7 6 5 4 3 2 1

ISBN: 0 7522 2265 1

Printed and bound in Great Britain by Redwood Books, Trowbridge Wiltshire.

A CIP catalogue record for this book is available from the British Library

I didn't forget this time, Pam.

Introduction

In the past few years several great cartoonists have decided to retire, much to the sadness of their fans. It makes me feel like the guy who took the home movies of the Kennedy assassination—the right side of my brain is saying, "What a horrible tragedy," while the left side is making those little cash register noises.

When the announcement of Bill Watterson's retirement came out several reporters called me to get my reaction. The phone conversations went like this:

Reporter: "What do you think about Watterson retiring?"

Me: "Hee hee. Oops."

Reporter: "Are you giggling?"

Me: "Um, no, I'm weeping over the loss of an excellent comic strip."

Reporter: "What's that music in the background?"

Me: "My cats are forming a conga line. They don't seem to appreciate the sadness of this situation."

Cats: "Tequila!!!!"

Maybe it didn't go exactly like that, but you get the general picture.

Anyway, the question I'm most often asked lately is whether I'm also "burned out" and planning to retire. The answer is no, I haven't made enough money to be "burned out" yet. I only have enough money to feel "tired" or maybe "overworked." And frankly, I blame you readers for that.

In any event, quitting just isn't my style. I'm more likely to hire illegal immigrants to do the writing and drawing for me. They might not bring the same wit and artistic integrity to the strip that I do … and it might not be in English … but let's face it, my work isn't a home run every single day either. It'll probably take a decade for anybody to notice. And by then maybe I'll be "burned out" too.

Speaking of home runs, you can still join Dogbert's New Ruling Class (DNRC) before Dogbert conquers the world and makes everybody else our domestic servants. As you might have noticed, the members of the DNRC are brighter and more attractive than the "induhviduals" who have not joined, so don't be an induhvidual.

To join the DNRC, simply put your name on the list for the free Dilbert Newsletter, published approximately "whenever I feel like it," or about four times a year.

If you want to receive the DNRC Newsletter via e-mail, send your e-mail address to:

ScottAdams@aol.com

If you prefer hard copies of the DNRC Newsletter, via snail mail, send your address to:

Dilbert Mailing List
c/o United Media
200 Madison Avenue
New York, NY 10016

S. Adams

http://www.unitedmedia.com/comics/dilbert/

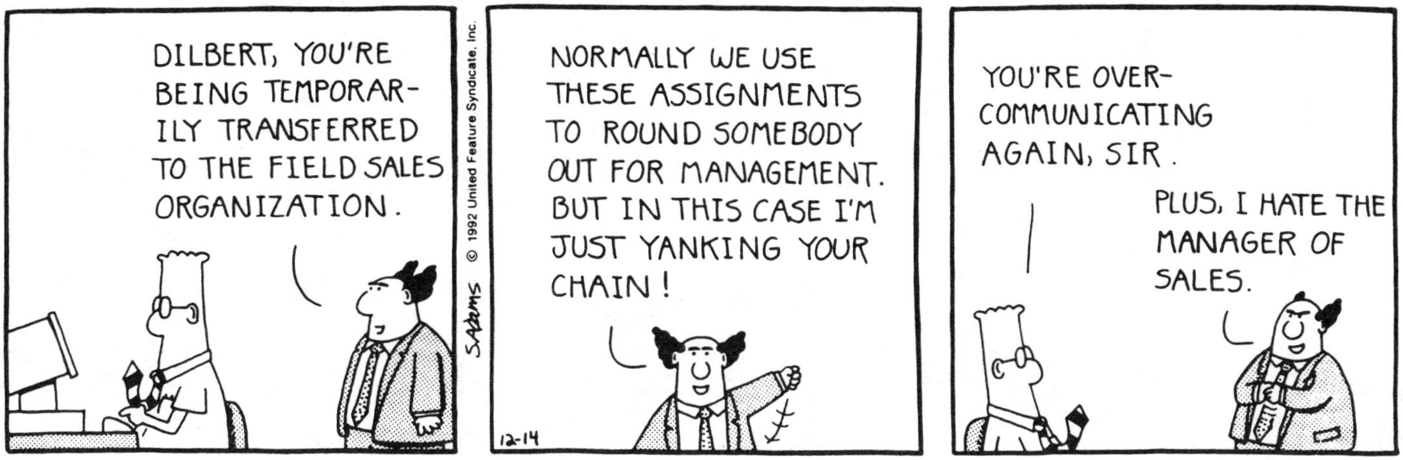
DILBERT, YOU'RE BEING TEMPORARILY TRANSFERRED TO THE FIELD SALES ORGANIZATION.
S.Adams © 1992 United Feature Syndicate, Inc.
NORMALLY WE USE THESE ASSIGNMENTS TO ROUND SOMEBODY OUT FOR MANAGEMENT. BUT IN THIS CASE I'M JUST YANKING YOUR CHAIN!
12-14
YOU'RE OVER-COMMUNICATING AGAIN, SIR.
PLUS, I HATE THE MANAGER OF SALES.

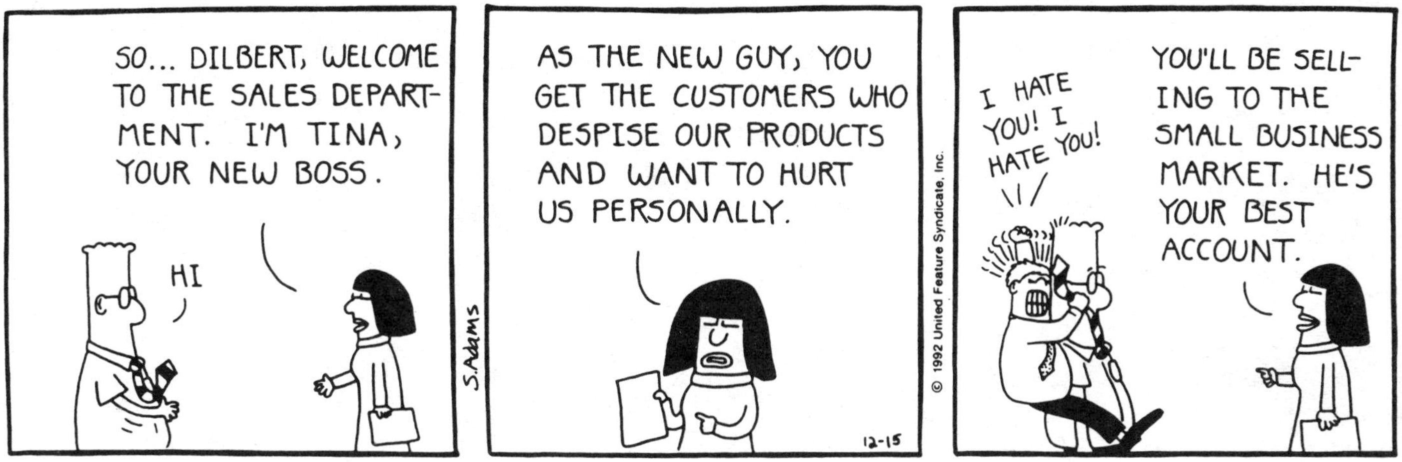
SO... DILBERT, WELCOME TO THE SALES DEPARTMENT. I'M TINA, YOUR NEW BOSS.
HI
S.Adams
AS THE NEW GUY, YOU GET THE CUSTOMERS WHO DESPISE OUR PRODUCTS AND WANT TO HURT US PERSONALLY.
12-15
© 1992 United Feature Syndicate, Inc.
I HATE YOU! I HATE YOU!
YOU'LL BE SELLING TO THE SMALL BUSINESS MARKET. HE'S YOUR BEST ACCOUNT.

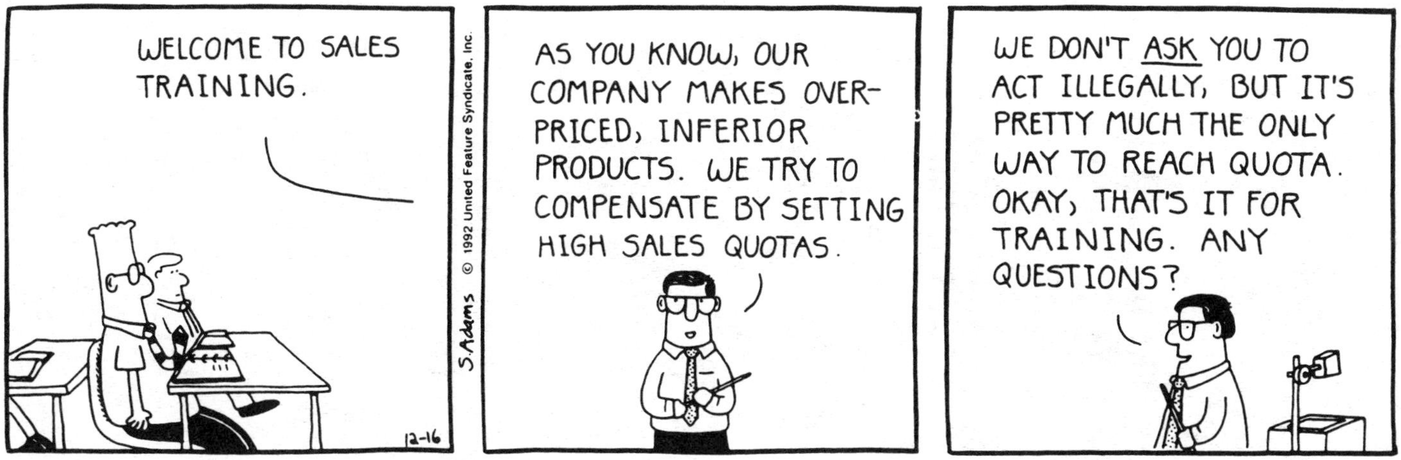
WELCOME TO SALES TRAINING.
12-16
S.Adams © 1992 United Feature Syndicate, Inc.
AS YOU KNOW, OUR COMPANY MAKES OVERPRICED, INFERIOR PRODUCTS. WE TRY TO COMPENSATE BY SETTING HIGH SALES QUOTAS.
WE DON'T ASK YOU TO ACT ILLEGALLY, BUT IT'S PRETTY MUCH THE ONLY WAY TO REACH QUOTA. OKAY, THAT'S IT FOR TRAINING. ANY QUESTIONS?

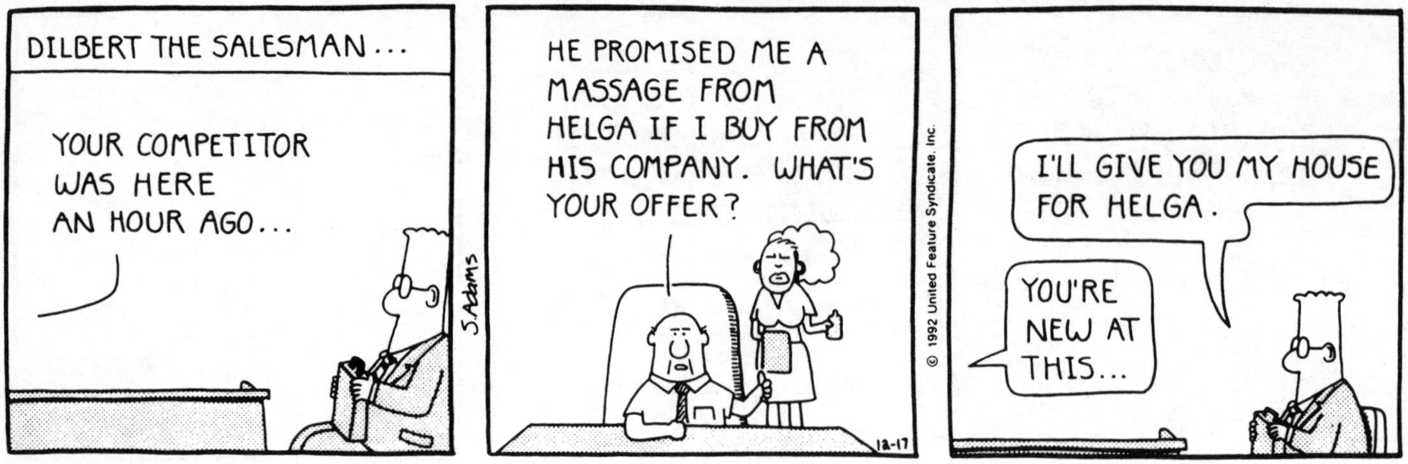
DILBERT THE SALESMAN...
YOUR COMPETITOR WAS HERE AN HOUR AGO...
S. Adams
HE PROMISED ME A MASSAGE FROM HELGA IF I BUY FROM HIS COMPANY. WHAT'S YOUR OFFER?
12-17
© 1992 United Feature Syndicate, Inc.
I'LL GIVE YOU MY HOUSE FOR HELGA.
YOU'RE NEW AT THIS...

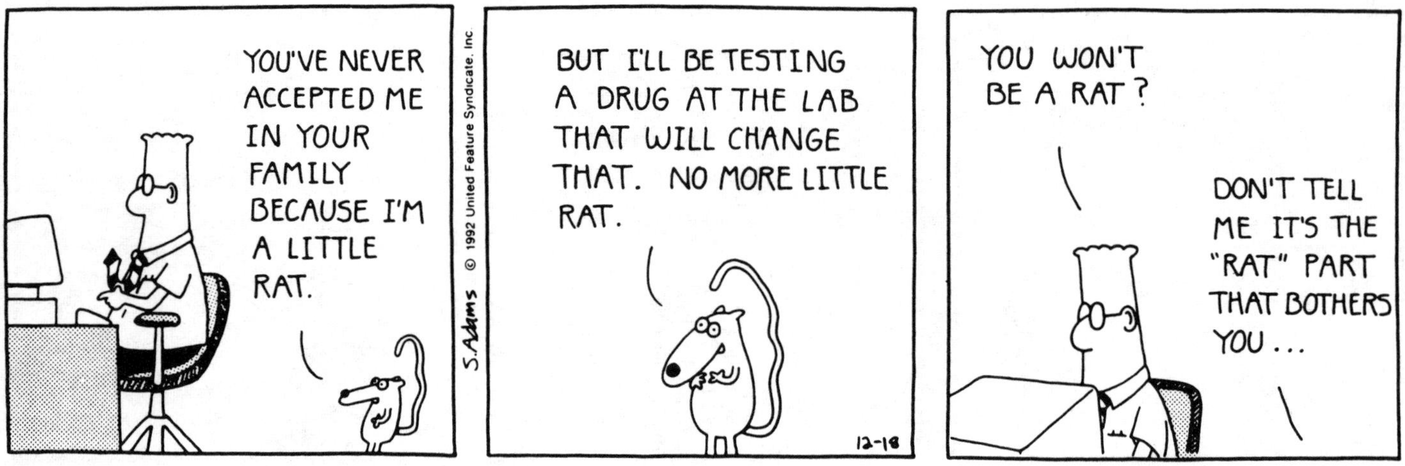
YOU'VE NEVER ACCEPTED ME IN YOUR FAMILY BECAUSE I'M A LITTLE RAT.
S. Adams © 1992 United Feature Syndicate, Inc.
BUT I'LL BE TESTING A DRUG AT THE LAB THAT WILL CHANGE THAT. NO MORE LITTLE RAT.
12-18
YOU WON'T BE A RAT?
DON'T TELL ME IT'S THE "RAT" PART THAT BOTHERS YOU...

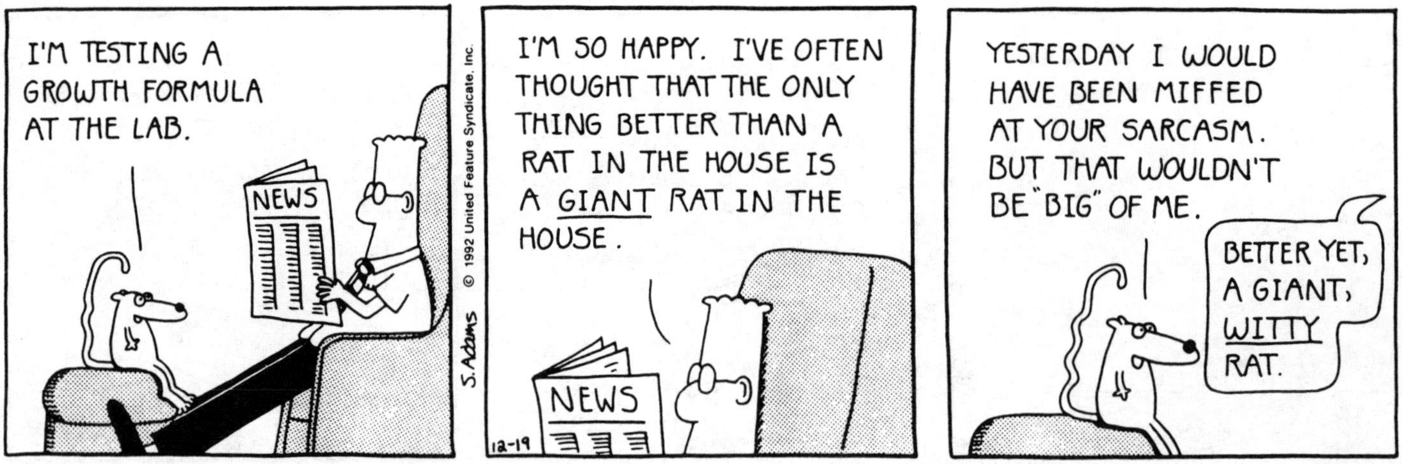
I'M TESTING A GROWTH FORMULA AT THE LAB.
NEWS
S. Adams © 1992 United Feature Syndicate, Inc.
I'M SO HAPPY. I'VE OFTEN THOUGHT THAT THE ONLY THING BETTER THAN A RAT IN THE HOUSE IS A GIANT RAT IN THE HOUSE.
NEWS
12-19
YESTERDAY I WOULD HAVE BEEN MIFFED AT YOUR SARCASM. BUT THAT WOULDN'T BE "BIG" OF ME.
BETTER YET, A GIANT, WITTY RAT.

I THOUGHT YOU MIGHT NEED HELP DECIDING WHAT TO GET ME FOR CHRISTMAS.
S. Adams
I STARTED BY DOING A COMPLETE ANALYSIS OF YOUR FINANCIAL SITUATION.
YOUR UTTER LACK OF A SOCIAL LIFE HAS RESULTED IN SIGNIFICANT CASH RESERVES.
THAT COMBINED WITH A SECOND MORTGAGE WOULD MAKE $50,000 AVAILABLE FOR MY GIFT.
I BOUGHT YOU A HAT.
IT WAS ON SALE.
© 1992 United Feature Syndicate, Inc.
12-10
IT SEEMS THAT EVERY YEAR AT ABOUT THIS TIME I FEEL LIKE BEATING SOMEBODY SENSELESS WITH A YULE LOG.

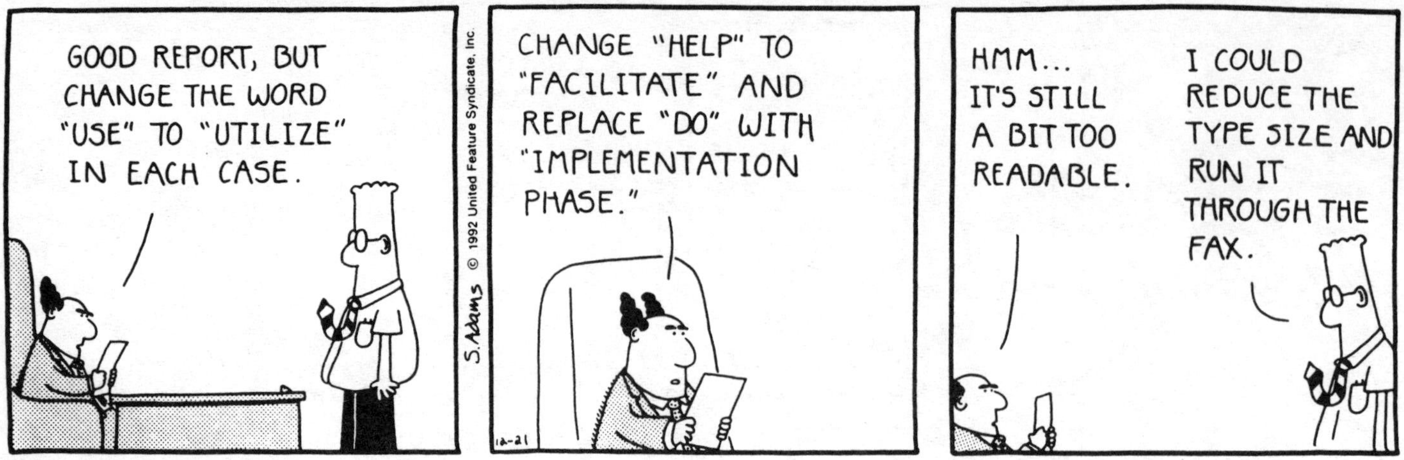
GOOD REPORT, BUT CHANGE THE WORD "USE" TO "UTILIZE" IN EACH CASE.
S. Adams © 1992 United Feature Syndicate, Inc.
CHANGE "HELP" TO "FACILITATE" AND REPLACE "DO" WITH "IMPLEMENTATION PHASE."
12-21
HMM... IT'S STILL A BIT TOO READABLE.
I COULD REDUCE THE TYPE SIZE AND RUN IT THROUGH THE FAX.

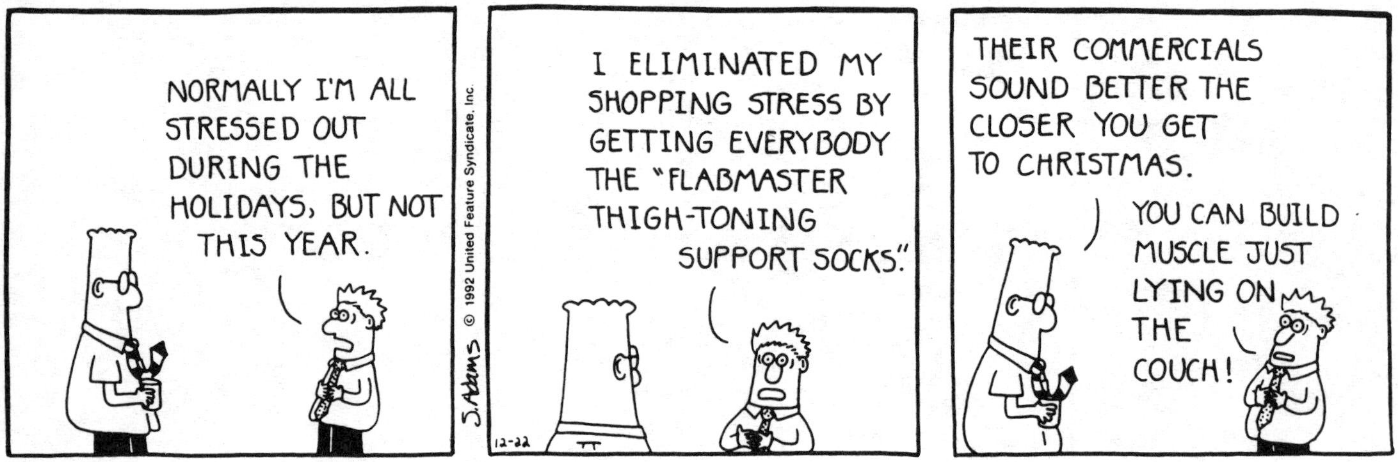
NORMALLY I'M ALL STRESSED OUT DURING THE HOLIDAYS, BUT NOT THIS YEAR.
S. Adams © 1992 United Feature Syndicate, Inc.
I ELIMINATED MY SHOPPING STRESS BY GETTING EVERYBODY THE "FLABMASTER THIGH-TONING SUPPORT SOCKS."
12-22
THEIR COMMERCIALS SOUND BETTER THE CLOSER YOU GET TO CHRISTMAS.
YOU CAN BUILD MUSCLE JUST LYING ON THE COUCH!

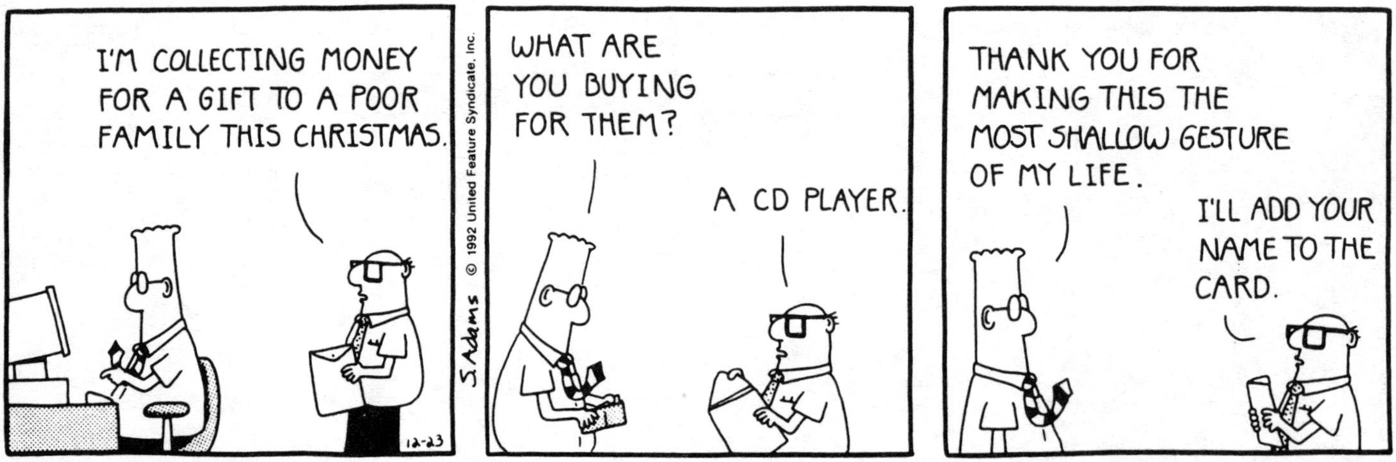
I'M COLLECTING MONEY FOR A GIFT TO A POOR FAMILY THIS CHRISTMAS.
12-23
S. Adams © 1992 United Feature Syndicate, Inc.
WHAT ARE YOU BUYING FOR THEM?
A CD PLAYER.
THANK YOU FOR MAKING THIS THE MOST SHALLOW GESTURE OF MY LIFE.
I'LL ADD YOUR NAME TO THE CARD.

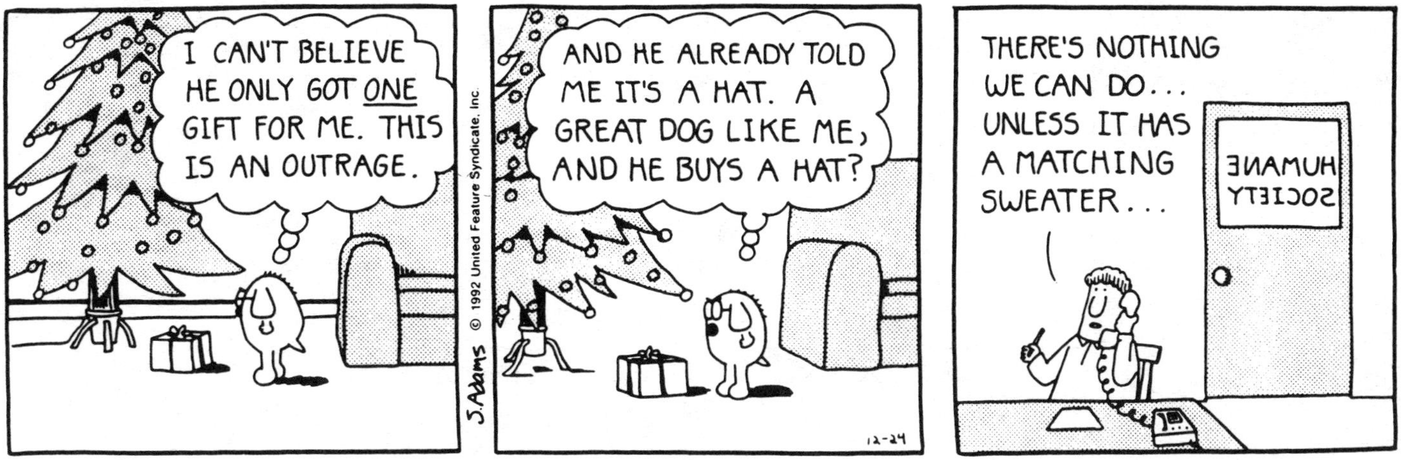
I CAN'T BELIEVE HE ONLY GOT ONE GIFT FOR ME. THIS IS AN OUTRAGE.
AND HE ALREADY TOLD ME IT'S A HAT. A GREAT DOG LIKE ME, AND HE BUYS A HAT?
THERE'S NOTHING WE CAN DO... UNLESS IT HAS A MATCHING SWEATER...
HUMANE SOCIETY

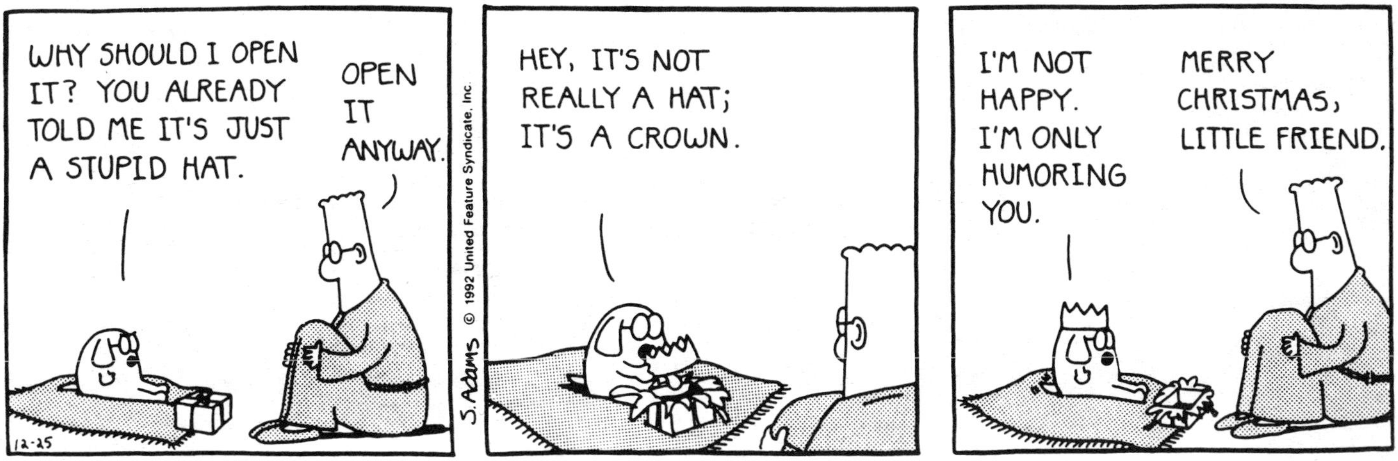
WHY SHOULD I OPEN IT? YOU ALREADY TOLD ME IT'S JUST A STUPID HAT.
OPEN IT ANYWAY.
HEY, IT'S NOT REALLY A HAT; IT'S A CROWN.
I'M NOT HAPPY. I'M ONLY HUMORING YOU.
MERRY CHRISTMAS, LITTLE FRIEND.

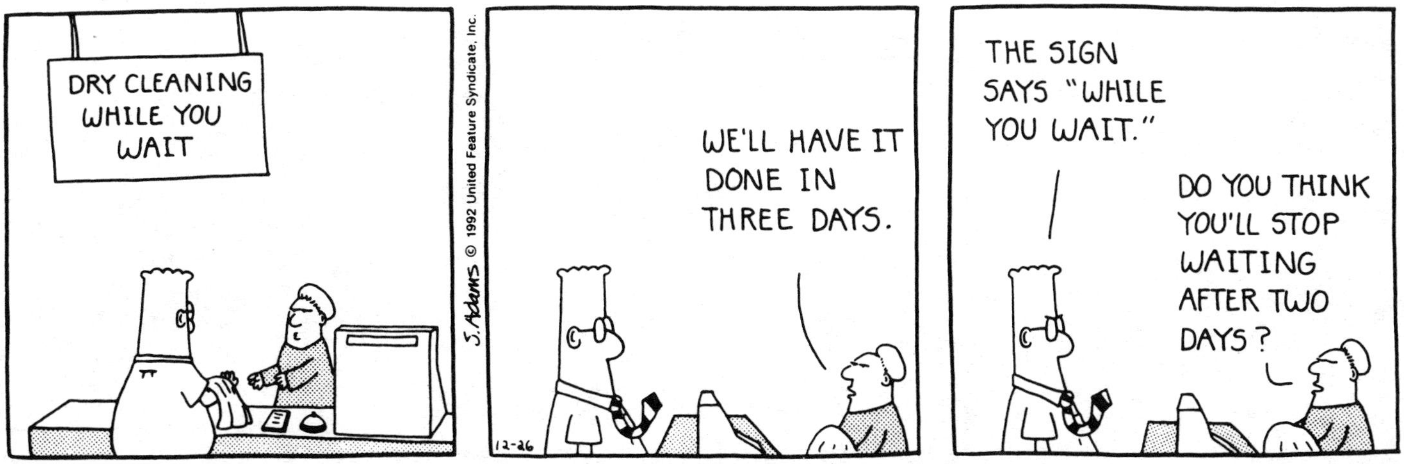
DRY CLEANING WHILE YOU WAIT
WE'LL HAVE IT DONE IN THREE DAYS.
THE SIGN SAYS "WHILE YOU WAIT."
DO YOU THINK YOU'LL STOP WAITING AFTER TWO DAYS?

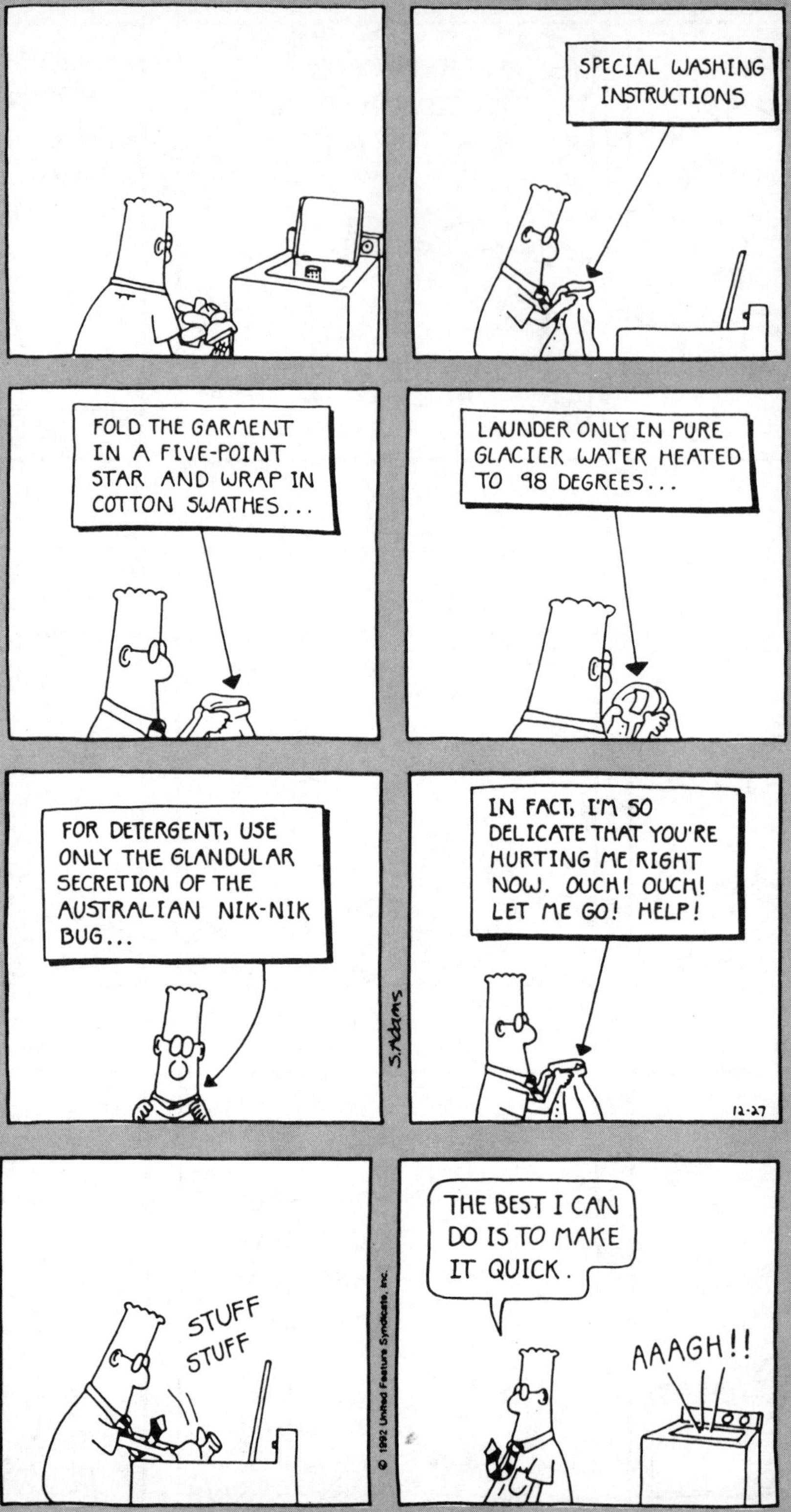
SPECIAL WASHING INSTRUCTIONS
FOLD THE GARMENT IN A FIVE-POINT STAR AND WRAP IN COTTON SWATHES...
LAUNDER ONLY IN PURE GLACIER WATER HEATED TO 98 DEGREES...
FOR DETERGENT, USE ONLY THE GLANDULAR SECRETION OF THE AUSTRALIAN NIK-NIK BUG...
S. Adams
IN FACT, I'M SO DELICATE THAT YOU'RE HURTING ME RIGHT NOW. OUCH! OUCH! LET ME GO! HELP!
12-27
STUFF STUFF
THE BEST I CAN DO IS TO MAKE IT QUICK.
AAAGH!!

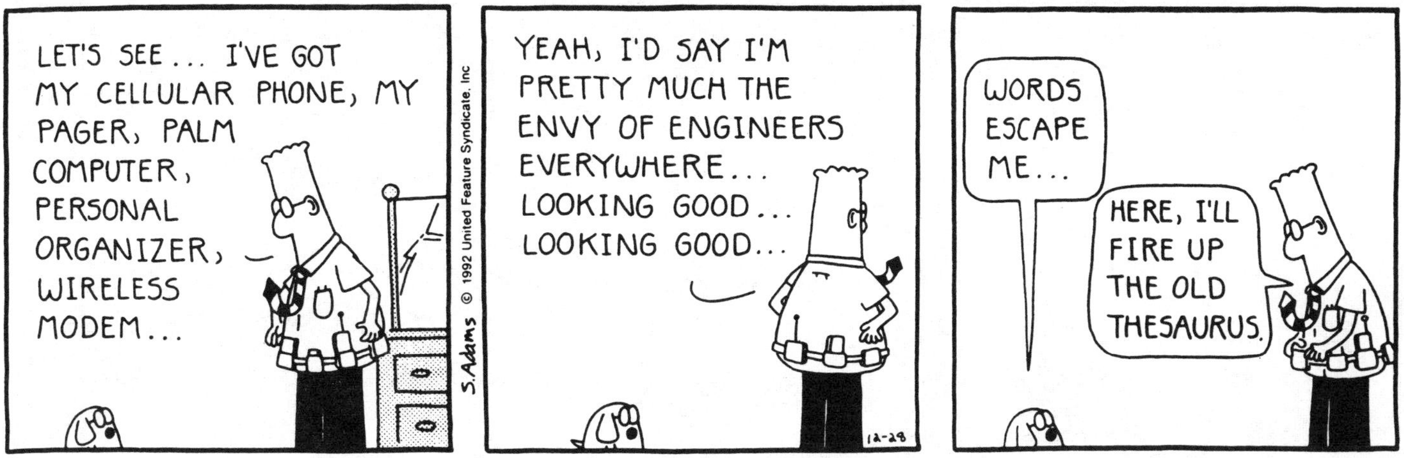
LET'S SEE... I'VE GOT MY CELLULAR PHONE, MY PAGER, PALM COMPUTER, PERSONAL ORGANIZER, WIRELESS MODEM...
S. Adams © 1992 United Feature Syndicate, Inc
YEAH, I'D SAY I'M PRETTY MUCH THE ENVY OF ENGINEERS EVERYWHERE... LOOKING GOOD... LOOKING GOOD...
12-28
WORDS ESCAPE ME...
HERE, I'LL FIRE UP THE OLD THESAURUS.

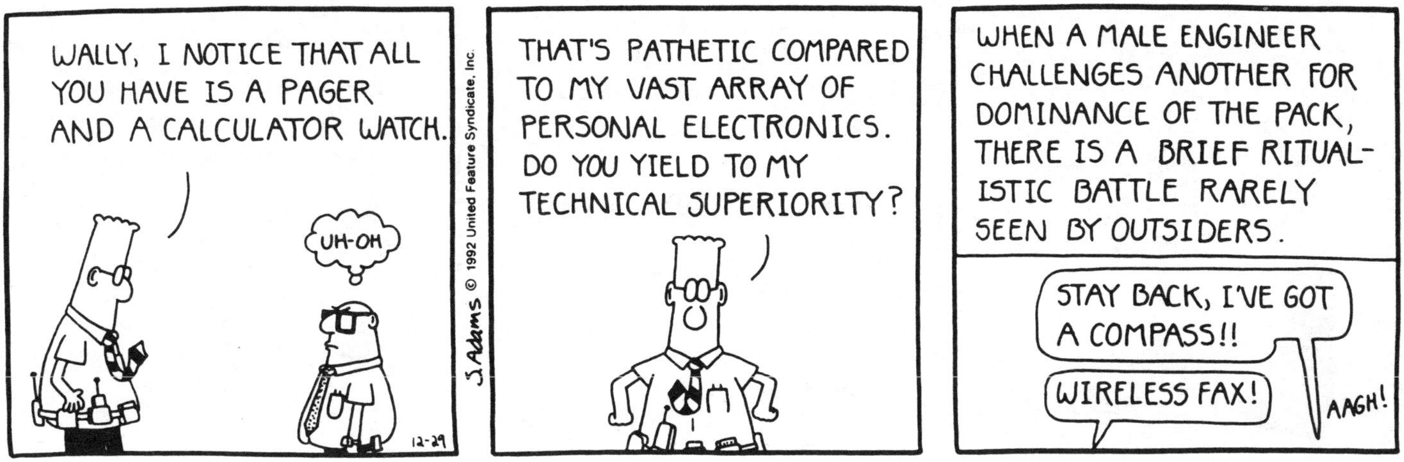
WALLY, I NOTICE THAT ALL YOU HAVE IS A PAGER AND A CALCULATOR WATCH.
UH-OH
12-29
S. Adams © 1992 United Feature Syndicate, Inc.
THAT'S PATHETIC COMPARED TO MY VAST ARRAY OF PERSONAL ELECTRONICS. DO YOU YIELD TO MY TECHNICAL SUPERIORITY?
WHEN A MALE ENGINEER CHALLENGES ANOTHER FOR DOMINANCE OF THE PACK, THERE IS A BRIEF RITUALISTIC BATTLE RARELY SEEN BY OUTSIDERS.
STAY BACK, I'VE GOT A COMPASS!!
WIRELESS FAX!
AAGH!

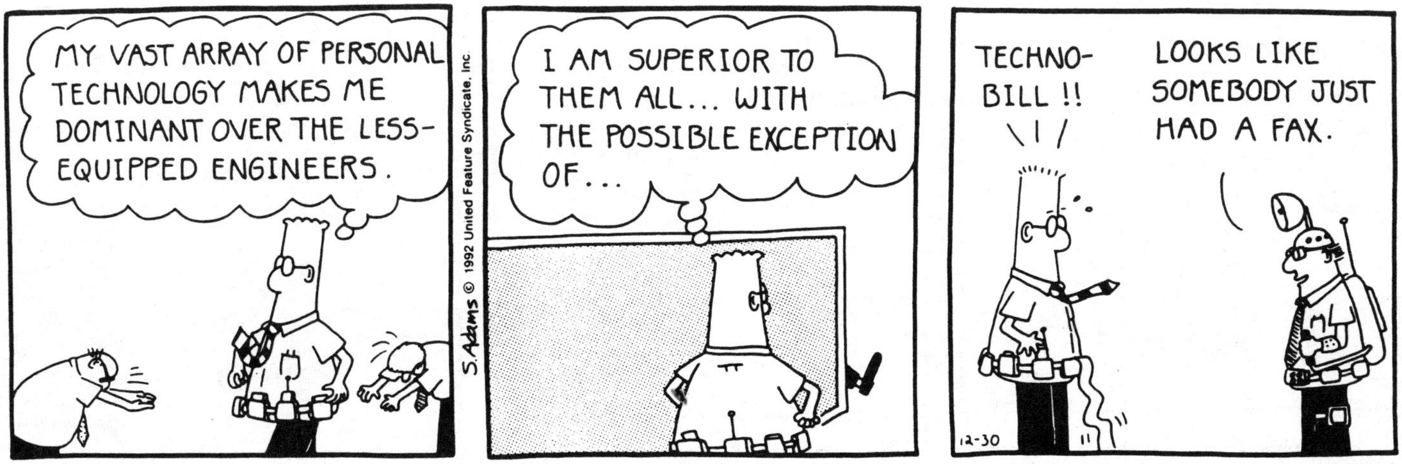
MY VAST ARRAY OF PERSONAL TECHNOLOGY MAKES ME DOMINANT OVER THE LESS-EQUIPPED ENGINEERS.
S. Adams © 1992 United Feature Syndicate, Inc.
I AM SUPERIOR TO THEM ALL... WITH THE POSSIBLE EXCEPTION OF...
TECHNO-BILL !!
LOOKS LIKE SOMEBODY JUST HAD A FAX.
12-30

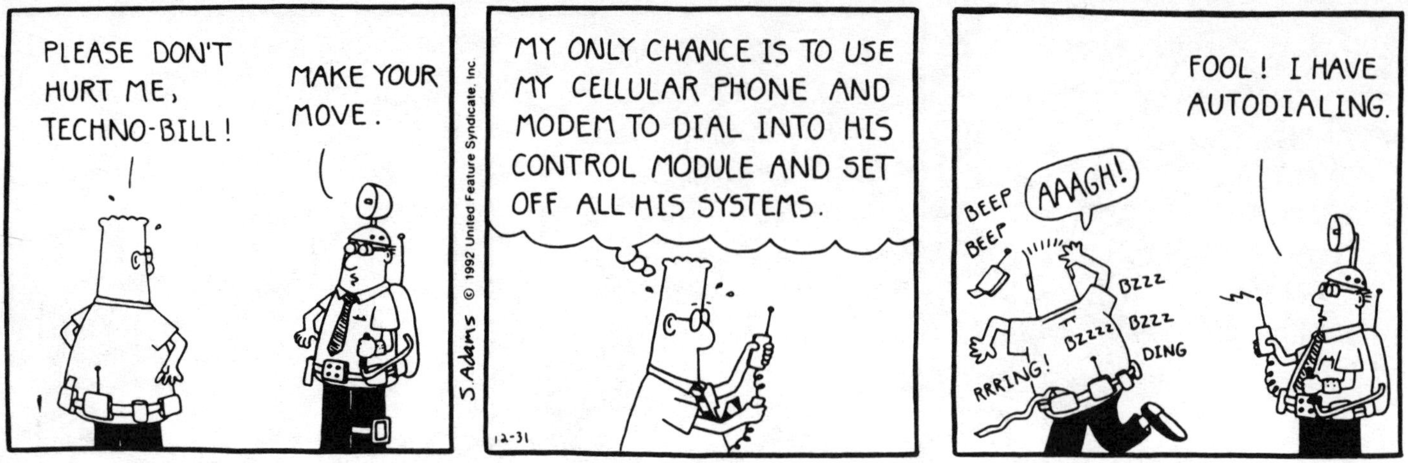
PLEASE DON'T HURT ME, TECHNO-BILL!
MAKE YOUR MOVE.
S. Adams © 1992 United Feature Syndicate, Inc.
MY ONLY CHANCE IS TO USE MY CELLULAR PHONE AND MODEM TO DIAL INTO HIS CONTROL MODULE AND SET OFF ALL HIS SYSTEMS.
12-31
FOOL! I HAVE AUTODIALING.
AAAGH!
BEEP BEEP
BZZZ
BZZZZ
BZZZ
DING
RRRING!

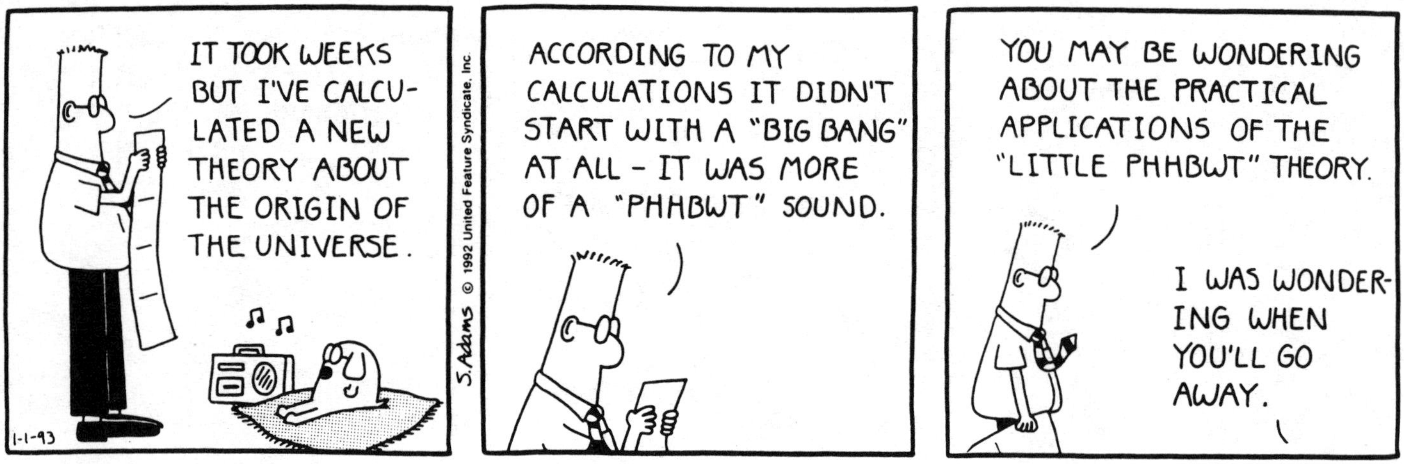
IT TOOK WEEKS BUT I'VE CALCULATED A NEW THEORY ABOUT THE ORIGIN OF THE UNIVERSE.
1-1-93
S. Adams © 1992 United Feature Syndicate, Inc.
ACCORDING TO MY CALCULATIONS IT DIDN'T START WITH A "BIG BANG" AT ALL – IT WAS MORE OF A "PHHBWT" SOUND.
YOU MAY BE WONDERING ABOUT THE PRACTICAL APPLICATIONS OF THE "LITTLE PHHBWT" THEORY.
I WAS WONDERING WHEN YOU'LL GO AWAY.

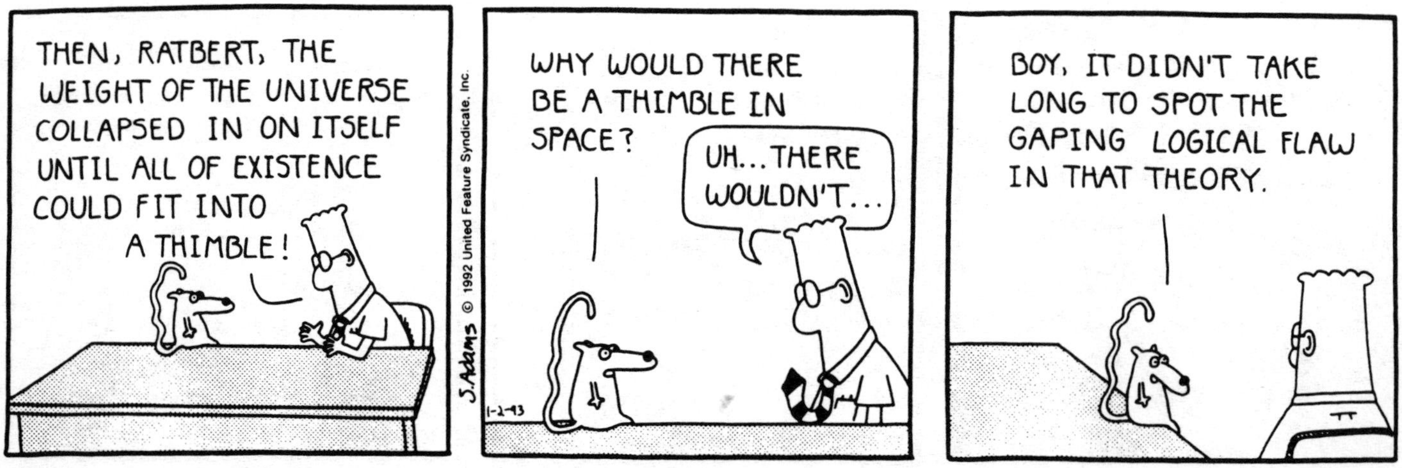
THEN, RATBERT, THE WEIGHT OF THE UNIVERSE COLLAPSED IN ON ITSELF UNTIL ALL OF EXISTENCE COULD FIT INTO A THIMBLE!
S. Adams © 1992 United Feature Syndicate, Inc.
WHY WOULD THERE BE A THIMBLE IN SPACE?
UH... THERE WOULDN'T...
1-2-93
BOY, IT DIDN'T TAKE LONG TO SPOT THE GAPING LOGICAL FLAW IN THAT THEORY.

FREE THERAPY
WHY IS IT FREE?
OUR THERAPISTS ARE FIRST YEAR PSYCHOLOGY STUDENTS.
WHAT HAVE I GOT TO LOSE?
SOMETIMES I HAVE LOW SELF-ESTEEM...
YOUR PROBLEM IS THAT YOU'RE UGLY. YOU SHOULD DRINK BEER UNTIL YOU FEEL HAND-SOME.
I THOUGHT YOU WOULD SAY SOME-THING ABOUT MY MOTHER.
S.Adams
1-3-93
GOOD POINT. YOUR MOTHER SHOULD DRINK BEER TOO. SHE'S PROBABLY AS UGLY AS YOU.
© 1992 United Feature Syndicate, Inc.
YOU'RE OVER-PRICED.
OOH, "MISTER LOW SELF-ESTEEM" IS UNHAPPY.

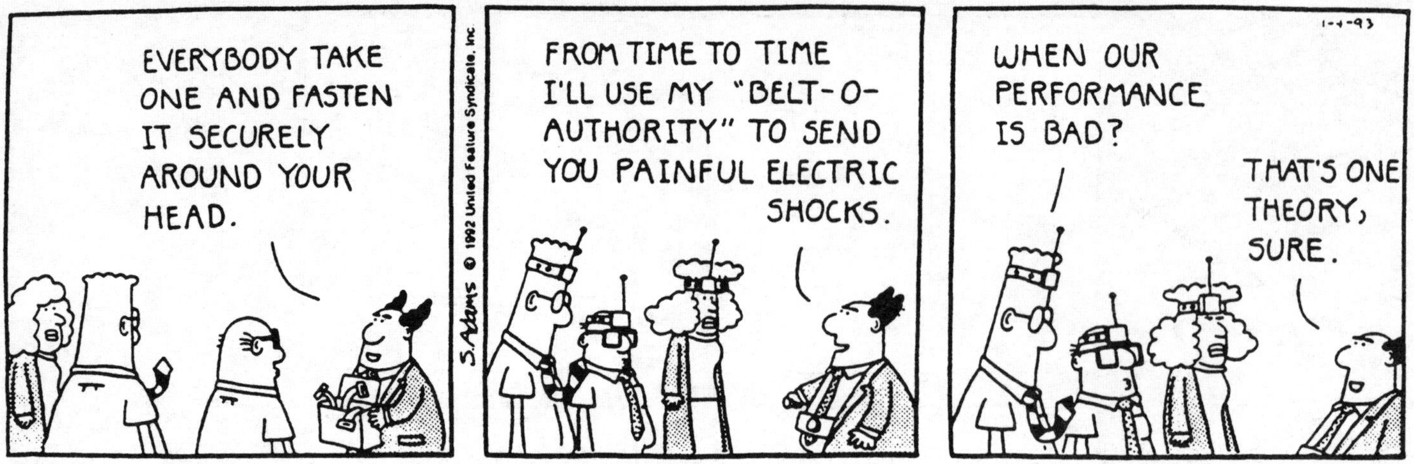
EVERYBODY TAKE ONE AND FASTEN IT SECURELY AROUND YOUR HEAD.
S. Adams © 1992 United Feature Syndicate, Inc.
FROM TIME TO TIME I'LL USE MY "BELT-O-AUTHORITY" TO SEND YOU PAINFUL ELECTRIC SHOCKS.
1-4-93
WHEN OUR PERFORMANCE IS BAD?
THAT'S ONE THEORY, SURE.

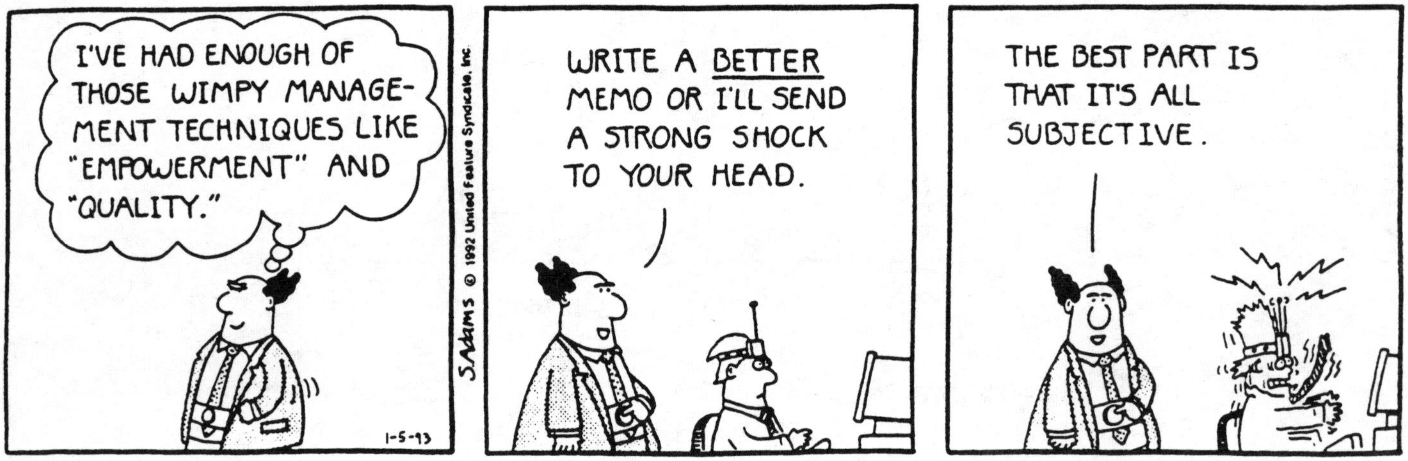
I'VE HAD ENOUGH OF THOSE WIMPY MANAGEMENT TECHNIQUES LIKE "EMPOWERMENT" AND "QUALITY."
1-5-93
S. Adams © 1992 United Feature Syndicate, Inc.
WRITE A BETTER MEMO OR I'LL SEND A STRONG SHOCK TO YOUR HEAD.
THE BEST PART IS THAT IT'S ALL SUBJECTIVE.

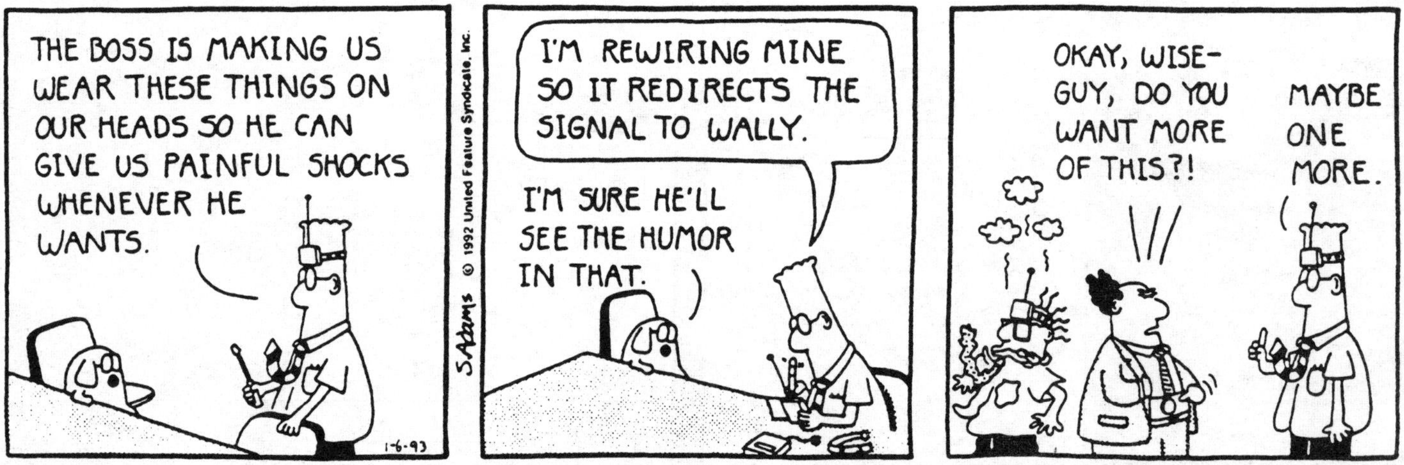
THE BOSS IS MAKING US WEAR THESE THINGS ON OUR HEADS SO HE CAN GIVE US PAINFUL SHOCKS WHENEVER HE WANTS.
1-6-93
S. Adams © 1992 United Feature Syndicate, Inc.
I'M REWIRING MINE SO IT REDIRECTS THE SIGNAL TO WALLY.
I'M SURE HE'LL SEE THE HUMOR IN THAT.
OKAY, WISE-GUY, DO YOU WANT MORE OF THIS?!
MAYBE ONE MORE.

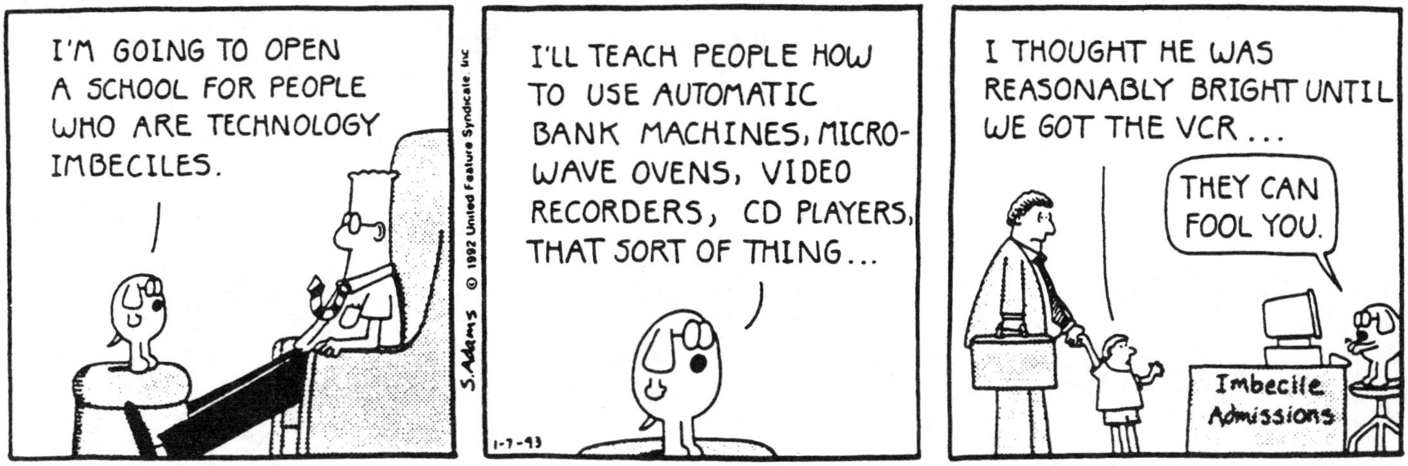
I'M GOING TO OPEN A SCHOOL FOR PEOPLE WHO ARE TECHNOLOGY IMBECILES.
S. Adams © 1992 United Feature Syndicate, Inc
I'LL TEACH PEOPLE HOW TO USE AUTOMATIC BANK MACHINES, MICRO-WAVE OVENS, VIDEO RECORDERS, CD PLAYERS, THAT SORT OF THING...
1-7-93
I THOUGHT HE WAS REASONABLY BRIGHT UNTIL WE GOT THE VCR...
THEY CAN FOOL YOU.
Imbecile Admissions

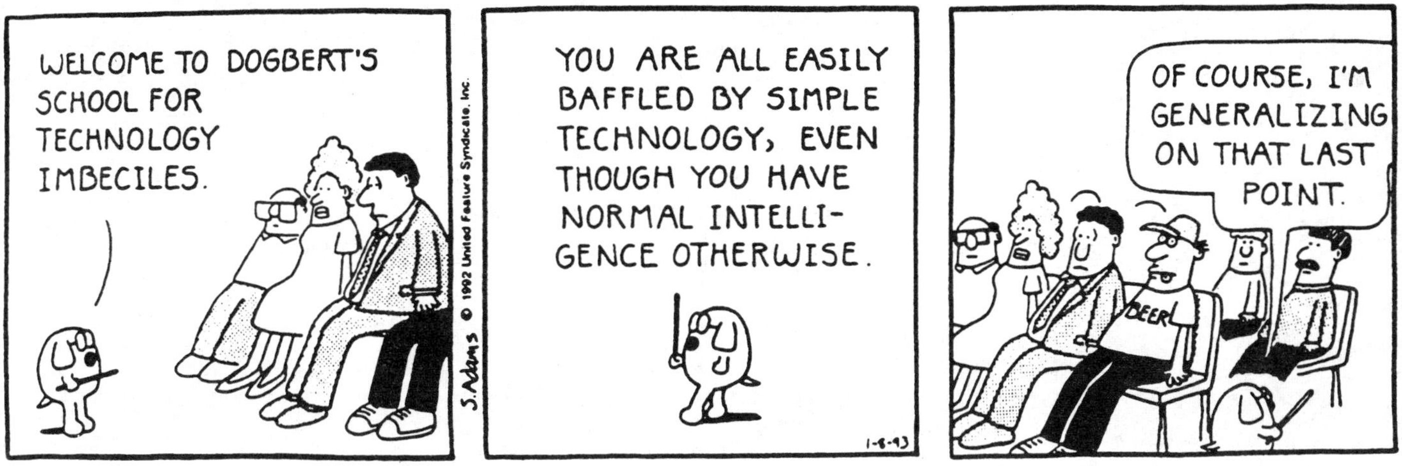
WELCOME TO DOGBERT'S SCHOOL FOR TECHNOLOGY IMBECILES.
S. Adams © 1992 United Feature Syndicate, Inc.
YOU ARE ALL EASILY BAFFLED BY SIMPLE TECHNOLOGY, EVEN THOUGH YOU HAVE NORMAL INTELLI-GENCE OTHERWISE.
1-8-93
OF COURSE, I'M GENERALIZING ON THAT LAST POINT.
BEER

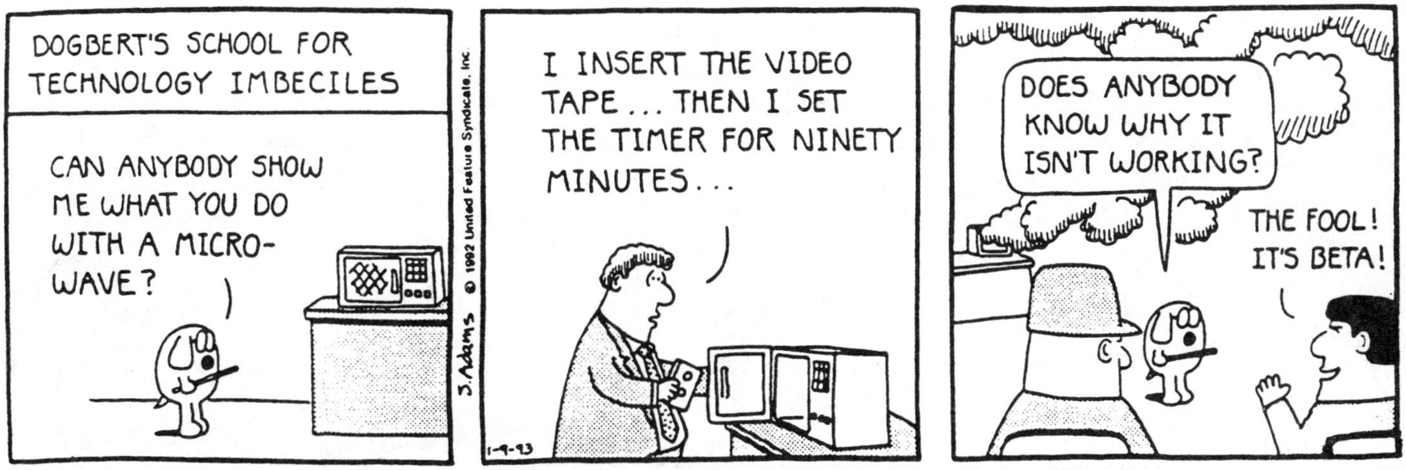
DOGBERT'S SCHOOL FOR TECHNOLOGY IMBECILES
CAN ANYBODY SHOW ME WHAT YOU DO WITH A MICRO-WAVE?
S. Adams © 1992 United Feature Syndicate, Inc.
I INSERT THE VIDEO TAPE... THEN I SET THE TIMER FOR NINETY MINUTES...
1-9-93
DOES ANYBODY KNOW WHY IT ISN'T WORKING?
THE FOOL! IT'S BETA!

DOGBERT, I'VE FOUND A WAY TO IMPROVE THE QUALITY OF LIFE AROUND HERE.
I'VE CATALOGUED AND PRIORITIZED ALL OF THE THINGS THAT BOTHER ME.
STUDY THE LIST SO YOU'LL KNOW WHAT BEHAVIORS ARE UNACCEPTABLE.
WOW! THANKS! THIS IS A REAL BONANZA!
YOU'RE RIGHT. THIS CERTAINLY WILL IMPROVE THE QUALITY OF MY LIFE!
I THINK I'LL DO A "TOP HUNDRED" COUNTDOWN. THIS COULD AMUSE ME FOR MONTHS.
S. Adams
1-10
THAT DIDN'T GO AS WELL AS I'D HOPED.
NUMBER 73: "CLIPPING MY TOENAILS NEAR YOUR SOUP."
THAT HAD BETTER BE AN ONION THERE.
© 1993 United Feature Syndicate, Inc.

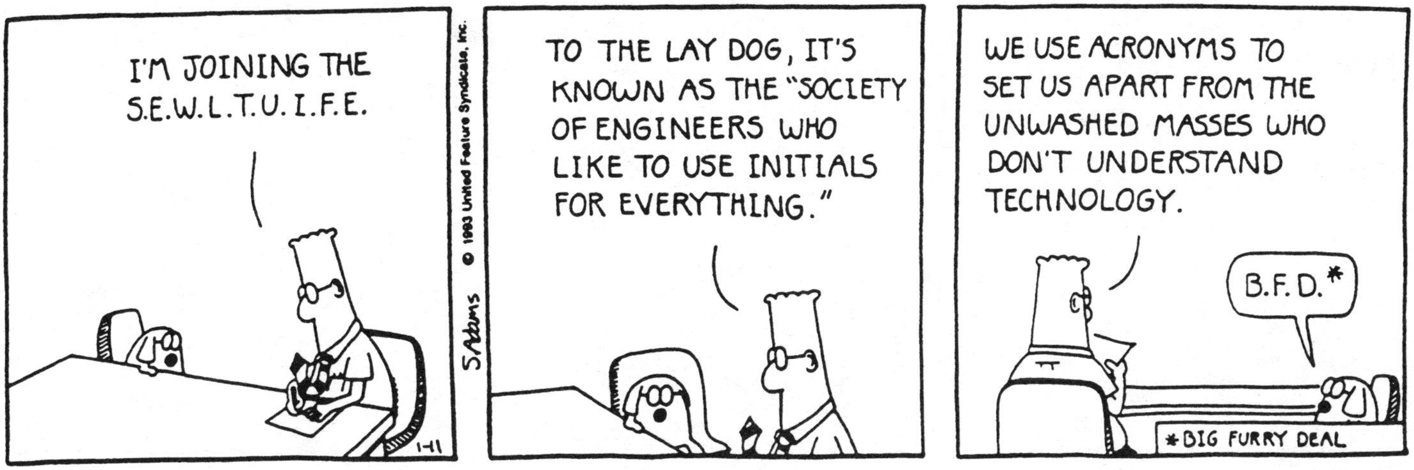
I'M JOINING THE S.E.W.L.T.U.I.F.E.
1-11
S.Adams © 1993 United Feature Syndicate, Inc.
TO THE LAY DOG, IT'S KNOWN AS THE "SOCIETY OF ENGINEERS WHO LIKE TO USE INITIALS FOR EVERYTHING."
WE USE ACRONYMS TO SET US APART FROM THE UNWASHED MASSES WHO DON'T UNDERSTAND TECHNOLOGY.
B.F.D.*
*BIG FURRY DEAL

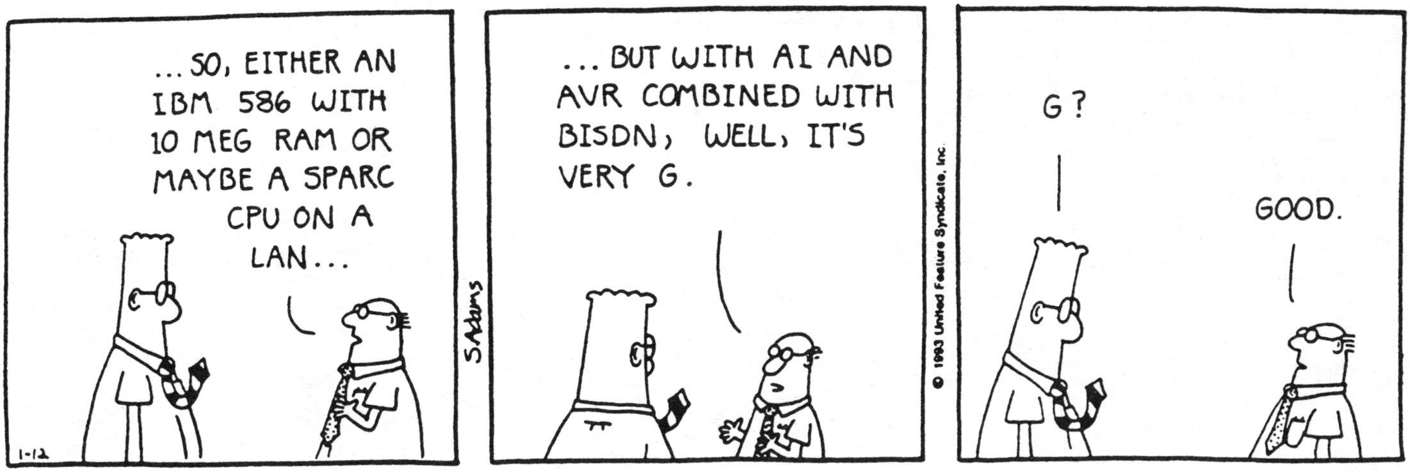
...SO, EITHER AN IBM 586 WITH 10 MEG RAM OR MAYBE A SPARC CPU ON A LAN...
1-12
S.Adams
...BUT WITH AI AND AVR COMBINED WITH BISDN, WELL, IT'S VERY G.
© 1993 United Feature Syndicate, Inc.
G?
GOOD.

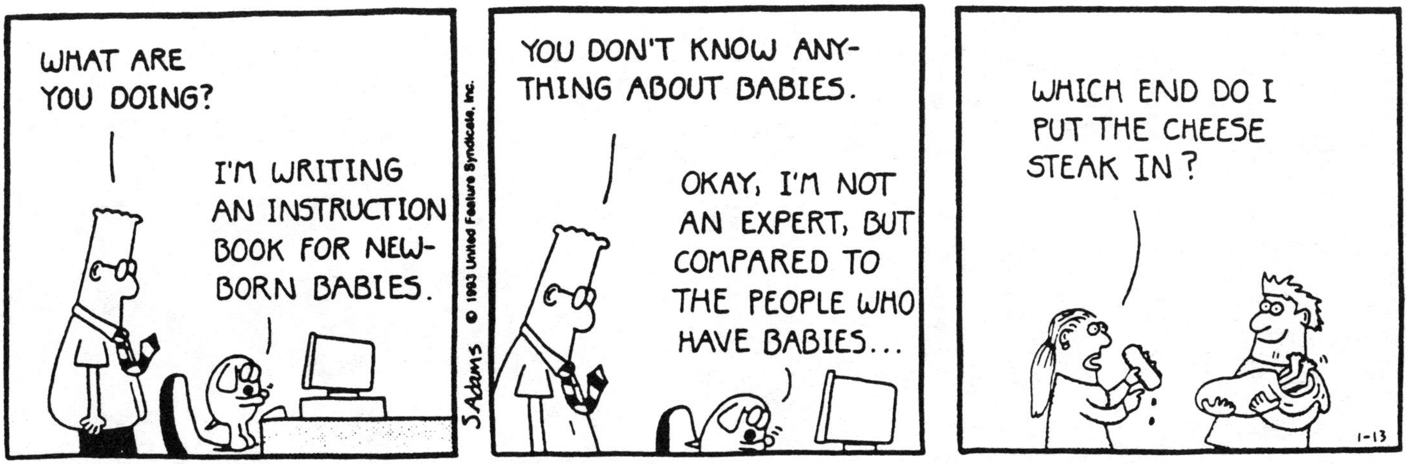
WHAT ARE YOU DOING?
I'M WRITING AN INSTRUCTION BOOK FOR NEW-BORN BABIES.
S.Adams © 1993 United Feature Syndicate, Inc.
YOU DON'T KNOW ANY-THING ABOUT BABIES.
OKAY, I'M NOT AN EXPERT, BUT COMPARED TO THE PEOPLE WHO HAVE BABIES...
WHICH END DO I PUT THE CHEESE STEAK IN?
1-13

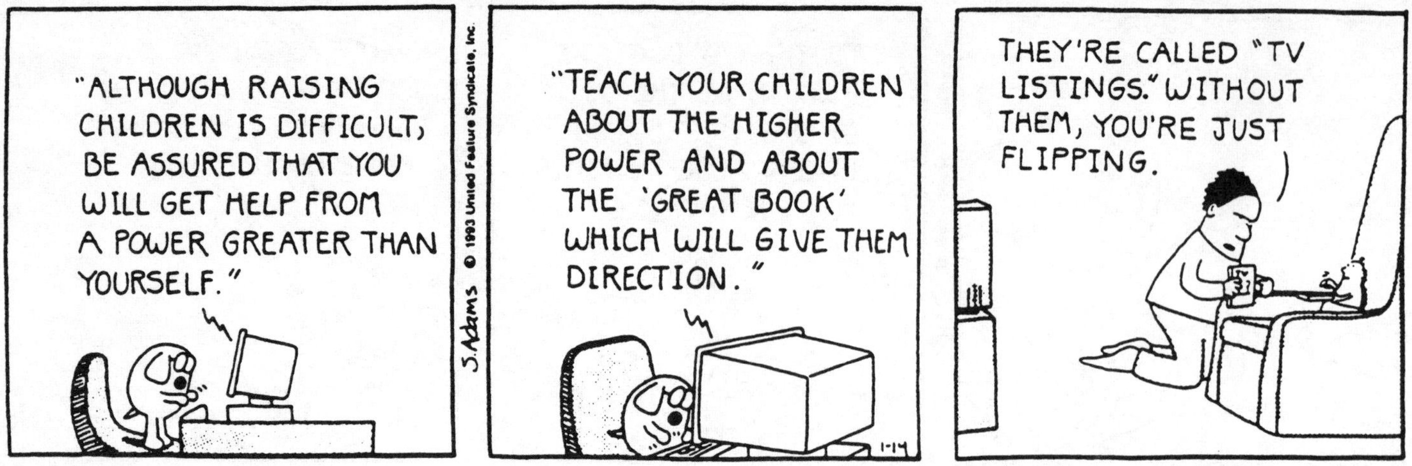
"ALTHOUGH RAISING CHILDREN IS DIFFICULT, BE ASSURED THAT YOU WILL GET HELP FROM A POWER GREATER THAN YOURSELF."
S. Adams © 1993 United Feature Syndicate, Inc.
"TEACH YOUR CHILDREN ABOUT THE HIGHER POWER AND ABOUT THE 'GREAT BOOK' WHICH WILL GIVE THEM DIRECTION."
1-14
THEY'RE CALLED "TV LISTINGS." WITHOUT THEM, YOU'RE JUST FLIPPING.

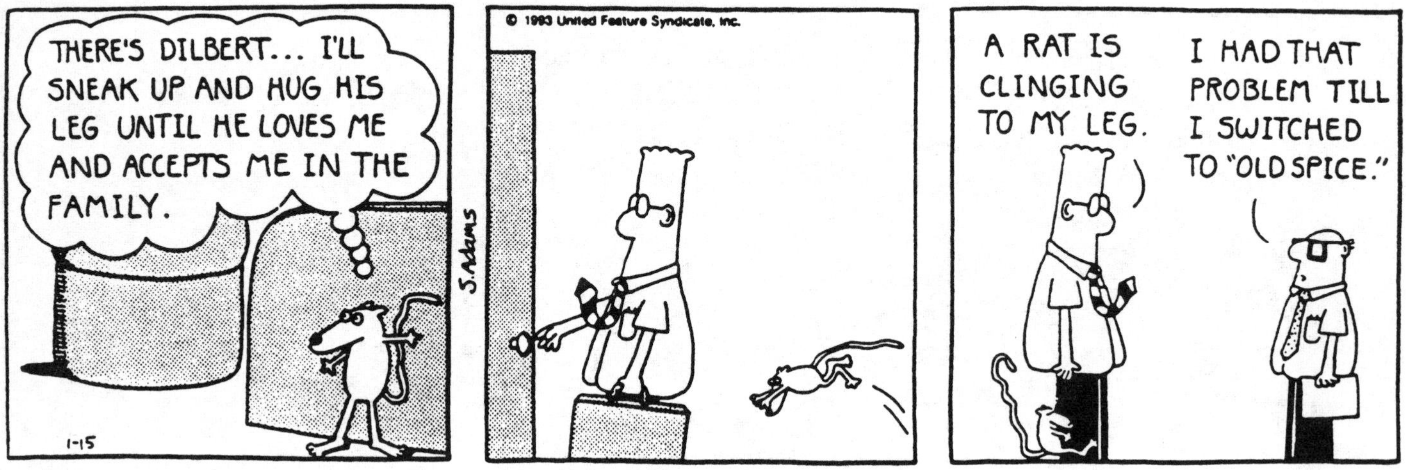
THERE'S DILBERT... I'LL SNEAK UP AND HUG HIS LEG UNTIL HE LOVES ME AND ACCEPTS ME IN THE FAMILY.
1-15
S. Adams
© 1993 United Feature Syndicate, Inc.
A RAT IS CLINGING TO MY LEG.
I HAD THAT PROBLEM TILL I SWITCHED TO "OLD SPICE."

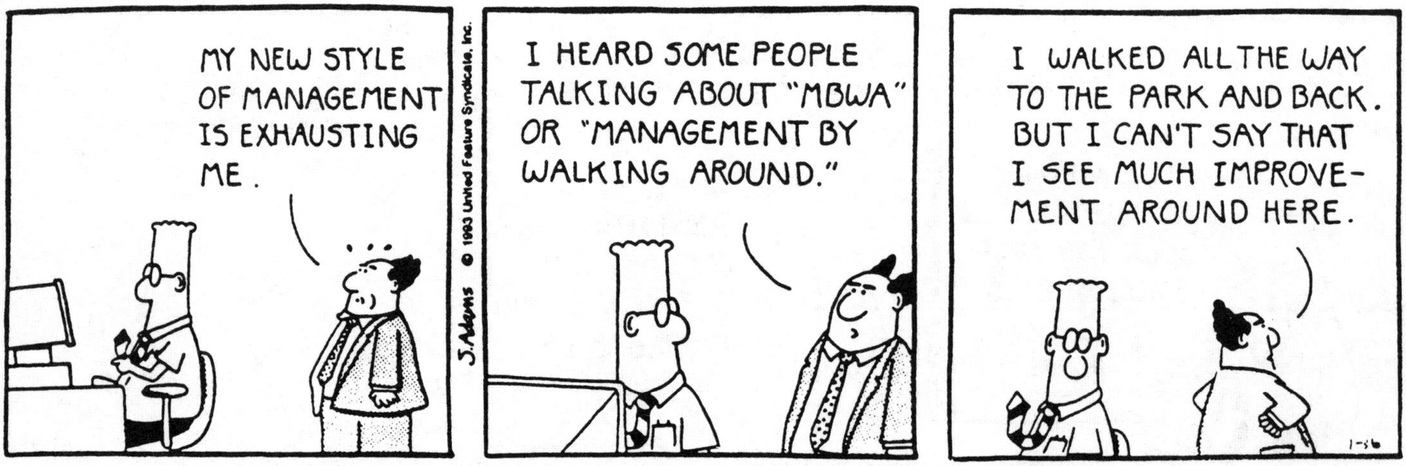
MY NEW STYLE OF MANAGEMENT IS EXHAUSTING ME.
S. Adams © 1993 United Feature Syndicate, Inc.
I HEARD SOME PEOPLE TALKING ABOUT "MBWA" OR "MANAGEMENT BY WALKING AROUND."
I WALKED ALL THE WAY TO THE PARK AND BACK. BUT I CAN'T SAY THAT I SEE MUCH IMPROVEMENT AROUND HERE.
1-16

HELP! DOGBERT, I'M BEING SUCKED INTO CYBERSPACE!
AAAAGH!!
LET'S HOPE YOU DON'T NEED PANTS IN CYBER-SPACE.
WOW! IT'S LIKE A "CALVIN AND HOBBES" FANTASY BUT WITHOUT THE ARTISTIC LOOK TO IT.
IT'S BEAUTIFUL! I'M INTERACT-ING WITH THE MINDS OF BRILLIANT PEOPLE FROM AROUND THE GLOBE.
INTERNET
S. Adams
I CAN SEE HOW ALL THEIR IDEAS AND KNOWLEDGE FIT TOGETHER! IT'S EXHILARATING!
E-MAIL
HOW CAN I EVER DESCRIBE THIS TO SOMEBODY WHO HASN'T BEEN HERE?
EXIT
1-17
© 1993 United Feature Syndicate, Inc.
...AND I DIDN'T EVEN NEED PANTS!!
SO, YOU'RE SOME KIND OF NERD, RIGHT?
INTERNET ID: SCOTTADAMS@AOL.COM

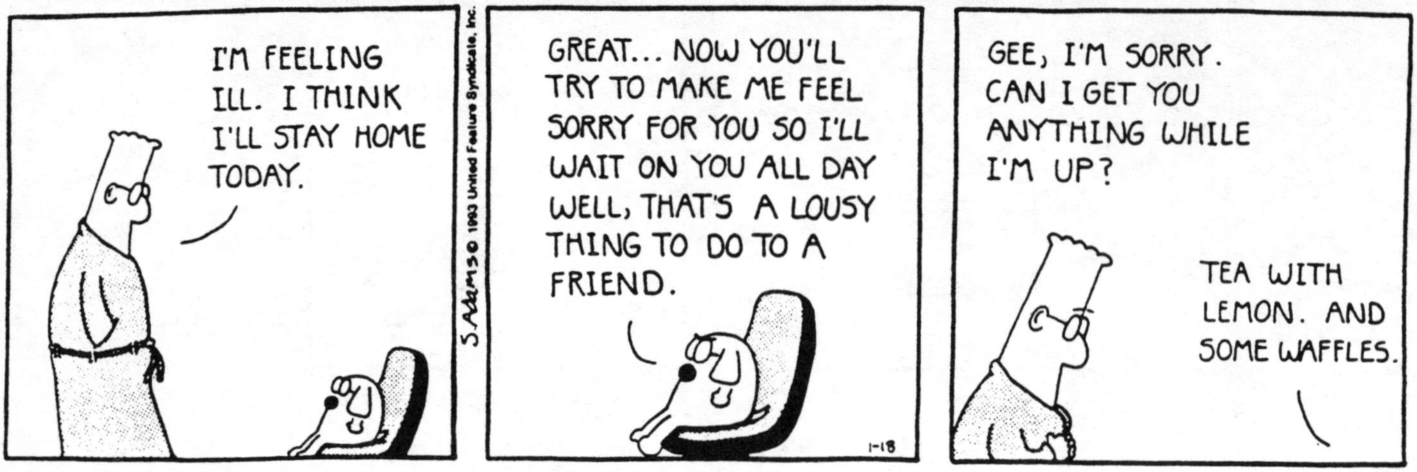
I'M FEELING ILL. I THINK I'LL STAY HOME TODAY.
S. Adams © 1993 United Feature Syndicate, Inc.
GREAT... NOW YOU'LL TRY TO MAKE ME FEEL SORRY FOR YOU SO I'LL WAIT ON YOU ALL DAY WELL, THAT'S A LOUSY THING TO DO TO A FRIEND.
1-18
GEE, I'M SORRY. CAN I GET YOU ANYTHING WHILE I'M UP?
TEA WITH LEMON. AND SOME WAFFLES.

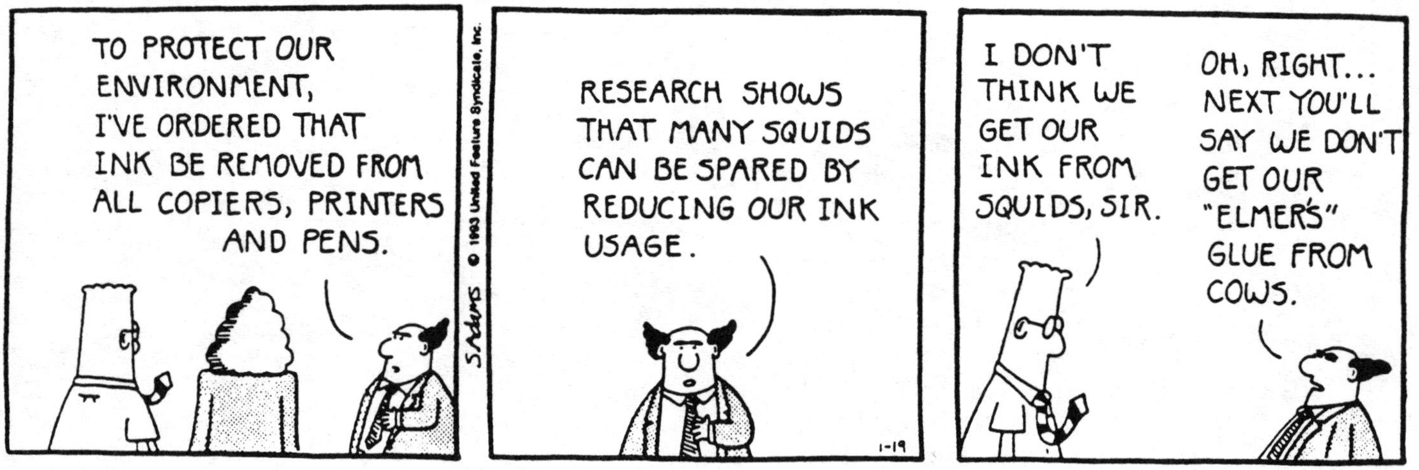
TO PROTECT OUR ENVIRONMENT, I'VE ORDERED THAT INK BE REMOVED FROM ALL COPIERS, PRINTERS AND PENS.
S. Adams © 1993 United Feature Syndicate, Inc.
RESEARCH SHOWS THAT MANY SQUIDS CAN BE SPARED BY REDUCING OUR INK USAGE.
1-19
I DON'T THINK WE GET OUR INK FROM SQUIDS, SIR.
OH, RIGHT... NEXT YOU'LL SAY WE DON'T GET OUR "ELMER'S" GLUE FROM COWS.

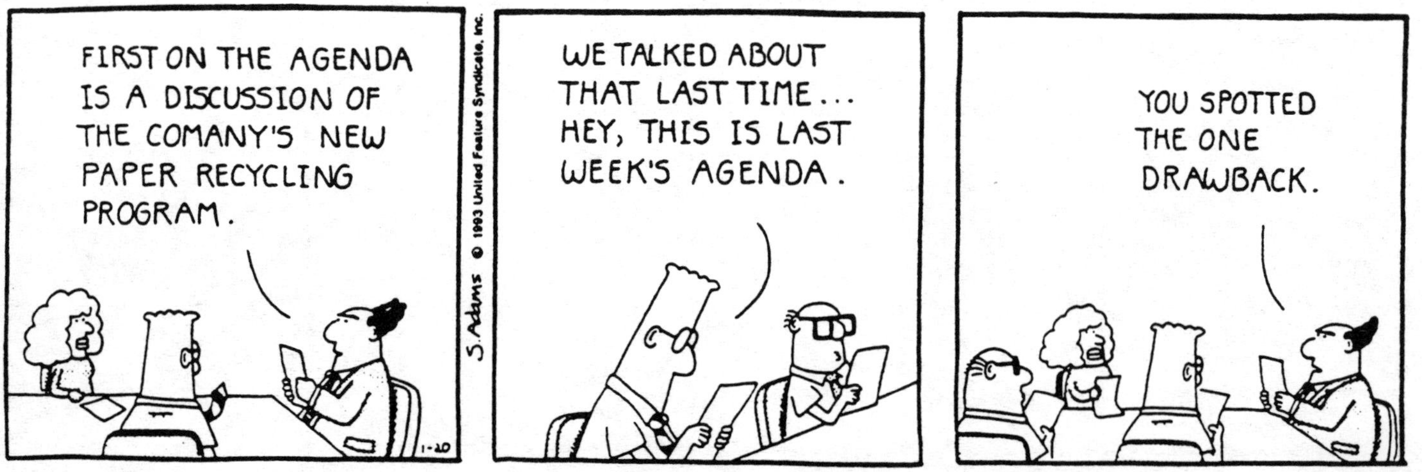
FIRST ON THE AGENDA IS A DISCUSSION OF THE COMANY'S NEW PAPER RECYCLING PROGRAM.
1-20
S. Adams © 1993 United Feature Syndicate, Inc.
WE TALKED ABOUT THAT LAST TIME... HEY, THIS IS LAST WEEK'S AGENDA.
YOU SPOTTED THE ONE DRAWBACK.

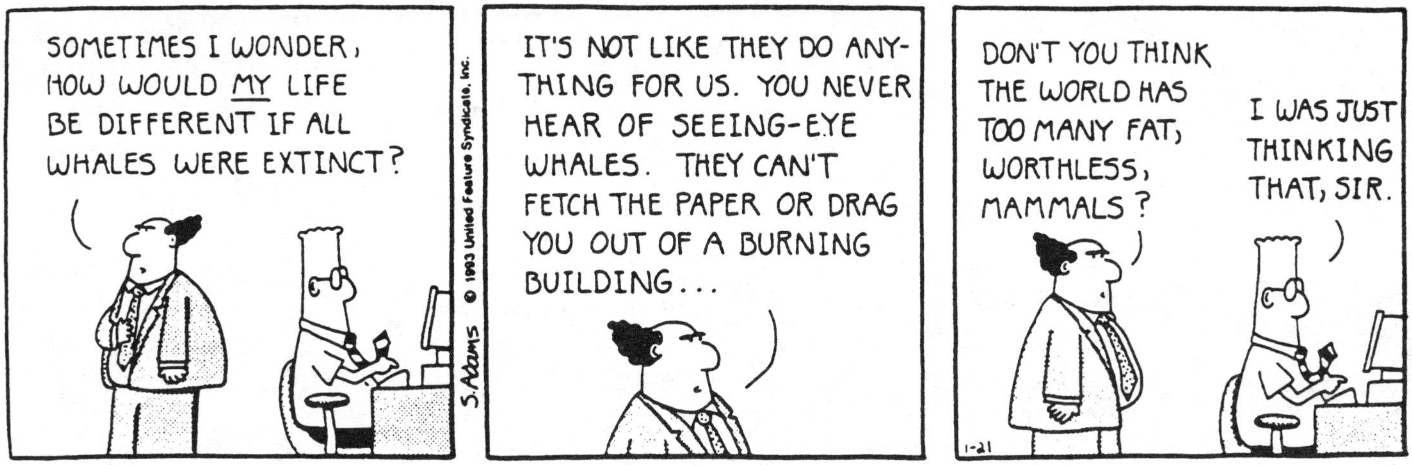
SOMETIMES I WONDER, HOW WOULD MY LIFE BE DIFFERENT IF ALL WHALES WERE EXTINCT?
S. Adams © 1993 United Feature Syndicate, Inc.
IT'S NOT LIKE THEY DO ANYTHING FOR US. YOU NEVER HEAR OF SEEING-EYE WHALES. THEY CAN'T FETCH THE PAPER OR DRAG YOU OUT OF A BURNING BUILDING...
DON'T YOU THINK THE WORLD HAS TOO MANY FAT, WORTHLESS, MAMMALS?
I WAS JUST THINKING THAT, SIR.
1-21

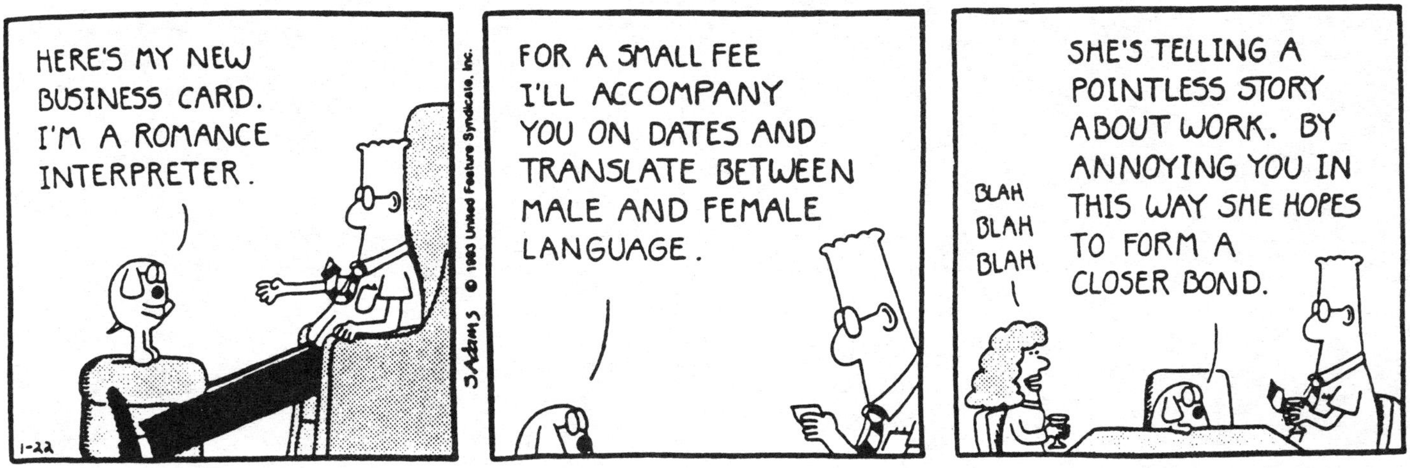
HERE'S MY NEW BUSINESS CARD. I'M A ROMANCE INTERPRETER.
1-22
S. Adams © 1993 United Feature Syndicate, Inc.
FOR A SMALL FEE I'LL ACCOMPANY YOU ON DATES AND TRANSLATE BETWEEN MALE AND FEMALE LANGUAGE.
BLAH BLAH BLAH
SHE'S TELLING A POINTLESS STORY ABOUT WORK. BY ANNOYING YOU IN THIS WAY SHE HOPES TO FORM A CLOSER BOND.

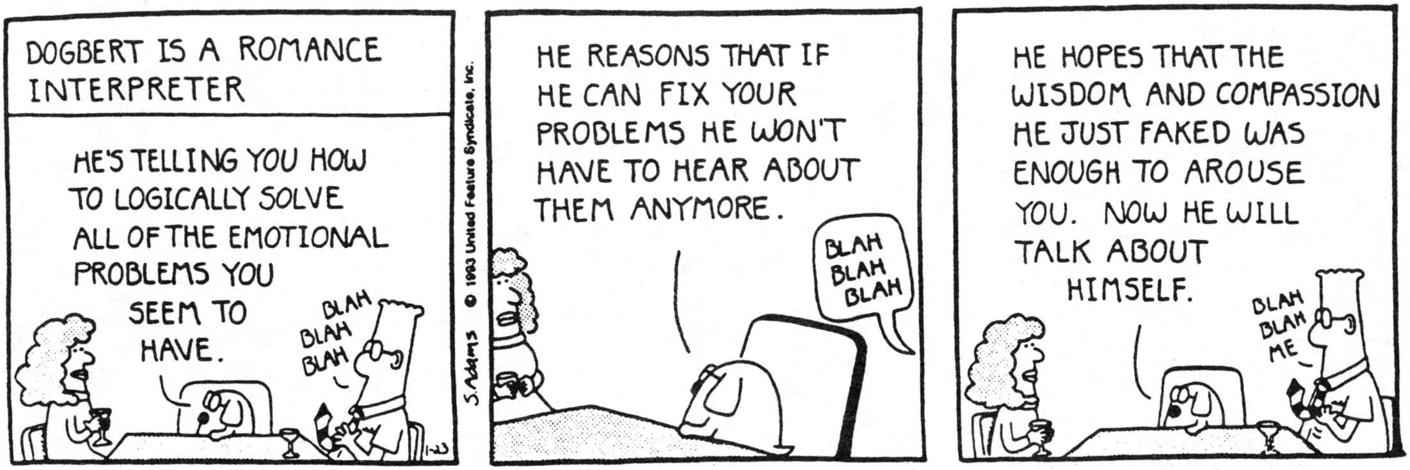
DOGBERT IS A ROMANCE INTERPRETER
HE'S TELLING YOU HOW TO LOGICALLY SOLVE ALL OF THE EMOTIONAL PROBLEMS YOU SEEM TO HAVE.
BLAH BLAH BLAH
1-23
S. Adams © 1993 United Feature Syndicate, Inc.
HE REASONS THAT IF HE CAN FIX YOUR PROBLEMS HE WON'T HAVE TO HEAR ABOUT THEM ANYMORE.
BLAH BLAH BLAH
HE HOPES THAT THE WISDOM AND COMPASSION HE JUST FAKED WAS ENOUGH TO AROUSE YOU. NOW HE WILL TALK ABOUT HIMSELF.
BLAH BLAH ME

MAYBE DILBERT CAN TELL US IF OUR PLAN IS TECHNI- CALLY FEASIBLE.
S.Adams
FOR DRAMATIC EFFECT I'LL SCOFF LOUDLY.
I'LL JUST SORT OF LAUGH AND SNORT AND TAKE A BREATH AT THE SAME TIME.
SNORK
OH-NO! SOME SPITTLE WENT DOWN MY AIR PIPE... I'M CHOKING.
1-24
MMPH
GAAK
SHOULD WE DO SOME- THING?
WE'RE OVER OUR HEAD- COUNT, YOU KNOW.
© 1993 United Feature Syndicate, Inc.
...AND SO I SURVIVED, BUT MY PROFESSIONAL CREDIBILITY TOOK A HIT.
YOU KNEW THE RISKS WHEN YOU BECAME AN ENGI- NEER.

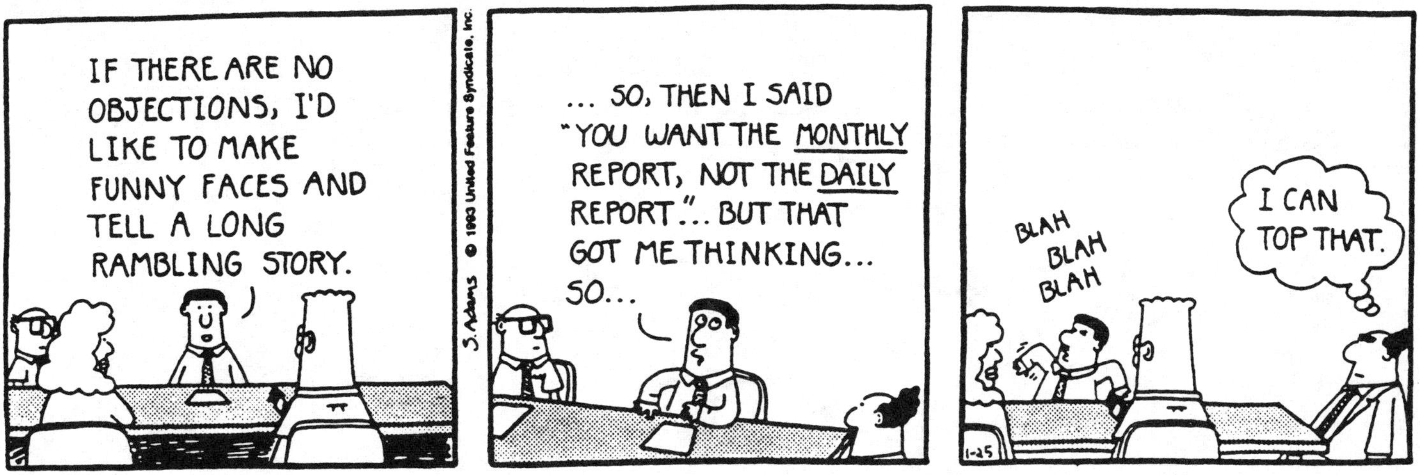
IF THERE ARE NO OBJECTIONS, I'D LIKE TO MAKE FUNNY FACES AND TELL A LONG RAMBLING STORY.
S. Adams © 1993 United Feature Syndicate, Inc.
... SO, THEN I SAID "YOU WANT THE MONTHLY REPORT, NOT THE DAILY REPORT."... BUT THAT GOT ME THINKING... SO...
BLAH BLAH BLAH
I CAN TOP THAT.
1-25

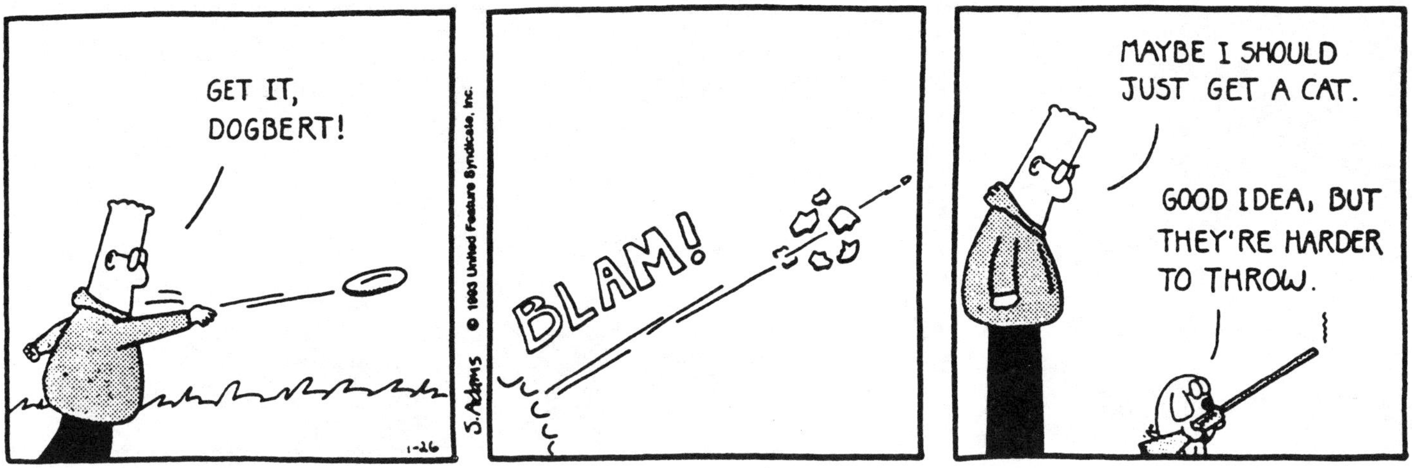
GET IT, DOGBERT!
1-26
S. Adams © 1993 United Feature Syndicate, Inc.
BLAM!
MAYBE I SHOULD JUST GET A CAT.
GOOD IDEA, BUT THEY'RE HARDER TO THROW.

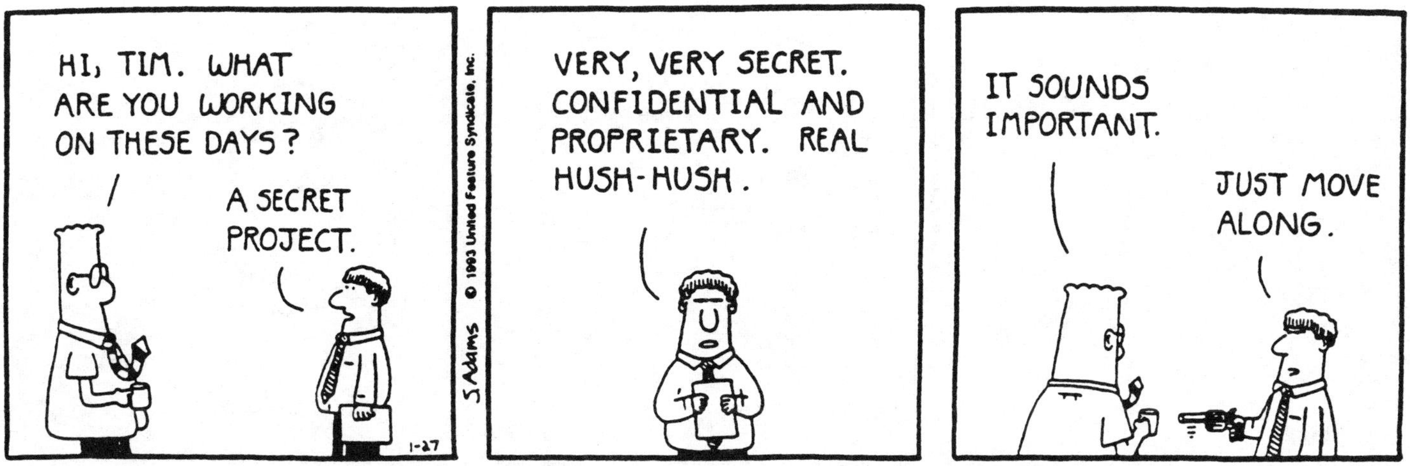
HI, TIM. WHAT ARE YOU WORKING ON THESE DAYS?
A SECRET PROJECT.
1-27
S. Adams © 1993 United Feature Syndicate, Inc.
VERY, VERY SECRET. CONFIDENTIAL AND PROPRIETARY. REAL HUSH-HUSH.
IT SOUNDS IMPORTANT.
JUST MOVE ALONG.

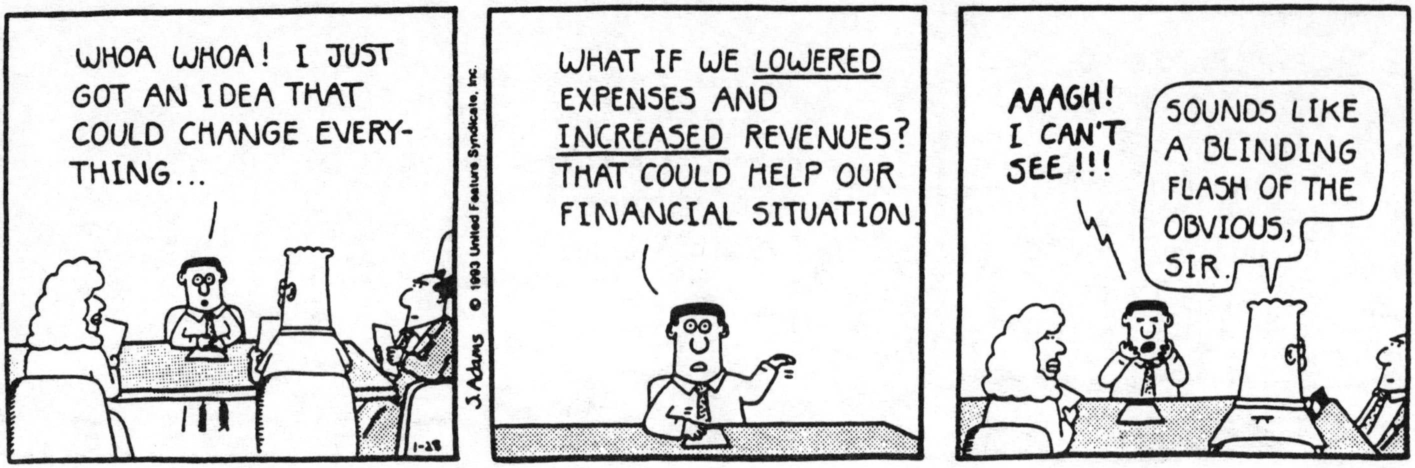
WHOA WHOA! I JUST GOT AN IDEA THAT COULD CHANGE EVERYTHING...
1-28
S. Adams © 1993 United Feature Syndicate, Inc.
WHAT IF WE LOWERED EXPENSES AND INCREASED REVENUES? THAT COULD HELP OUR FINANCIAL SITUATION.
AAAGH! I CAN'T SEE!!!
SOUNDS LIKE A BLINDING FLASH OF THE OBVIOUS, SIR.

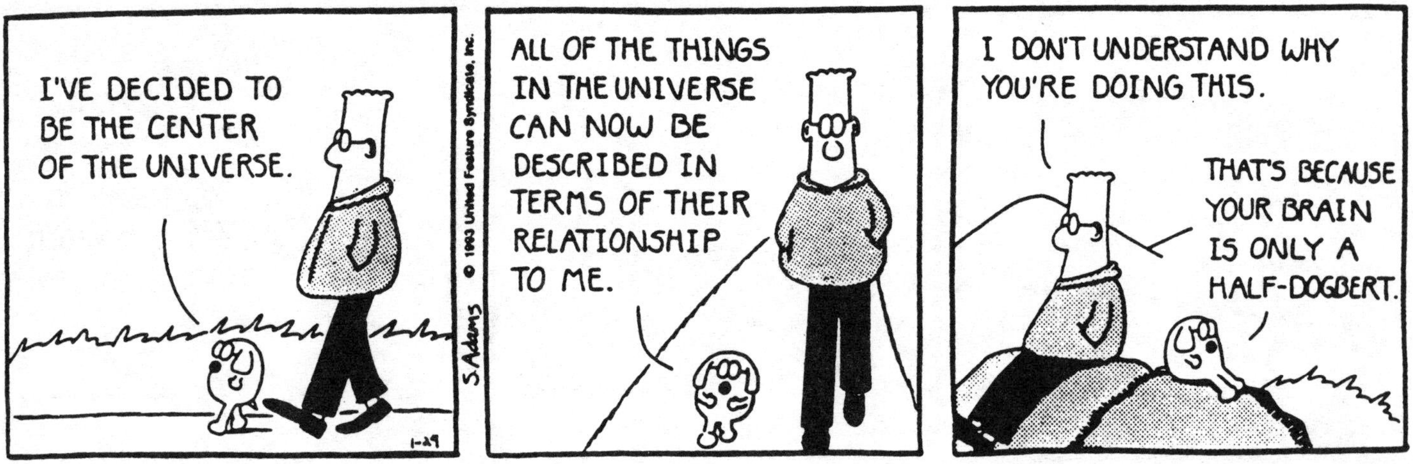
I'VE DECIDED TO BE THE CENTER OF THE UNIVERSE.
1-29
S. Adams © 1993 United Feature Syndicate, Inc.
ALL OF THE THINGS IN THE UNIVERSE CAN NOW BE DESCRIBED IN TERMS OF THEIR RELATIONSHIP TO ME.
I DON'T UNDERSTAND WHY YOU'RE DOING THIS.
THAT'S BECAUSE YOUR BRAIN IS ONLY A HALF-DOGBERT.

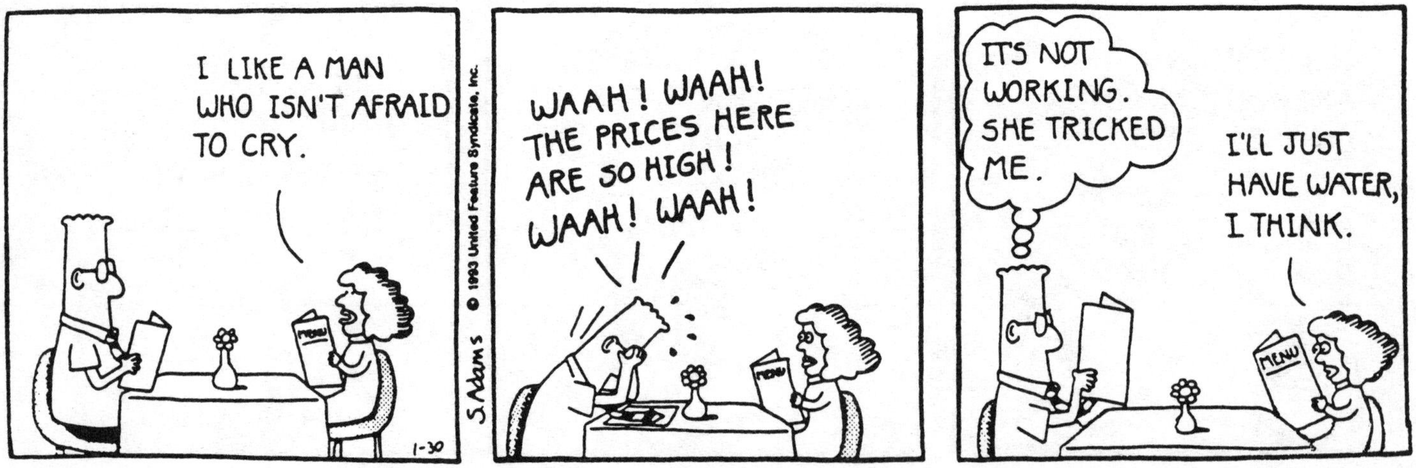
I LIKE A MAN WHO ISN'T AFRAID TO CRY.
MENU
1-30
S. Adams © 1993 United Feature Syndicate, Inc.
WAAH! WAAH! THE PRICES HERE ARE SO HIGH! WAAH! WAAH!
IT'S NOT WORKING. SHE TRICKED ME.
I'LL JUST HAVE WATER, I THINK.

BEFORE I READ YOUR PROPOSAL, RUN IT PAST OUR LEGAL DEPARTMENT.
GROAN
S. Adams
THAT'S THE END OF THAT.
I DIDN'T HAVE TO BECOME A CORPORATE LAWYER. I COULD BE A TRIAL LAWYER OR A JUDGE, YOU KNOW.
BUT I CHOSE TO WORK HERE AT THIS UNGLAMOR-OUS POSITION.
CONSEQUENTLY, I HAVE A BAD ATTITUDE AND I'M GOING TO TAKE IT OUT ON YOU.
YOUR PROPOSAL DOES NOTHING TO HELP MY CAREER. AND IF I APPROVE IT AND WE GET SUED LATER, THEN I'LL GET IN TROUBLE.
1-31
IN A MONTH OR SO, I'LL FORMALLY REJECT YOUR IDEA WITH A NEATLY TYPED BUT ODDLY WORD-ED MEMO.
© 1993 United Feature Syndicate, Inc.
DID HE REJECT YOUR PROPOSAL YET?
YEAH. AND HE FILED A LAW-SUIT AGAINST ME.

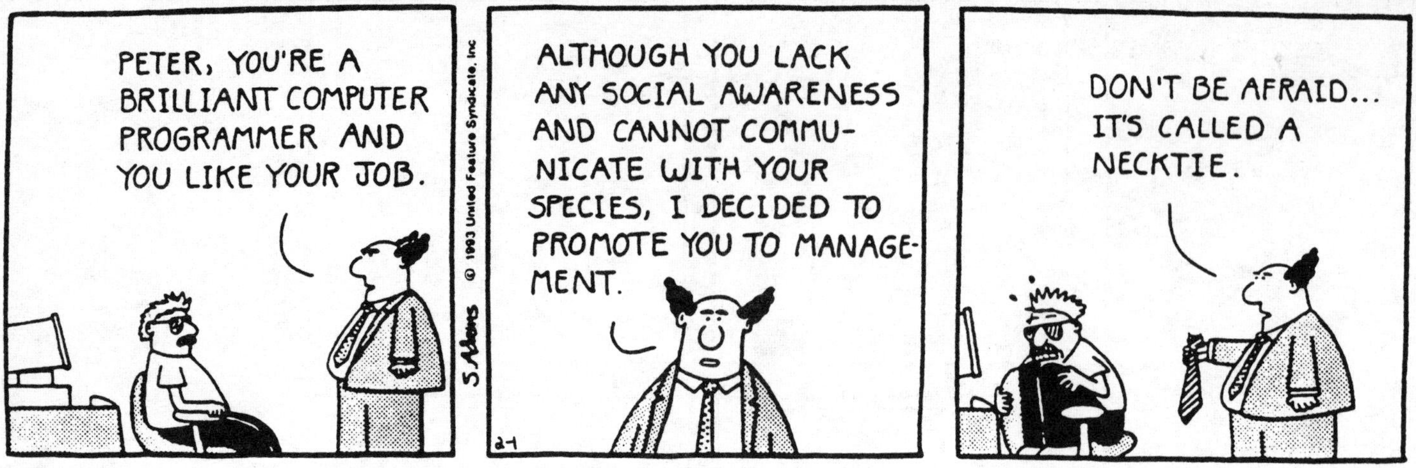
PETER, YOU'RE A BRILLIANT COMPUTER PROGRAMMER AND YOU LIKE YOUR JOB.
S. Adams © 1993 United Feature Syndicate, Inc
ALTHOUGH YOU LACK ANY SOCIAL AWARENESS AND CANNOT COMMUNICATE WITH YOUR SPECIES, I DECIDED TO PROMOTE YOU TO MANAGEMENT.
DON'T BE AFRAID... IT'S CALLED A NECKTIE.

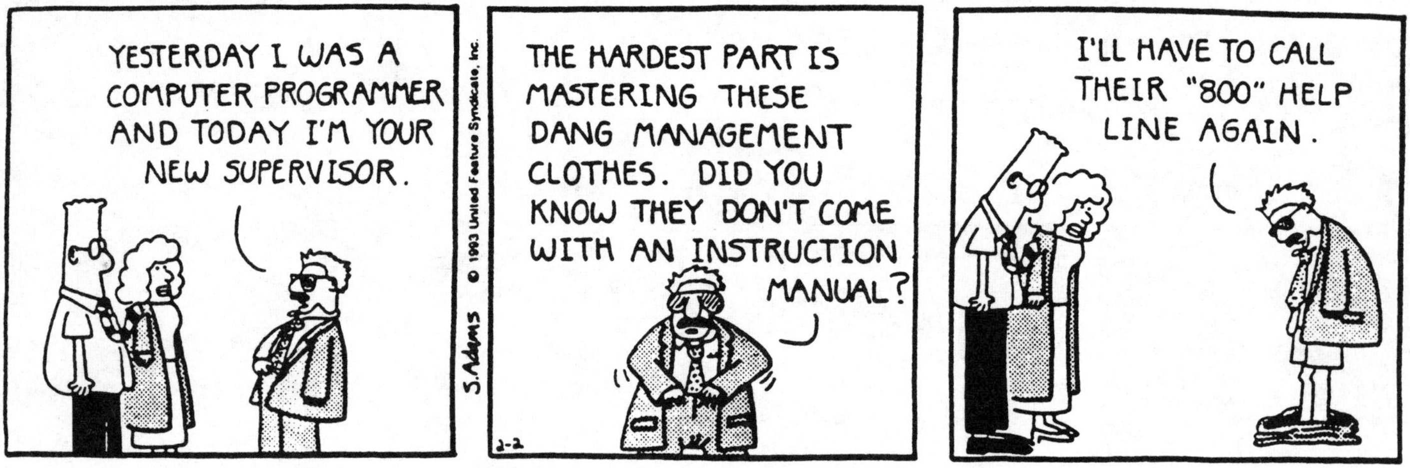
YESTERDAY I WAS A COMPUTER PROGRAMMER AND TODAY I'M YOUR NEW SUPERVISOR.
S. Adams © 1993 United Feature Syndicate, Inc.
THE HARDEST PART IS MASTERING THESE DANG MANAGEMENT CLOTHES. DID YOU KNOW THEY DON'T COME WITH AN INSTRUCTION MANUAL?
I'LL HAVE TO CALL THEIR "800" HELP LINE AGAIN.

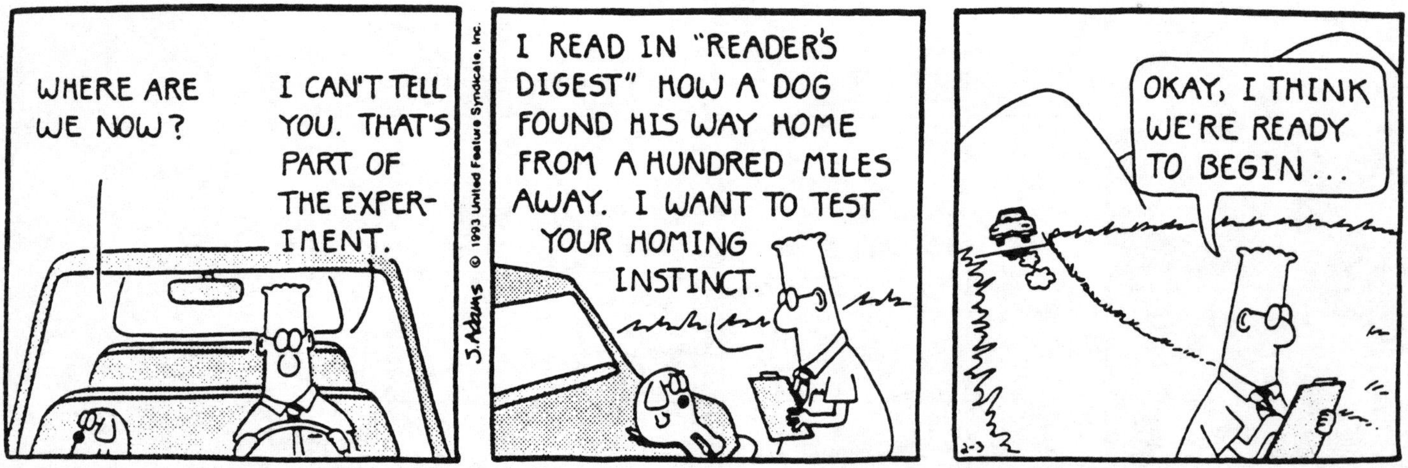
WHERE ARE WE NOW?
I CAN'T TELL YOU. THAT'S PART OF THE EXPERIMENT.
S. Adams © 1993 United Feature Syndicate, Inc.
I READ IN "READER'S DIGEST" HOW A DOG FOUND HIS WAY HOME FROM A HUNDRED MILES AWAY. I WANT TO TEST YOUR HOMING INSTINCT.
OKAY, I THINK WE'RE READY TO BEGIN...

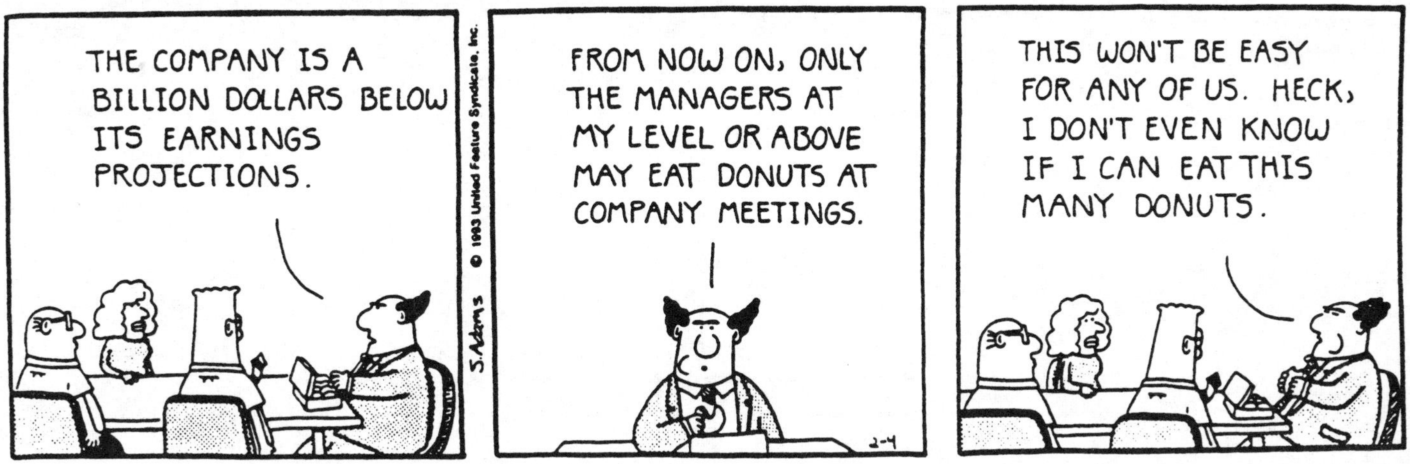
THE COMPANY IS A BILLION DOLLARS BELOW ITS EARNINGS PROJECTIONS.
FROM NOW ON, ONLY THE MANAGERS AT MY LEVEL OR ABOVE MAY EAT DONUTS AT COMPANY MEETINGS.
THIS WON'T BE EASY FOR ANY OF US. HECK, I DON'T EVEN KNOW IF I CAN EAT THIS MANY DONUTS.

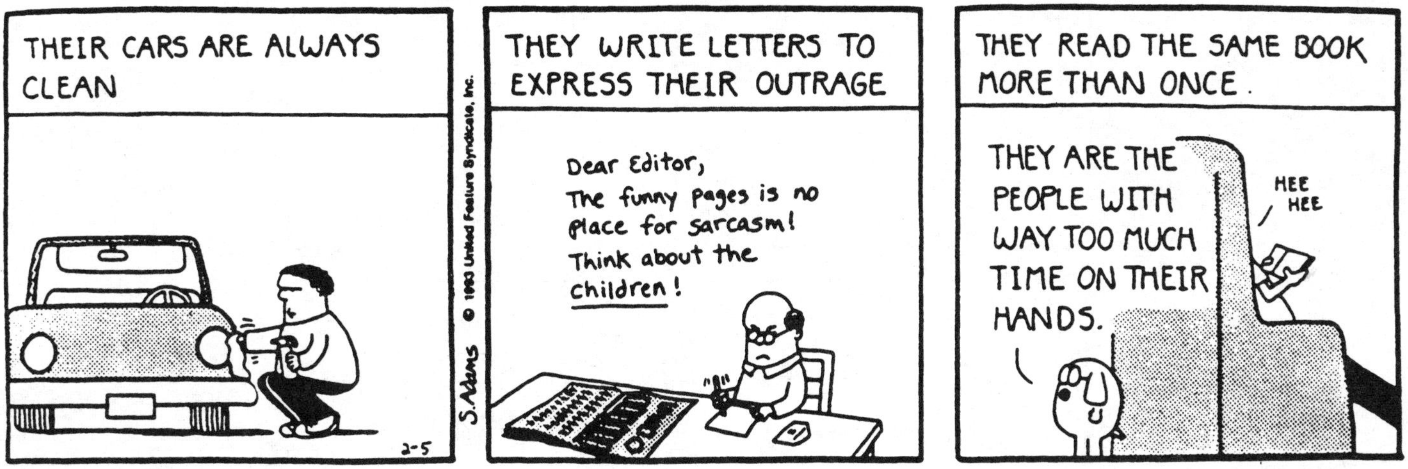
THEIR CARS ARE ALWAYS CLEAN
THEY WRITE LETTERS TO EXPRESS THEIR OUTRAGE
Dear Editor, The funny pages is no place for sarcasm! Think about the children!
THEY READ THE SAME BOOK MORE THAN ONCE.
THEY ARE THE PEOPLE WITH WAY TOO MUCH TIME ON THEIR HANDS.
HEE HEE

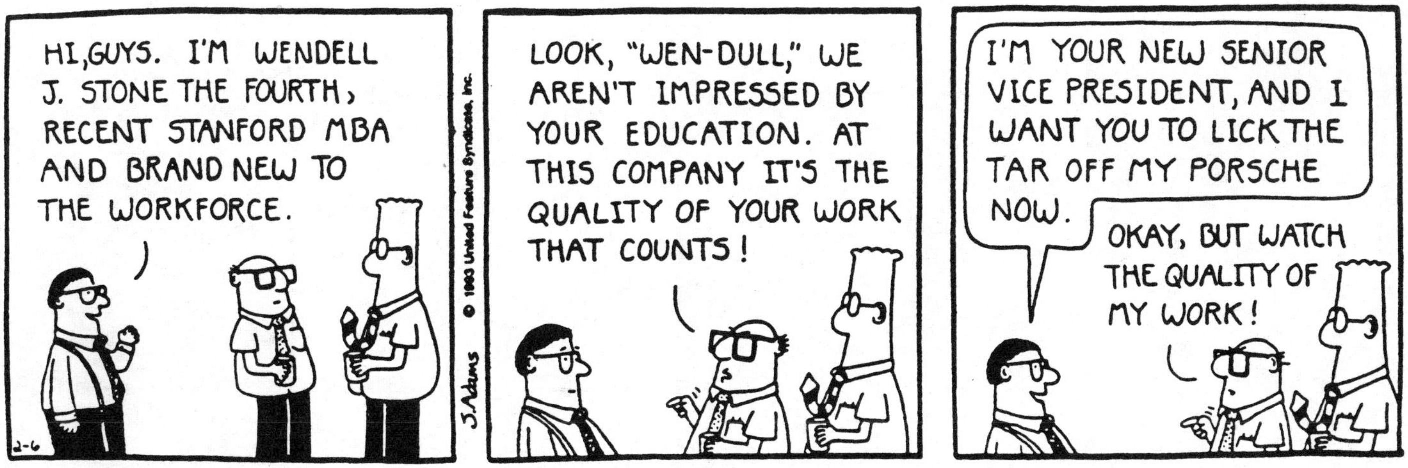
HI, GUYS. I'M WENDELL J. STONE THE FOURTH, RECENT STANFORD MBA AND BRAND NEW TO THE WORKFORCE.
LOOK, "WEN-DULL," WE AREN'T IMPRESSED BY YOUR EDUCATION. AT THIS COMPANY IT'S THE QUALITY OF YOUR WORK THAT COUNTS!
I'M YOUR NEW SENIOR VICE PRESIDENT, AND I WANT YOU TO LICK THE TAR OFF MY PORSCHE NOW.
OKAY, BUT WATCH THE QUALITY OF MY WORK!

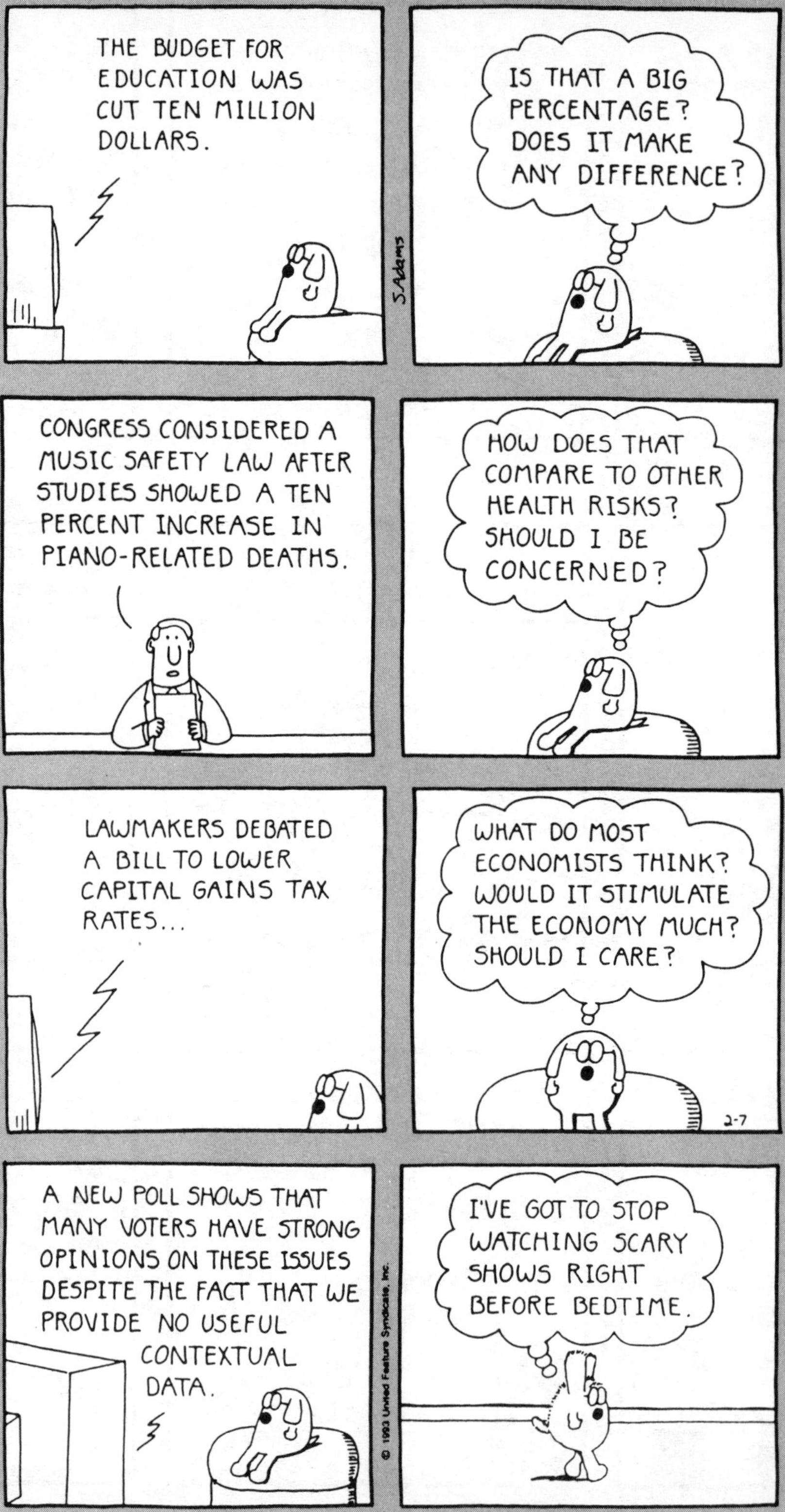
THE BUDGET FOR EDUCATION WAS CUT TEN MILLION DOLLARS.
IS THAT A BIG PERCENTAGE? DOES IT MAKE ANY DIFFERENCE?
CONGRESS CONSIDERED A MUSIC SAFETY LAW AFTER STUDIES SHOWED A TEN PERCENT INCREASE IN PIANO-RELATED DEATHS.
HOW DOES THAT COMPARE TO OTHER HEALTH RISKS? SHOULD I BE CONCERNED?
LAWMAKERS DEBATED A BILL TO LOWER CAPITAL GAINS TAX RATES...
WHAT DO MOST ECONOMISTS THINK? WOULD IT STIMULATE THE ECONOMY MUCH? SHOULD I CARE?
A NEW POLL SHOWS THAT MANY VOTERS HAVE STRONG OPINIONS ON THESE ISSUES DESPITE THE FACT THAT WE PROVIDE NO USEFUL CONTEXTUAL DATA.
I'VE GOT TO STOP WATCHING SCARY SHOWS RIGHT BEFORE BEDTIME.
© 1993 United Feature Syndicate, Inc.

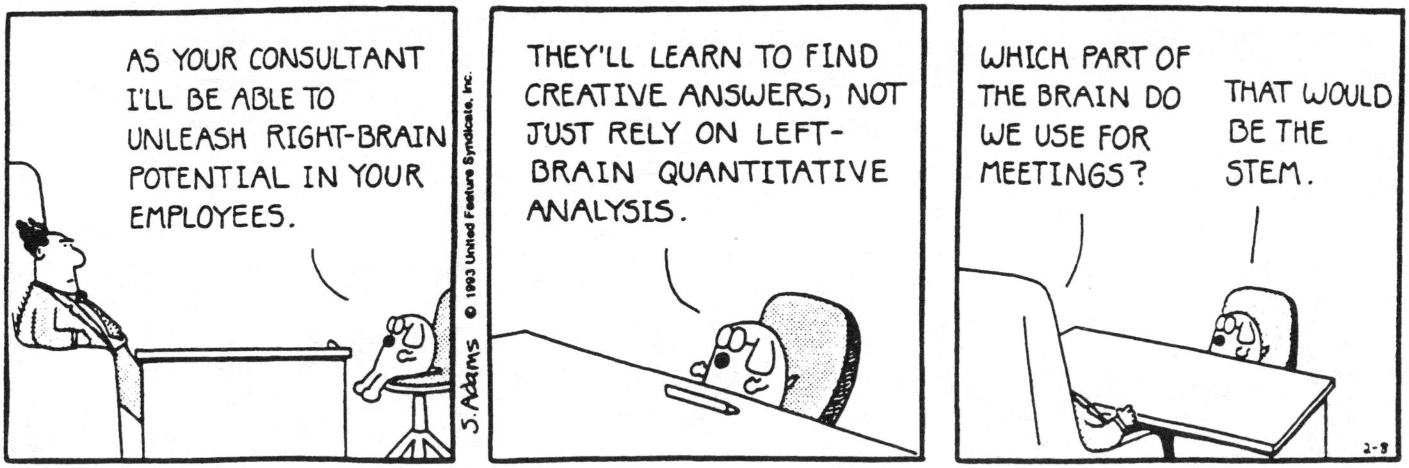
AS YOUR CONSULTANT I'LL BE ABLE TO UNLEASH RIGHT-BRAIN POTENTIAL IN YOUR EMPLOYEES.
S. Adams © 1993 United Feature Syndicate, Inc.
THEY'LL LEARN TO FIND CREATIVE ANSWERS, NOT JUST RELY ON LEFT-BRAIN QUANTITATIVE ANALYSIS.
WHICH PART OF THE BRAIN DO WE USE FOR MEETINGS?
THAT WOULD BE THE STEM.
2-8

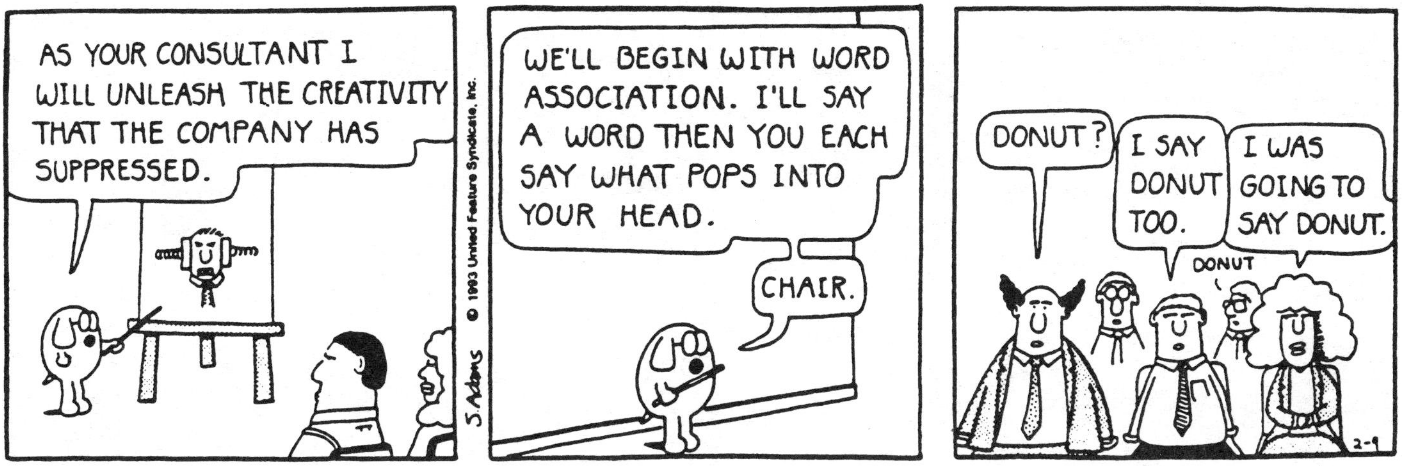
AS YOUR CONSULTANT I WILL UNLEASH THE CREATIVITY THAT THE COMPANY HAS SUPPRESSED.
S. Adams © 1993 United Feature Syndicate, Inc.
WE'LL BEGIN WITH WORD ASSOCIATION. I'LL SAY A WORD THEN YOU EACH SAY WHAT POPS INTO YOUR HEAD.
CHAIR.
DONUT?
I SAY DONUT TOO.
DONUT
I WAS GOING TO SAY DONUT.
2-9

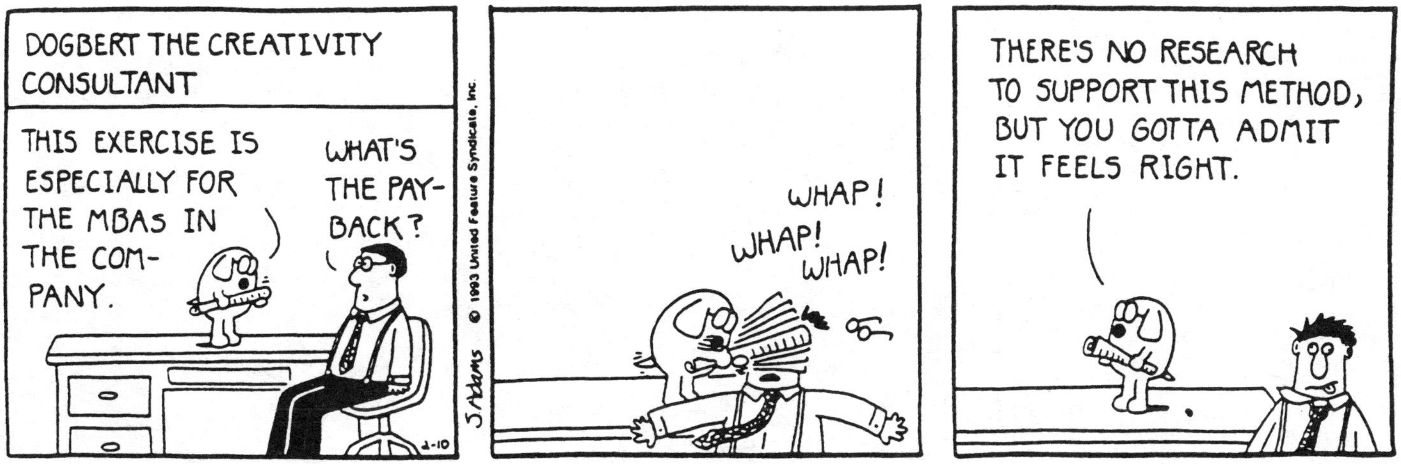
DOGBERT THE CREATIVITY CONSULTANT
THIS EXERCISE IS ESPECIALLY FOR THE MBAS IN THE COMPANY.
WHAT'S THE PAY-BACK?
2-10
S. Adams © 1993 United Feature Syndicate, Inc.
WHAP!
WHAP!
WHAP!
THERE'S NO RESEARCH TO SUPPORT THIS METHOD, BUT YOU GOTTA ADMIT IT FEELS RIGHT.

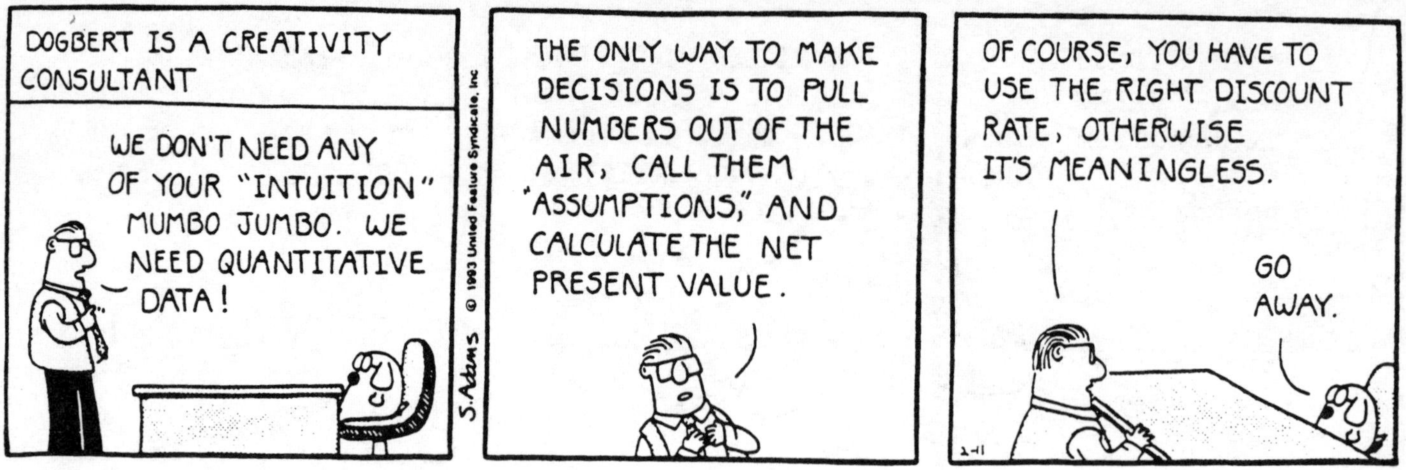
DOGBERT IS A CREATIVITY CONSULTANT
WE DON'T NEED ANY OF YOUR "INTUITION" MUMBO JUMBO. WE NEED QUANTITATIVE DATA!
S. Adams
© 1993 United Feature Syndicate, Inc
THE ONLY WAY TO MAKE DECISIONS IS TO PULL NUMBERS OUT OF THE AIR, CALL THEM "ASSUMPTIONS," AND CALCULATE THE NET PRESENT VALUE.
OF COURSE, YOU HAVE TO USE THE RIGHT DISCOUNT RATE, OTHERWISE IT'S MEANINGLESS.
GO AWAY.
2-11

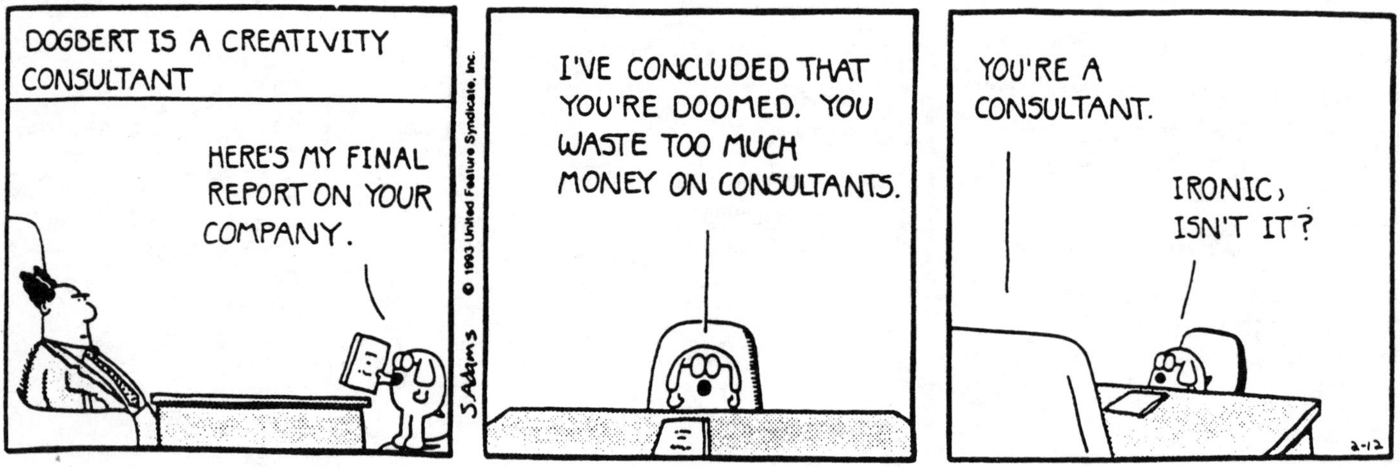
DOGBERT IS A CREATIVITY CONSULTANT
HERE'S MY FINAL REPORT ON YOUR COMPANY.
S. Adams
© 1993 United Feature Syndicate, Inc.
I'VE CONCLUDED THAT YOU'RE DOOMED. YOU WASTE TOO MUCH MONEY ON CONSULTANTS.
YOU'RE A CONSULTANT.
IRONIC, ISN'T IT?
2-12

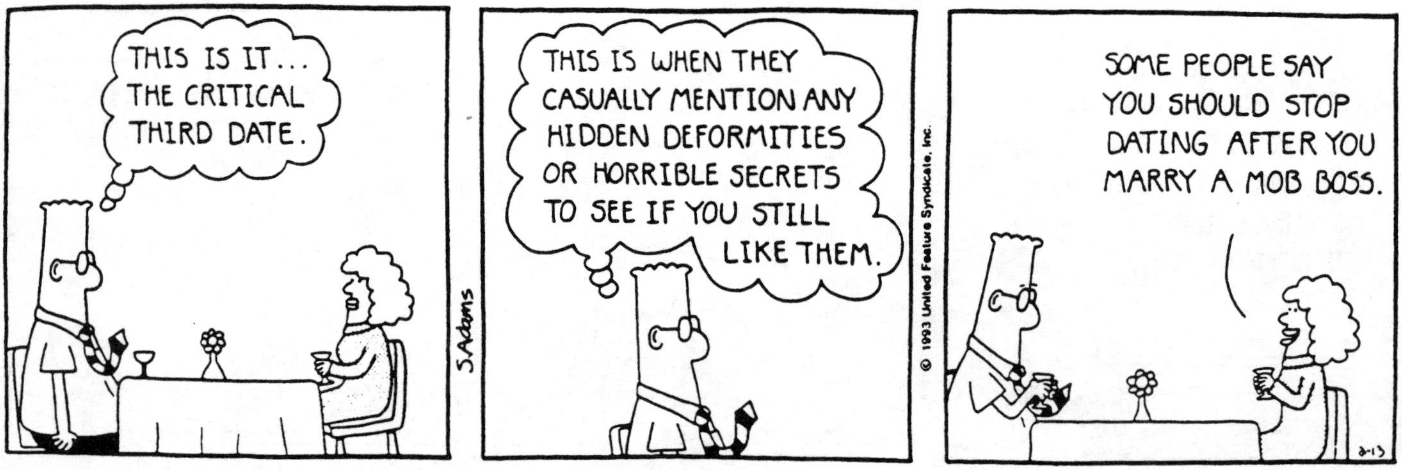
THIS IS IT... THE CRITICAL THIRD DATE.
S. Adams
THIS IS WHEN THEY CASUALLY MENTION ANY HIDDEN DEFORMITIES OR HORRIBLE SECRETS TO SEE IF YOU STILL LIKE THEM.
© 1993 United Feature Syndicate, Inc.
SOME PEOPLE SAY YOU SHOULD STOP DATING AFTER YOU MARRY A MOB BOSS.
2-13

DILBERT, I WANT YOU TO INTERVIEW THE JOB APPLICANT WHO'S COMING IN TODAY.
SEE IF HE'S GOT WHAT IT TAKES TO BE AN ENGINEER.
S.Adams
HI, KARL. WE'LL START WITH THE STANDARD ENGINEERING TEST.
OKEY-DOKEY.
I HAVE THIRTY-FIVE PENS AND PENCILS HERE. HOW MANY ARE REALLY NEEDED TO PERFORM YOUR JOB?
ALL OF THEM.
CORRECT... NOW, WHAT IS THE PROPER WAY TO CARRY THEM WITH YOU?
2-14
© 1993 United Feature Syndicate, Inc.
RIGHT AGAIN. LAST QUESTION: WHAT IS THE ADVANTAGE OF WEARING NATURAL FABRICS?
UH-OH... PANIC SITUATION.
I... I DON'T KNOW.
THAT'S OKAY. I WAS TESTING YOUR HAIR. YOU'RE AN ENGINEER.

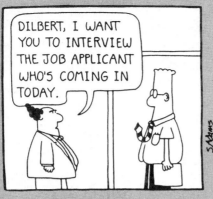

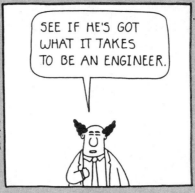

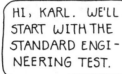

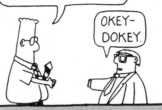

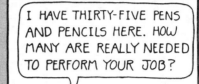

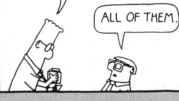

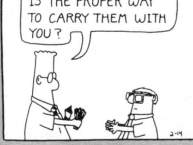

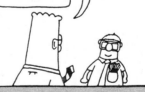

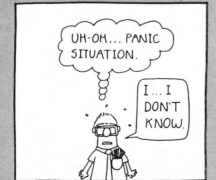

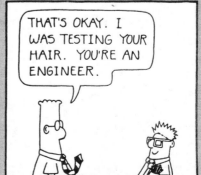

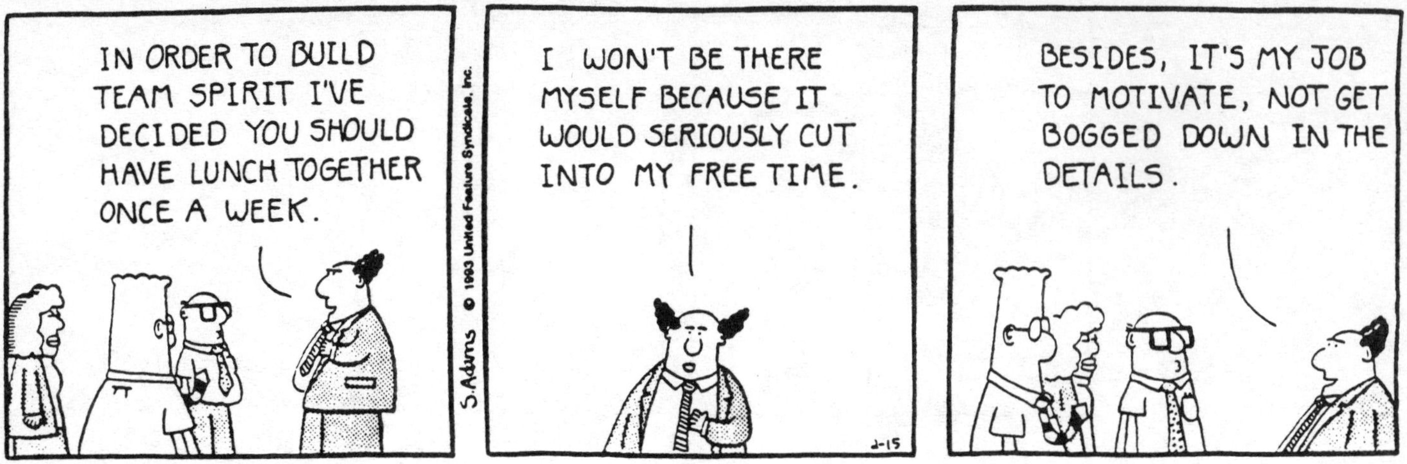
IN ORDER TO BUILD TEAM SPIRIT I'VE DECIDED YOU SHOULD HAVE LUNCH TOGETHER ONCE A WEEK.
S. Adams © 1993 United Feature Syndicate, Inc.
I WON'T BE THERE MYSELF BECAUSE IT WOULD SERIOUSLY CUT INTO MY FREE TIME.
2-15
BESIDES, IT'S MY JOB TO MOTIVATE, NOT GET BOGGED DOWN IN THE DETAILS.

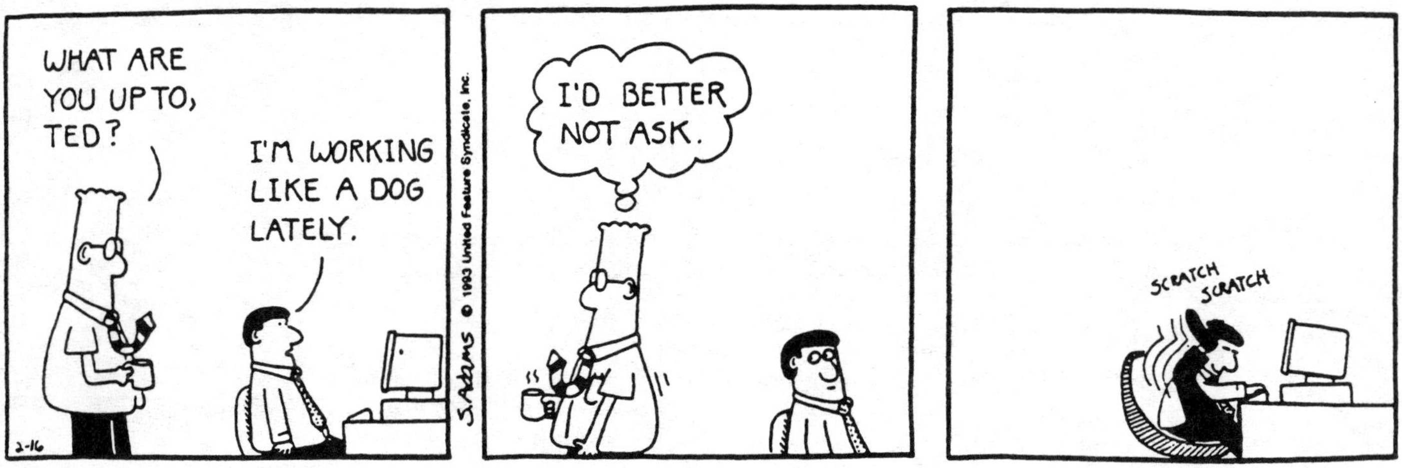
WHAT ARE YOU UP TO, TED?
I'M WORKING LIKE A DOG LATELY.
2-16
S. Adams © 1993 United Feature Syndicate, Inc.
I'D BETTER NOT ASK.
SCRATCH SCRATCH

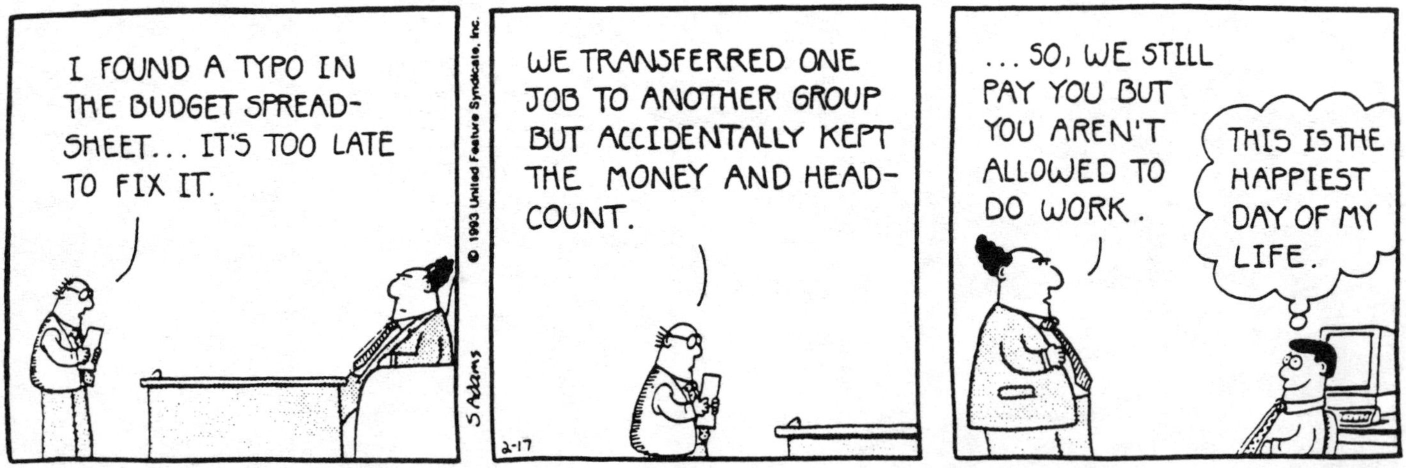
I FOUND A TYPO IN THE BUDGET SPREAD-SHEET... IT'S TOO LATE TO FIX IT.
S. Adams © 1993 United Feature Syndicate, Inc.
WE TRANSFERRED ONE JOB TO ANOTHER GROUP BUT ACCIDENTALLY KEPT THE MONEY AND HEAD-COUNT.
2-17
...SO, WE STILL PAY YOU BUT YOU AREN'T ALLOWED TO DO WORK.
THIS IS THE HAPPIEST DAY OF MY LIFE.

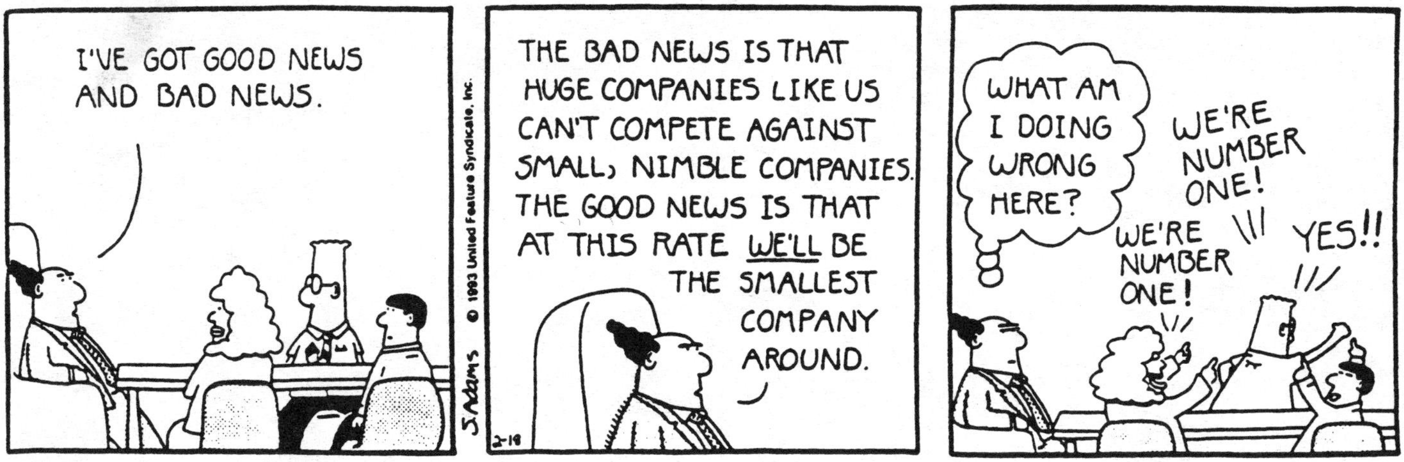
I'VE GOT GOOD NEWS AND BAD NEWS.
THE BAD NEWS IS THAT HUGE COMPANIES LIKE US CAN'T COMPETE AGAINST SMALL, NIMBLE COMPANIES. THE GOOD NEWS IS THAT AT THIS RATE WE'LL BE THE SMALLEST COMPANY AROUND.
S. Adams
© 1993 United Feature Syndicate, Inc.
2-18
WHAT AM I DOING WRONG HERE?
WE'RE NUMBER ONE!
WE'RE NUMBER ONE!
YES!!

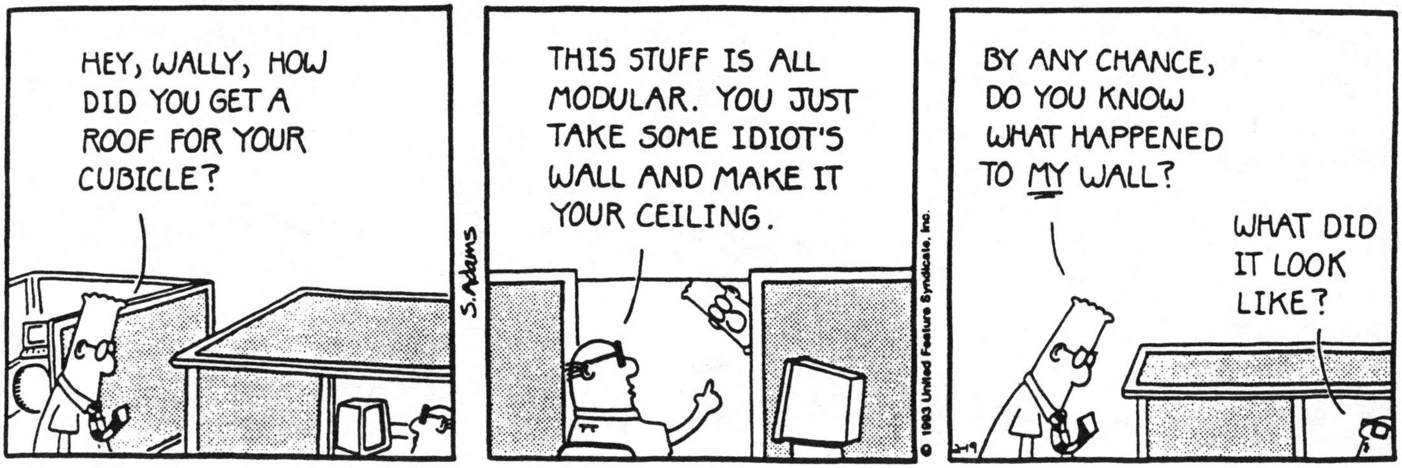
HEY, WALLY, HOW DID YOU GET A ROOF FOR YOUR CUBICLE?
S. Adams
THIS STUFF IS ALL MODULAR. YOU JUST TAKE SOME IDIOT'S WALL AND MAKE IT YOUR CEILING.
© 1993 United Feature Syndicate, Inc.
BY ANY CHANCE, DO YOU KNOW WHAT HAPPENED TO MY WALL?
WHAT DID IT LOOK LIKE?
2-19

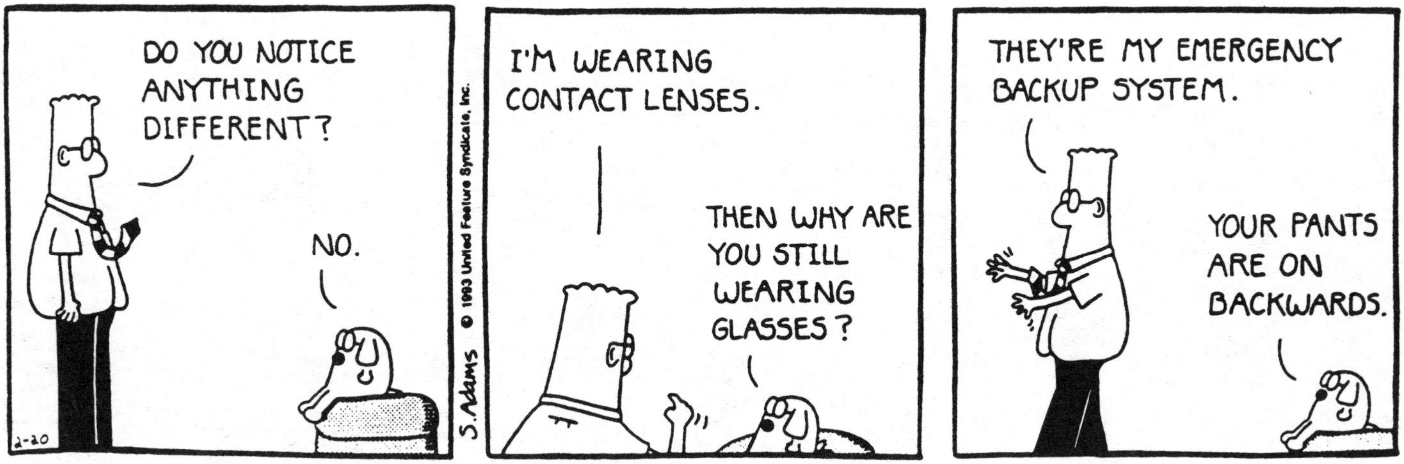
DO YOU NOTICE ANYTHING DIFFERENT?
NO.
2-20
S. Adams
© 1993 United Feature Syndicate, Inc.
I'M WEARING CONTACT LENSES.
THEN WHY ARE YOU STILL WEARING GLASSES?
THEY'RE MY EMERGENCY BACKUP SYSTEM.
YOUR PANTS ARE ON BACKWARDS.

DOGBERT'S DIGITAL DATING SERVICE
I'M A LOSER. SIGN ME UP.
SAY "VELVEETA."
NOW WE DIGITIZE YOUR PICTURE FOR THE DATABASE.
I COULD ADD SOME DIGITAL HAIR.
GOOD IDEA.
MAYBE I SHOULD BOB YOUR NOSE AND GIVE YOU A TAN.
THAT'S FAIR.
WHITEN TEETH?
YES
SMOOTH WRINKLES?
YES
HIDE STOMACH?
YES
THICKEN LIPS?
YES
I LOOK LIKE SANDRA BERNHARD.
YEAH, BUT YOU HAVE TO ADMIT IT IMPROVES YOUR ODDS.
S.Adams © 1993 United Feature Syndicate, Inc.
2-21

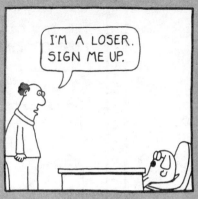

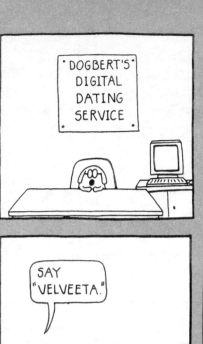

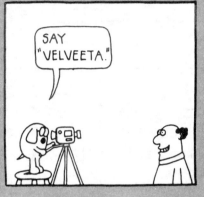

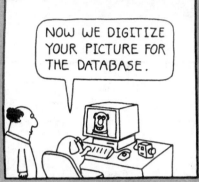

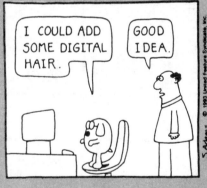

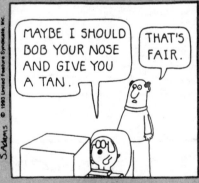

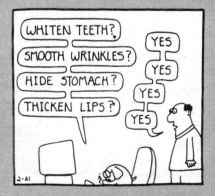

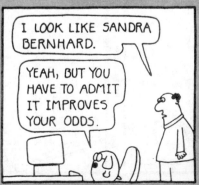

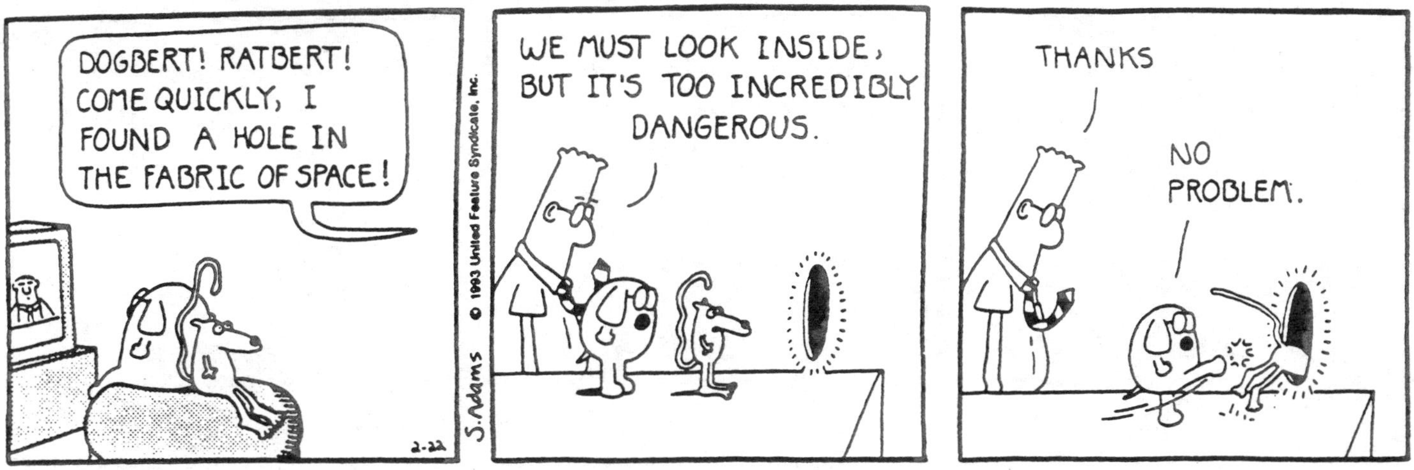
DOGBERT! RATBERT! COME QUICKLY, I FOUND A HOLE IN THE FABRIC OF SPACE!
WE MUST LOOK INSIDE, BUT IT'S TOO INCREDIBLY DANGEROUS.
S. Adams © 1993 United Feature Syndicate, Inc.
THANKS
NO PROBLEM.

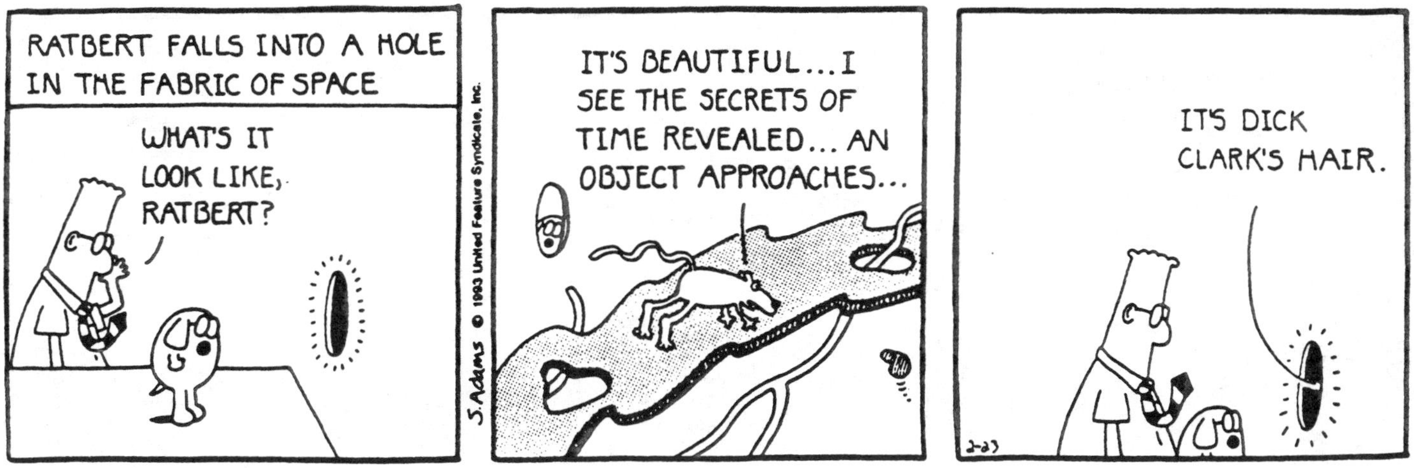
RATBERT FALLS INTO A HOLE IN THE FABRIC OF SPACE
WHAT'S IT LOOK LIKE, RATBERT?
IT'S BEAUTIFUL... I SEE THE SECRETS OF TIME REVEALED... AN OBJECT APPROACHES...
S. Adams © 1993 United Feature Syndicate, Inc.
IT'S DICK CLARK'S HAIR.

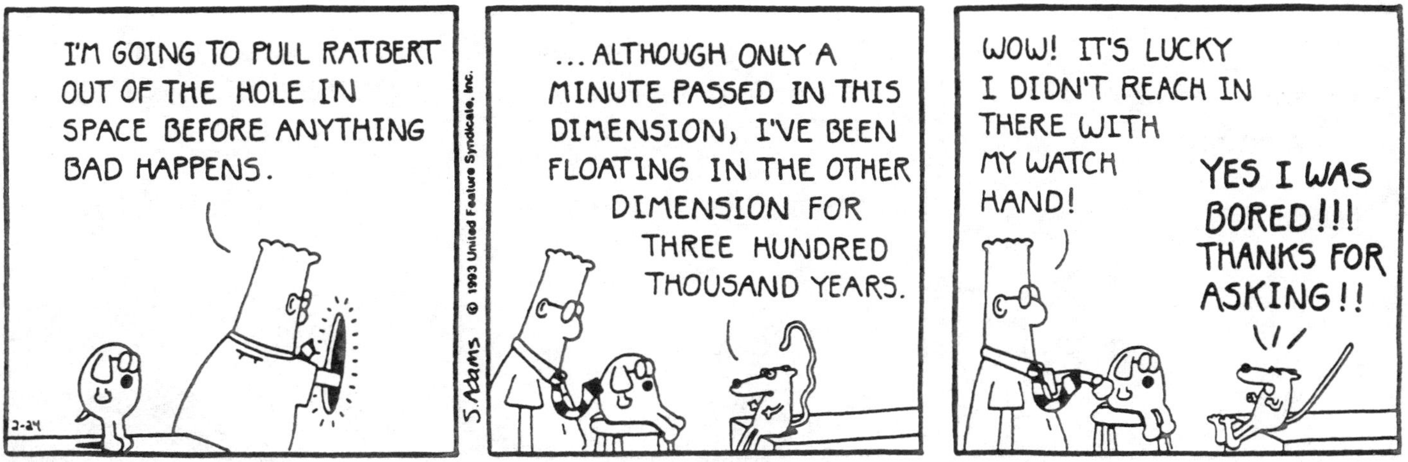
I'M GOING TO PULL RATBERT OUT OF THE HOLE IN SPACE BEFORE ANYTHING BAD HAPPENS.
...ALTHOUGH ONLY A MINUTE PASSED IN THIS DIMENSION, I'VE BEEN FLOATING IN THE OTHER DIMENSION FOR THREE HUNDRED THOUSAND YEARS.
S. Adams © 1993 United Feature Syndicate, Inc.
WOW! IT'S LUCKY I DIDN'T REACH IN THERE WITH MY WATCH HAND!
YES I WAS BORED!!! THANKS FOR ASKING!!

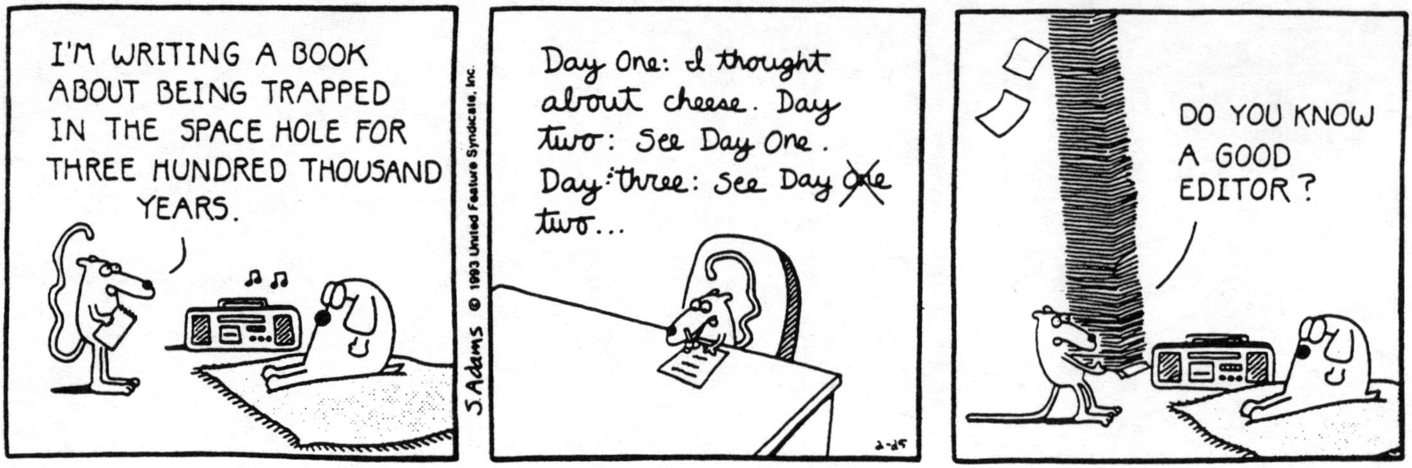
I'M WRITING A BOOK ABOUT BEING TRAPPED IN THE SPACE HOLE FOR THREE HUNDRED THOUSAND YEARS.
S. Adams © 1993 United Feature Syndicate, Inc.
Day One: I thought about cheese. Day two: See Day One. Day three: See Day ~~One~~ two...
2-25
DO YOU KNOW A GOOD EDITOR?

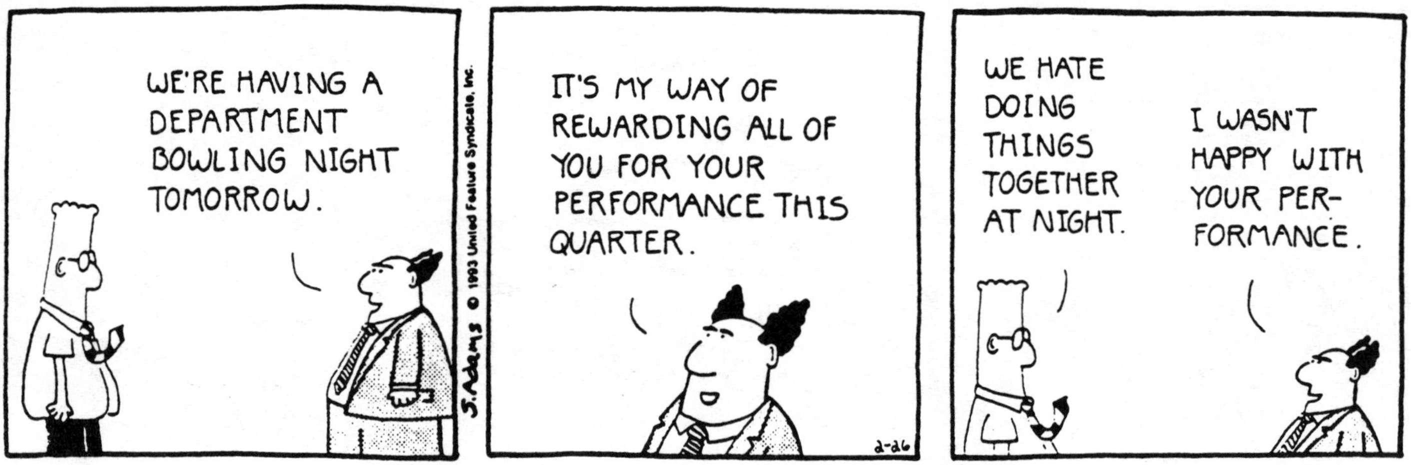
WE'RE HAVING A DEPARTMENT BOWLING NIGHT TOMORROW.
S. Adams © 1993 United Feature Syndicate, Inc.
IT'S MY WAY OF REWARDING ALL OF YOU FOR YOUR PERFORMANCE THIS QUARTER.
2-26
WE HATE DOING THINGS TOGETHER AT NIGHT.
I WASN'T HAPPY WITH YOUR PERFORMANCE.

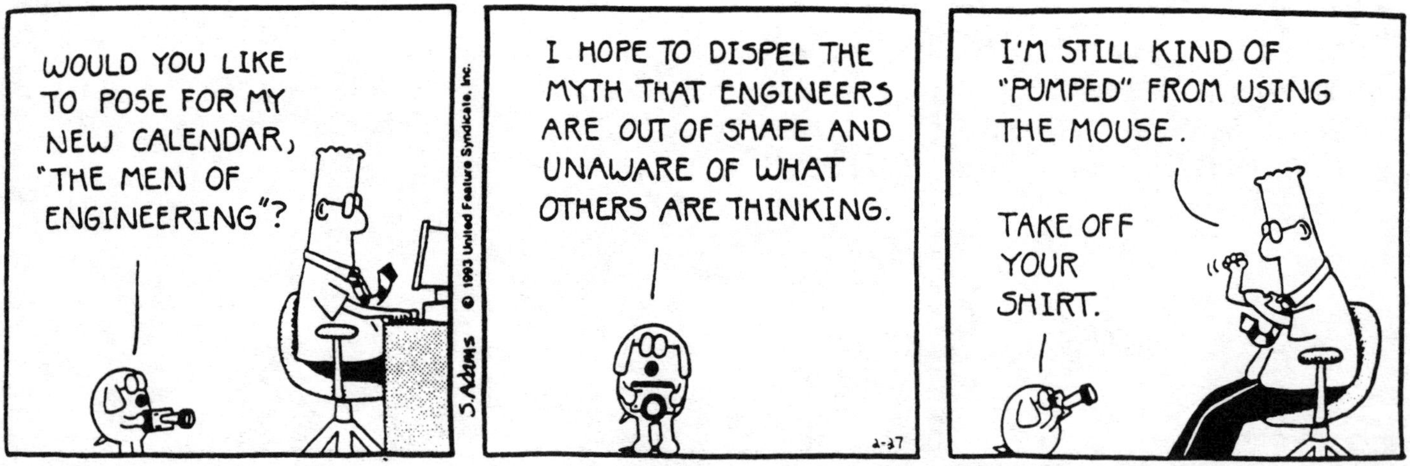
WOULD YOU LIKE TO POSE FOR MY NEW CALENDAR, "THE MEN OF ENGINEERING"?
S. Adams © 1993 United Feature Syndicate, Inc.
I HOPE TO DISPEL THE MYTH THAT ENGINEERS ARE OUT OF SHAPE AND UNAWARE OF WHAT OTHERS ARE THINKING.
2-27
I'M STILL KIND OF "PUMPED" FROM USING THE MOUSE.
TAKE OFF YOUR SHIRT.

LET'S TAKE A TEN-MINUTE BREAK.
UH-OH
$
I'VE GOT TO USE THE RESTROOM AND GET BACK BEFORE ALL THE MINGLE GROUPS HAVE SOLIDIFIED.
OH NO, IT'S AN AIR DRYER, AN UNEXPECTED DELAY!
I'M TOO LATE. ALL THE MINGLERS HAVE FORMED IMPENETRABLE GROUPS.
I'LL PRETEND TO STUDY THE AGENDA SO IT LOOKS LIKE I HAVE A REASON TO BE ALONE.
© 1993 United Feature Syndicate, Inc.
EVERYBODY KNOWS IT DOESN'T TAKE THIS LONG TO READ AN AGENDA. NOW WHAT DO I DO??
I'VE GOT TO STAND HERE ALONE, TOTALLY NON-MINGLED, FOR FIVE MORE MINUTES.
2-28
TOUGH DAY AT WORK?
JUST THE BREAKS.

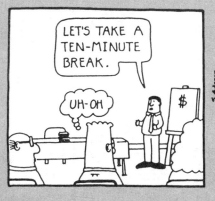

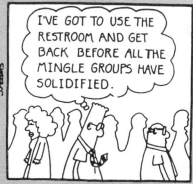

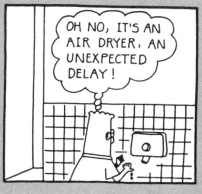

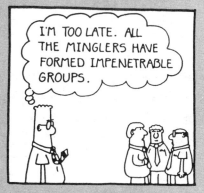

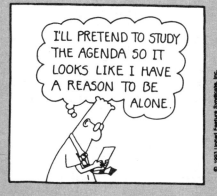

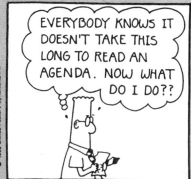

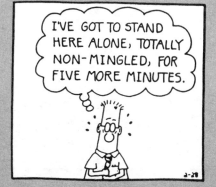

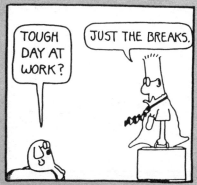

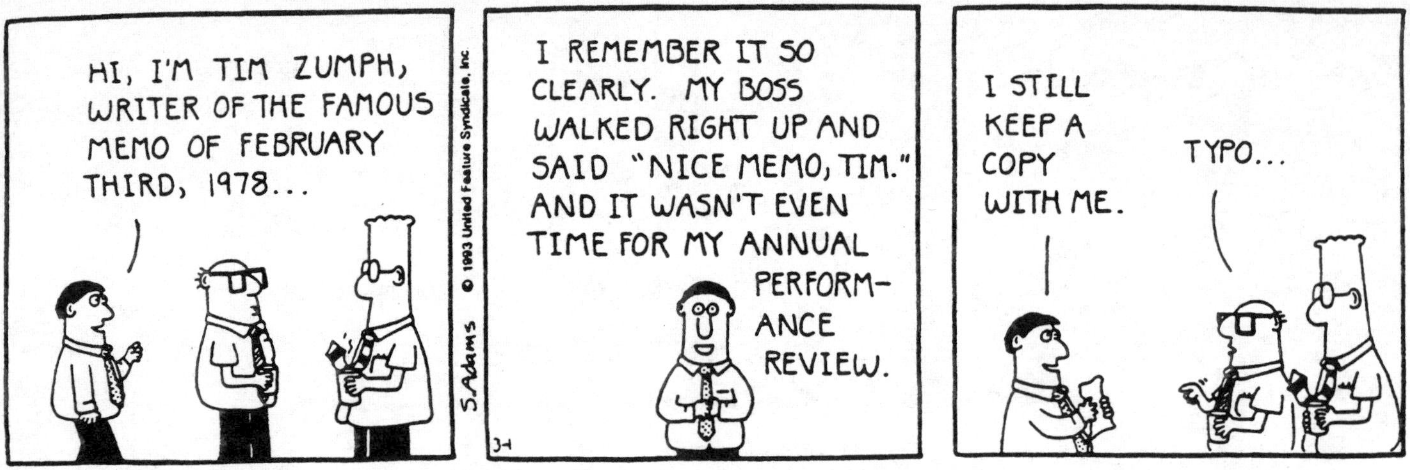
HI, I'M TIM ZUMPH, WRITER OF THE FAMOUS MEMO OF FEBRUARY THIRD, 1978...
S. Adams © 1993 United Feature Syndicate, Inc.
I REMEMBER IT SO CLEARLY. MY BOSS WALKED RIGHT UP AND SAID "NICE MEMO, TIM." AND IT WASN'T EVEN TIME FOR MY ANNUAL PERFORMANCE REVIEW.
3-1
I STILL KEEP A COPY WITH ME.
TYPO...

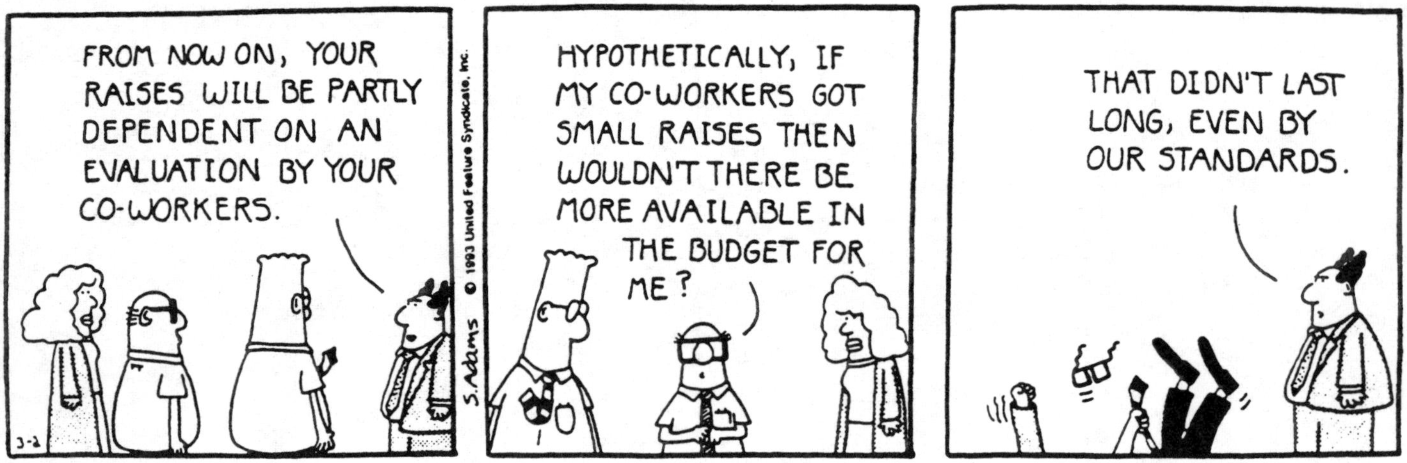
FROM NOW ON, YOUR RAISES WILL BE PARTLY DEPENDENT ON AN EVALUATION BY YOUR CO-WORKERS.
3-2
S. Adams © 1993 United Feature Syndicate, Inc.
HYPOTHETICALLY, IF MY CO-WORKERS GOT SMALL RAISES THEN WOULDN'T THERE BE MORE AVAILABLE IN THE BUDGET FOR ME?
THAT DIDN'T LAST LONG, EVEN BY OUR STANDARDS.

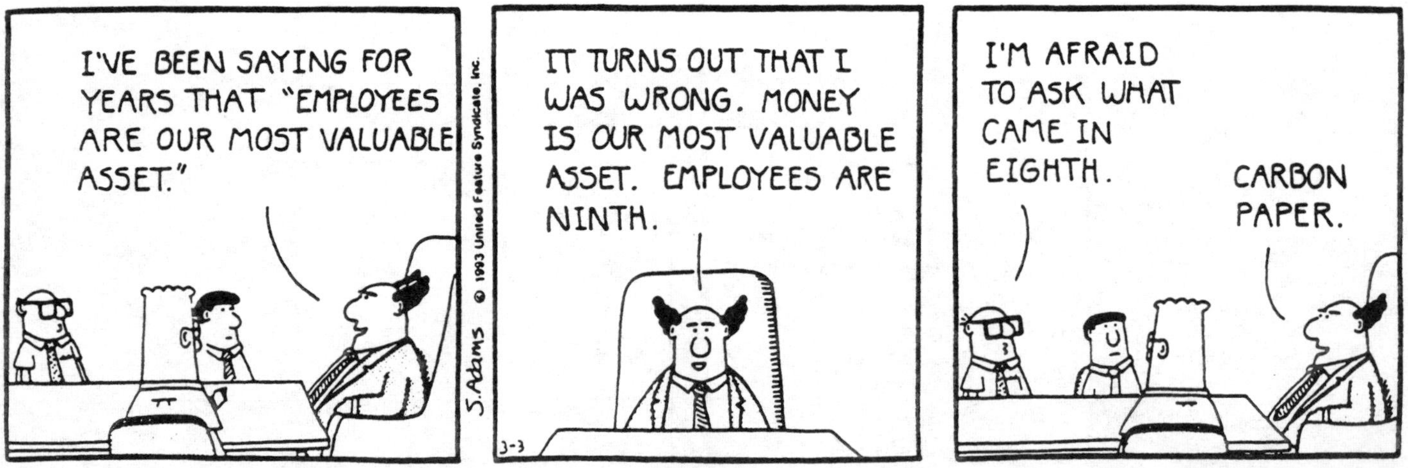
I'VE BEEN SAYING FOR YEARS THAT "EMPLOYEES ARE OUR MOST VALUABLE ASSET."
S. Adams © 1993 United Feature Syndicate, Inc.
IT TURNS OUT THAT I WAS WRONG. MONEY IS OUR MOST VALUABLE ASSET. EMPLOYEES ARE NINTH.
3-3
I'M AFRAID TO ASK WHAT CAME IN EIGHTH.
CARBON PAPER.

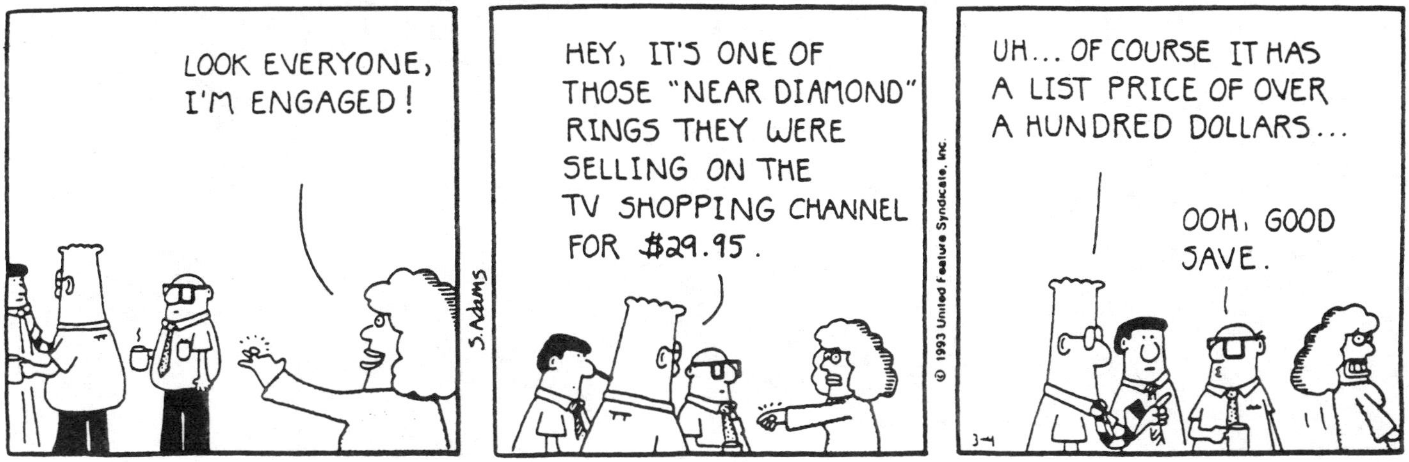
LOOK EVERYONE, I'M ENGAGED!
S. Adams
HEY, IT'S ONE OF THOSE "NEAR DIAMOND" RINGS THEY WERE SELLING ON THE TV SHOPPING CHANNEL FOR $29.95.
© 1993 United Feature Syndicate, Inc.
UH... OF COURSE IT HAS A LIST PRICE OF OVER A HUNDRED DOLLARS...
OOH, GOOD SAVE.
3-4

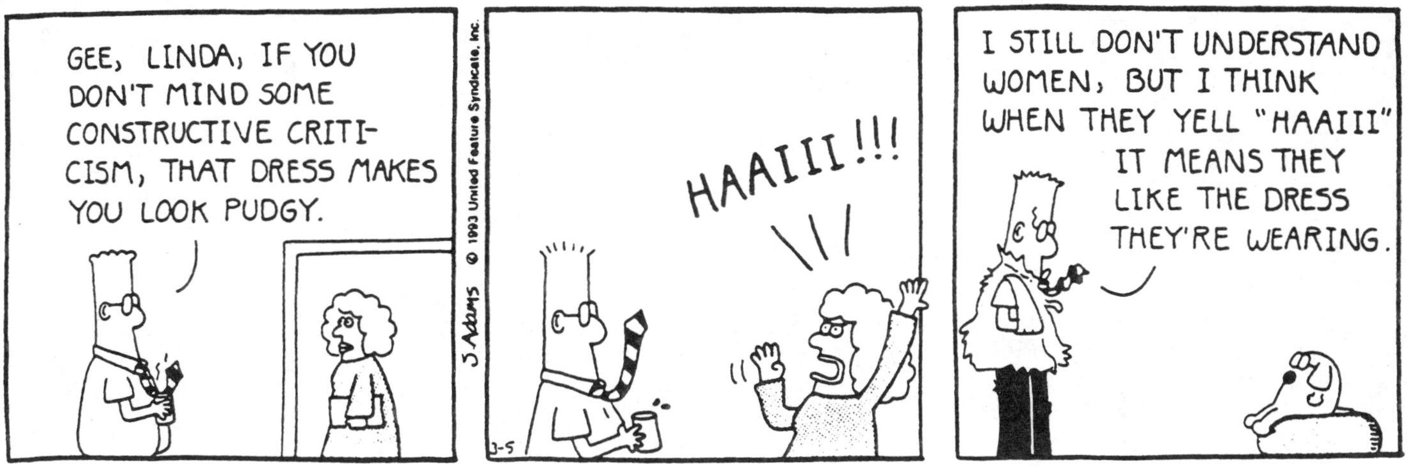
GEE, LINDA, IF YOU DON'T MIND SOME CONSTRUCTIVE CRITI-CISM, THAT DRESS MAKES YOU LOOK PUDGY.
S. Adams © 1993 United Feature Syndicate, Inc.
HAAIII!!!
3-5
I STILL DON'T UNDERSTAND WOMEN, BUT I THINK WHEN THEY YELL "HAAIII" IT MEANS THEY LIKE THE DRESS THEY'RE WEARING.

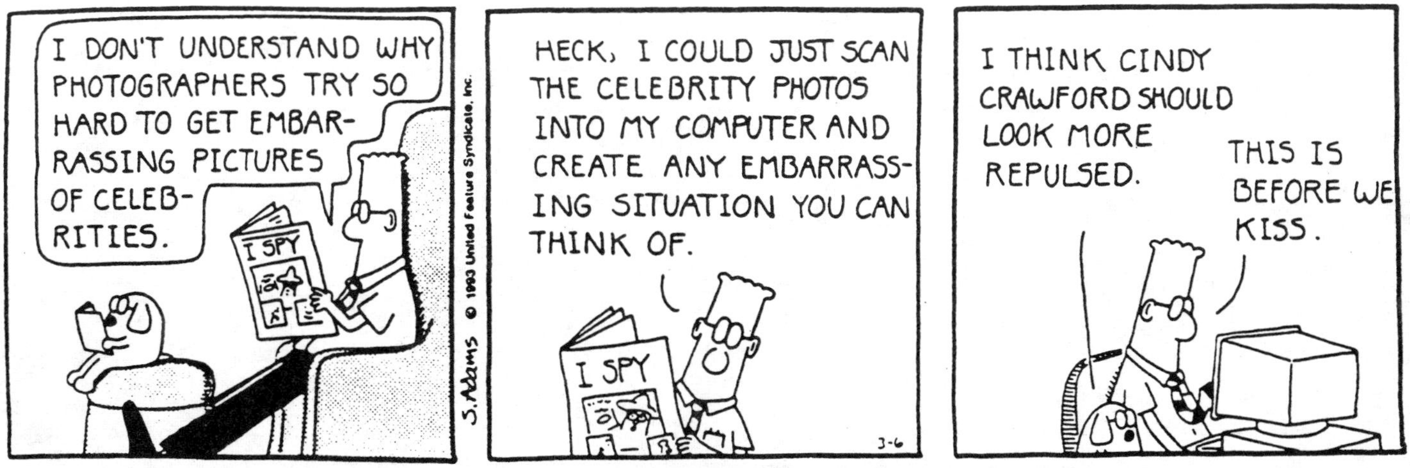
I DON'T UNDERSTAND WHY PHOTOGRAPHERS TRY SO HARD TO GET EMBAR-RASSING PICTURES OF CELEB-RITIES.
I SPY
S. Adams © 1993 United Feature Syndicate, Inc.
HECK, I COULD JUST SCAN THE CELEBRITY PHOTOS INTO MY COMPUTER AND CREATE ANY EMBARRASS-ING SITUATION YOU CAN THINK OF.
I SPY
3-6
I THINK CINDY CRAWFORD SHOULD LOOK MORE REPULSED.
THIS IS BEFORE WE KISS.

I SEE SOME NEW FACES. LET'S GO AROUND THE TABLE AND INTRODUCE OURSELVES.
I HATE THIS. I'M ALWAYS AFRAID I'LL FORGET MY NAME WHEN THE PRESSURE IS ON ME.
...AND I'VE BEEN IN THE INTEGRATED DESIGN DISTRICT FOR FOUR YEARS.
UH-OH
PEOPLE ARE SAYING WHERE THEY WORK. I CAN'T REMEMBER THE NAME OF MY DISTRICT.
...AND THERE YOU HAVE IT! HA HA!
AAAGH! NOW THEY'RE ADDING WITTY COMMENTS.
S.Adams © 1993 United Feature Syndicate, Inc.
3-7
I'M DRAWING A BLANK. MY ONLY CHANCE IS TO PRETEND I ONLY SPEAK NORWEGIAN.
NORNA BORNA CORNA DORNA FIORD CAJORDA HA HA HA!
THE AMAZING THING IS THAT I GET PAID THE SAME NO MATTER WHAT I DO.
THANK GOD FOR THAT.

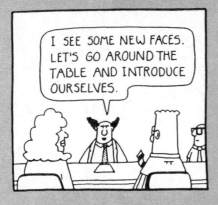

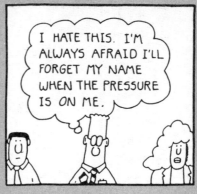

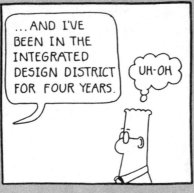

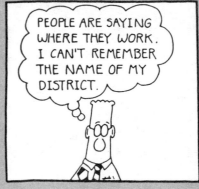

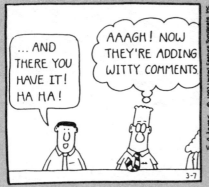

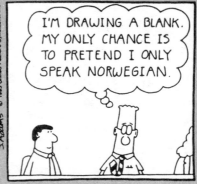

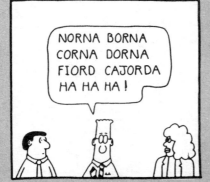

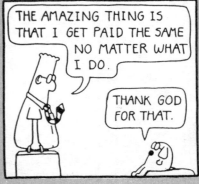

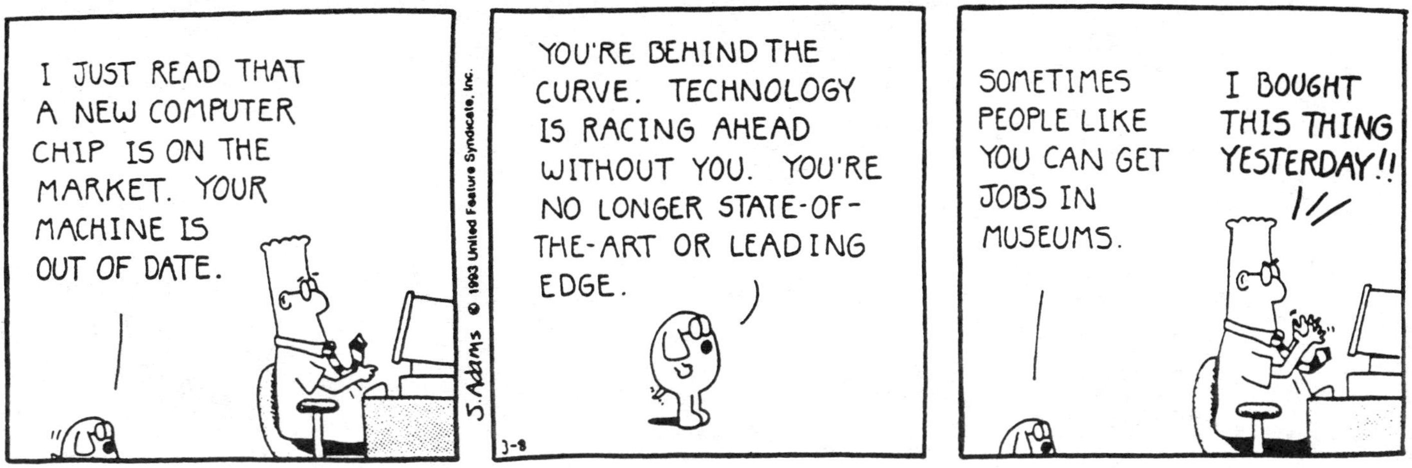
I JUST READ THAT A NEW COMPUTER CHIP IS ON THE MARKET. YOUR MACHINE IS OUT OF DATE.
S. Adams © 1993 United Feature Syndicate, Inc.
YOU'RE BEHIND THE CURVE. TECHNOLOGY IS RACING AHEAD WITHOUT YOU. YOU'RE NO LONGER STATE-OF-THE-ART OR LEADING EDGE.
3-8
SOMETIMES PEOPLE LIKE YOU CAN GET JOBS IN MUSEUMS.
I BOUGHT THIS THING YESTERDAY!!

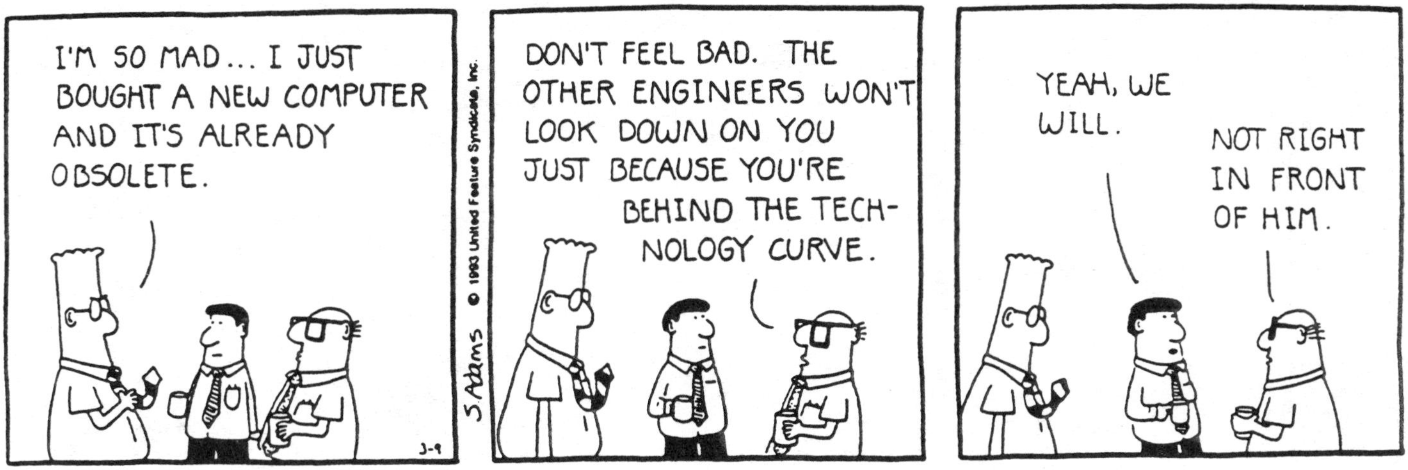
I'M SO MAD... I JUST BOUGHT A NEW COMPUTER AND IT'S ALREADY OBSOLETE.
3-9
S. Adams © 1993 United Feature Syndicate, Inc.
DON'T FEEL BAD. THE OTHER ENGINEERS WON'T LOOK DOWN ON YOU JUST BECAUSE YOU'RE BEHIND THE TECHNOLOGY CURVE.
YEAH, WE WILL.
NOT RIGHT IN FRONT OF HIM.

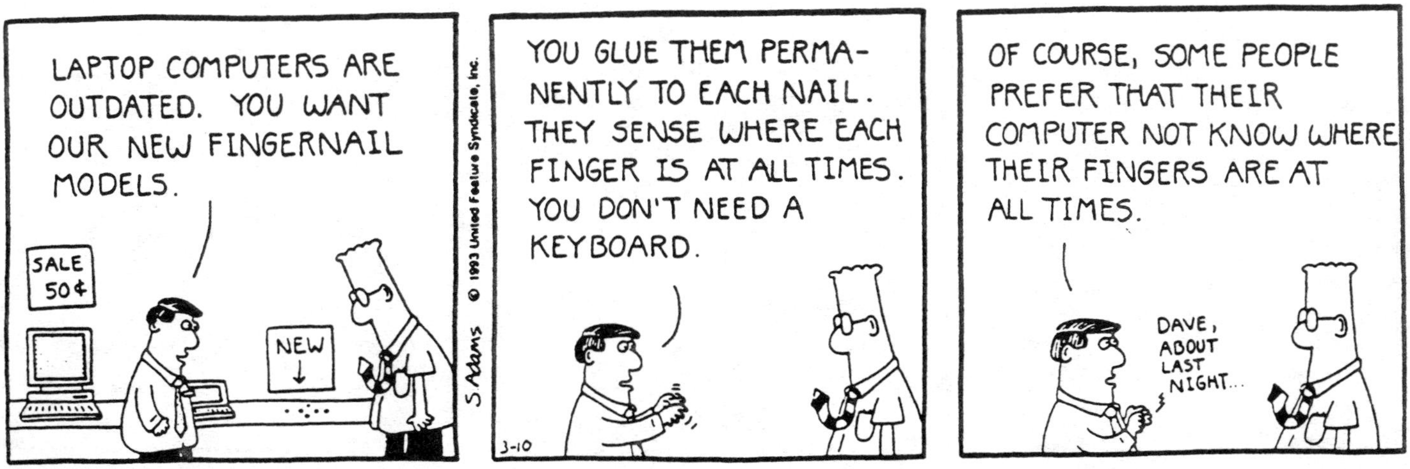
LAPTOP COMPUTERS ARE OUTDATED. YOU WANT OUR NEW FINGERNAIL MODELS.
SALE 50¢
NEW ↓
S. Adams © 1993 United Feature Syndicate, Inc.
YOU GLUE THEM PERMANENTLY TO EACH NAIL. THEY SENSE WHERE EACH FINGER IS AT ALL TIMES. YOU DON'T NEED A KEYBOARD.
3-10
OF COURSE, SOME PEOPLE PREFER THAT THEIR COMPUTER NOT KNOW WHERE THEIR FINGERS ARE AT ALL TIMES.
DAVE, ABOUT LAST NIGHT...

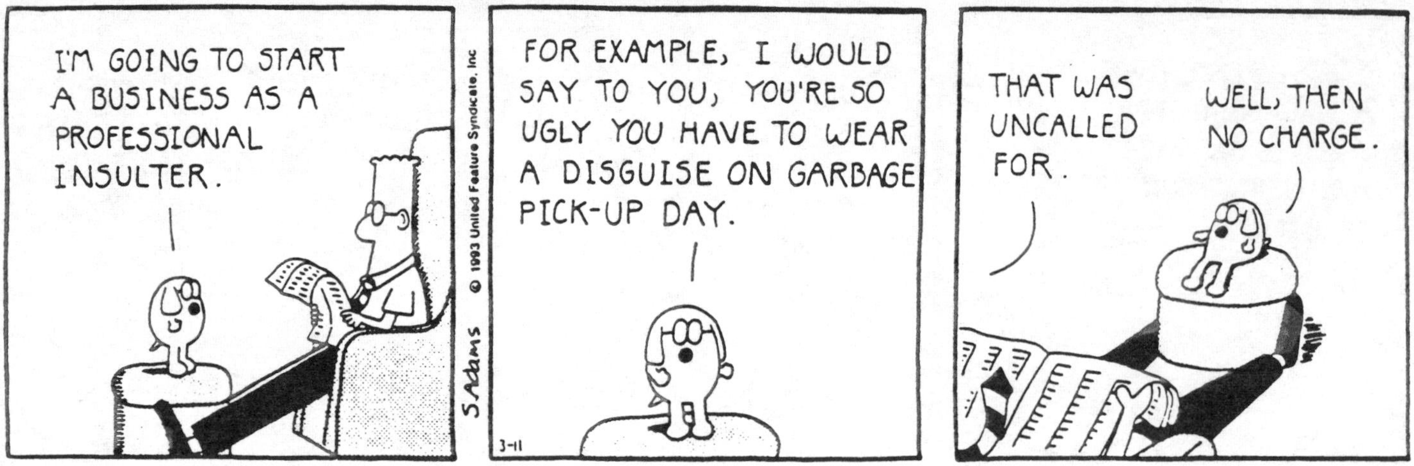
I'M GOING TO START A BUSINESS AS A PROFESSIONAL INSULTER.
FOR EXAMPLE, I WOULD SAY TO YOU, YOU'RE SO UGLY YOU HAVE TO WEAR A DISGUISE ON GARBAGE PICK-UP DAY.
THAT WAS UNCALLED FOR.
WELL, THEN NO CHARGE.
S. Adams © 1993 United Feature Syndicate, Inc
3-11

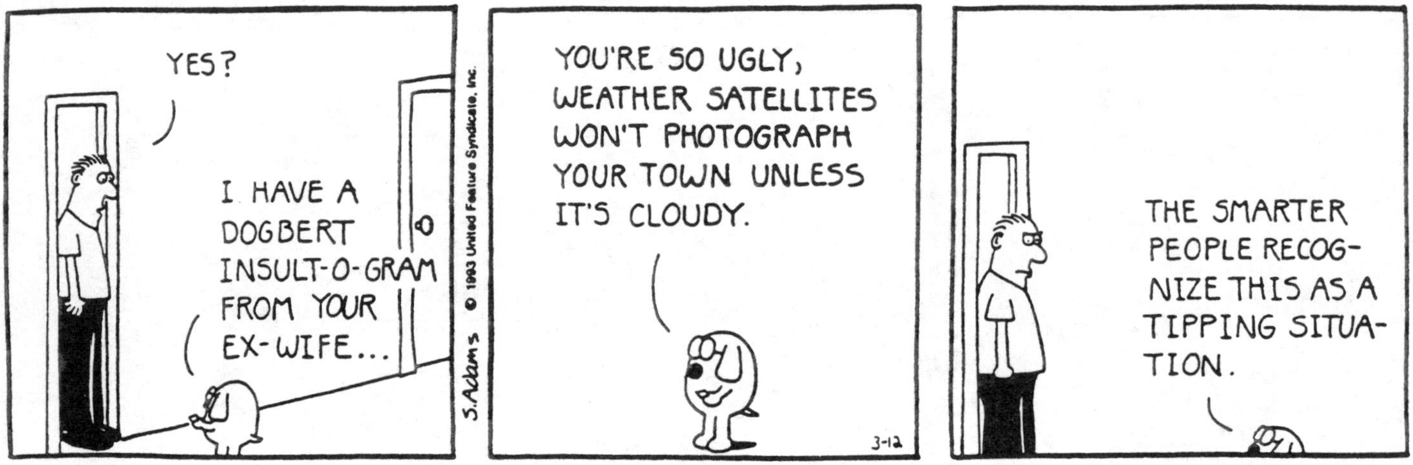
YES?
I HAVE A DOGBERT INSULT-O-GRAM FROM YOUR EX-WIFE...
YOU'RE SO UGLY, WEATHER SATELLITES WON'T PHOTOGRAPH YOUR TOWN UNLESS IT'S CLOUDY.
THE SMARTER PEOPLE RECOGNIZE THIS AS A TIPPING SITUATION.
S. Adams © 1993 United Feature Syndicate, Inc.
3-12

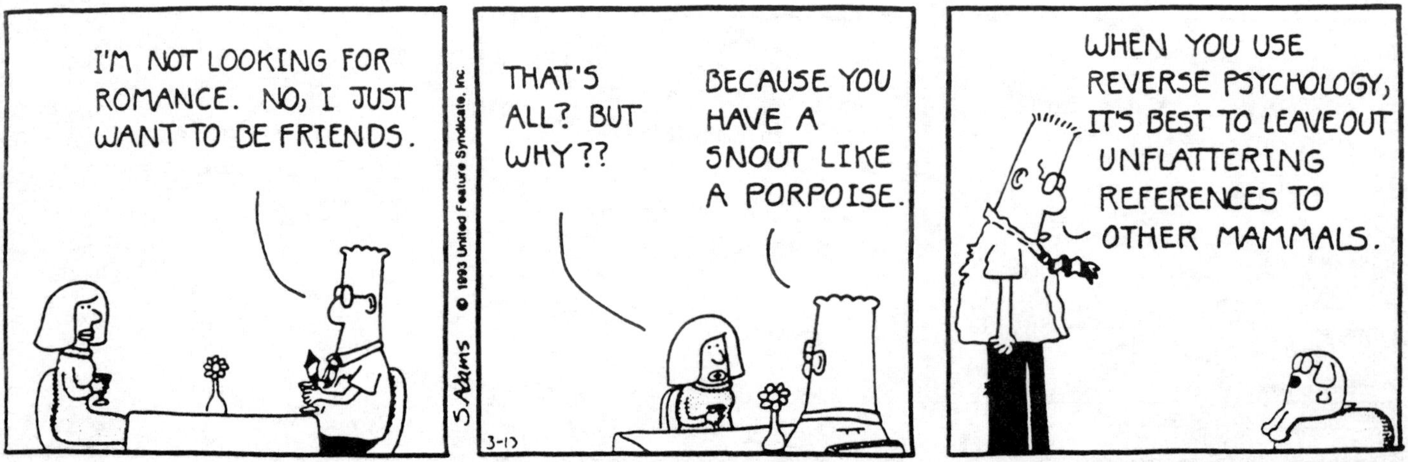
I'M NOT LOOKING FOR ROMANCE. NO, I JUST WANT TO BE FRIENDS.
THAT'S ALL? BUT WHY??
BECAUSE YOU HAVE A SNOUT LIKE A PORPOISE.
WHEN YOU USE REVERSE PSYCHOLOGY, IT'S BEST TO LEAVE OUT UNFLATTERING REFERENCES TO OTHER MAMMALS.
S. Adams © 1993 United Feature Syndicate, Inc
3-13

UH... LISA, I WAS WONDERING IF YOU'D LIKE TO GO ON A DATE WITH ME.
S. Adams
I CAN ONLY DATE YOU IF YOU SURVIVE THE "CHALLENGE OF FEAR."
WHAT IS THE "CHALLENGE OF FEAR"?
IT'S A TEST OF YOUR MANLINESS.
FIRST YOU MUST STICK YOUR HEAD IN THE DRAWER AS I SLAM IT SHUT.
THEN I STAPLE YOU TO THE EMPLOYEE BULLETIN BOARD.
© 1993 United Feature Syndicate, Inc
LIVE WEASELS ARE STUFFED IN YOUR PANTS.
FINALLY, YOU MUST FLING YOURSELF DOWN THE ELEVATOR SHAFT!
3-14
THE WEIRD THING IS THAT THEY RULE THE WORLD.
READY

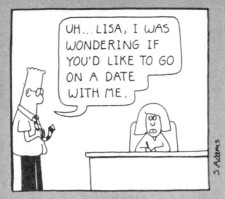

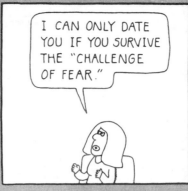

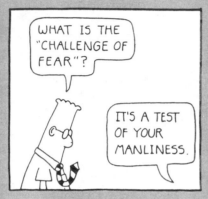

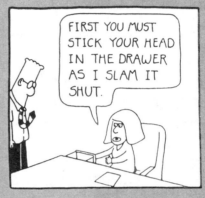

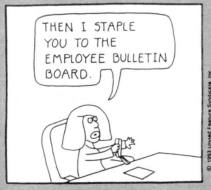

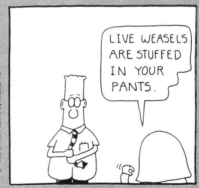

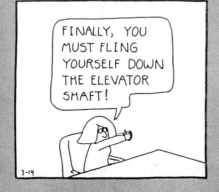

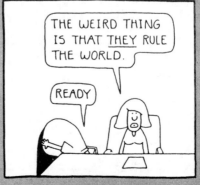

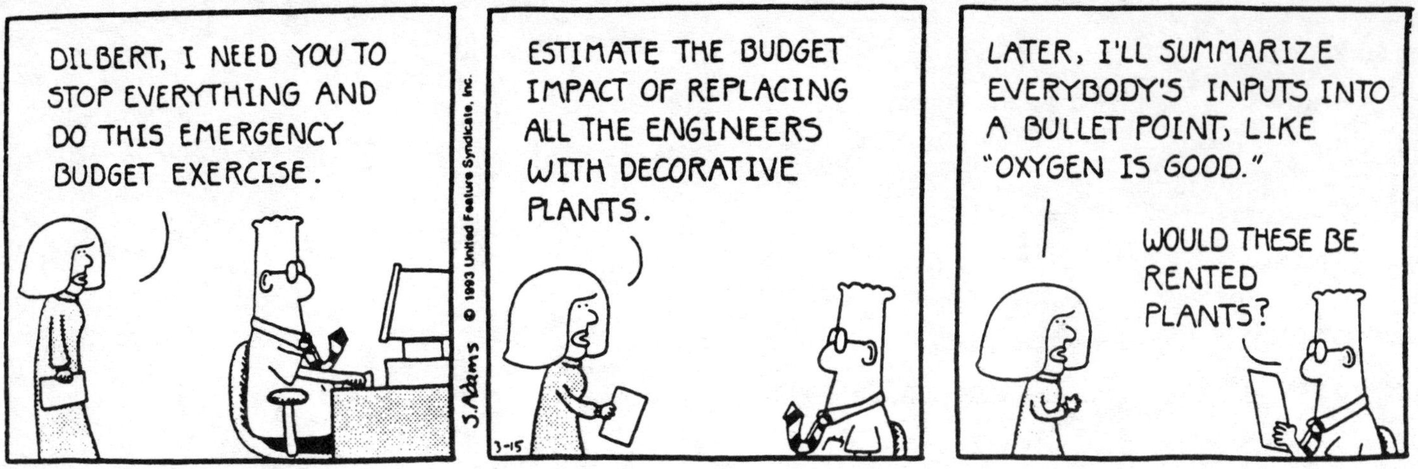
DILBERT, I NEED YOU TO STOP EVERYTHING AND DO THIS EMERGENCY BUDGET EXERCISE.
ESTIMATE THE BUDGET IMPACT OF REPLACING ALL THE ENGINEERS WITH DECORATIVE PLANTS.
LATER, I'LL SUMMARIZE EVERYBODY'S INPUTS INTO A BULLET POINT, LIKE "OXYGEN IS GOOD."
WOULD THESE BE RENTED PLANTS?
S. Adams © 1993 United Feature Syndicate, Inc.
3-15

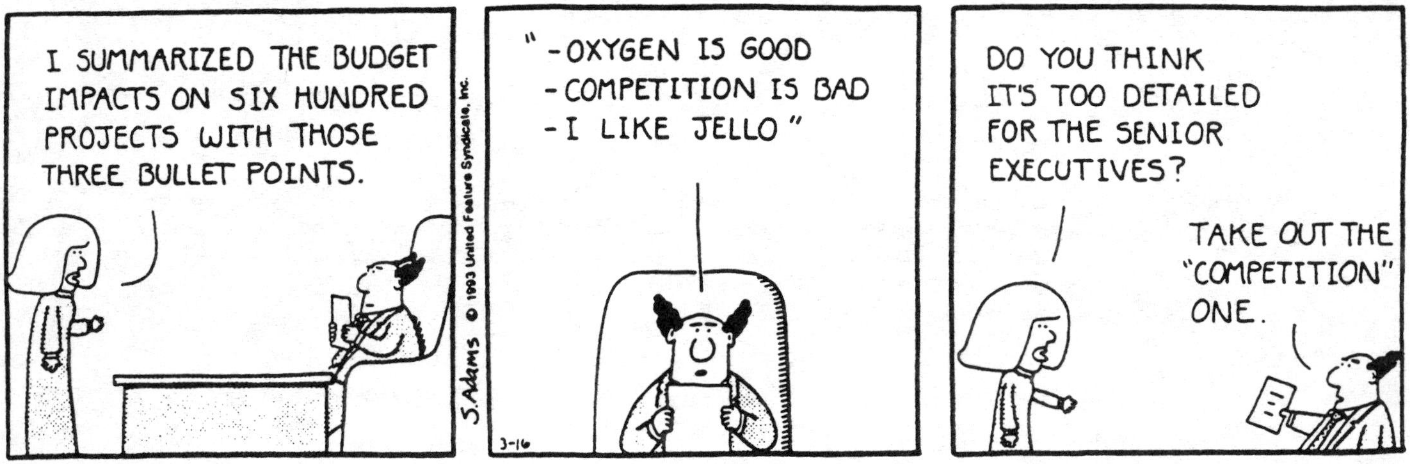
I SUMMARIZED THE BUDGET IMPACTS ON SIX HUNDRED PROJECTS WITH THOSE THREE BULLET POINTS.
" -OXYGEN IS GOOD
-COMPETITION IS BAD
-I LIKE JELLO "
DO YOU THINK IT'S TOO DETAILED FOR THE SENIOR EXECUTIVES?
TAKE OUT THE "COMPETITION" ONE.
S. Adams © 1993 United Feature Syndicate, Inc.
3-16

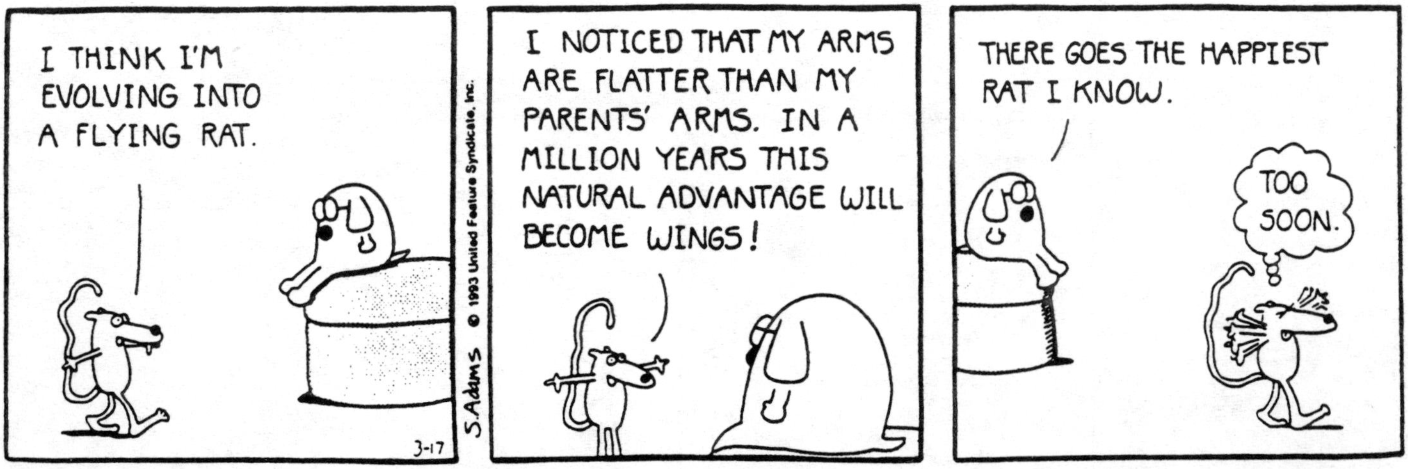
I THINK I'M EVOLVING INTO A FLYING RAT.
I NOTICED THAT MY ARMS ARE FLATTER THAN MY PARENTS' ARMS. IN A MILLION YEARS THIS NATURAL ADVANTAGE WILL BECOME WINGS!
THERE GOES THE HAPPIEST RAT I KNOW.
TOO SOON.
S. Adams © 1993 United Feature Syndicate, Inc.
3-17

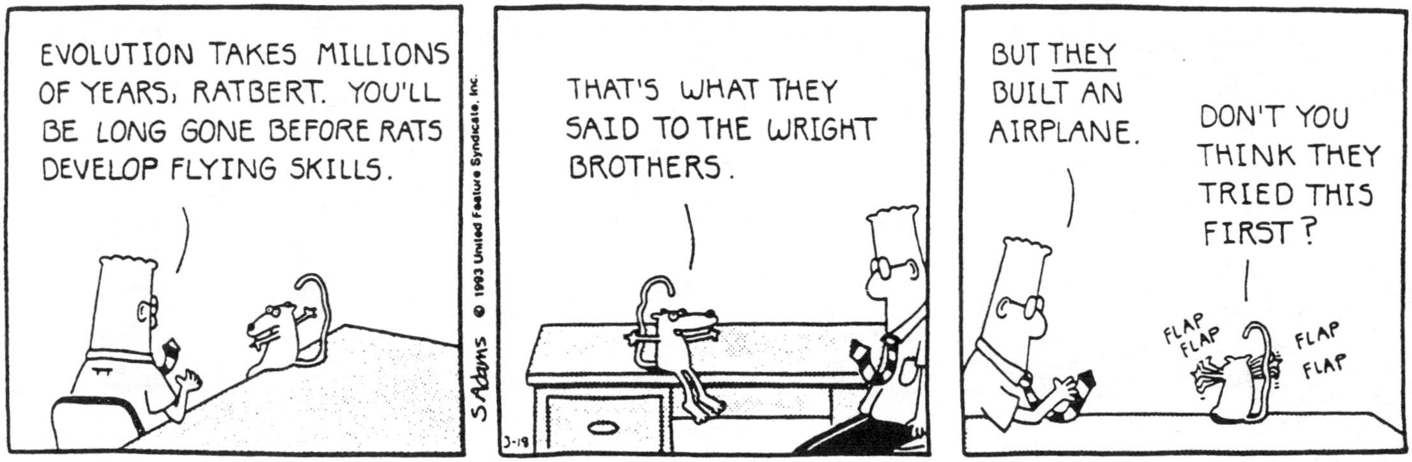
EVOLUTION TAKES MILLIONS OF YEARS, RATBERT. YOU'LL BE LONG GONE BEFORE RATS DEVELOP FLYING SKILLS.
S. Adams © 1993 United Feature Syndicate, Inc.
3-18
THAT'S WHAT THEY SAID TO THE WRIGHT BROTHERS.
BUT THEY BUILT AN AIRPLANE.
DON'T YOU THINK THEY TRIED THIS FIRST?
FLAP FLAP
FLAP FLAP

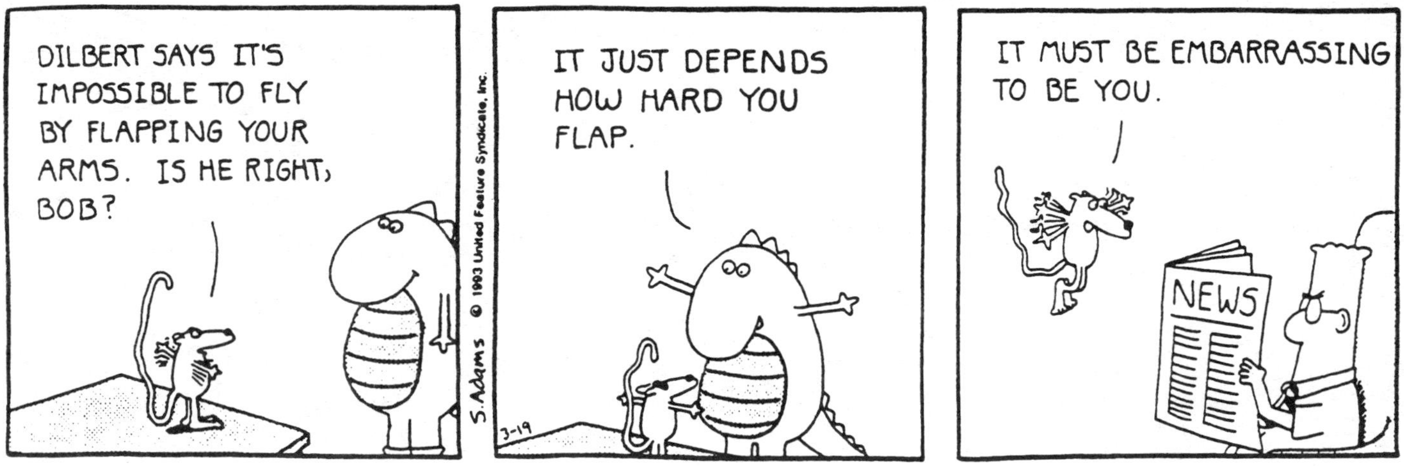
DILBERT SAYS IT'S IMPOSSIBLE TO FLY BY FLAPPING YOUR ARMS. IS HE RIGHT, BOB?
S. Adams © 1993 United Feature Syndicate, Inc.
3-19
IT JUST DEPENDS HOW HARD YOU FLAP.
IT MUST BE EMBARRASSING TO BE YOU.
NEWS

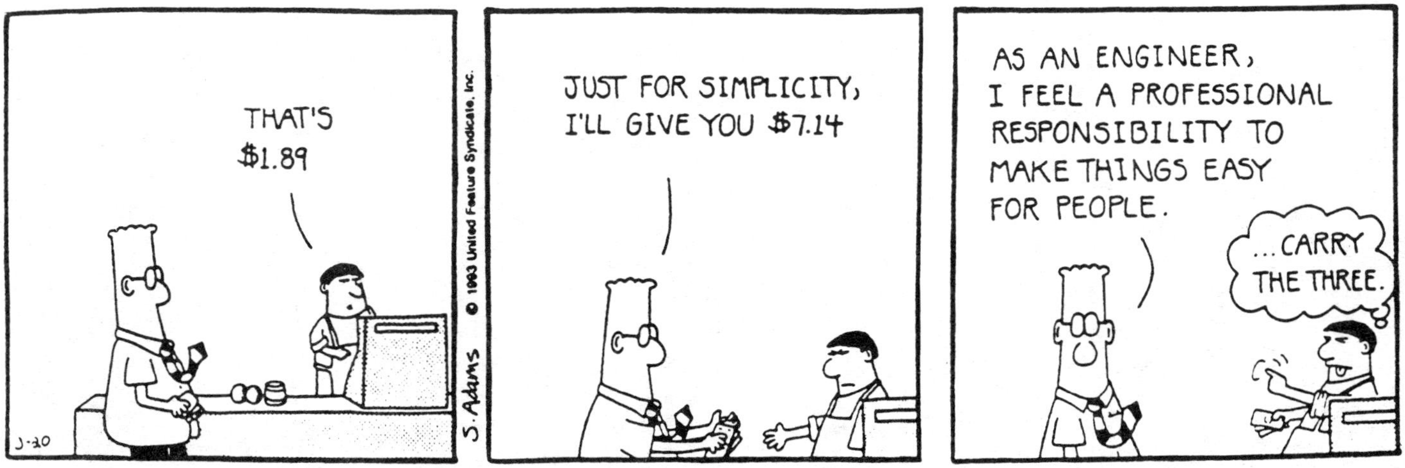
THAT'S $1.89
3-20
S. Adams © 1993 United Feature Syndicate, Inc.
JUST FOR SIMPLICITY, I'LL GIVE YOU $7.14
AS AN ENGINEER, I FEEL A PROFESSIONAL RESPONSIBILITY TO MAKE THINGS EASY FOR PEOPLE.
...CARRY THE THREE.

HAVE YOU EVER NOTICED HOW CRABBY PEOPLE ALWAYS GET WHAT THEY WANT?
S. Adams
IT DEFIES ALL REASON. SOCIETY SHOULD PUNISH THE CRABBY, BUT INSTEAD THEY GET REWARDED.
SO WHY FIGHT IT? I'VE DECIDED TO TRY THE POWER OF CRABDOM MYSELF.
I'M WORKING. COULD WE TALK LATER?
LATER?! LATER?! IS MY TIME WORTHLESS TO YOU? WHAT ABOUT MY NEEDS?
© 1993 United Feature Syndicate, Inc
WE'LL TALK NOW OR WE WON'T EVER TALK AGAIN!!
3-21
OKAY, OKAY! LET'S TALK.
OR WERE YOU JUST TESTING THE POWER OF CRABDOM?
NOW YOU WILL DANCE FOR ME.

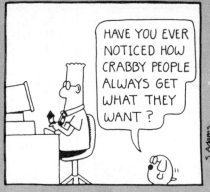

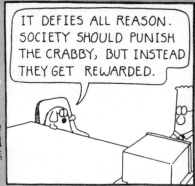

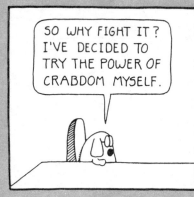

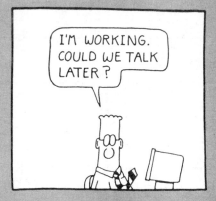

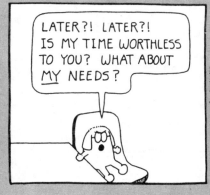

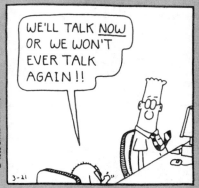

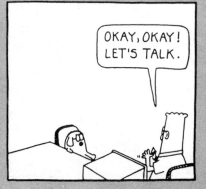

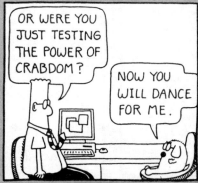

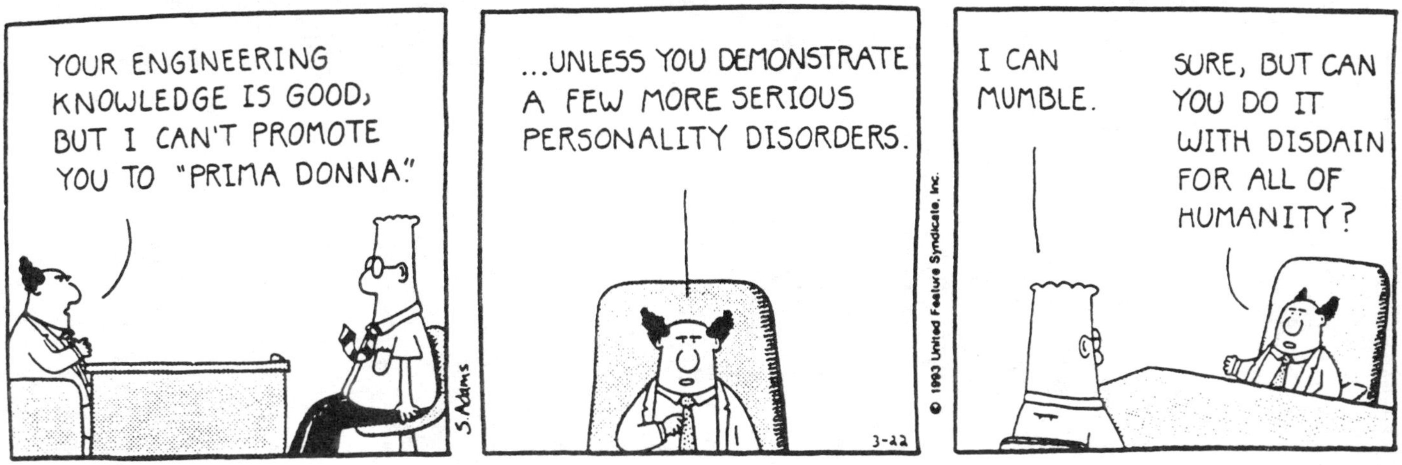
YOUR ENGINEERING KNOWLEDGE IS GOOD, BUT I CAN'T PROMOTE YOU TO "PRIMA DONNA."
...UNLESS YOU DEMONSTRATE A FEW MORE SERIOUS PERSONALITY DISORDERS.
I CAN MUMBLE.
SURE, BUT CAN YOU DO IT WITH DISDAIN FOR ALL OF HUMANITY?

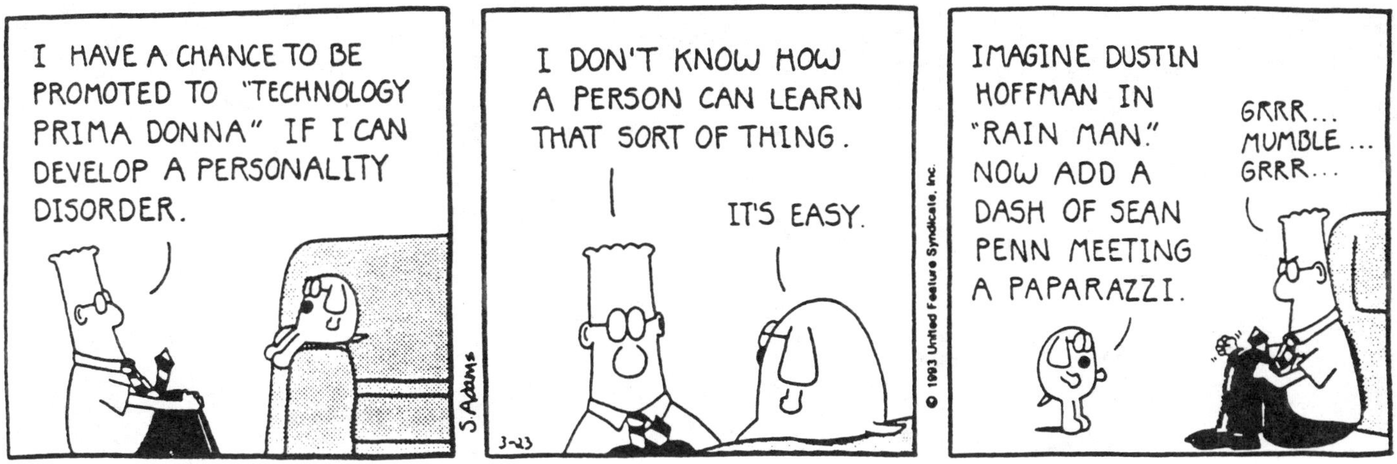
I HAVE A CHANCE TO BE PROMOTED TO "TECHNOLOGY PRIMA DONNA" IF I CAN DEVELOP A PERSONALITY DISORDER.
I DON'T KNOW HOW A PERSON CAN LEARN THAT SORT OF THING.
IT'S EASY.
IMAGINE DUSTIN HOFFMAN IN "RAIN MAN." NOW ADD A DASH OF SEAN PENN MEETING A PAPARAZZI.
GRRR... MUMBLE... GRRR...

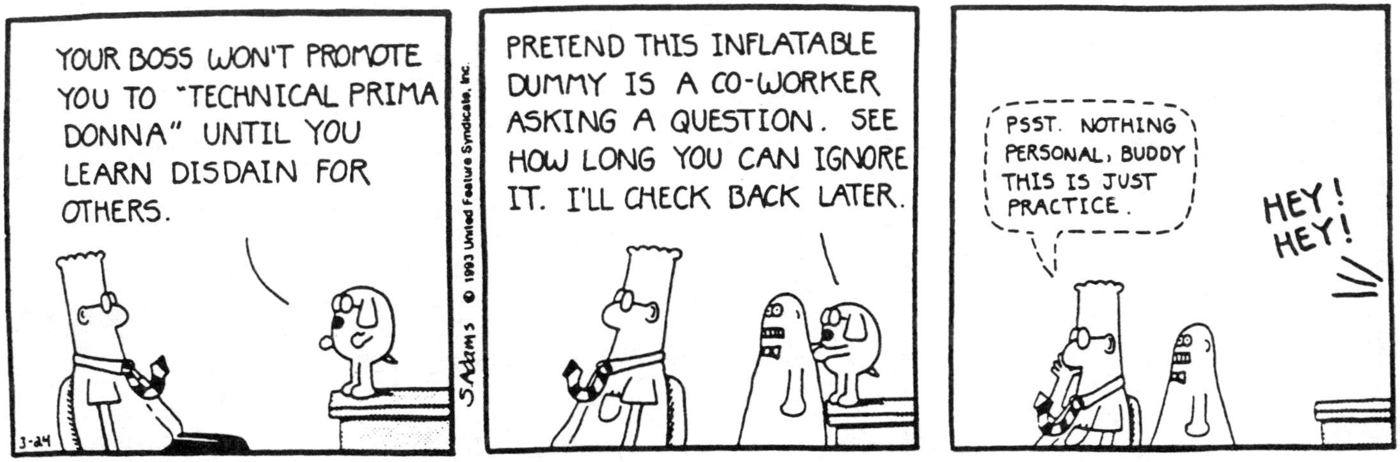
YOUR BOSS WON'T PROMOTE YOU TO "TECHNICAL PRIMA DONNA" UNTIL YOU LEARN DISDAIN FOR OTHERS.
PRETEND THIS INFLATABLE DUMMY IS A CO-WORKER ASKING A QUESTION. SEE HOW LONG YOU CAN IGNORE IT. I'LL CHECK BACK LATER.
PSST. NOTHING PERSONAL, BUDDY THIS IS JUST PRACTICE.
HEY! HEY!

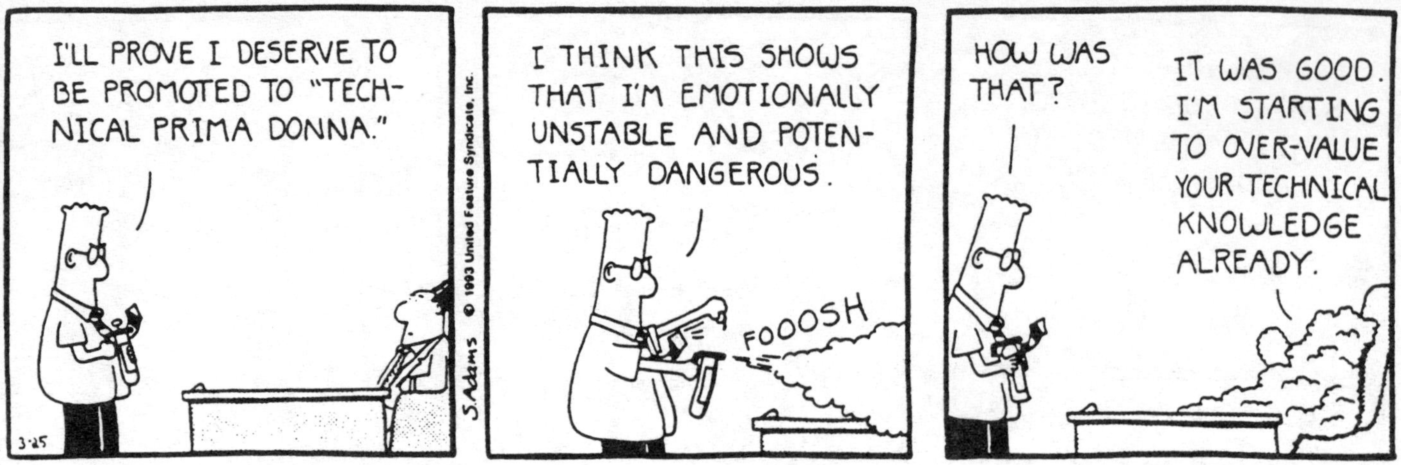
I'LL PROVE I DESERVE TO BE PROMOTED TO "TECHNICAL PRIMA DONNA."
I THINK THIS SHOWS THAT I'M EMOTIONALLY UNSTABLE AND POTENTIALLY DANGEROUS.
FOOOSH
HOW WAS THAT?
IT WAS GOOD. I'M STARTING TO OVER-VALUE YOUR TECHNICAL KNOWLEDGE ALREADY.
S. Adams
© 1993 United Feature Syndicate, Inc.
3-25

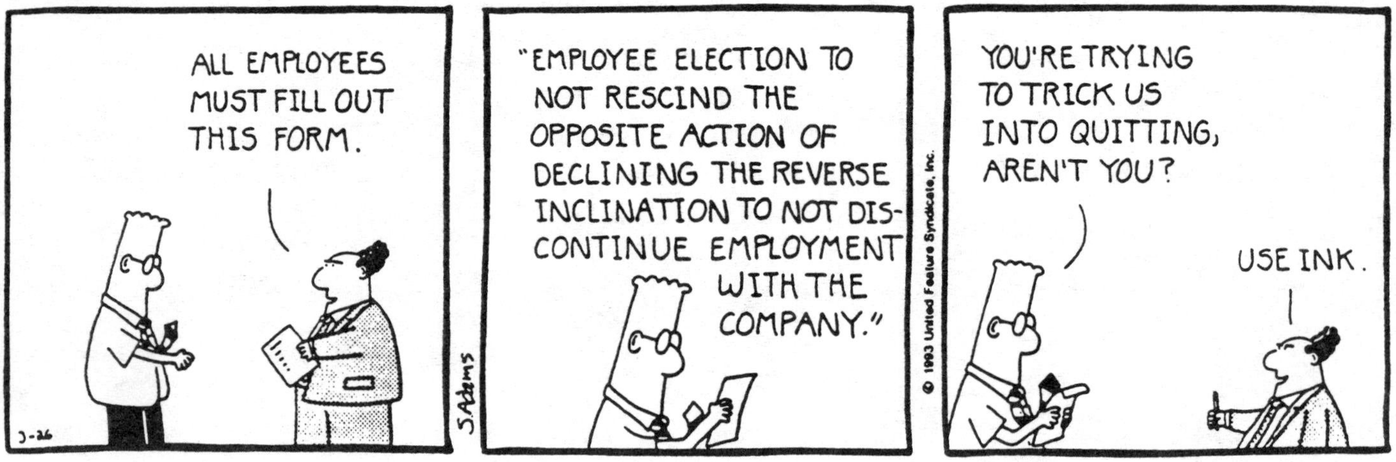
ALL EMPLOYEES MUST FILL OUT THIS FORM.
"EMPLOYEE ELECTION TO NOT RESCIND THE OPPOSITE ACTION OF DECLINING THE REVERSE INCLINATION TO NOT DISCONTINUE EMPLOYMENT WITH THE COMPANY."
YOU'RE TRYING TO TRICK US INTO QUITTING, AREN'T YOU?
USE INK.
S. Adams
© 1993 United Feature Syndicate, Inc.
3-26

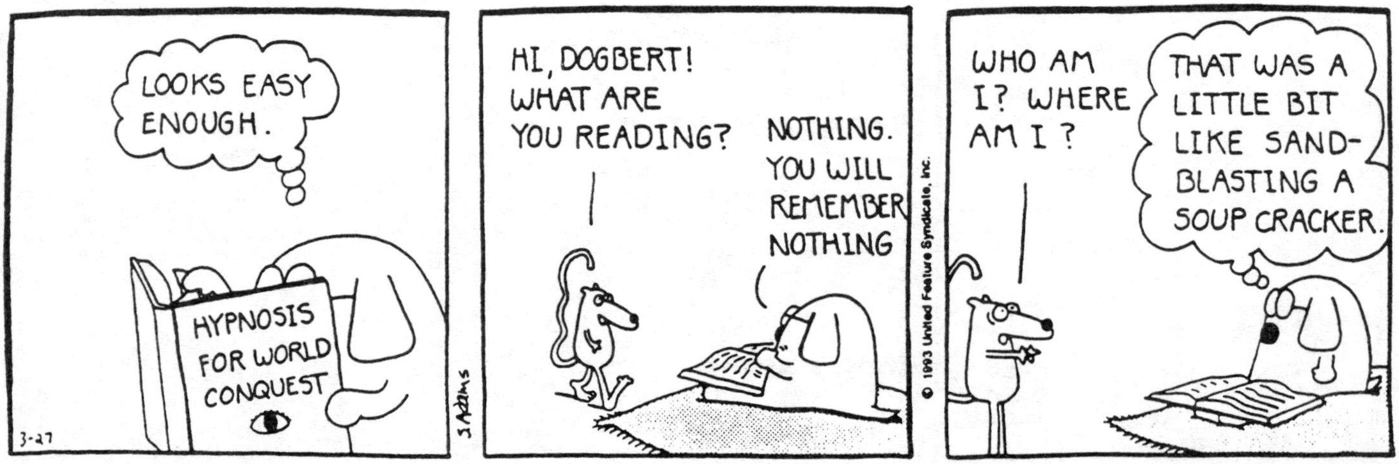
LOOKS EASY ENOUGH.
HYPNOSIS FOR WORLD CONQUEST
HI, DOGBERT! WHAT ARE YOU READING?
NOTHING. YOU WILL REMEMBER NOTHING
WHO AM I? WHERE AM I?
THAT WAS A LITTLE BIT LIKE SAND-BLASTING A SOUP CRACKER.
S. Adams
© 1993 United Feature Syndicate, Inc.
3-27

DO YOU HAVE A MINUTE?
UH-OH, IT'S TOUCHY-FEELY STUFF.
WHAT'S GOING TO HAPPEN TO OUR DEPARTMENT? THE RUMORS ARE FLYING.
WHAT HAVE YOU HEARD?
RUMOR HAS IT THAT FLYING LIZARDS FROM THE PLANET ZORB WILL BUY THE COMPANY.
THEY PLAN TO TURN THE EMPLOYEES INTO GIANT CORN DOGS ON STICKS.
S. Adams © 1993 United Feature Syndicate, Inc
DON'T WORRY ABOUT RUMORS. IT'S BUSINESS AS USUAL FOR NOW.
3-28
GULP
I THINK I HANDLED THAT PRETTY WELL.
ARE YOU SURE THIS WILL IMPRESS THE ZORBIANS?
I HEAR THEY LIKE TEAM PLAYERS.

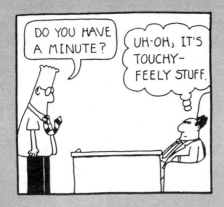

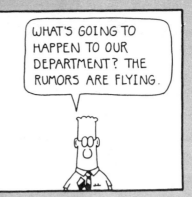

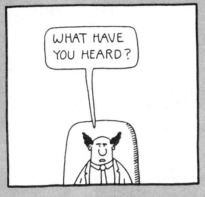

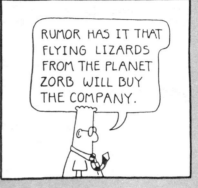

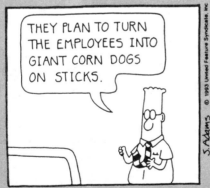

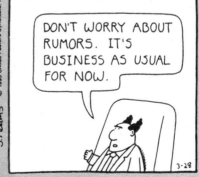

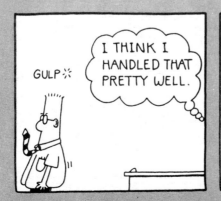

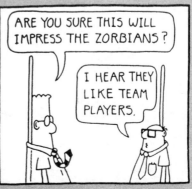

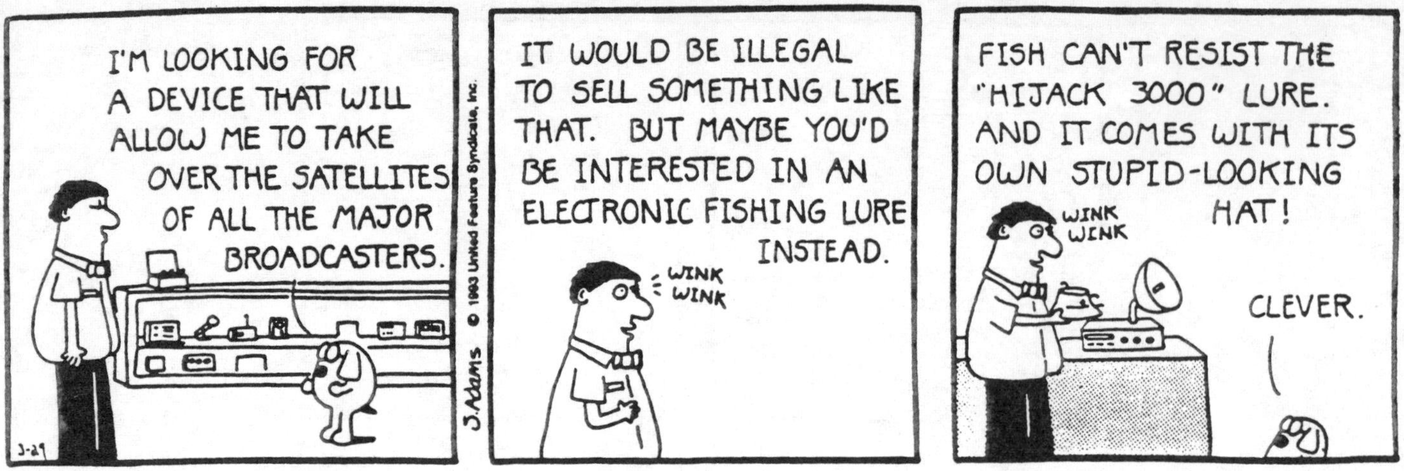
I'M LOOKING FOR A DEVICE THAT WILL ALLOW ME TO TAKE OVER THE SATELLITES OF ALL THE MAJOR BROADCASTERS.
3-29
S. Adams
© 1993 United Feature Syndicate, Inc.
IT WOULD BE ILLEGAL TO SELL SOMETHING LIKE THAT. BUT MAYBE YOU'D BE INTERESTED IN AN ELECTRONIC FISHING LURE INSTEAD.
WINK WINK
FISH CAN'T RESIST THE "HIJACK 3000" LURE. AND IT COMES WITH ITS OWN STUPID-LOOKING HAT!
WINK WINK
CLEVER.

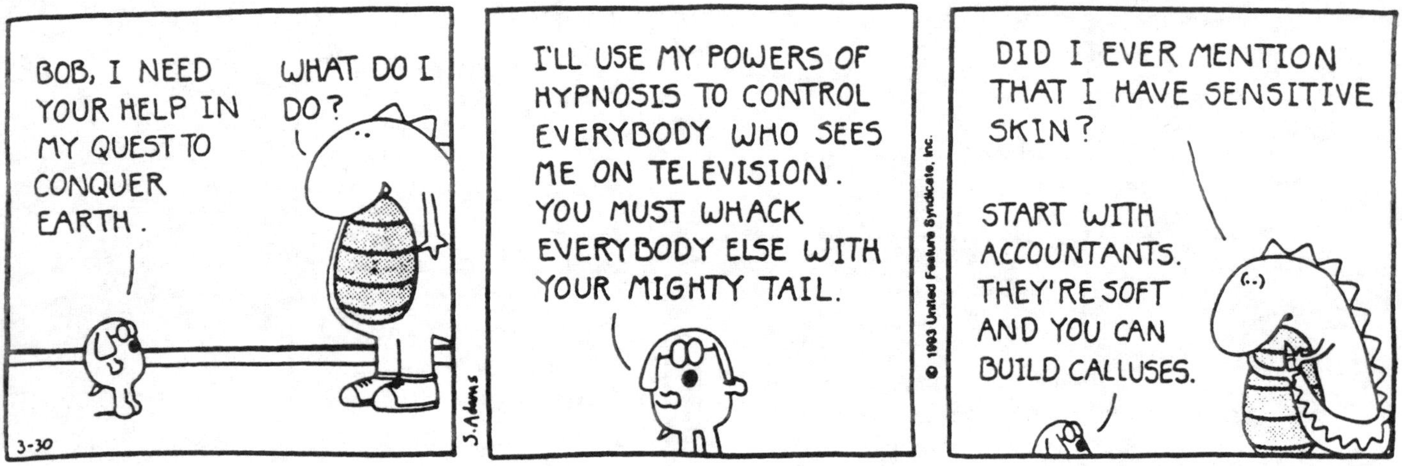
BOB, I NEED YOUR HELP IN MY QUEST TO CONQUER EARTH.
WHAT DO I DO?
3-30
S. Adams
I'LL USE MY POWERS OF HYPNOSIS TO CONTROL EVERYBODY WHO SEES ME ON TELEVISION. YOU MUST WHACK EVERYBODY ELSE WITH YOUR MIGHTY TAIL.
© 1993 United Feature Syndicate, Inc.
DID I EVER MENTION THAT I HAVE SENSITIVE SKIN?
START WITH ACCOUNTANTS. THEY'RE SOFT AND YOU CAN BUILD CALLUSES.

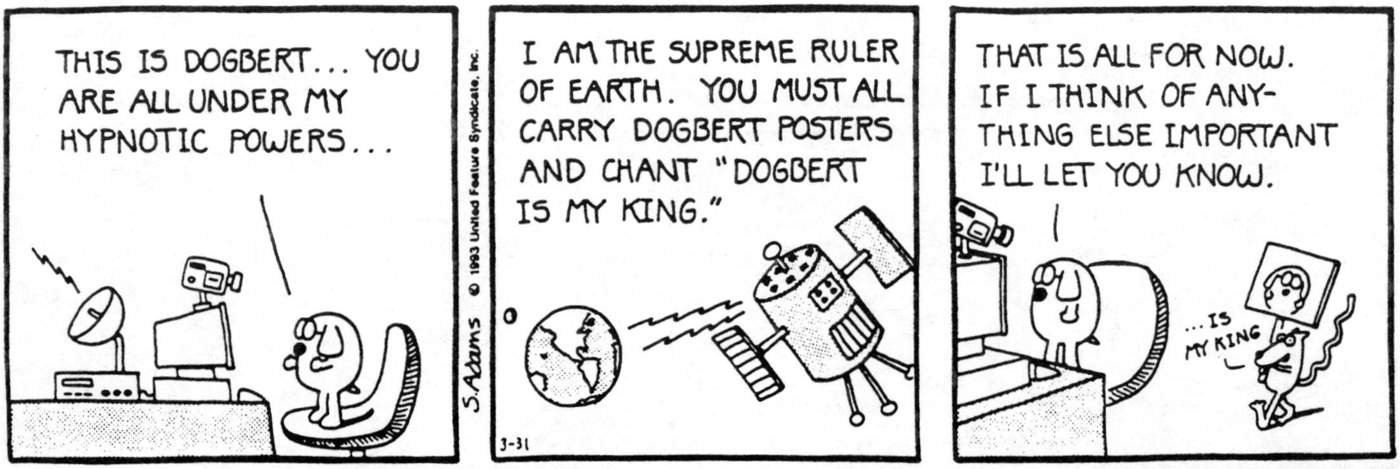
THIS IS DOGBERT... YOU ARE ALL UNDER MY HYPNOTIC POWERS...
S. Adams
© 1993 United Feature Syndicate, Inc.
I AM THE SUPREME RULER OF EARTH. YOU MUST ALL CARRY DOGBERT POSTERS AND CHANT "DOGBERT IS MY KING."
3-31
THAT IS ALL FOR NOW. IF I THINK OF ANYTHING ELSE IMPORTANT I'LL LET YOU KNOW.
... IS MY KING

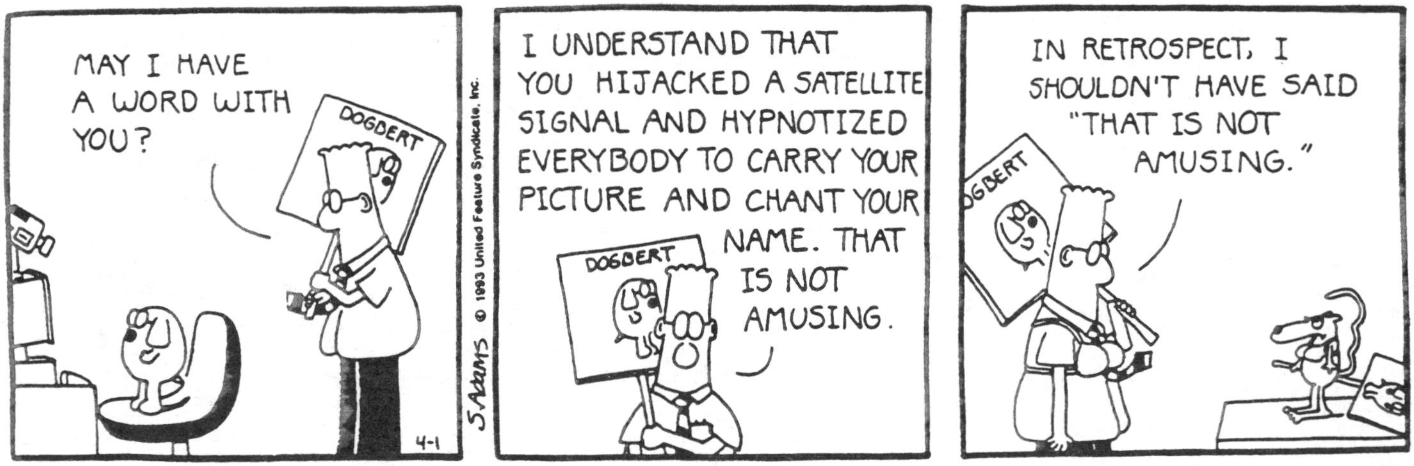
MAY I HAVE A WORD WITH YOU?
DOGBERT
© 1993 United Feature Syndicate, Inc.
S.Adams
4-1
I UNDERSTAND THAT YOU HIJACKED A SATELLITE SIGNAL AND HYPNOTIZED EVERYBODY TO CARRY YOUR PICTURE AND CHANT YOUR NAME. THAT IS NOT AMUSING.
DOGBERT
IN RETROSPECT, I SHOULDN'T HAVE SAID "THAT IS NOT AMUSING."

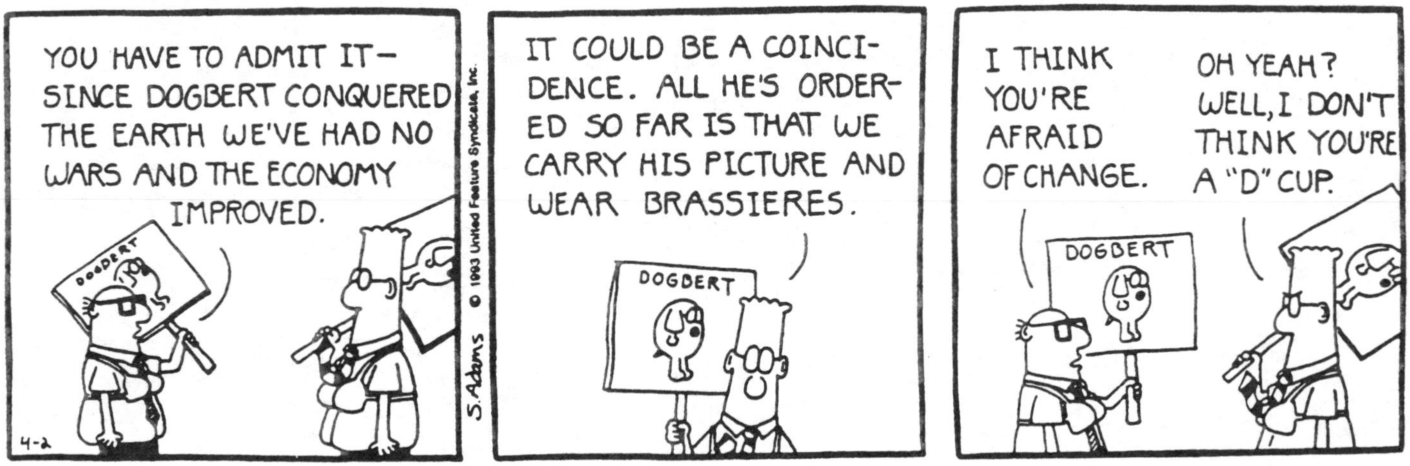
YOU HAVE TO ADMIT IT— SINCE DOGBERT CONQUERED THE EARTH WE'VE HAD NO WARS AND THE ECONOMY IMPROVED.
DOGBERT
4-2
© 1993 United Feature Syndicate, Inc.
S.Adams
IT COULD BE A COINCIDENCE. ALL HE'S ORDERED SO FAR IS THAT WE CARRY HIS PICTURE AND WEAR BRASSIERES.
DOGBERT
I THINK YOU'RE AFRAID OF CHANGE.
OH YEAH? WELL, I DON'T THINK YOU'RE A "D" CUP.
DOGBERT

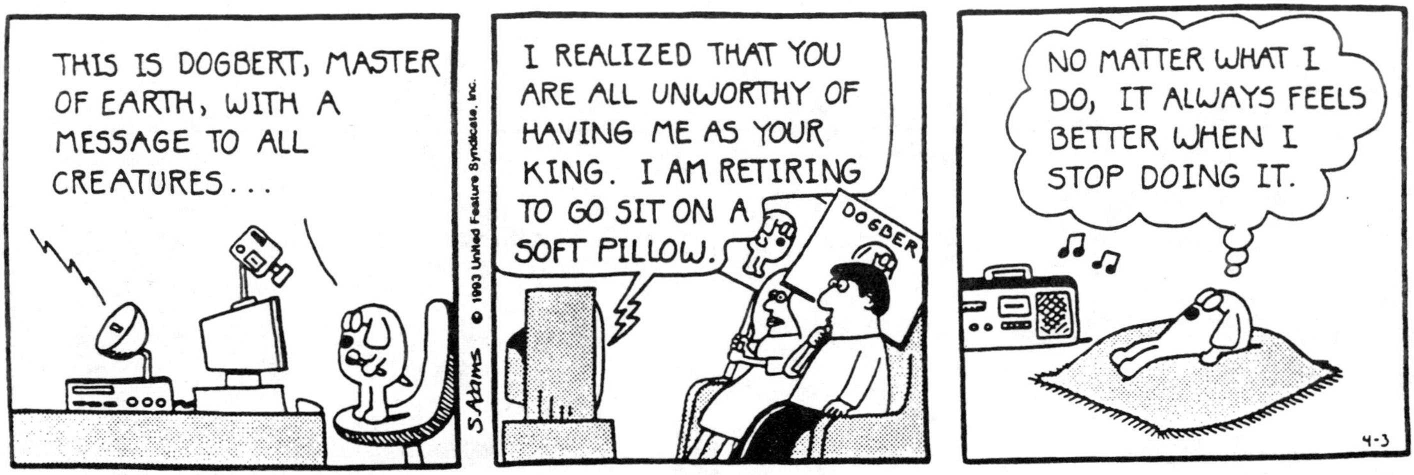
THIS IS DOGBERT, MASTER OF EARTH, WITH A MESSAGE TO ALL CREATURES...
© 1993 United Feature Syndicate, Inc.
S.Adams
I REALIZED THAT YOU ARE ALL UNWORTHY OF HAVING ME AS YOUR KING. I AM RETIRING TO GO SIT ON A SOFT PILLOW.
DOGBER
NO MATTER WHAT I DO, IT ALWAYS FEELS BETTER WHEN I STOP DOING IT.
4-3

ELECTRON HUT
OPEN
I'M LOOKING FOR A P-CONNECT ADAPTER POST.
WE DON'T HAVE ANY.
THERE'S A WHOLE SHELF OF THEM RIGHT BEHIND YOU.
THEY'RE ONLY FIVE CENTS APIECE. I CAN'T WASTE MY TIME SELLING THEM.
I'M THE ONLY CUSTOMER IN THE STORE! BESIDES, WHY DO YOU STOCK SOME-THING YOU DON'T WANT TO SELL?
S Adams
HERE! TAKE THREE! AND STOP WASTING MY TIME!
4-4
© 1993 United Feature Syndicate, Inc.
WHILE YOU'RE HERE, HAVE YOU SEEN OUR FINE LINE OF COMPUTERS?

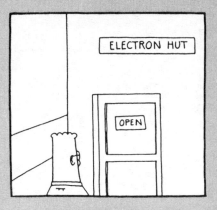

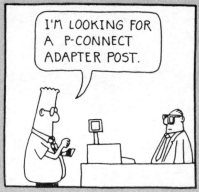

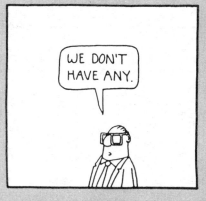

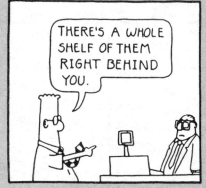

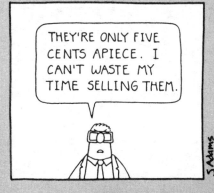

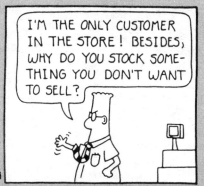

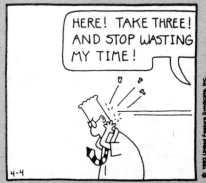

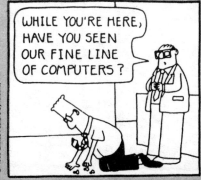

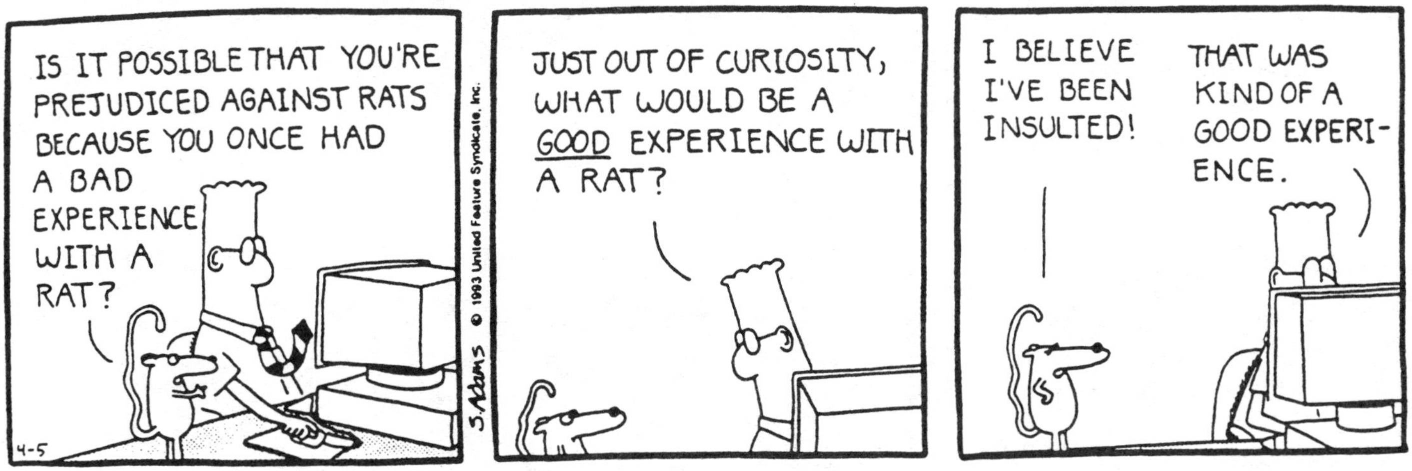
IS IT POSSIBLE THAT YOU'RE PREJUDICED AGAINST RATS BECAUSE YOU ONCE HAD A BAD EXPERIENCE WITH A RAT?
JUST OUT OF CURIOSITY, WHAT WOULD BE A GOOD EXPERIENCE WITH A RAT?
I BELIEVE I'VE BEEN INSULTED!
THAT WAS KIND OF A GOOD EXPERIENCE.
S. Adams © 1993 United Feature Syndicate, Inc.
4-5

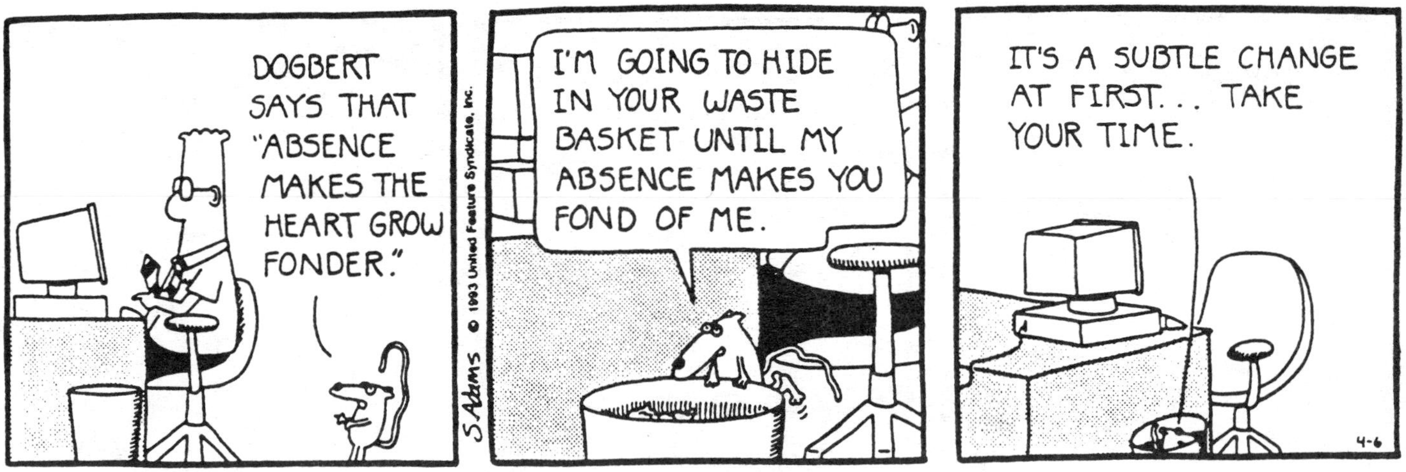
DOGBERT SAYS THAT "ABSENCE MAKES THE HEART GROW FONDER."
I'M GOING TO HIDE IN YOUR WASTE BASKET UNTIL MY ABSENCE MAKES YOU FOND OF ME.
IT'S A SUBTLE CHANGE AT FIRST... TAKE YOUR TIME.
S. Adams © 1993 United Feature Syndicate, Inc.
4-6

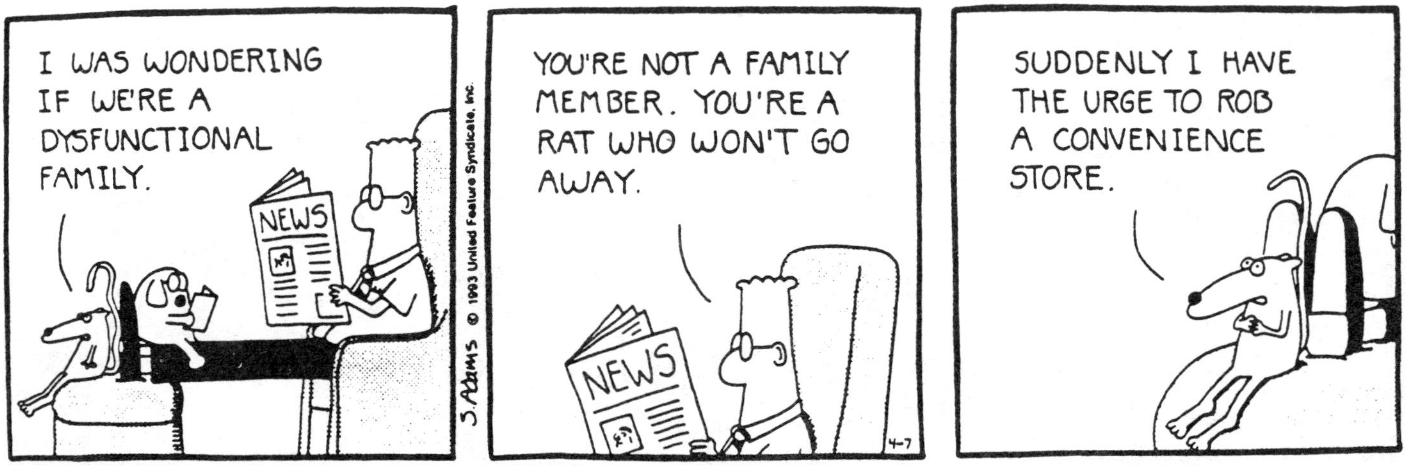
I WAS WONDERING IF WE'RE A DYSFUNCTIONAL FAMILY.
NEWS
YOU'RE NOT A FAMILY MEMBER. YOU'RE A RAT WHO WON'T GO AWAY.
NEWS
SUDDENLY I HAVE THE URGE TO ROB A CONVENIENCE STORE.
S. Adams © 1993 United Feature Syndicate, Inc.
4-7

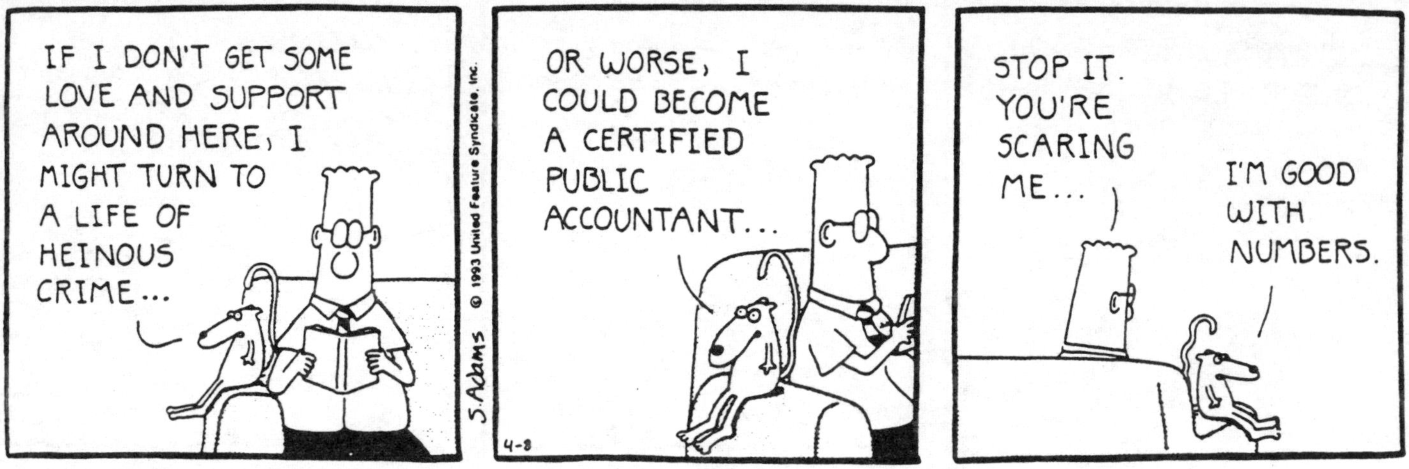
IF I DON'T GET SOME LOVE AND SUPPORT AROUND HERE, I MIGHT TURN TO A LIFE OF HEINOUS CRIME...
S. Adams © 1993 United Feature Syndicate, Inc.
OR WORSE, I COULD BECOME A CERTIFIED PUBLIC ACCOUNTANT...
4-8
STOP IT. YOU'RE SCARING ME...
I'M GOOD WITH NUMBERS.

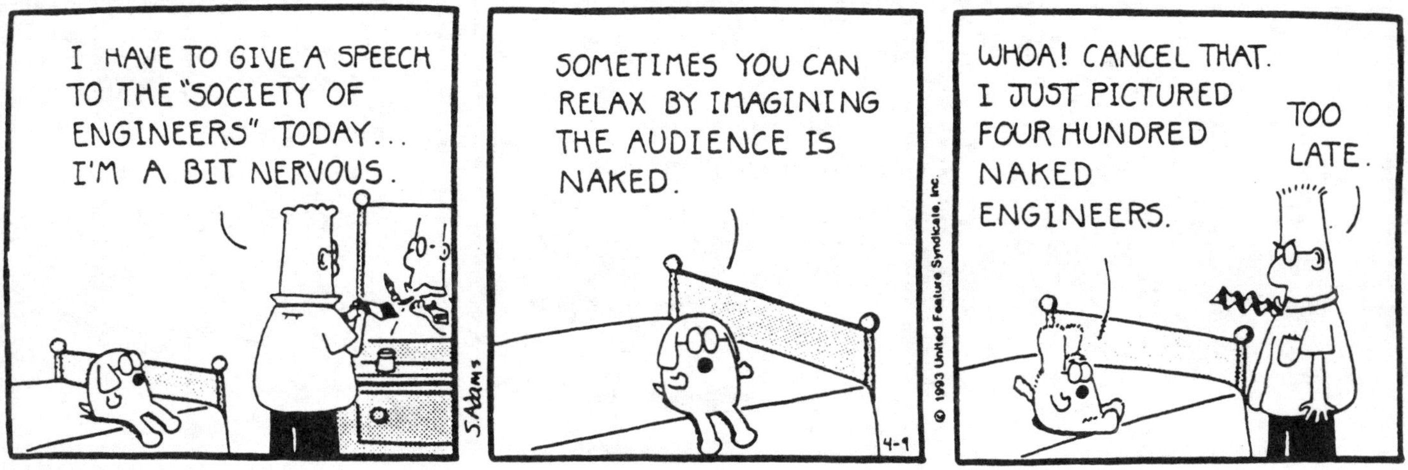
I HAVE TO GIVE A SPEECH TO THE "SOCIETY OF ENGINEERS" TODAY... I'M A BIT NERVOUS.
S. Adams
SOMETIMES YOU CAN RELAX BY IMAGINING THE AUDIENCE IS NAKED.
4-9
© 1993 United Feature Syndicate, Inc.
WHOA! CANCEL THAT. I JUST PICTURED FOUR HUNDRED NAKED ENGINEERS.
TOO LATE.

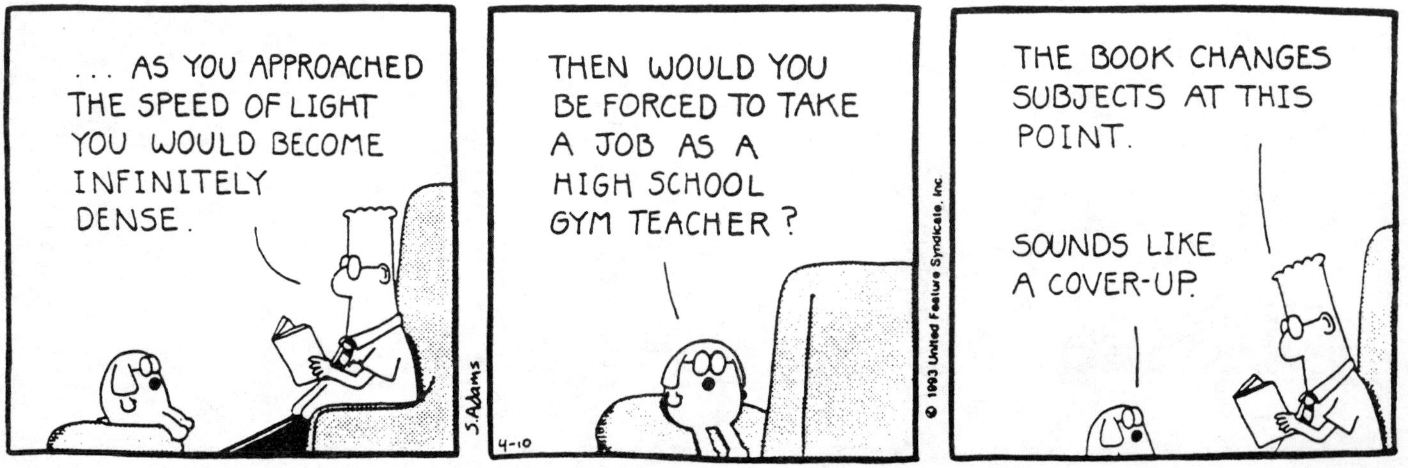
... AS YOU APPROACHED THE SPEED OF LIGHT YOU WOULD BECOME INFINITELY DENSE.
S. Adams
THEN WOULD YOU BE FORCED TO TAKE A JOB AS A HIGH SCHOOL GYM TEACHER?
4-10
© 1993 United Feature Syndicate, Inc.
THE BOOK CHANGES SUBJECTS AT THIS POINT.
SOUNDS LIKE A COVER-UP.

A SMALL BAND OF THE CREATURES WERE KNOWN TO LIVE HIGH IN AN ARTIFICIAL STRUCTURE.
S.Adams © 1993 United Feature Syndicate, Inc.
ON MY WAY TO STUDY THEM I TOOK NOTE OF THE NATIVE VEGETATION.
RENTED
THE YOUNGER MALES WERE AT PLAY. THEY BECAME SELF-CONSCIOUS WHEN WATCHED.
THE DOMINANT MALE HAD A GRAY BACK. HE CONTROLLED THE OTHERS BY WAVING LITTLE ENVELOPES.
THERE WERE FEW FEMALES IN THE GROUP. THE LESS DOMINANT MALES HAD NO CHANCE OF MATING.
UNLIKE OTHER SPECIES THEY HAD NO INSTINCT FOR GROOMING.
WANT TO GROOM?
DROP DEAD.
4-11
MY TIME WAS UP. BUT I WILL MISS THEM, THOSE . . .
ENGINEERS IN THE MIST
HOW LONG ARE YOU SUPPOSED TO MICROWAVE POPCORN?

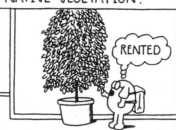

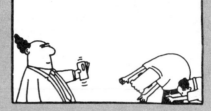

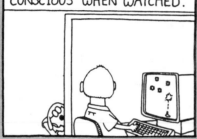

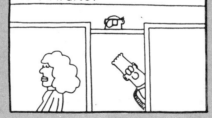

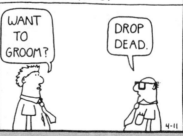

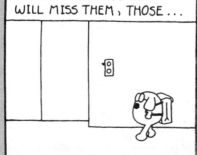

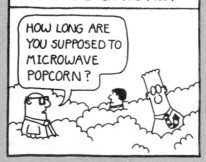

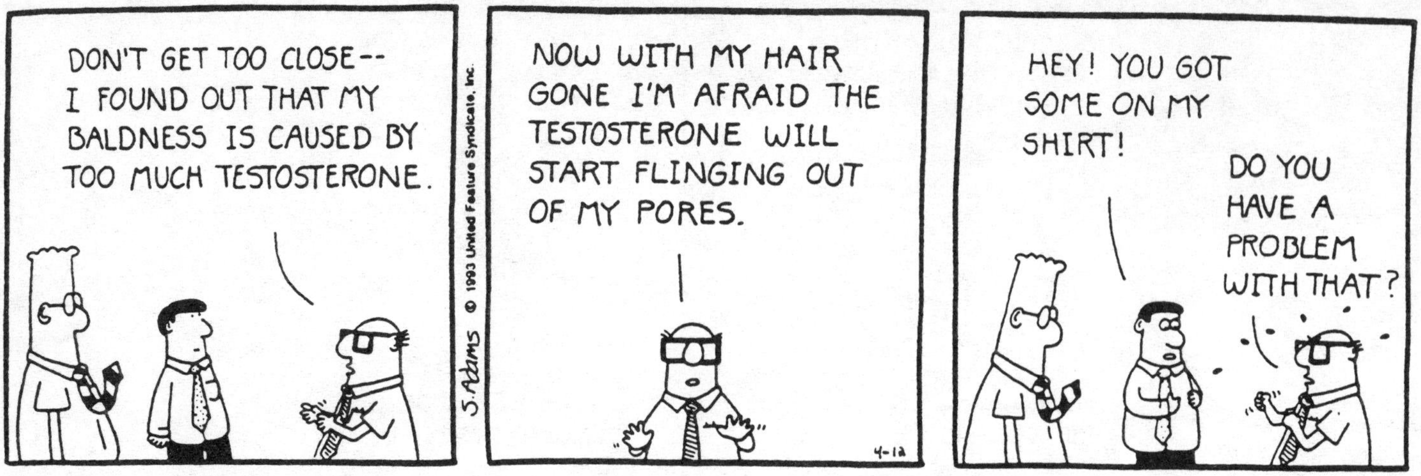
DON'T GET TOO CLOSE-- I FOUND OUT THAT MY BALDNESS IS CAUSED BY TOO MUCH TESTOSTERONE.
S. Adams © 1993 United Feature Syndicate, Inc.
NOW WITH MY HAIR GONE I'M AFRAID THE TESTOSTERONE WILL START FLINGING OUT OF MY PORES.
4-12
HEY! YOU GOT SOME ON MY SHIRT!
DO YOU HAVE A PROBLEM WITH THAT?

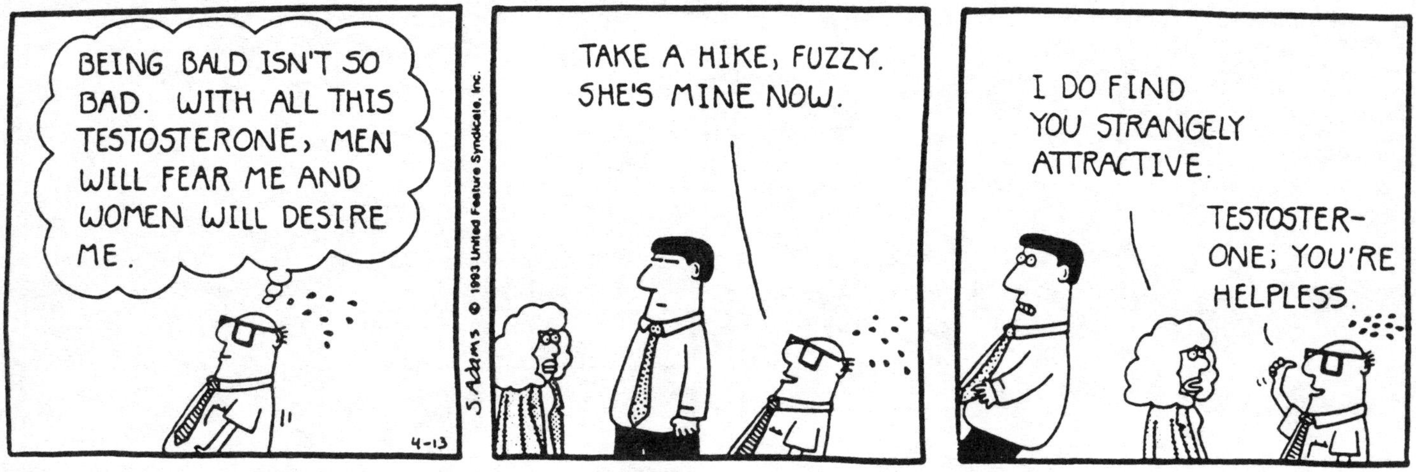
BEING BALD ISN'T SO BAD. WITH ALL THIS TESTOSTERONE, MEN WILL FEAR ME AND WOMEN WILL DESIRE ME.
4-13
S. Adams © 1993 United Feature Syndicate, Inc.
TAKE A HIKE, FUZZY. SHE'S MINE NOW.
I DO FIND YOU STRANGELY ATTRACTIVE.
TESTOSTER-ONE; YOU'RE HELPLESS.

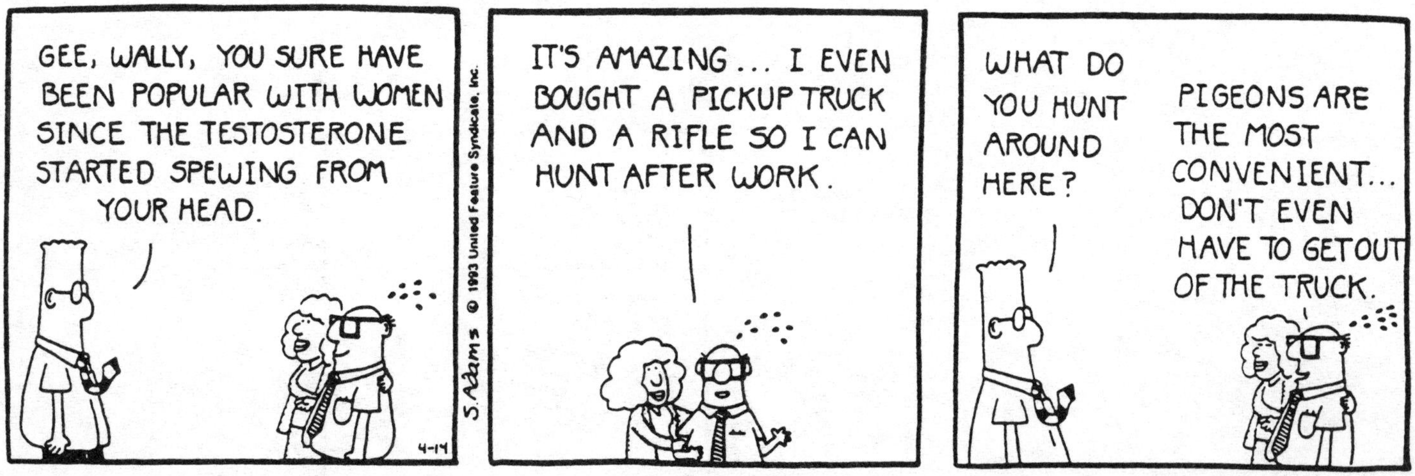
GEE, WALLY, YOU SURE HAVE BEEN POPULAR WITH WOMEN SINCE THE TESTOSTERONE STARTED SPEWING FROM YOUR HEAD.
4-14
S. Adams © 1993 United Feature Syndicate, Inc.
IT'S AMAZING... I EVEN BOUGHT A PICKUP TRUCK AND A RIFLE SO I CAN HUNT AFTER WORK.
WHAT DO YOU HUNT AROUND HERE?
PIGEONS ARE THE MOST CONVENIENT... DON'T EVEN HAVE TO GET OUT OF THE TRUCK.

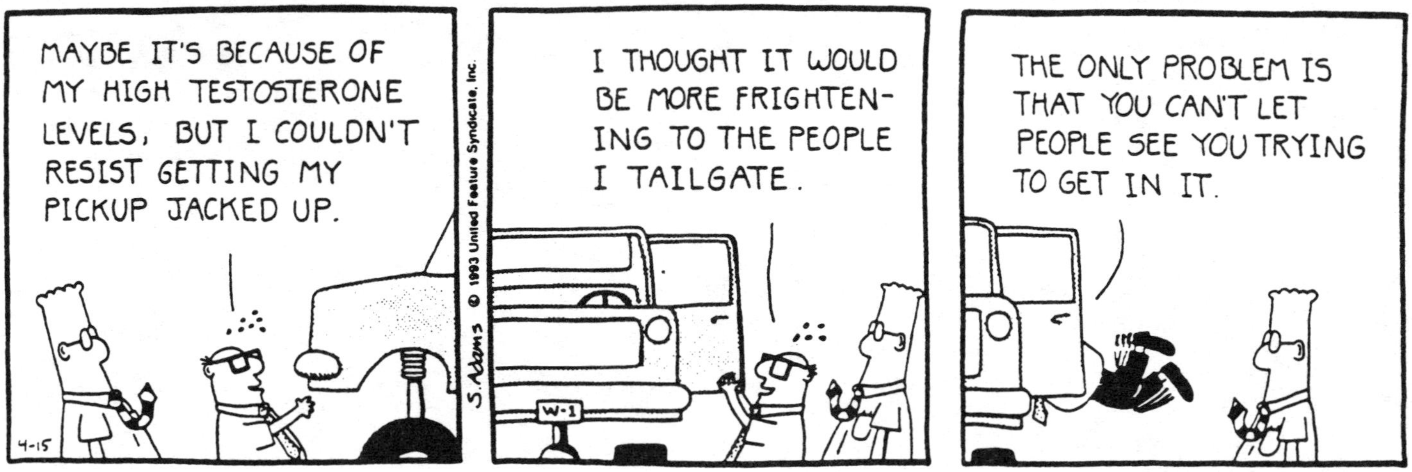
MAYBE IT'S BECAUSE OF MY HIGH TESTOSTERONE LEVELS, BUT I COULDN'T RESIST GETTING MY PICKUP JACKED UP.
4-15
© 1993 United Feature Syndicate, Inc.
S. Adams
I THOUGHT IT WOULD BE MORE FRIGHTENING TO THE PEOPLE I TAILGATE.
W-1
THE ONLY PROBLEM IS THAT YOU CAN'T LET PEOPLE SEE YOU TRYING TO GET IN IT.

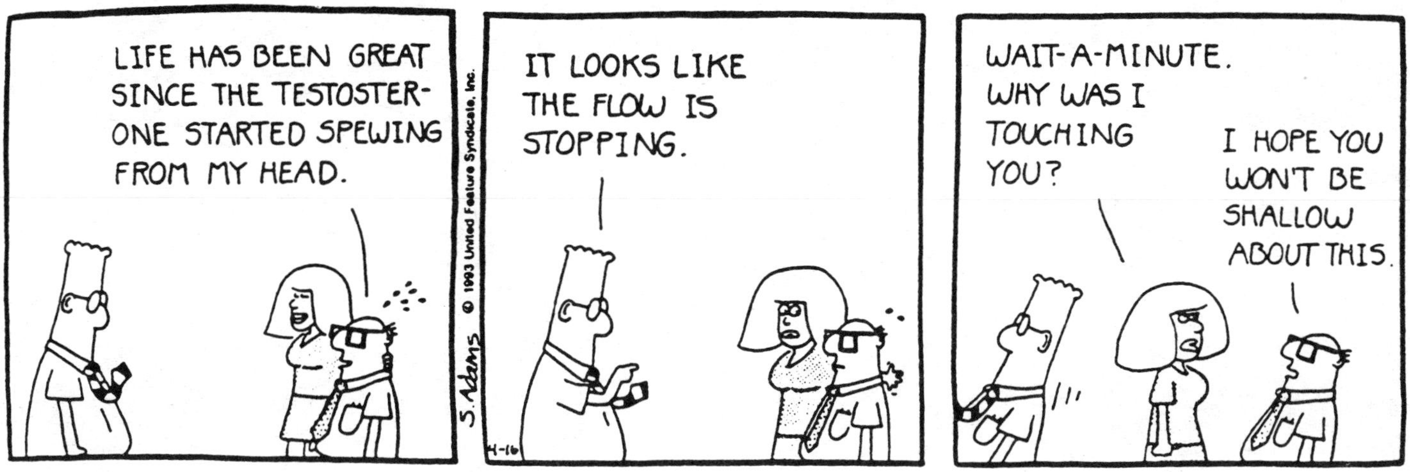
LIFE HAS BEEN GREAT SINCE THE TESTOSTERONE STARTED SPEWING FROM MY HEAD.
© 1993 United Feature Syndicate, Inc.
S. Adams
4-16
IT LOOKS LIKE THE FLOW IS STOPPING.
WAIT-A-MINUTE. WHY WAS I TOUCHING YOU?
I HOPE YOU WON'T BE SHALLOW ABOUT THIS.

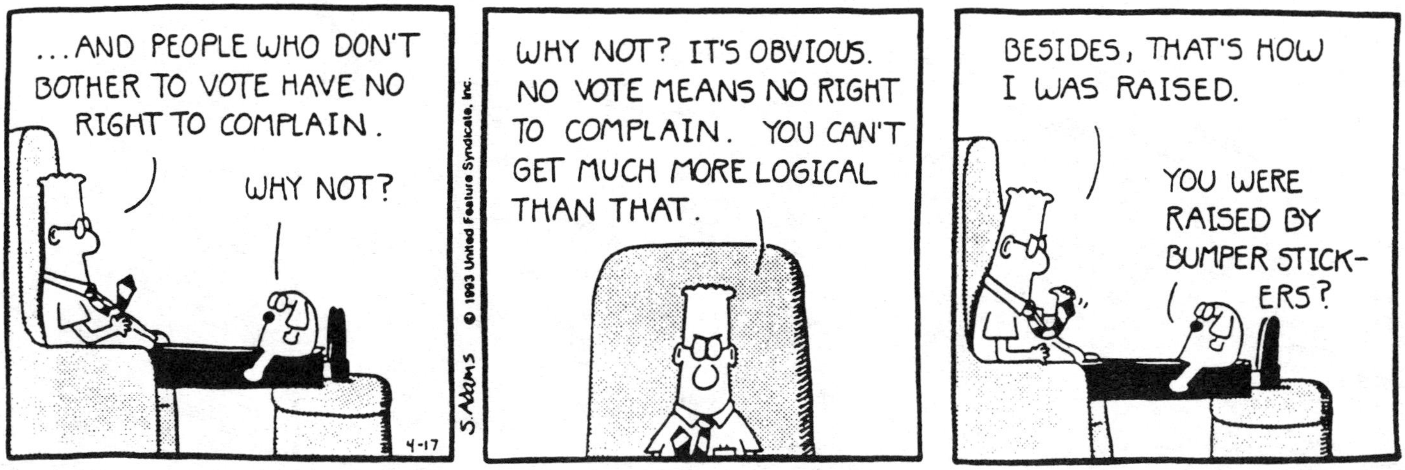
...AND PEOPLE WHO DON'T BOTHER TO VOTE HAVE NO RIGHT TO COMPLAIN.
WHY NOT?
4-17
© 1993 United Feature Syndicate, Inc.
S. Adams
WHY NOT? IT'S OBVIOUS. NO VOTE MEANS NO RIGHT TO COMPLAIN. YOU CAN'T GET MUCH MORE LOGICAL THAN THAT.
BESIDES, THAT'S HOW I WAS RAISED.
YOU WERE RAISED BY BUMPER STICKERS?

THANKS FOR ASKING ME TO DINNER, DILBERT.
IT'S MY PLEAS...
© 1993 United Feature Syndicate, Inc.
I LOVE EATING OUT. WHAT KIND OF TABLECLOTH IS THIS? I SAW A MOVIE LAST MONTH.
UH-OH... SHE'S A SERIAL YAKKER.
YAK YAK YAK BLAH BLAH YAK YAK BLAH YAK
SHE CHANGES TOPICS WITHOUT EVEN PAUSING TO BREATHE.
YAK YAK YAK YAK YAK YAK YAK YAK YAK YAK YAK YAK YAK YAK
IT'S TOO HARD TO LISTEN. I'M SLIPPING INTO A COMA.
YAK YAK YAK YAK YAK YAK YAK YAK YAK YAK
IS THERE SOME PROBLEM?
R-U-U-U-N! SAVE YOURSELF!
YAK YAK BLAH BLAH YAK YAK YAK YAK BLAH BLAH
SERIAL YAKKER!
. . .
4-18
S. Adams
HELP ME.
SHHH! I'M TRYING TO PLAY DEAD.

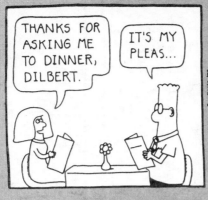

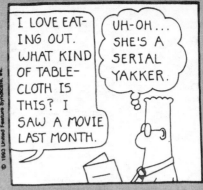

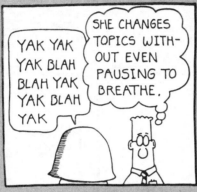

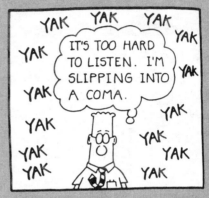

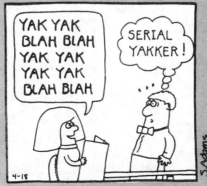

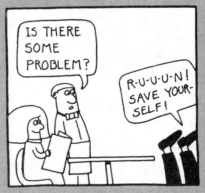

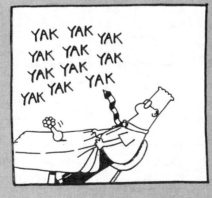

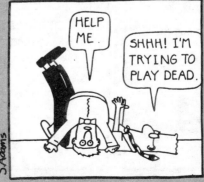

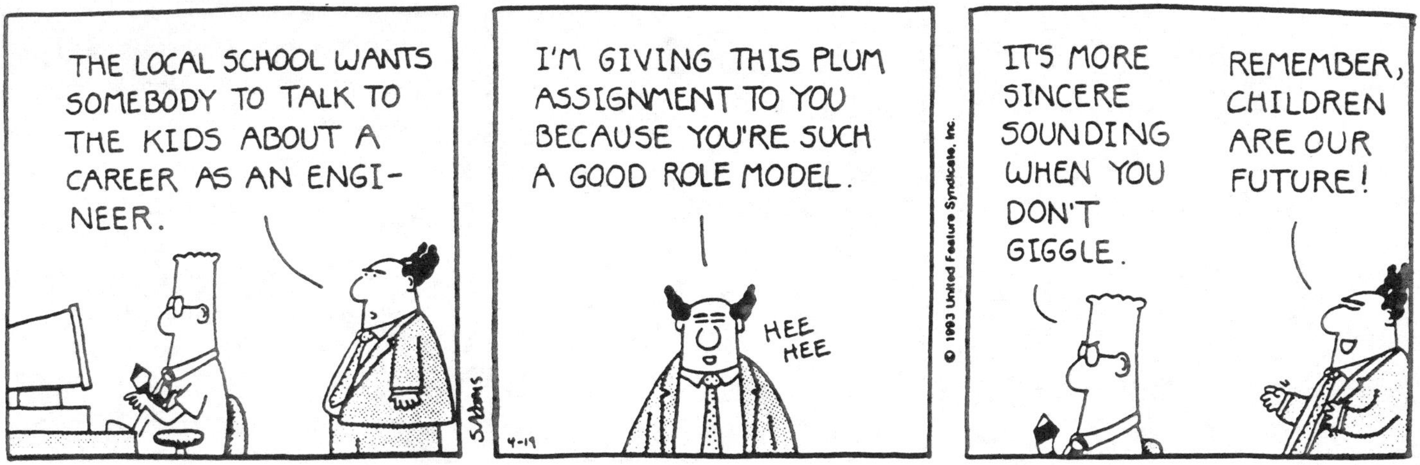
THE LOCAL SCHOOL WANTS SOMEBODY TO TALK TO THE KIDS ABOUT A CAREER AS AN ENGI- NEER.
I'M GIVING THIS PLUM ASSIGNMENT TO YOU BECAUSE YOU'RE SUCH A GOOD ROLE MODEL.
HEE HEE
IT'S MORE SINCERE SOUNDING WHEN YOU DON'T GIGGLE.
REMEMBER, CHILDREN ARE OUR FUTURE!
© 1993 United Feature Syndicate, Inc.
4-19

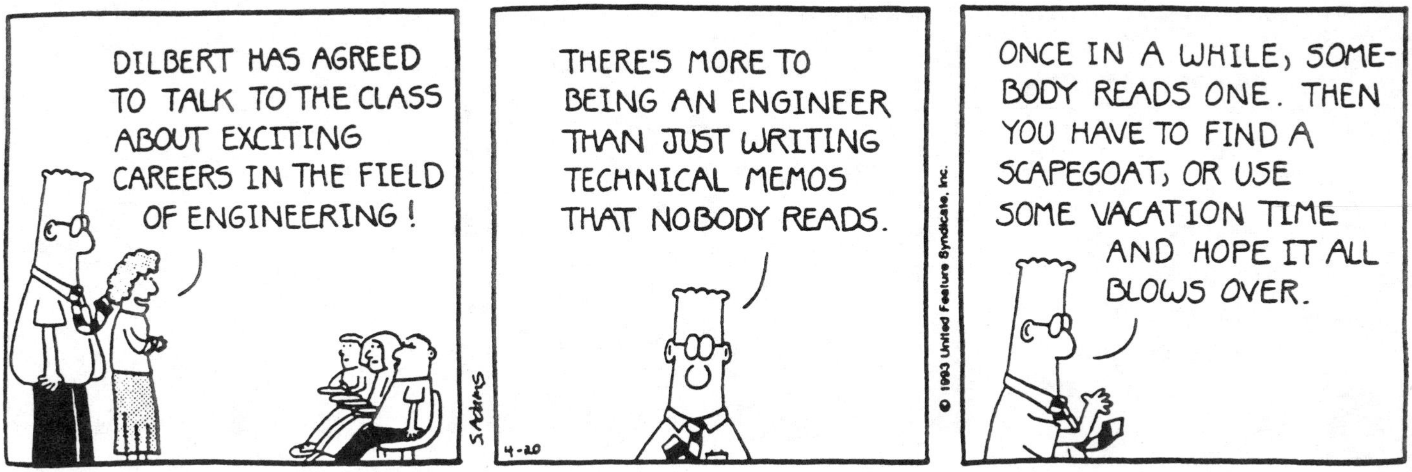
DILBERT HAS AGREED TO TALK TO THE CLASS ABOUT EXCITING CAREERS IN THE FIELD OF ENGINEERING!
THERE'S MORE TO BEING AN ENGINEER THAN JUST WRITING TECHNICAL MEMOS THAT NOBODY READS.
ONCE IN A WHILE, SOME- BODY READS ONE. THEN YOU HAVE TO FIND A SCAPEGOAT, OR USE SOME VACATION TIME AND HOPE IT ALL BLOWS OVER.
© 1993 United Feature Syndicate, Inc.
4-20

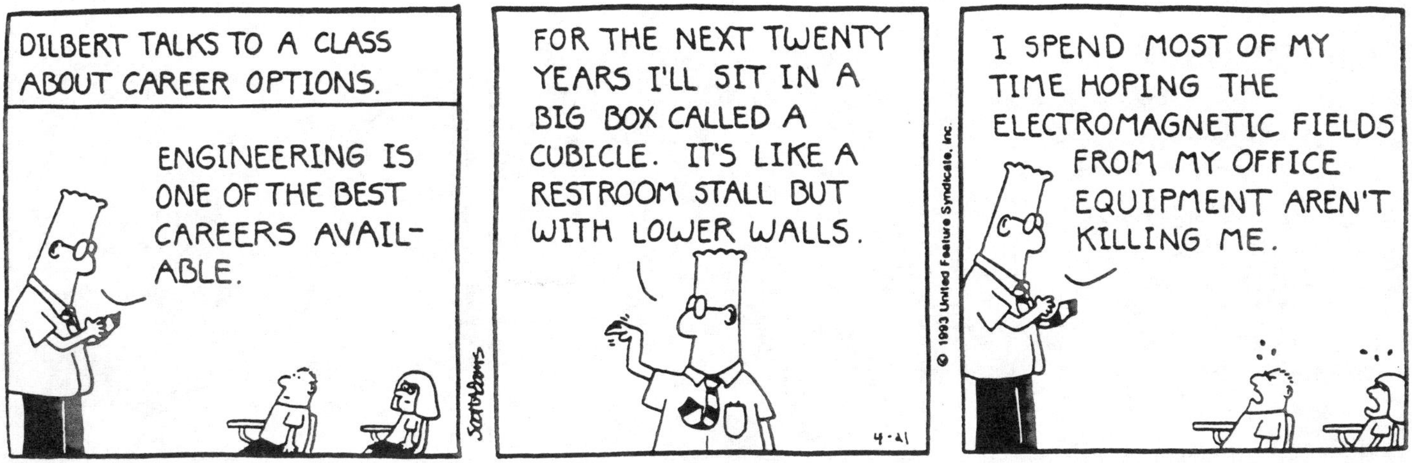
DILBERT TALKS TO A CLASS ABOUT CAREER OPTIONS.
ENGINEERING IS ONE OF THE BEST CAREERS AVAIL- ABLE.
FOR THE NEXT TWENTY YEARS I'LL SIT IN A BIG BOX CALLED A CUBICLE. IT'S LIKE A RESTROOM STALL BUT WITH LOWER WALLS.
I SPEND MOST OF MY TIME HOPING THE ELECTROMAGNETIC FIELDS FROM MY OFFICE EQUIPMENT AREN'T KILLING ME.
© 1993 United Feature Syndicate, Inc.
4-21

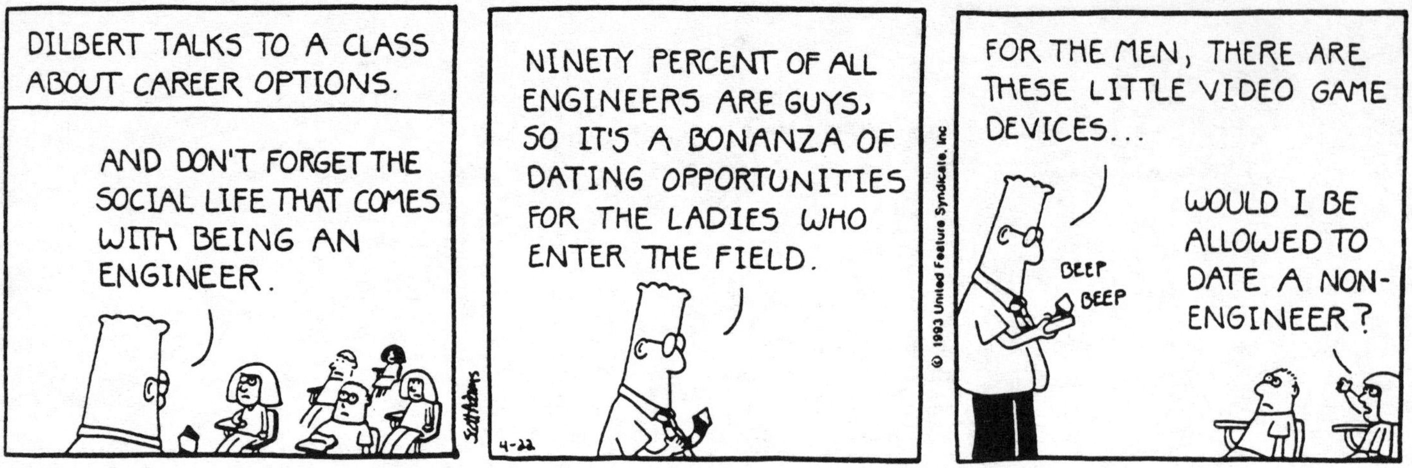
DILBERT TALKS TO A CLASS ABOUT CAREER OPTIONS.
AND DON'T FORGET THE SOCIAL LIFE THAT COMES WITH BEING AN ENGINEER.
NINETY PERCENT OF ALL ENGINEERS ARE GUYS, SO IT'S A BONANZA OF DATING OPPORTUNITIES FOR THE LADIES WHO ENTER THE FIELD.
FOR THE MEN, THERE ARE THESE LITTLE VIDEO GAME DEVICES...
BEEP BEEP
WOULD I BE ALLOWED TO DATE A NON-ENGINEER?
© 1993 United Feature Syndicate, Inc

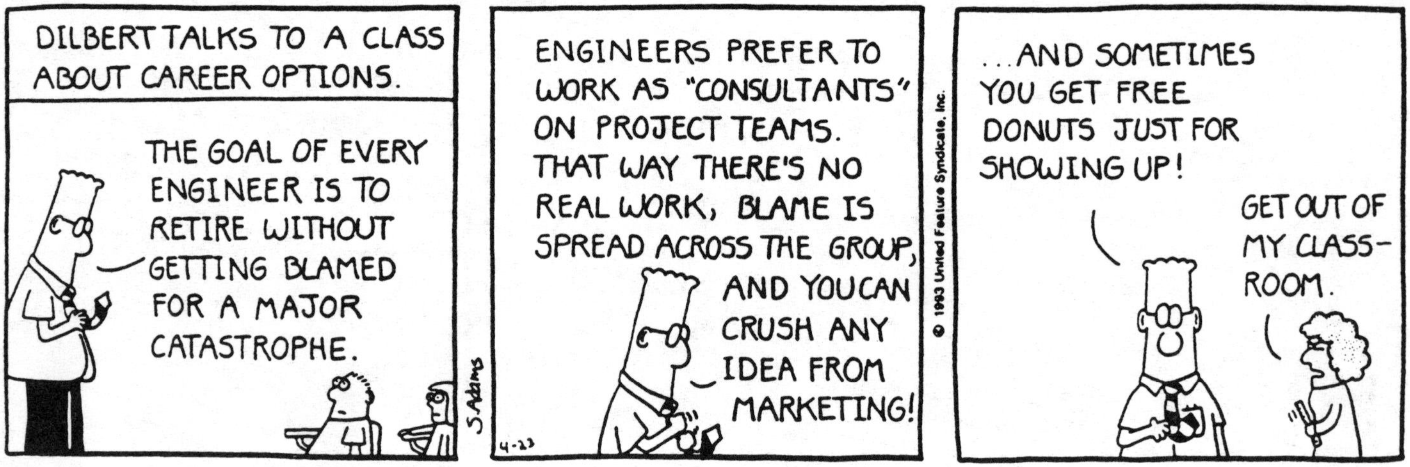
DILBERT TALKS TO A CLASS ABOUT CAREER OPTIONS.
THE GOAL OF EVERY ENGINEER IS TO RETIRE WITHOUT GETTING BLAMED FOR A MAJOR CATASTROPHE.
ENGINEERS PREFER TO WORK AS "CONSULTANTS" ON PROJECT TEAMS. THAT WAY THERE'S NO REAL WORK, BLAME IS SPREAD ACROSS THE GROUP, AND YOU CAN CRUSH ANY IDEA FROM MARKETING!
...AND SOMETIMES YOU GET FREE DONUTS JUST FOR SHOWING UP!
GET OUT OF MY CLASSROOM.
© 1993 United Feature Syndicate, Inc.

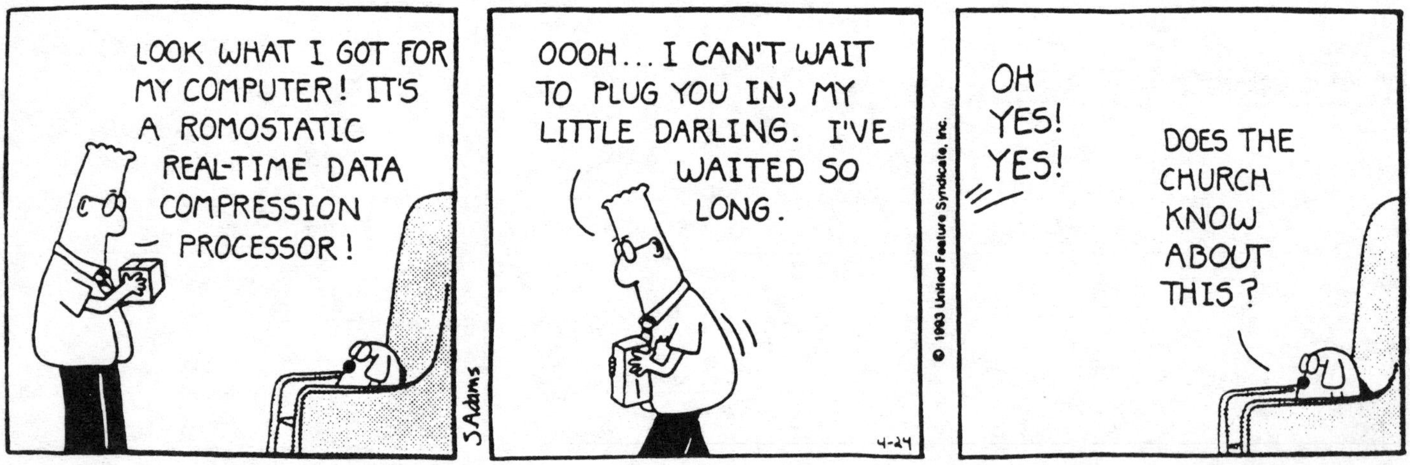
LOOK WHAT I GOT FOR MY COMPUTER! IT'S A ROMOSTATIC REAL-TIME DATA COMPRESSION PROCESSOR!
OOOH... I CAN'T WAIT TO PLUG YOU IN, MY LITTLE DARLING. I'VE WAITED SO LONG.
OH YES! YES!
DOES THE CHURCH KNOW ABOUT THIS?
© 1993 United Feature Syndicate, Inc.

GOVERNMENT STATISTICS SHOW THAT OFFICE PRODUCTIVITY WENT DOWN AS COMPUTERS BECAME WIDELY USED.
© 1993 United Feature Syndicate, Inc
BUT I DIDN'T BELIEVE IT.
SO I WROTE A LITTLE SOFTWARE PROGRAM TO TEST THAT CONCLUSION.
IT ONLY TOOK A MONTH, BUT IT PRODUCED SOME IMPRESSIVE DATA.
IN FACT, IT WAS SO IMPRESSIVE IT TOOK A WEEK TO FIGURE OUT HOW TO PRINT IT.
S.Adams
BUT BEFORE I COULD PRINT, MY COMPUTER CRASHED AND I DIDN'T HAVE BACKUP COPIES.
4-25
SO, IT SEEMS THE GOVERNMENT WAS RIGHT; COMPUTERS ARE TO BLAME FOR THE DECLINE IN PRODUCTIVITY.
DO YOU THINK THE EMPLOYEES COULD BE PARTLY RESPONSIBLE?
SURE, FIND A SCAPEGOAT.

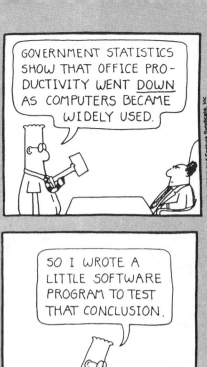

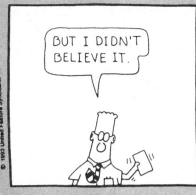

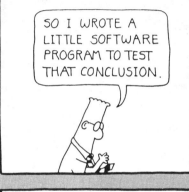

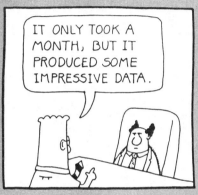

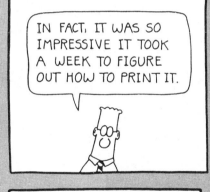

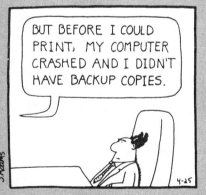

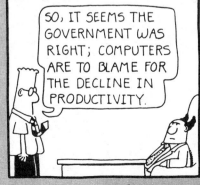

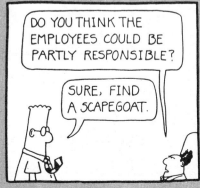

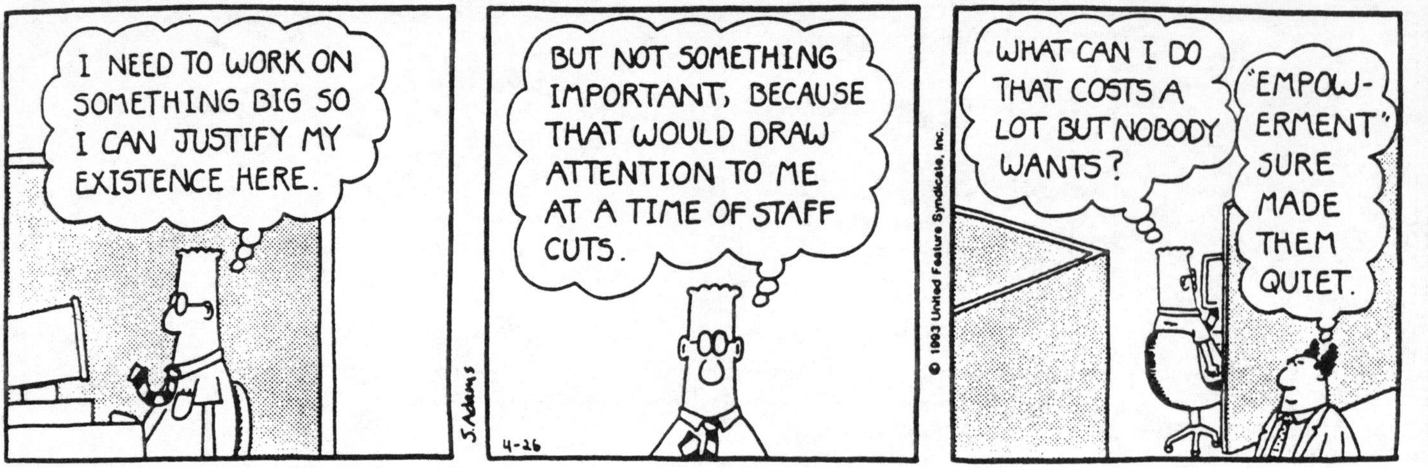
I NEED TO WORK ON SOMETHING BIG SO I CAN JUSTIFY MY EXISTENCE HERE.
S. Adams
BUT NOT SOMETHING IMPORTANT, BECAUSE THAT WOULD DRAW ATTENTION TO ME AT A TIME OF STAFF CUTS.
4-26
© 1993 United Feature Syndicate, Inc.
WHAT CAN I DO THAT COSTS A LOT BUT NOBODY WANTS?
"EMPOWERMENT" SURE MADE THEM QUIET.

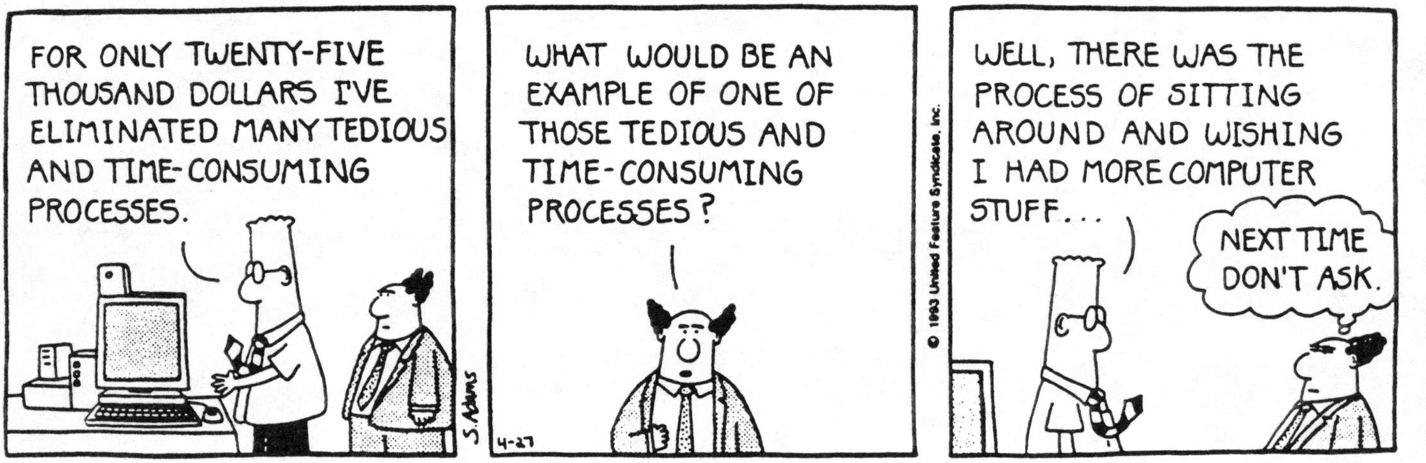
FOR ONLY TWENTY-FIVE THOUSAND DOLLARS I'VE ELIMINATED MANY TEDIOUS AND TIME-CONSUMING PROCESSES.
S. Adams
WHAT WOULD BE AN EXAMPLE OF ONE OF THOSE TEDIOUS AND TIME-CONSUMING PROCESSES?
4-27
© 1993 United Feature Syndicate, Inc.
WELL, THERE WAS THE PROCESS OF SITTING AROUND AND WISHING I HAD MORE COMPUTER STUFF...
NEXT TIME DON'T ASK.

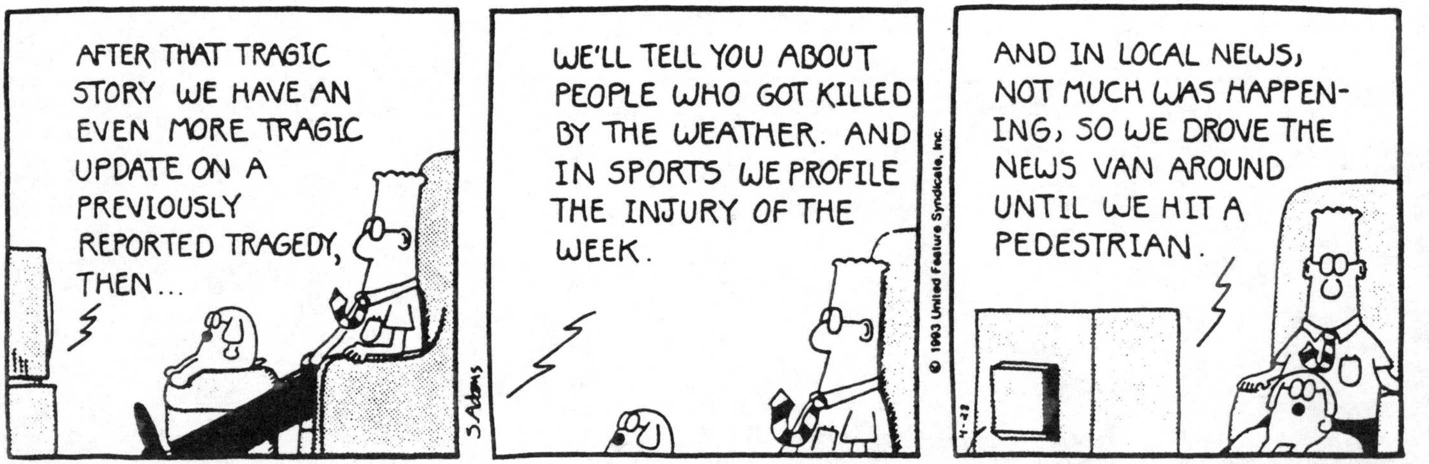
AFTER THAT TRAGIC STORY WE HAVE AN EVEN MORE TRAGIC UPDATE ON A PREVIOUSLY REPORTED TRAGEDY, THEN...
S. Adams
WE'LL TELL YOU ABOUT PEOPLE WHO GOT KILLED BY THE WEATHER. AND IN SPORTS WE PROFILE THE INJURY OF THE WEEK.
© 1993 United Feature Syndicate, Inc.
AND IN LOCAL NEWS, NOT MUCH WAS HAPPENING, SO WE DROVE THE NEWS VAN AROUND UNTIL WE HIT A PEDESTRIAN.

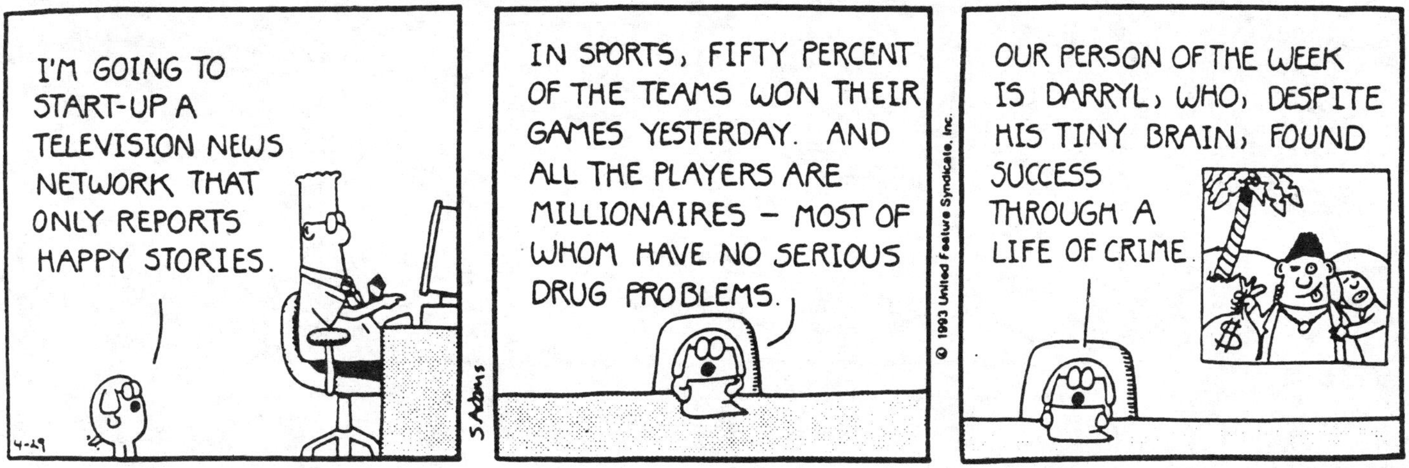
I'M GOING TO START-UP A TELEVISION NEWS NETWORK THAT ONLY REPORTS HAPPY STORIES.
IN SPORTS, FIFTY PERCENT OF THE TEAMS WON THEIR GAMES YESTERDAY. AND ALL THE PLAYERS ARE MILLIONAIRES – MOST OF WHOM HAVE NO SERIOUS DRUG PROBLEMS.
OUR PERSON OF THE WEEK IS DARRYL, WHO, DESPITE HIS TINY BRAIN, FOUND SUCCESS THROUGH A LIFE OF CRIME.
© 1993 United Feature Syndicate, Inc.

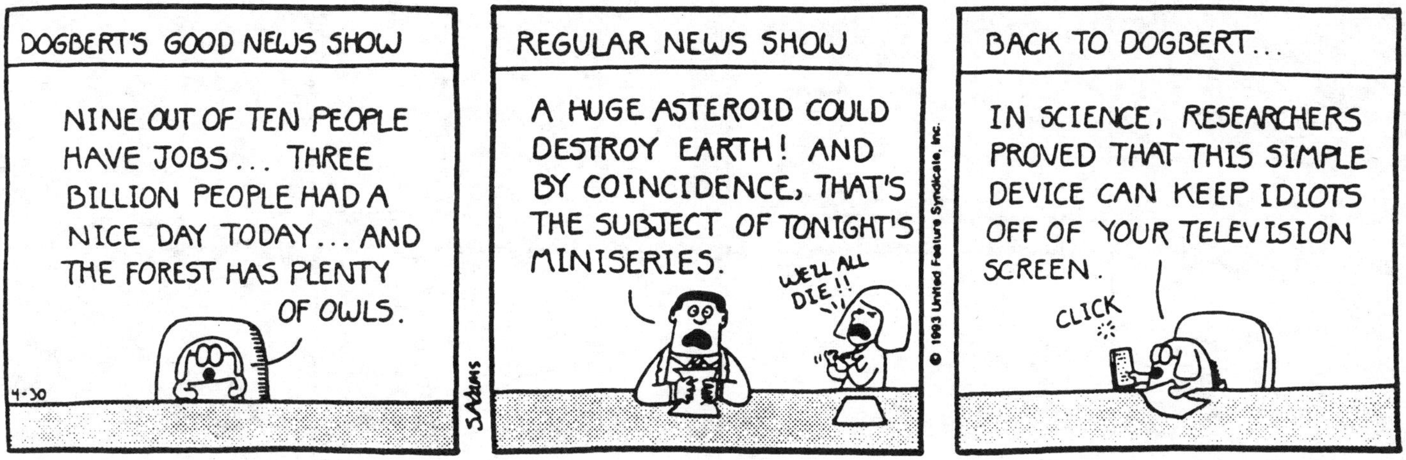
DOGBERT'S GOOD NEWS SHOW
NINE OUT OF TEN PEOPLE HAVE JOBS... THREE BILLION PEOPLE HAD A NICE DAY TODAY... AND THE FOREST HAS PLENTY OF OWLS.
REGULAR NEWS SHOW
A HUGE ASTEROID COULD DESTROY EARTH! AND BY COINCIDENCE, THAT'S THE SUBJECT OF TONIGHT'S MINISERIES.
WE'LL ALL DIE!!
BACK TO DOGBERT...
IN SCIENCE, RESEARCHERS PROVED THAT THIS SIMPLE DEVICE CAN KEEP IDIOTS OFF OF YOUR TELEVISION SCREEN.
CLICK
© 1993 United Feature Syndicate, Inc.

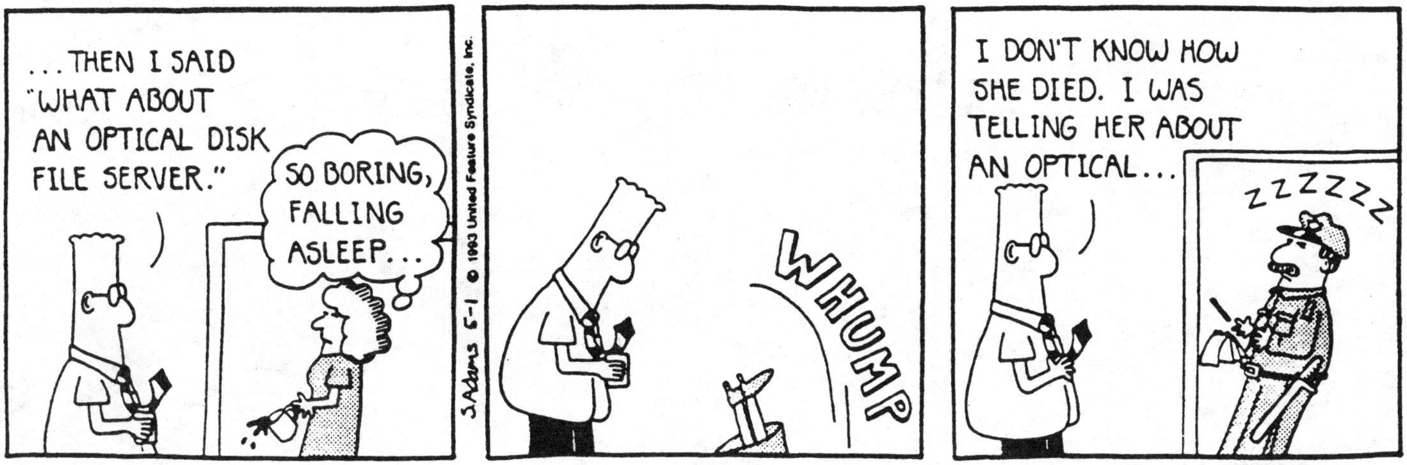
...THEN I SAID "WHAT ABOUT AN OPTICAL DISK FILE SERVER."
SO BORING, FALLING ASLEEP...
WHUMP
I DON'T KNOW HOW SHE DIED. I WAS TELLING HER ABOUT AN OPTICAL...
ZZZZZZ
© 1993 United Feature Syndicate, Inc.

IT'S THE MANLY THING TO DO.
BUNGEE JUMP $10
I'D LIKE TO EXPOSE MYSELF TO AVOIDABLE DANGER.
SIT RIGHT DOWN.
I NEED TO KNOW YOUR WEIGHT SO I CAN ADJUST THE BUNGEE CORD.
BE SURE YOU DON'T UNDER-ESTIMATE YOUR WEIGHT OR ELSE YOUR HEAD WILL HIT THE GROUND LIKE AN OVER-RIPE CANTALOUPE.
SEVEN HUNDRED POUNDS.
COUNT TO THREE AND JUMP.
5-2
I DIDN'T KNOW YOU COULD DO THIS ON A HILL.
S. Adams
TODAY, I AM A MAN.
FOR A HUNDRED BUCKS I'LL PULL YOU BACK.

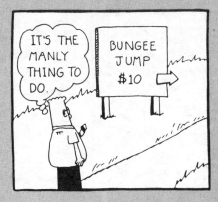

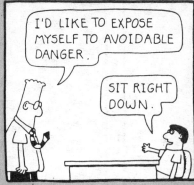

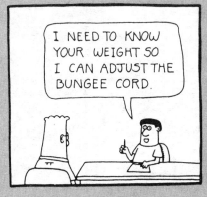

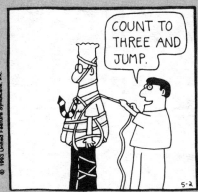

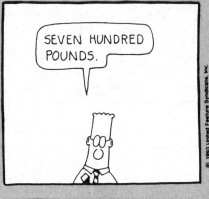

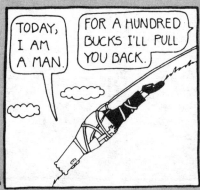

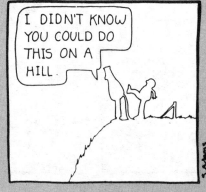

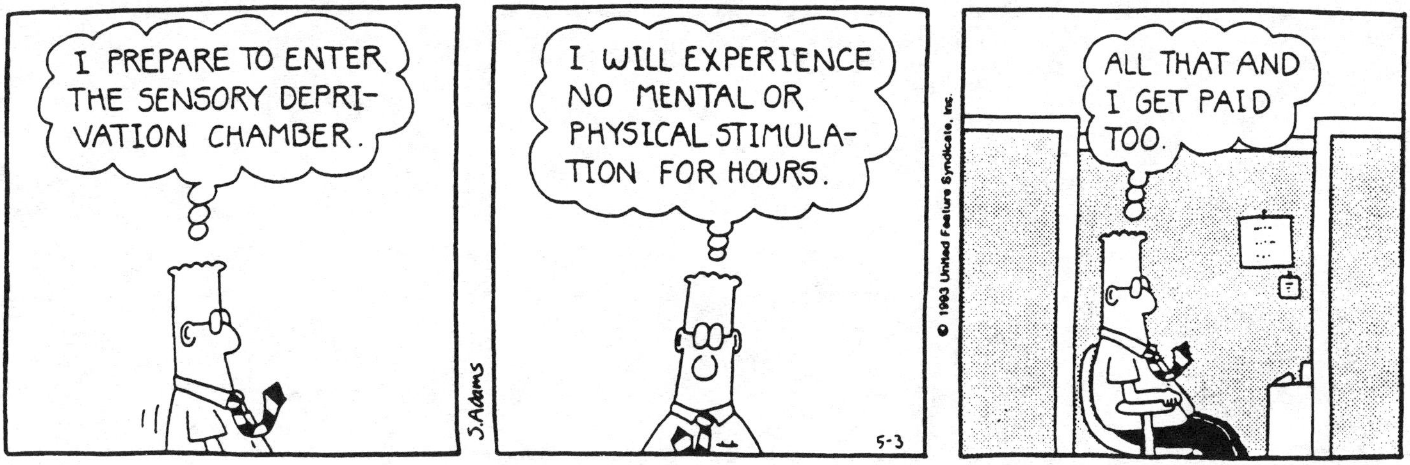
I PREPARE TO ENTER THE SENSORY DEPRIVATION CHAMBER.
S. Adams
I WILL EXPERIENCE NO MENTAL OR PHYSICAL STIMULATION FOR HOURS.
5-3
© 1993 United Feature Syndicate, Inc.
ALL THAT AND I GET PAID TOO.

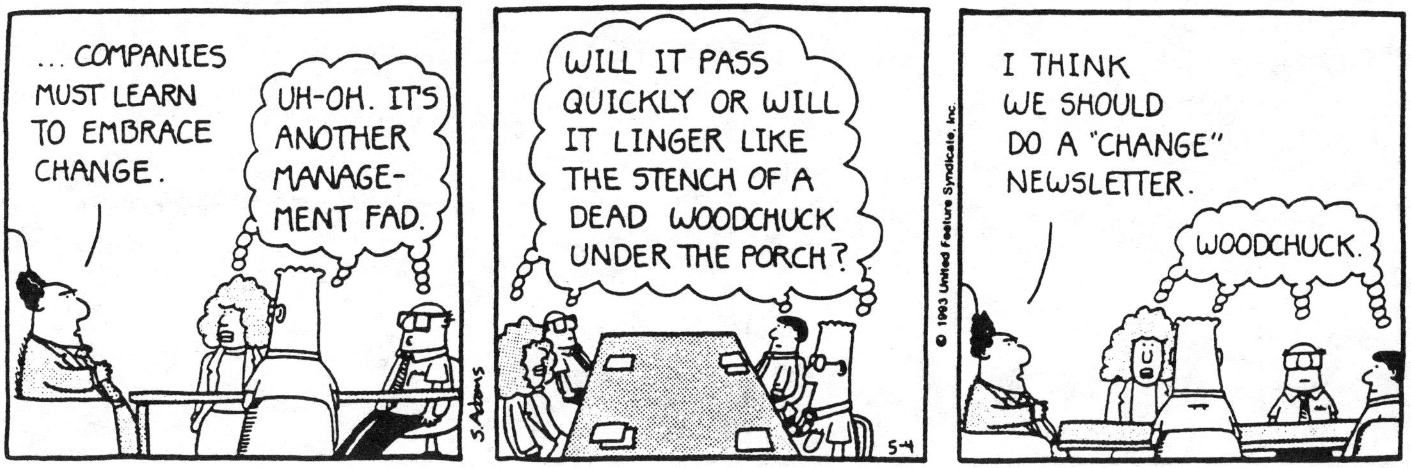
... COMPANIES MUST LEARN TO EMBRACE CHANGE.
UH-OH. IT'S ANOTHER MANAGEMENT FAD.
S. Adams
WILL IT PASS QUICKLY OR WILL IT LINGER LIKE THE STENCH OF A DEAD WOODCHUCK UNDER THE PORCH?
5-4
© 1993 United Feature Syndicate, Inc.
I THINK WE SHOULD DO A "CHANGE" NEWSLETTER.
WOODCHUCK.

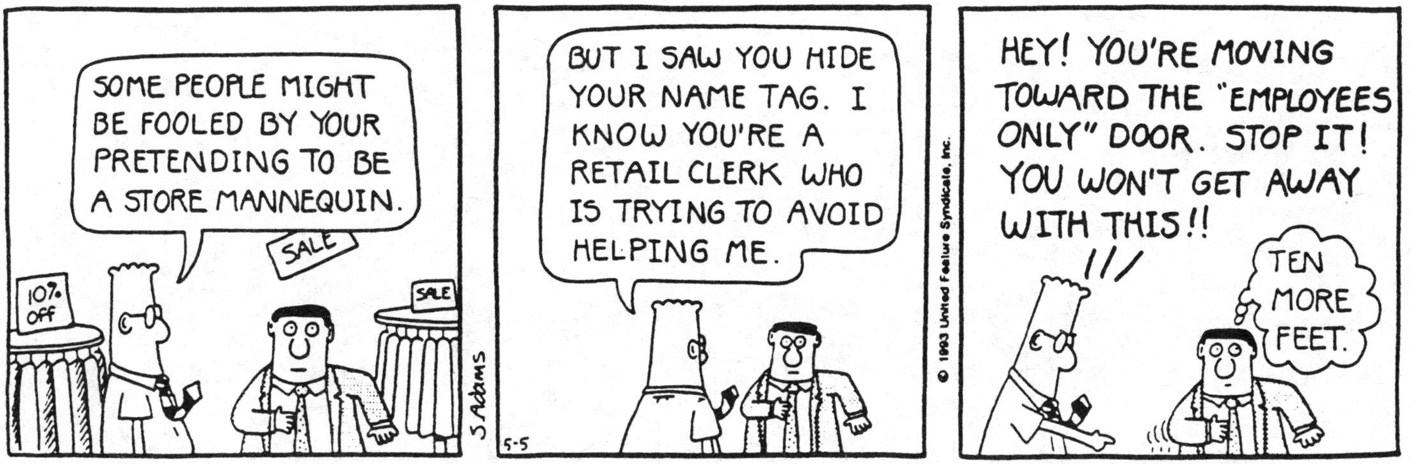
SOME PEOPLE MIGHT BE FOOLED BY YOUR PRETENDING TO BE A STORE MANNEQUIN.
10% OFF
SALE
SALE
S. Adams
BUT I SAW YOU HIDE YOUR NAME TAG. I KNOW YOU'RE A RETAIL CLERK WHO IS TRYING TO AVOID HELPING ME.
5-5
© 1993 United Feature Syndicate, Inc.
HEY! YOU'RE MOVING TOWARD THE "EMPLOYEES ONLY" DOOR. STOP IT! YOU WON'T GET AWAY WITH THIS!!
TEN MORE FEET.

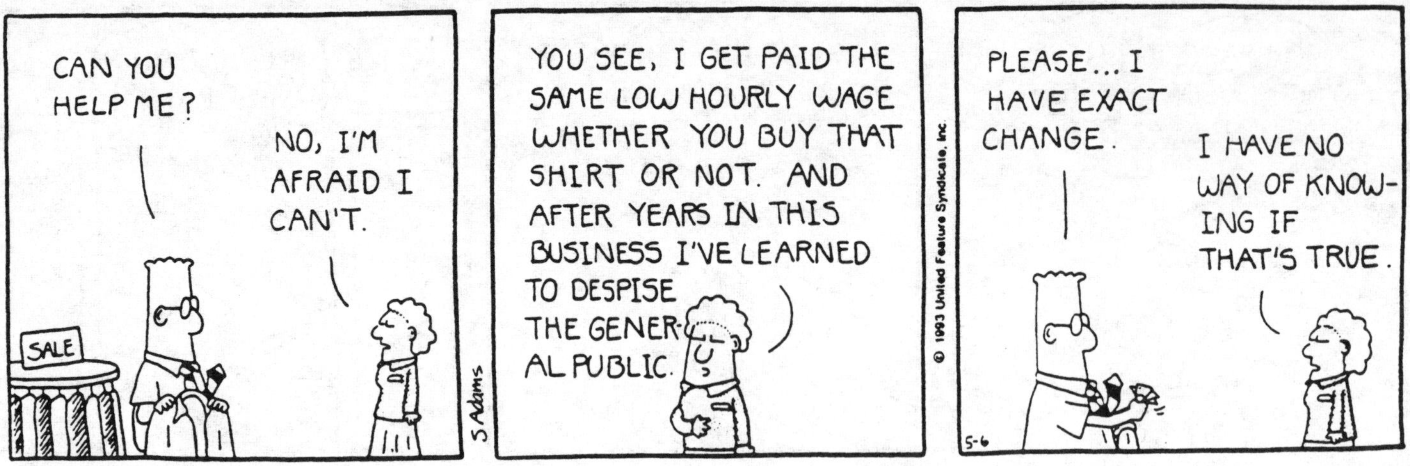
CAN YOU HELP ME?
NO, I'M AFRAID I CAN'T.
YOU SEE, I GET PAID THE SAME LOW HOURLY WAGE WHETHER YOU BUY THAT SHIRT OR NOT. AND AFTER YEARS IN THIS BUSINESS I'VE LEARNED TO DESPISE THE GENERAL PUBLIC.
PLEASE... I HAVE EXACT CHANGE.
I HAVE NO WAY OF KNOWING IF THAT'S TRUE.
S. Adams
© 1993 United Feature Syndicate, Inc.
5-6

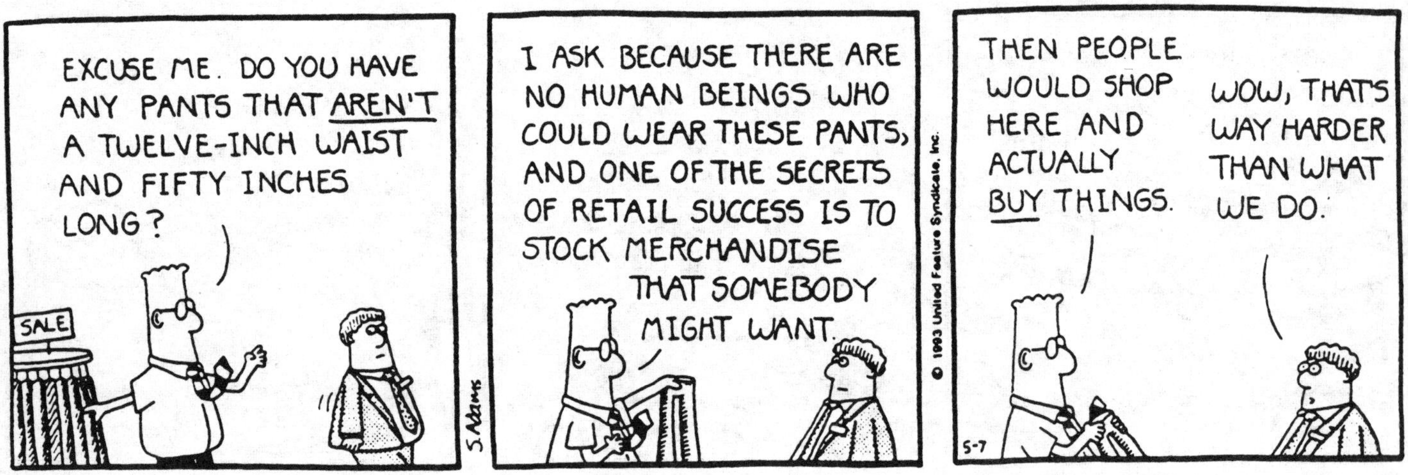
EXCUSE ME. DO YOU HAVE ANY PANTS THAT AREN'T A TWELVE-INCH WAIST AND FIFTY INCHES LONG?
SALE
I ASK BECAUSE THERE ARE NO HUMAN BEINGS WHO COULD WEAR THESE PANTS, AND ONE OF THE SECRETS OF RETAIL SUCCESS IS TO STOCK MERCHANDISE THAT SOMEBODY MIGHT WANT.
THEN PEOPLE WOULD SHOP HERE AND ACTUALLY BUY THINGS.
WOW, THAT'S WAY HARDER THAN WHAT WE DO.
S. Adams
© 1993 United Feature Syndicate, Inc.
5-7

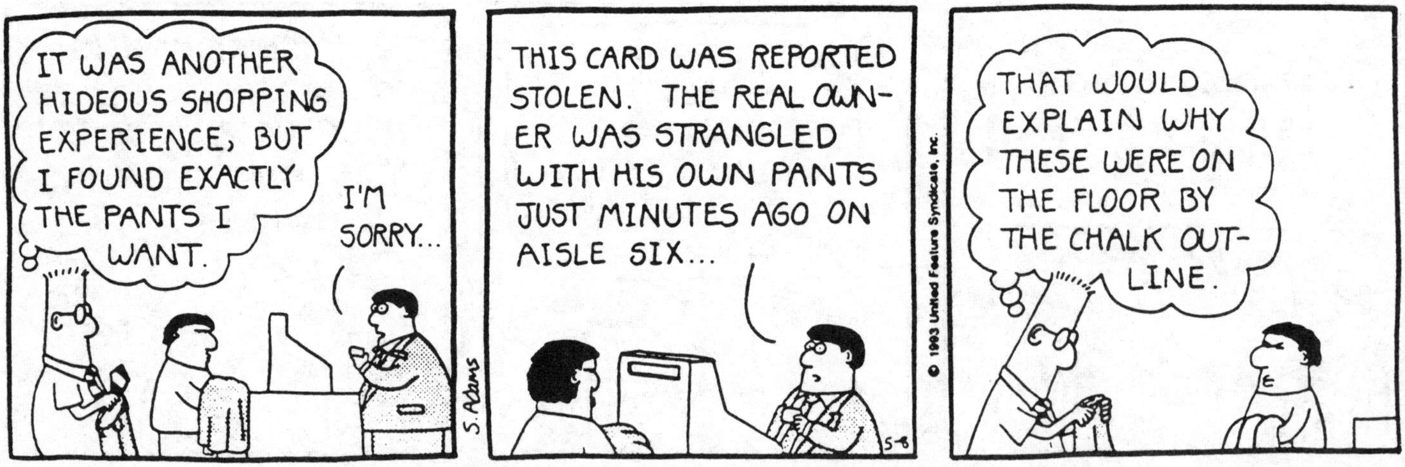
IT WAS ANOTHER HIDEOUS SHOPPING EXPERIENCE, BUT I FOUND EXACTLY THE PANTS I WANT.
I'M SORRY...
THIS CARD WAS REPORTED STOLEN. THE REAL OWNER WAS STRANGLED WITH HIS OWN PANTS JUST MINUTES AGO ON AISLE SIX...
THAT WOULD EXPLAIN WHY THESE WERE ON THE FLOOR BY THE CHALK OUTLINE.
S. Adams
© 1993 United Feature Syndicate, Inc.
5-8

DID YOU KNOW THAT TWENTY PERCENT OF ALL MICROFLEEMS ARE SUBRADIANTE?
S. Adams
UH-OH. THE BOSS HAS LATCHED ONTO SOME OBSCURE ENGINEERING FACT.
THIS IS GOING TO BE PAINFUL.
JUST THINK OF THE IMPLICATIONS. IT MEANS EIGHTY PERCENT OF MICROFLEEMS ARE NOT SUBRADIANTE.
MAYBE I CAN HIDE UNDER THE DESK UNTIL THIS BLOWS OVER.
DON'T YOU THINK IT'S FASCINATING? I MEAN, WHAT WITH THE IMPLICATIONS AND ALL...
OKAY, OKAY. I ACKNOWLEDGE YOUR INCREDIBLE GRASP OF TECH-NOLOGY ISSUES.
© 1993 United Feature Syndicate, Inc.
IT ALMOST MAKES ME CURIOUS WHAT A MICROFLEEM IS.
5-9

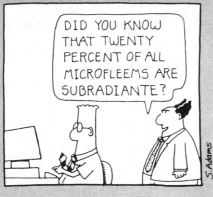

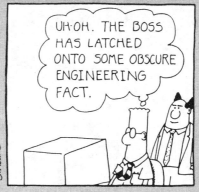

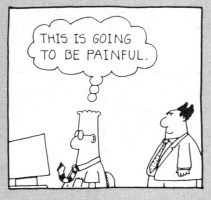

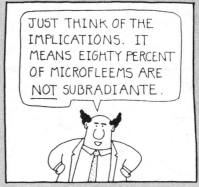

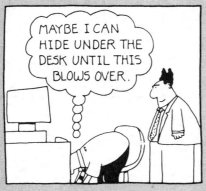

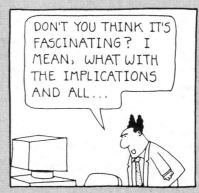

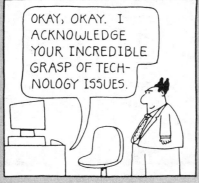

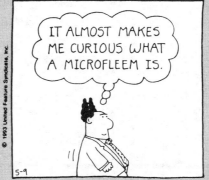

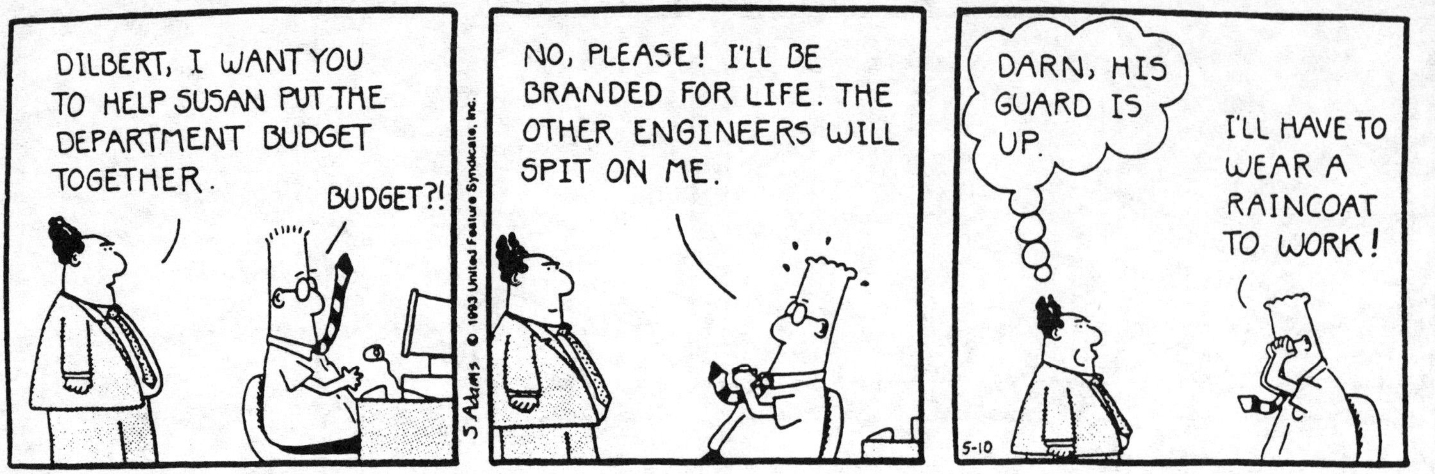
DILBERT, I WANT YOU TO HELP SUSAN PUT THE DEPARTMENT BUDGET TOGETHER.
BUDGET?!
S. Adams © 1993 United Feature Syndicate, Inc.
NO, PLEASE! I'LL BE BRANDED FOR LIFE. THE OTHER ENGINEERS WILL SPIT ON ME.
DARN, HIS GUARD IS UP.
I'LL HAVE TO WEAR A RAINCOAT TO WORK!
5-10

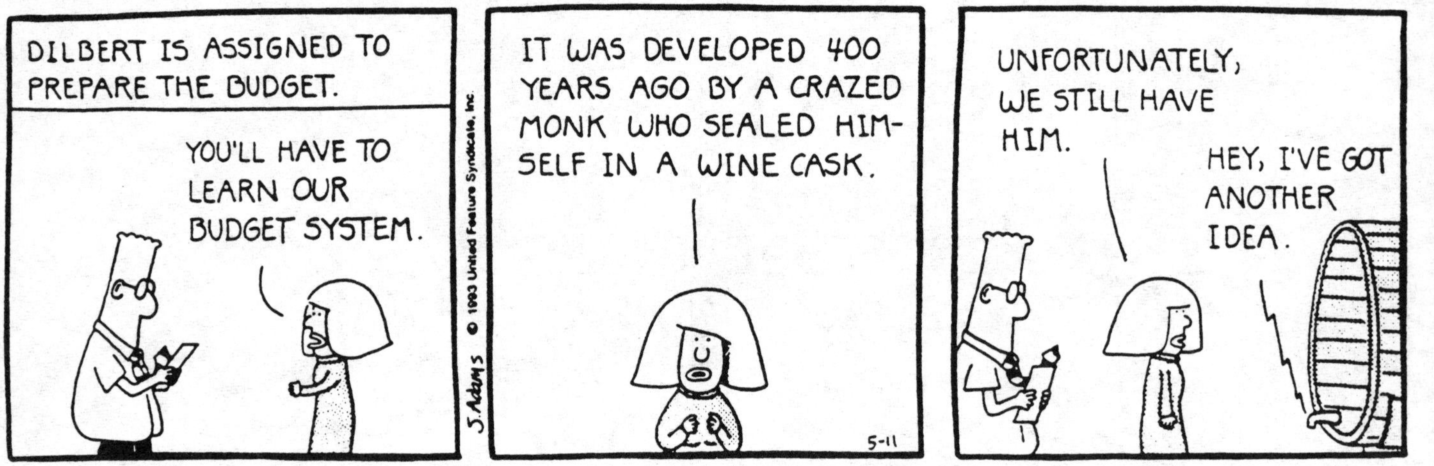
DILBERT IS ASSIGNED TO PREPARE THE BUDGET.
YOU'LL HAVE TO LEARN OUR BUDGET SYSTEM.
S. Adams © 1993 United Feature Syndicate, Inc.
IT WAS DEVELOPED 400 YEARS AGO BY A CRAZED MONK WHO SEALED HIMSELF IN A WINE CASK.
5-11
UNFORTUNATELY, WE STILL HAVE HIM.
HEY, I'VE GOT ANOTHER IDEA.

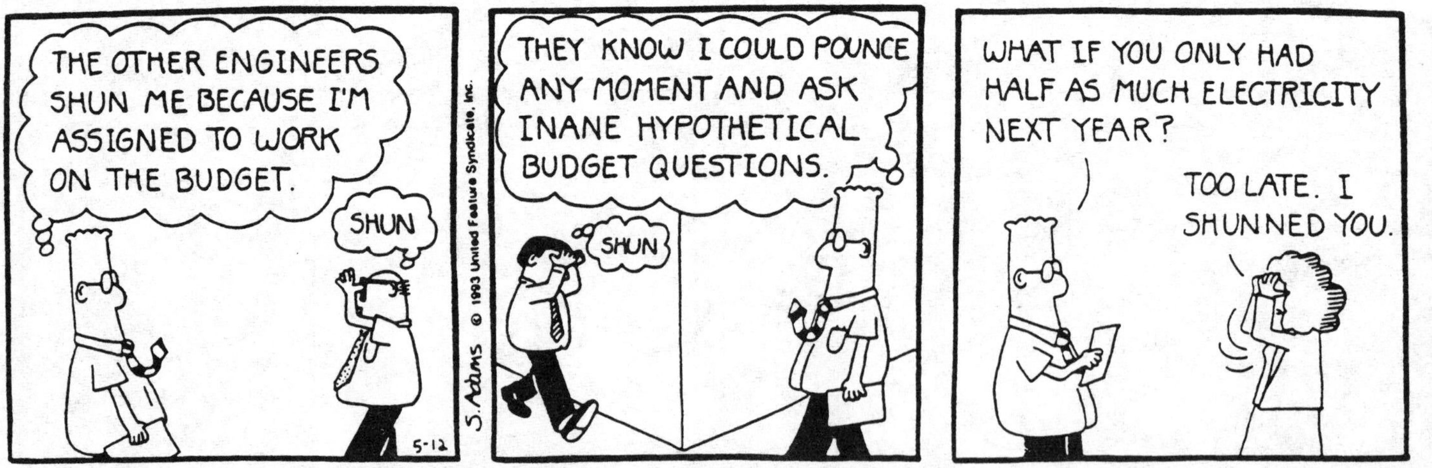
THE OTHER ENGINEERS SHUN ME BECAUSE I'M ASSIGNED TO WORK ON THE BUDGET.
SHUN
5-12
S. Adams © 1993 United Feature Syndicate, Inc.
THEY KNOW I COULD POUNCE ANY MOMENT AND ASK INANE HYPOTHETICAL BUDGET QUESTIONS.
SHUN
WHAT IF YOU ONLY HAD HALF AS MUCH ELECTRICITY NEXT YEAR?
TOO LATE. I SHUNNED YOU.

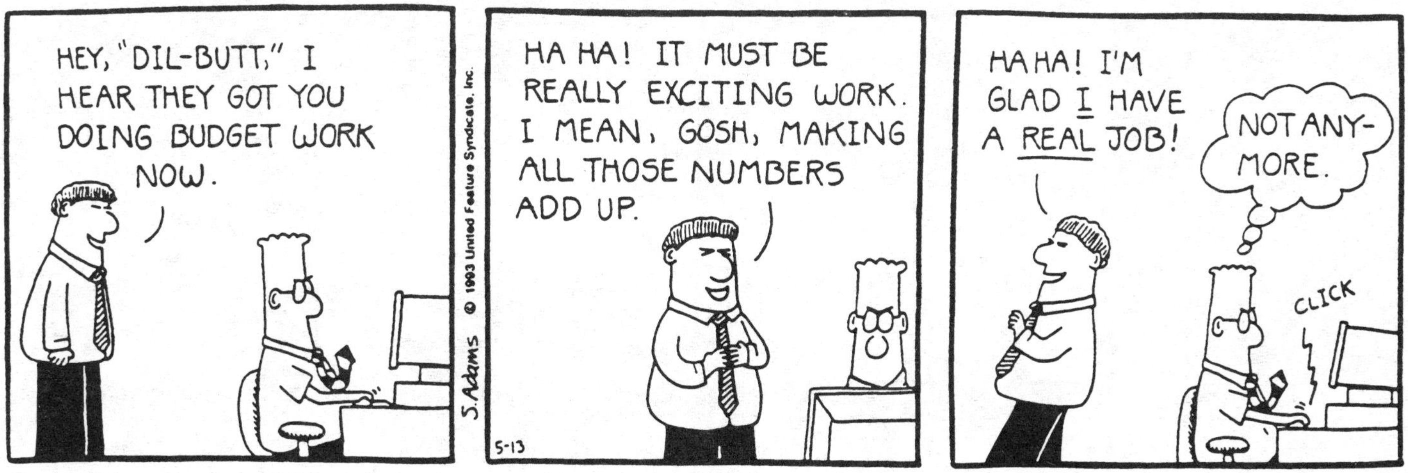
HEY, "DIL-BUTT," I HEAR THEY GOT YOU DOING BUDGET WORK NOW.
S. Adams
© 1993 United Feature Syndicate, Inc.
5-13
HA HA! IT MUST BE REALLY EXCITING WORK. I MEAN, GOSH, MAKING ALL THOSE NUMBERS ADD UP.
HA HA! I'M GLAD I HAVE A REAL JOB!
NOT ANY-MORE.
CLICK

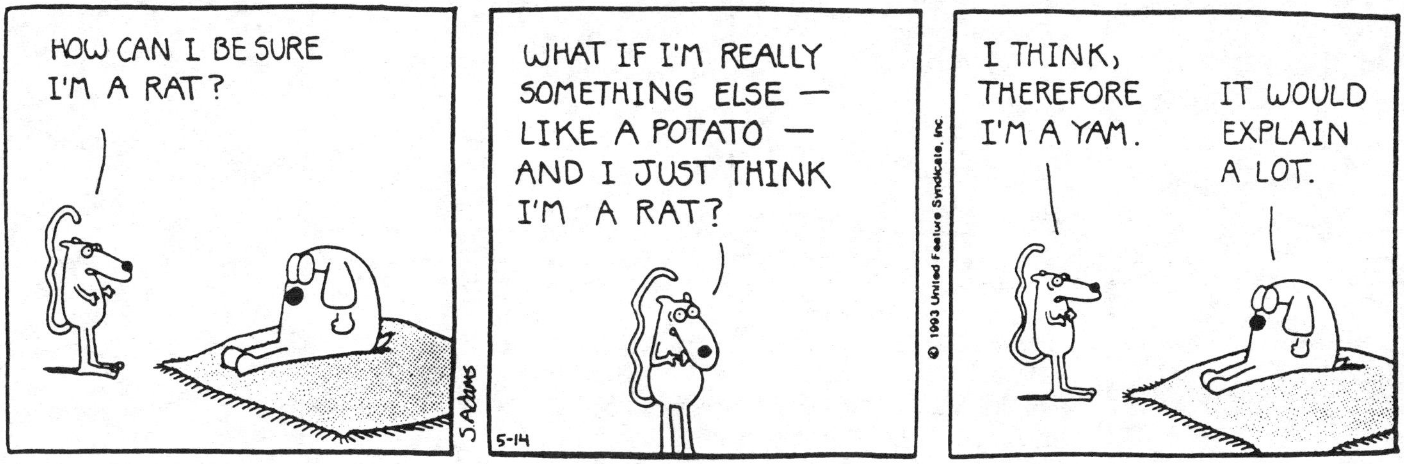
HOW CAN I BE SURE I'M A RAT?
S. Adams
5-14
WHAT IF I'M REALLY SOMETHING ELSE — LIKE A POTATO — AND I JUST THINK I'M A RAT?
© 1993 United Feature Syndicate, Inc.
I THINK, THEREFORE I'M A YAM.
IT WOULD EXPLAIN A LOT.

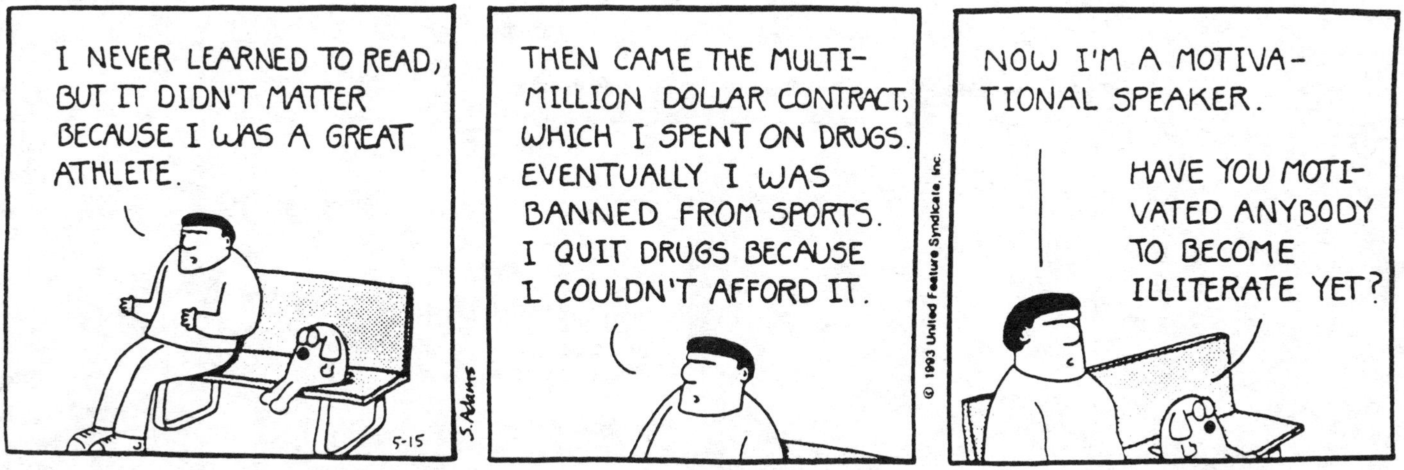
I NEVER LEARNED TO READ, BUT IT DIDN'T MATTER BECAUSE I WAS A GREAT ATHLETE.
5-15
S. Adams
THEN CAME THE MULTI-MILLION DOLLAR CONTRACT, WHICH I SPENT ON DRUGS. EVENTUALLY I WAS BANNED FROM SPORTS. I QUIT DRUGS BECAUSE I COULDN'T AFFORD IT.
© 1993 United Feature Syndicate, Inc.
NOW I'M A MOTIVA-TIONAL SPEAKER.
HAVE YOU MOTI-VATED ANYBODY TO BECOME ILLITERATE YET?

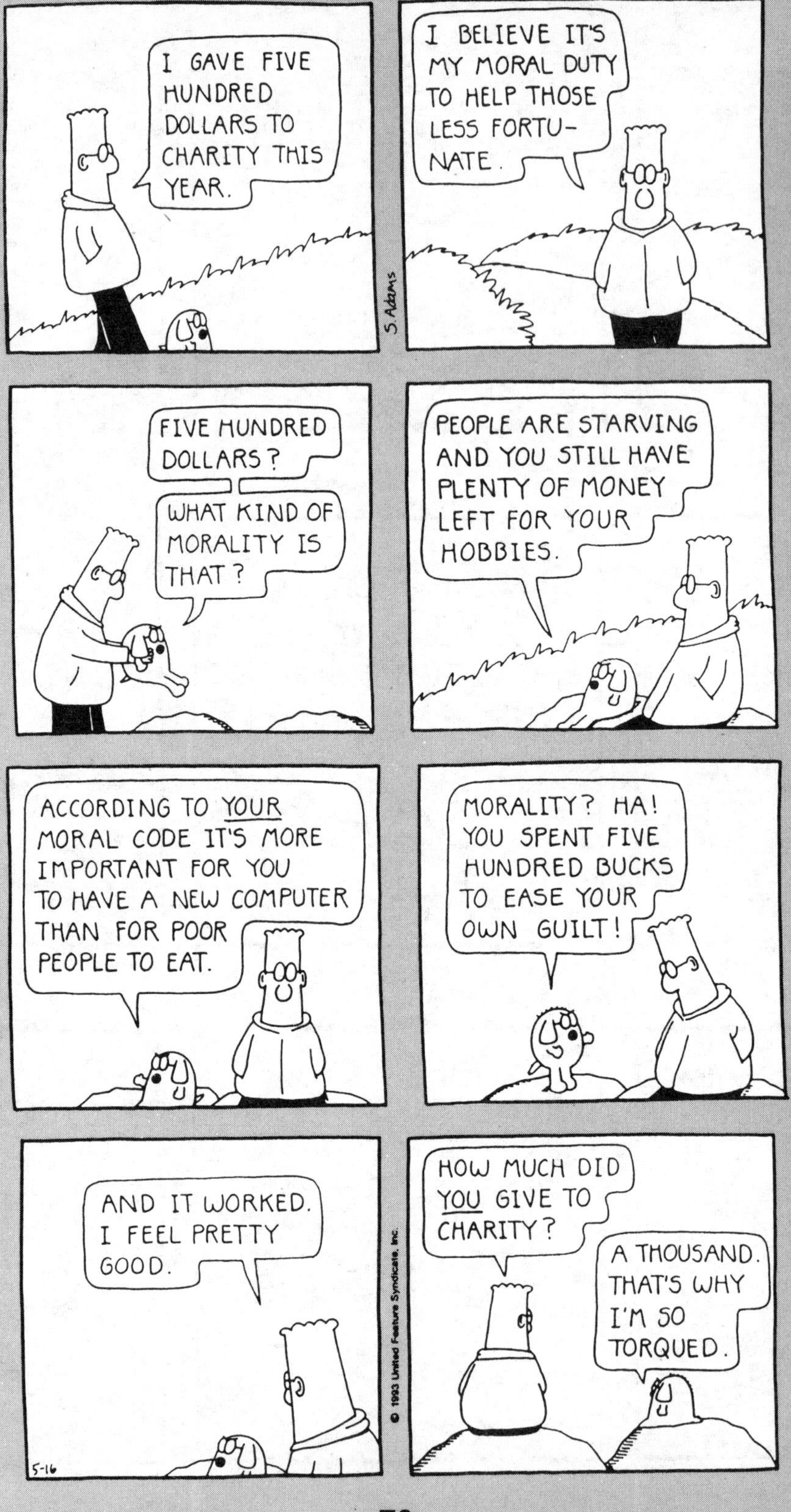

I GAVE FIVE HUNDRED DOLLARS TO CHARITY THIS YEAR.
I BELIEVE IT'S MY MORAL DUTY TO HELP THOSE LESS FORTUNATE.
FIVE HUNDRED DOLLARS?
WHAT KIND OF MORALITY IS THAT?
PEOPLE ARE STARVING AND YOU STILL HAVE PLENTY OF MONEY LEFT FOR YOUR HOBBIES.
ACCORDING TO YOUR MORAL CODE IT'S MORE IMPORTANT FOR YOU TO HAVE A NEW COMPUTER THAN FOR POOR PEOPLE TO EAT.
MORALITY? HA! YOU SPENT FIVE HUNDRED BUCKS TO EASE YOUR OWN GUILT!
AND IT WORKED. I FEEL PRETTY GOOD.
HOW MUCH DID YOU GIVE TO CHARITY?
A THOUSAND. THAT'S WHY I'M SO TORQUED.
S. Adams
© 1993 United Feature Syndicate, Inc.
5-16

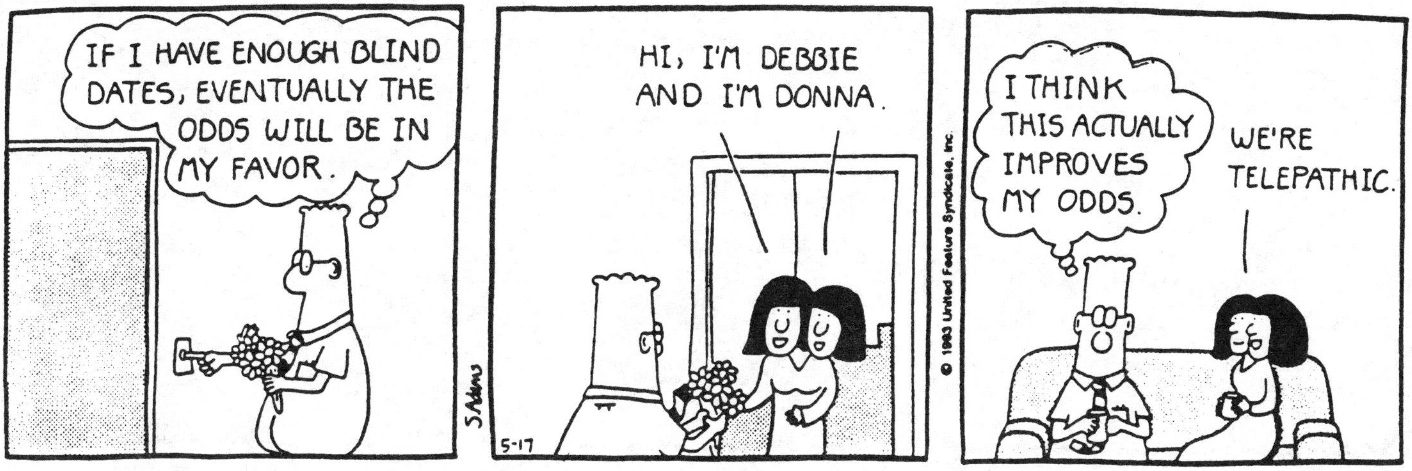
IF I HAVE ENOUGH BLIND DATES, EVENTUALLY THE ODDS WILL BE IN MY FAVOR.
HI, I'M DEBBIE
AND I'M DONNA.
I THINK THIS ACTUALLY IMPROVES MY ODDS.
WE'RE TELEPATHIC.
S. Adams
5-17
© 1993 United Feature Syndicate, Inc.

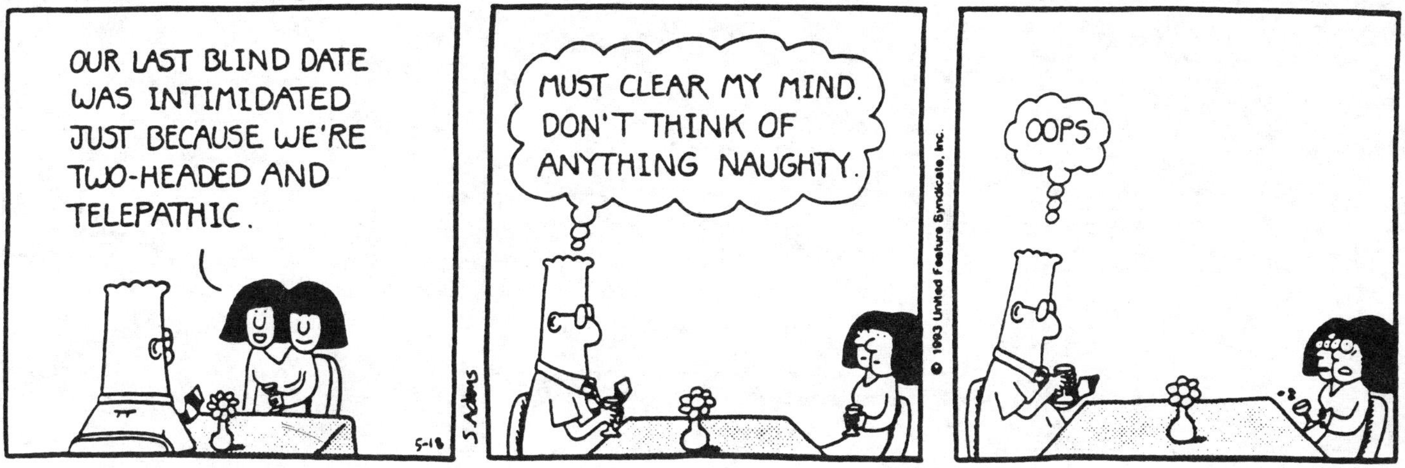
OUR LAST BLIND DATE WAS INTIMIDATED JUST BECAUSE WE'RE TWO-HEADED AND TELEPATHIC.
MUST CLEAR MY MIND. DON'T THINK OF ANYTHING NAUGHTY.
OOPS
S. Adams
5-18
© 1993 United Feature Syndicate, Inc.

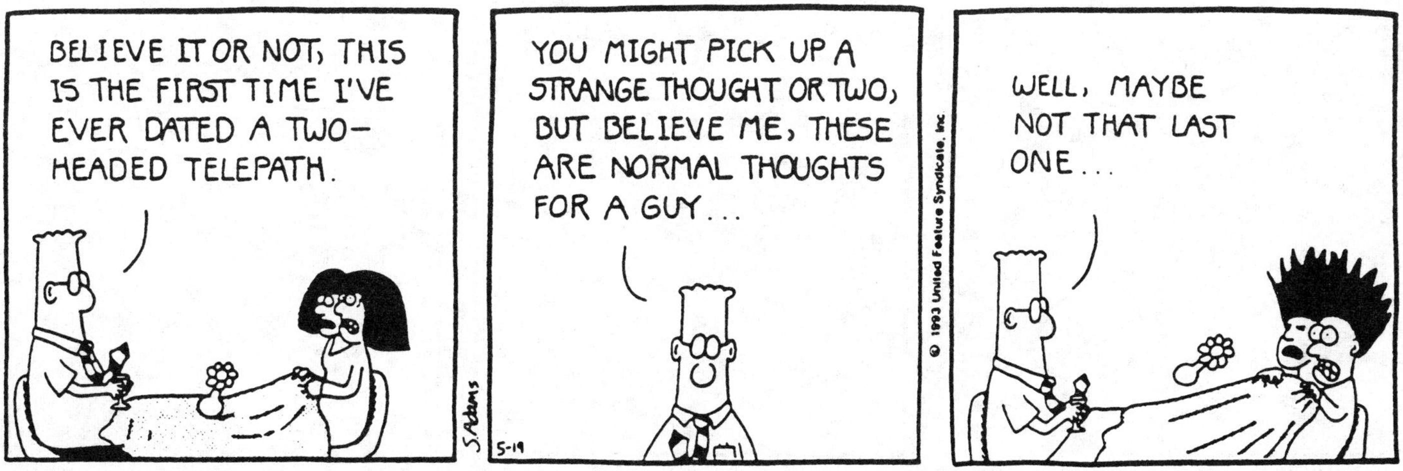
BELIEVE IT OR NOT, THIS IS THE FIRST TIME I'VE EVER DATED A TWO-HEADED TELEPATH.
YOU MIGHT PICK UP A STRANGE THOUGHT OR TWO, BUT BELIEVE ME, THESE ARE NORMAL THOUGHTS FOR A GUY...
WELL, MAYBE NOT THAT LAST ONE...
S. Adams
5-19
© 1993 United Feature Syndicate, Inc.

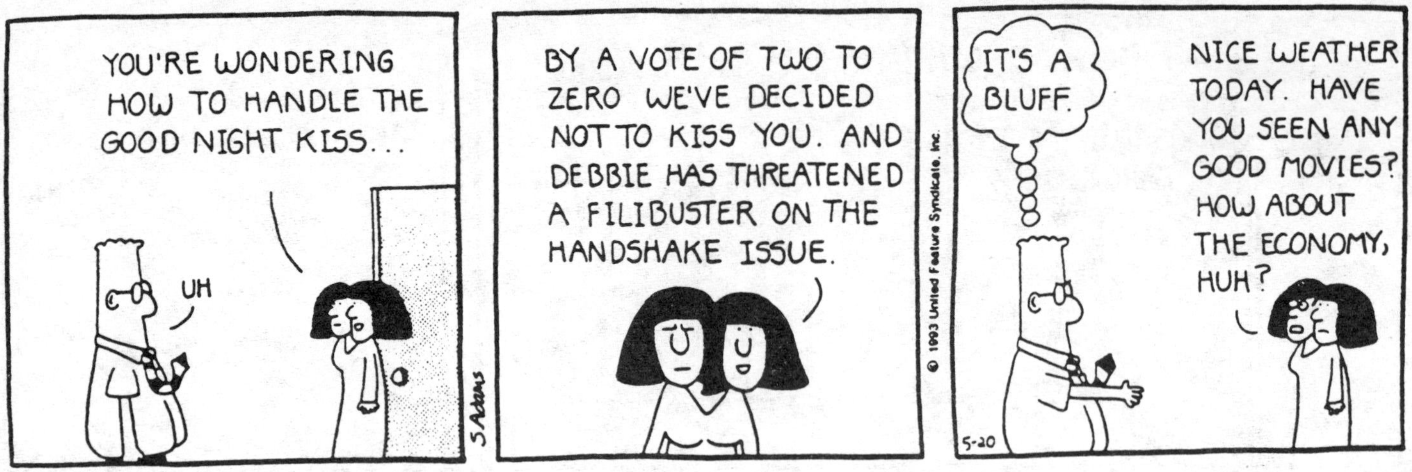
YOU'RE WONDERING HOW TO HANDLE THE GOOD NIGHT KISS...
UH
S. Adams
BY A VOTE OF TWO TO ZERO WE'VE DECIDED NOT TO KISS YOU. AND DEBBIE HAS THREATENED A FILIBUSTER ON THE HANDSHAKE ISSUE.
© 1993 United Feature Syndicate, Inc.
IT'S A BLUFF.
NICE WEATHER TODAY. HAVE YOU SEEN ANY GOOD MOVIES? HOW ABOUT THE ECONOMY, HUH?
5-20

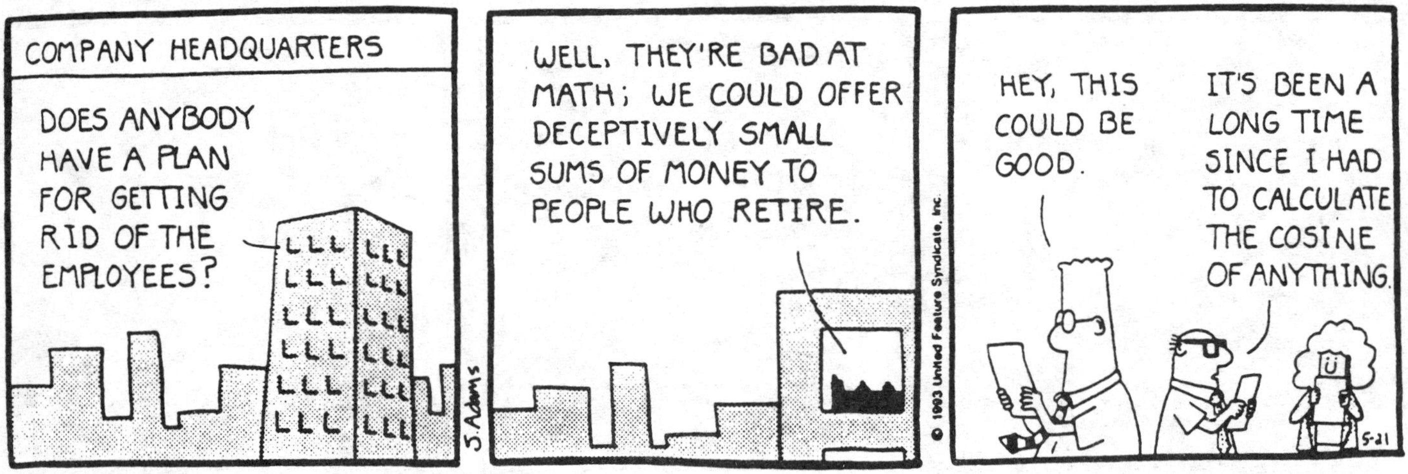
COMPANY HEADQUARTERS
DOES ANYBODY HAVE A PLAN FOR GETTING RID OF THE EMPLOYEES?
S. Adams
WELL, THEY'RE BAD AT MATH; WE COULD OFFER DECEPTIVELY SMALL SUMS OF MONEY TO PEOPLE WHO RETIRE.
© 1993 United Feature Syndicate, Inc.
HEY, THIS COULD BE GOOD.
IT'S BEEN A LONG TIME SINCE I HAD TO CALCULATE THE COSINE OF ANYTHING.
5-21

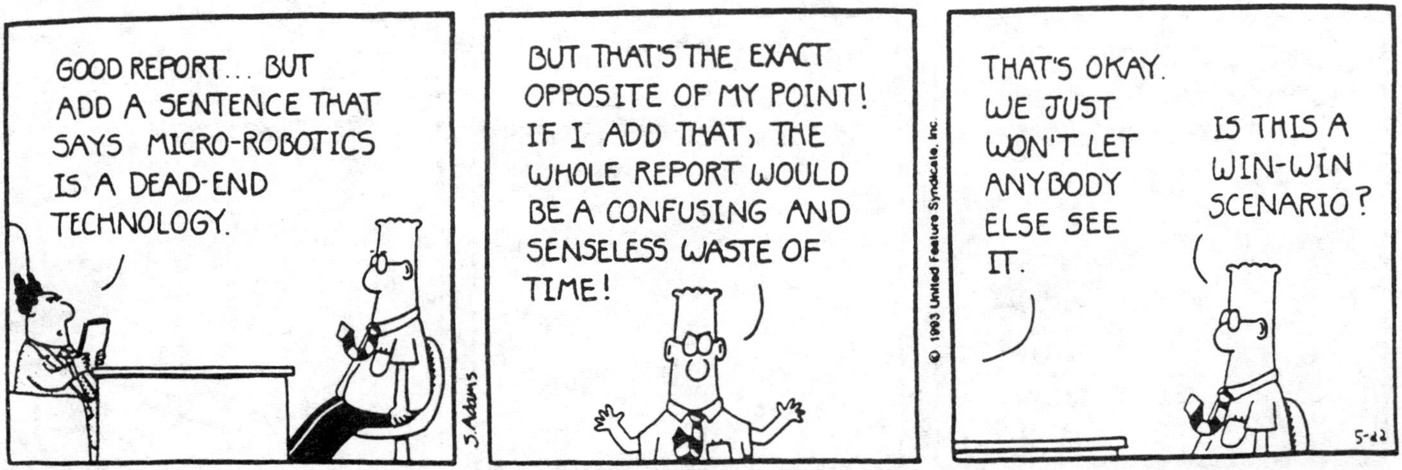
GOOD REPORT... BUT ADD A SENTENCE THAT SAYS MICRO-ROBOTICS IS A DEAD-END TECHNOLOGY.
S. Adams
BUT THAT'S THE EXACT OPPOSITE OF MY POINT! IF I ADD THAT, THE WHOLE REPORT WOULD BE A CONFUSING AND SENSELESS WASTE OF TIME!
© 1993 United Feature Syndicate, Inc.
THAT'S OKAY. WE JUST WON'T LET ANYBODY ELSE SEE IT.
IS THIS A WIN-WIN SCENARIO?
5-22

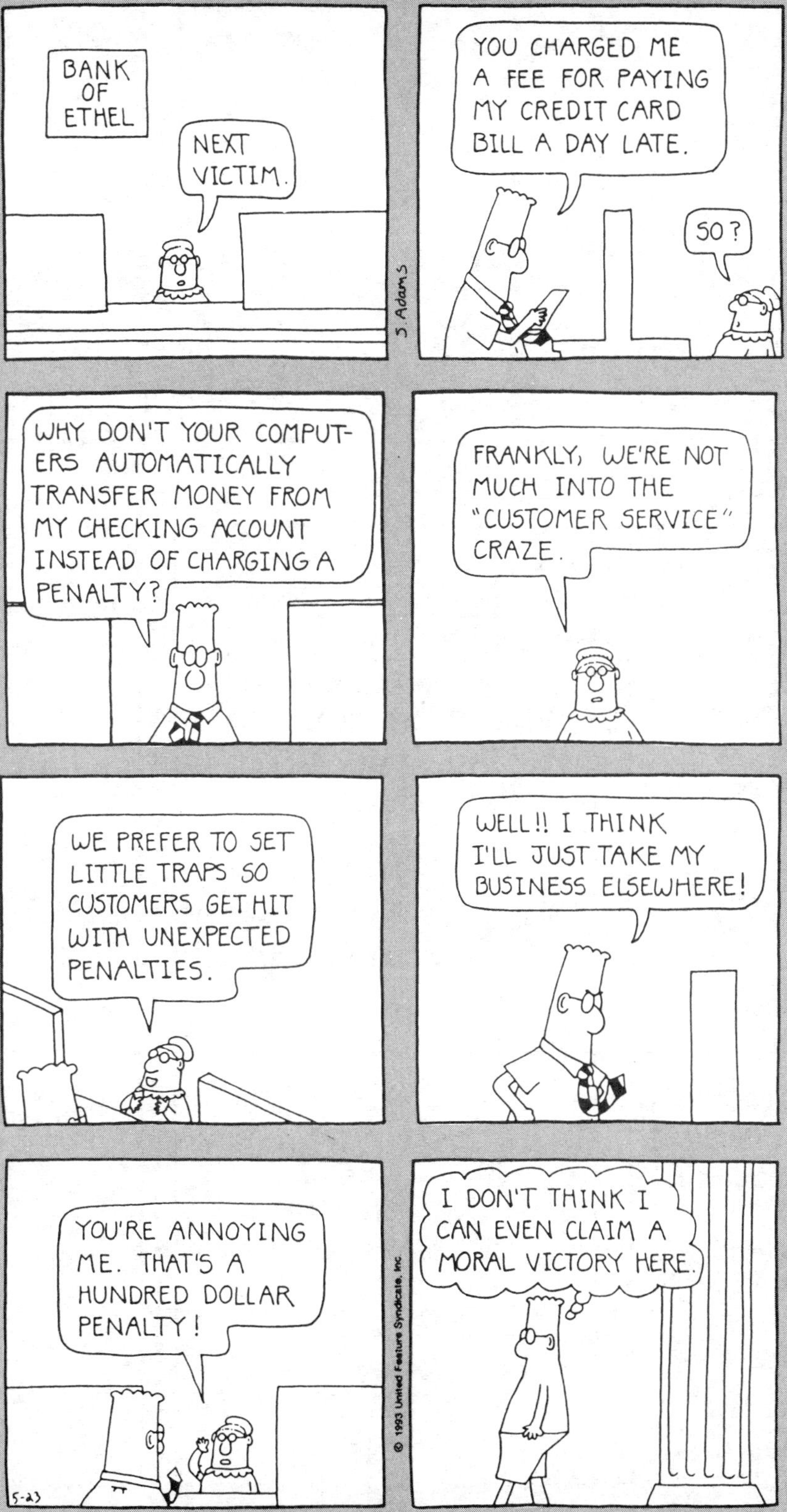
BANK OF ETHEL
NEXT VICTIM.
YOU CHARGED ME A FEE FOR PAYING MY CREDIT CARD BILL A DAY LATE.
SO?
S. Adams
WHY DON'T YOUR COMPUTERS AUTOMATICALLY TRANSFER MONEY FROM MY CHECKING ACCOUNT INSTEAD OF CHARGING A PENALTY?
FRANKLY, WE'RE NOT MUCH INTO THE "CUSTOMER SERVICE" CRAZE.
WE PREFER TO SET LITTLE TRAPS SO CUSTOMERS GET HIT WITH UNEXPECTED PENALTIES.
WELL!! I THINK I'LL JUST TAKE MY BUSINESS ELSEWHERE!
YOU'RE ANNOYING ME. THAT'S A HUNDRED DOLLAR PENALTY!
5-23
© 1993 United Feature Syndicate, Inc.
I DON'T THINK I CAN EVEN CLAIM A MORAL VICTORY HERE.

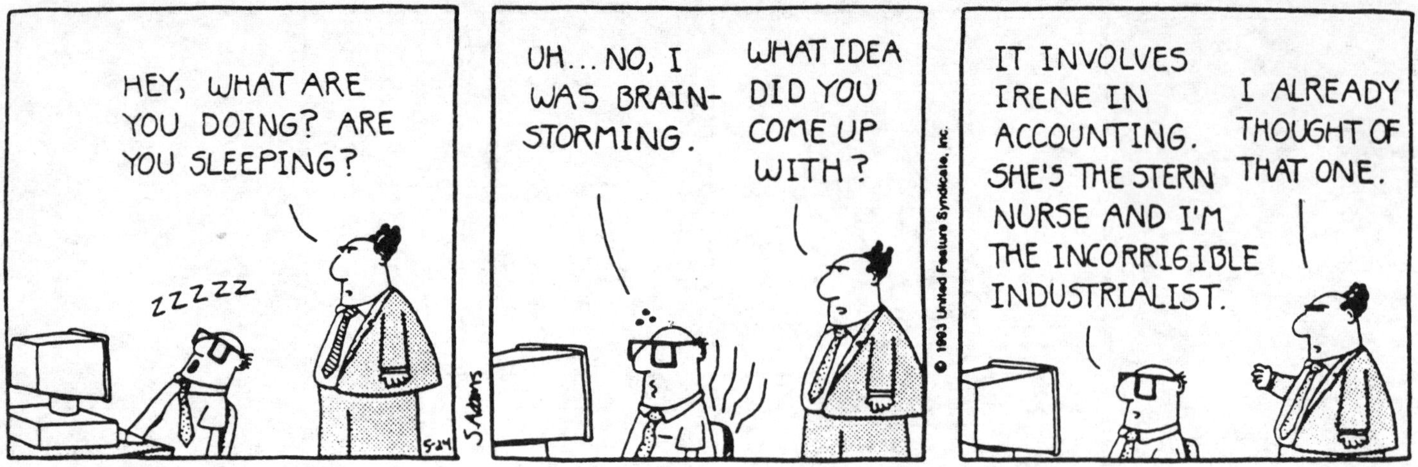
HEY, WHAT ARE YOU DOING? ARE YOU SLEEPING?
ZZZZZ
UH... NO, I WAS BRAIN-STORMING.
WHAT IDEA DID YOU COME UP WITH?
IT INVOLVES IRENE IN ACCOUNTING. SHE'S THE STERN NURSE AND I'M THE INCORRIGIBLE INDUSTRIALIST.
I ALREADY THOUGHT OF THAT ONE.
S. Adams
5-24
© 1993 United Feature Syndicate, Inc.

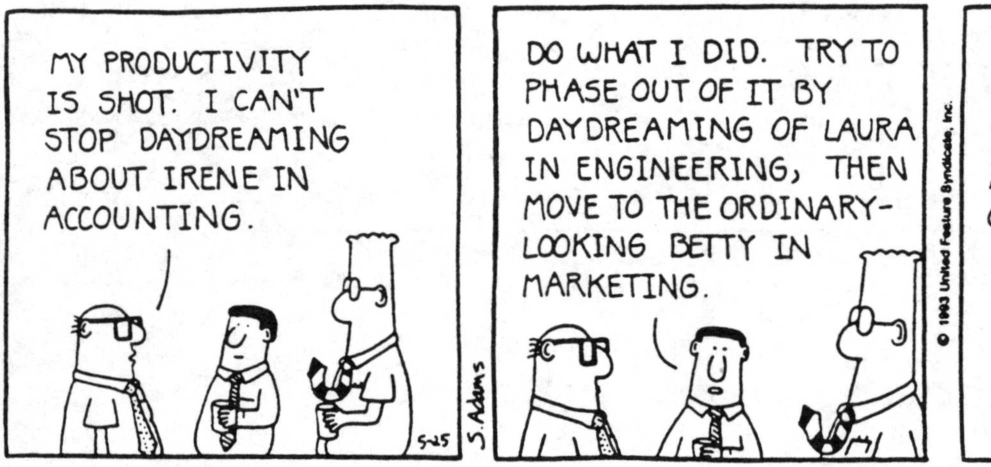
MY PRODUCTIVITY IS SHOT. I CAN'T STOP DAYDREAMING ABOUT IRENE IN ACCOUNTING.
DO WHAT I DID. TRY TO PHASE OUT OF IT BY DAYDREAMING OF LAURA IN ENGINEERING, THEN MOVE TO THE ORDINARY-LOOKING BETTY IN MARKETING.
NOW I'M DAYDREAMING ABOUT ALL THREE OF THEM.
SAME THING HAPPENED TO ME.
S. Adams
5-25
© 1993 United Feature Syndicate, Inc.

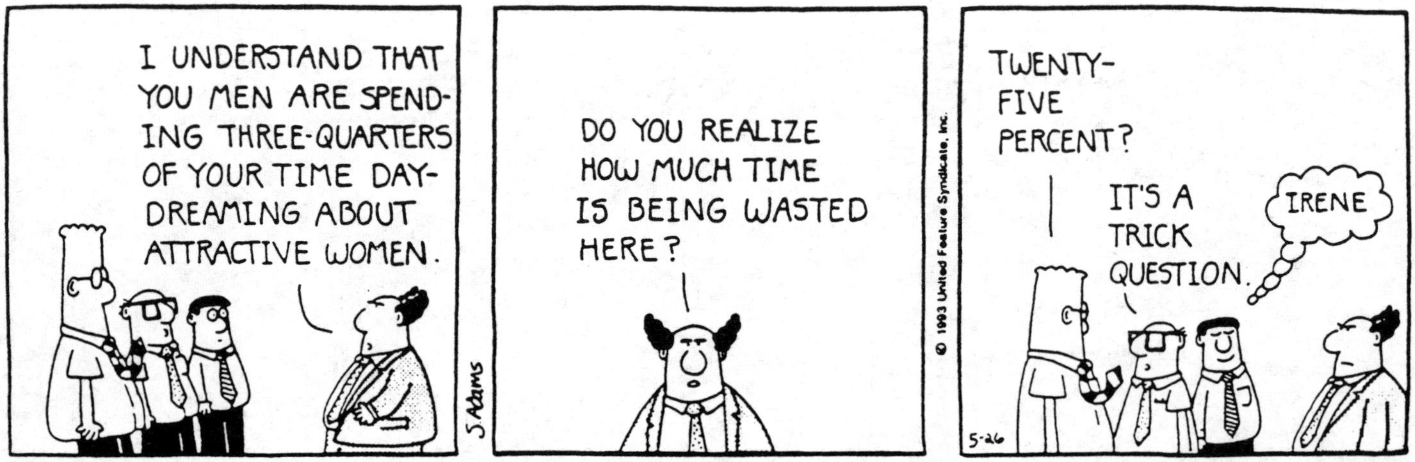
I UNDERSTAND THAT YOU MEN ARE SPENDING THREE-QUARTERS OF YOUR TIME DAYDREAMING ABOUT ATTRACTIVE WOMEN.
DO YOU REALIZE HOW MUCH TIME IS BEING WASTED HERE?
TWENTY-FIVE PERCENT?
IT'S A TRICK QUESTION.
IRENE
S. Adams
5-26
© 1993 United Feature Syndicate, Inc.

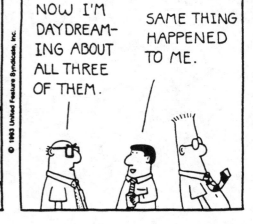

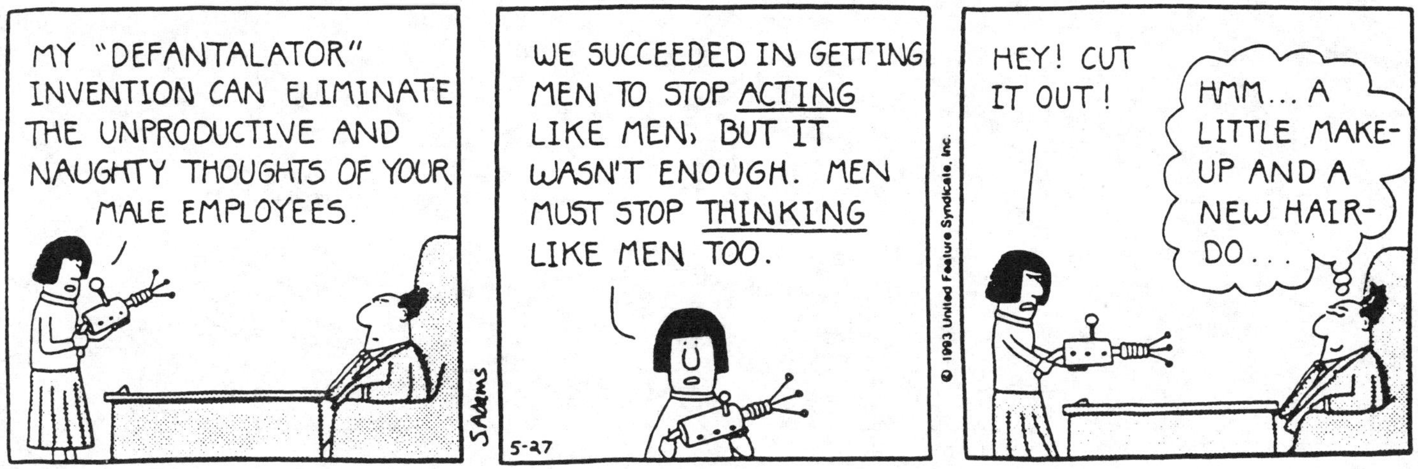
MY "DEFANTALATOR" INVENTION CAN ELIMINATE THE UNPRODUCTIVE AND NAUGHTY THOUGHTS OF YOUR MALE EMPLOYEES.
S.Adams
WE SUCCEEDED IN GETTING MEN TO STOP ACTING LIKE MEN, BUT IT WASN'T ENOUGH. MEN MUST STOP THINKING LIKE MEN TOO.
5-27
© 1993 United Feature Syndicate, Inc.
HEY! CUT IT OUT!
HMM... A LITTLE MAKE-UP AND A NEW HAIR-DO...

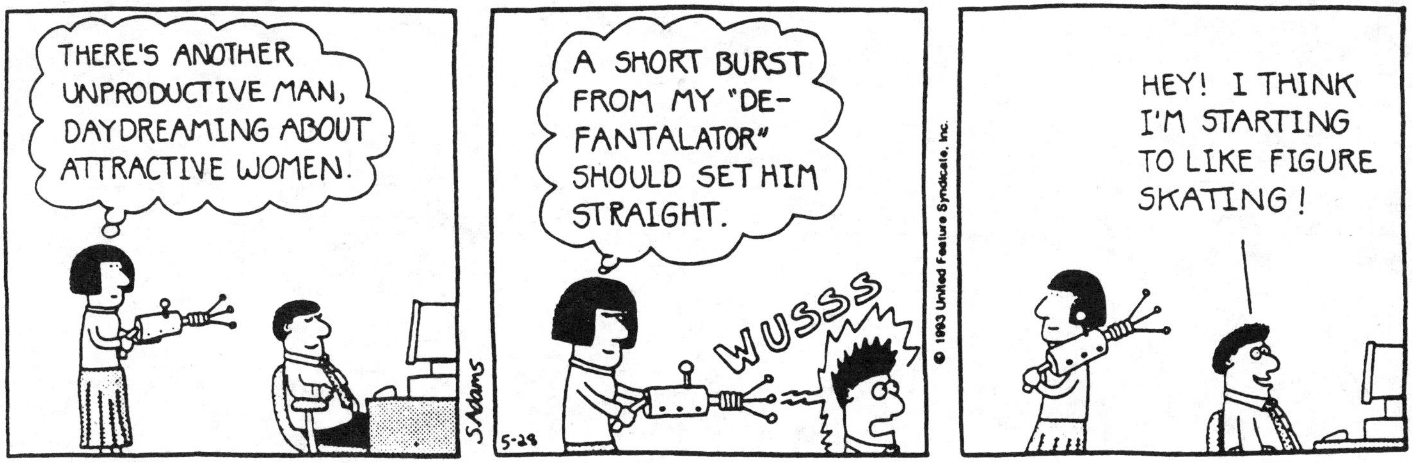
THERE'S ANOTHER UNPRODUCTIVE MAN, DAYDREAMING ABOUT ATTRACTIVE WOMEN.
S.Adams
A SHORT BURST FROM MY "DE-FANTALATOR" SHOULD SET HIM STRAIGHT.
WUSSS
5-28
© 1993 United Feature Syndicate, Inc.
HEY! I THINK I'M STARTING TO LIKE FIGURE SKATING!

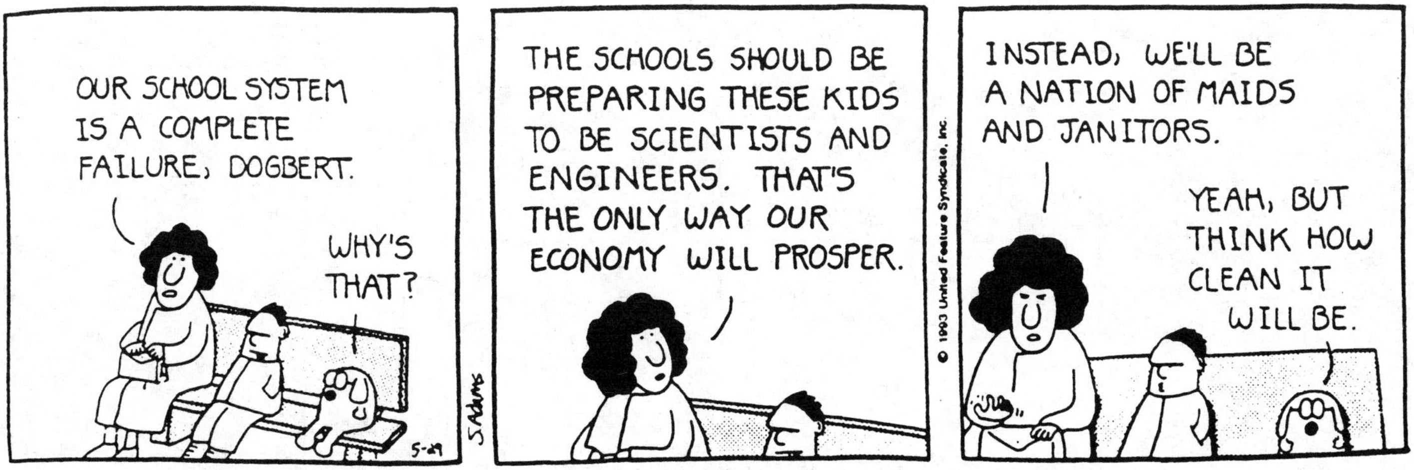
OUR SCHOOL SYSTEM IS A COMPLETE FAILURE, DOGBERT.
WHY'S THAT?
5-29
S.Adams
THE SCHOOLS SHOULD BE PREPARING THESE KIDS TO BE SCIENTISTS AND ENGINEERS. THAT'S THE ONLY WAY OUR ECONOMY WILL PROSPER.
© 1993 United Feature Syndicate, Inc.
INSTEAD, WE'LL BE A NATION OF MAIDS AND JANITORS.
YEAH, BUT THINK HOW CLEAN IT WILL BE.

DO YOU THINK THE CHEMISTRY OF THE BRAIN CONTROLS WHAT PEOPLE DO?
OF COURSE.
S. Adams
THEN HOW CAN WE BLAME PEOPLE FOR THEIR ACTIONS?
BECAUSE PEOPLE HAVE FREE WILL TO DO AS THEY CHOOSE.
ARE YOU SAYING THAT "FREE WILL" IS NOT PART OF THE BRAIN?
OF COURSE IT IS. BUT IT'S THE PART OF THE BRAIN THAT'S OUT THERE JUST BEING KIND OF FREE.
SO, YOU'RE SAYING THE "FREE WILL" PART OF THE BRAIN IS EXEMPT FROM THE NATURAL LAWS OF PHYSICS.
OBVIOUSLY. OTHERWISE WE COULDN'T BLAME PEOPLE FOR ANYTHING THEY DO.
5-30
© 1993 United Feature Syndicate, Inc.
DO YOU THINK THE "FREE WILL" PART OF THE BRAIN IS ATTACHED OR DOES IT JUST FLOAT NEARBY?
SHUT UP.

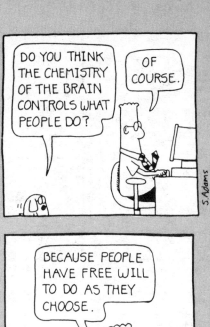

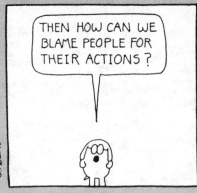

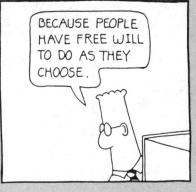

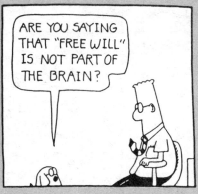

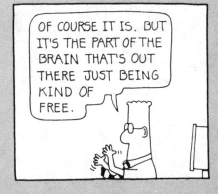

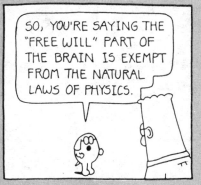

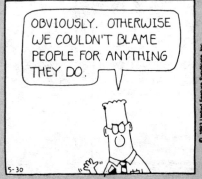

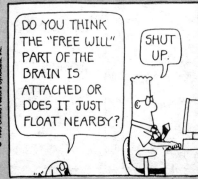

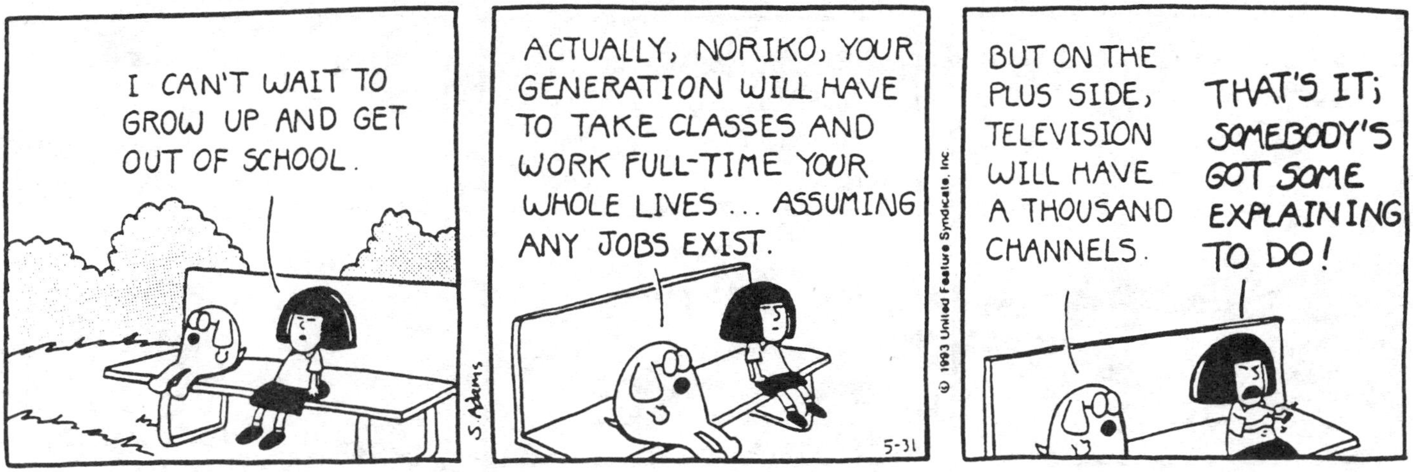
I CAN'T WAIT TO GROW UP AND GET OUT OF SCHOOL.
S. Adams
ACTUALLY, NORIKO, YOUR GENERATION WILL HAVE TO TAKE CLASSES AND WORK FULL-TIME YOUR WHOLE LIVES ... ASSUMING ANY JOBS EXIST.
5-31
© 1993 United Feature Syndicate, Inc
BUT ON THE PLUS SIDE, TELEVISION WILL HAVE A THOUSAND CHANNELS.
THAT'S IT; SOMEBODY'S GOT SOME EXPLAINING TO DO!

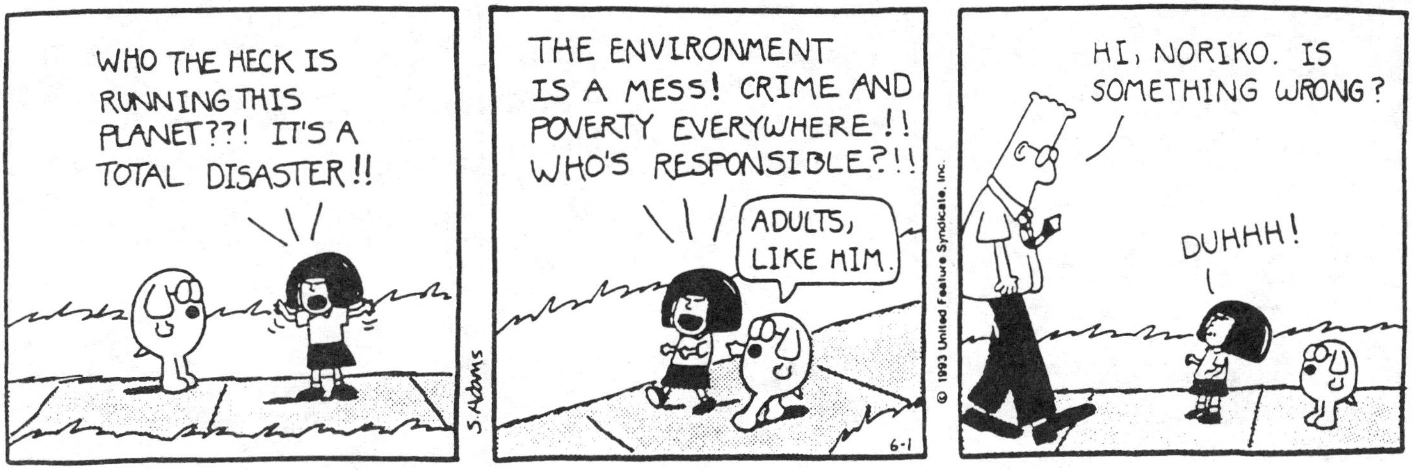
WHO THE HECK IS RUNNING THIS PLANET??! IT'S A TOTAL DISASTER!!
S. Adams
THE ENVIRONMENT IS A MESS! CRIME AND POVERTY EVERYWHERE!! WHO'S RESPONSIBLE?!!
ADULTS, LIKE HIM.
6-1
© 1993 United Feature Syndicate, Inc.
HI, NORIKO. IS SOMETHING WRONG?
DUHHH!

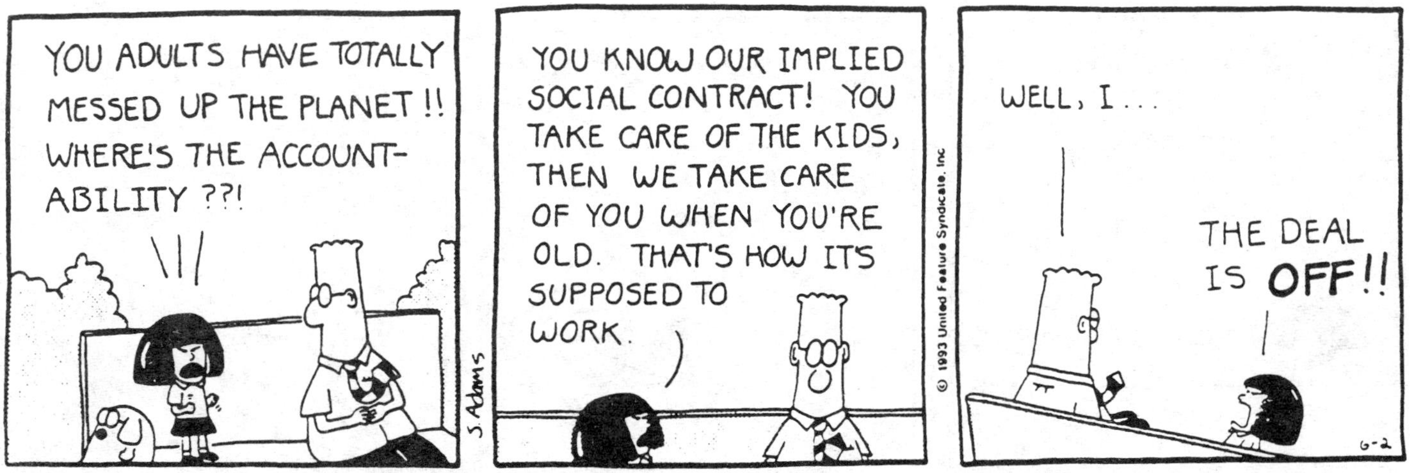
YOU ADULTS HAVE TOTALLY MESSED UP THE PLANET!! WHERE'S THE ACCOUNT-ABILITY??!
S. Adams
YOU KNOW OUR IMPLIED SOCIAL CONTRACT! YOU TAKE CARE OF THE KIDS, THEN WE TAKE CARE OF YOU WHEN YOU'RE OLD. THAT'S HOW IT'S SUPPOSED TO WORK.
© 1993 United Feature Syndicate, Inc
WELL, I...
THE DEAL IS OFF!!
6-2

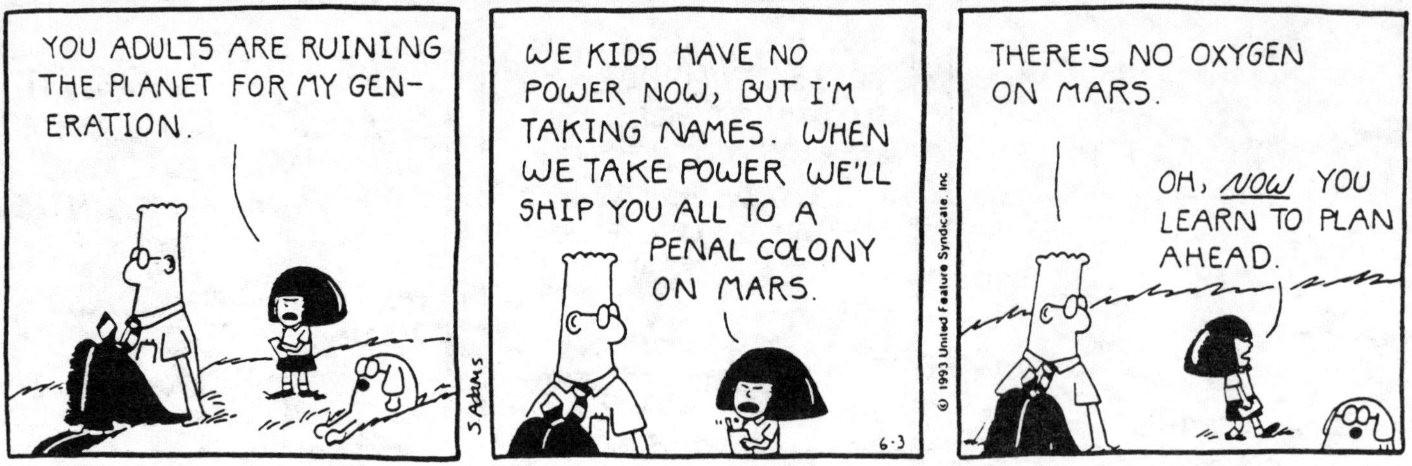
YOU ADULTS ARE RUINING THE PLANET FOR MY GENERATION.
S. Adams
WE KIDS HAVE NO POWER NOW, BUT I'M TAKING NAMES. WHEN WE TAKE POWER WE'LL SHIP YOU ALL TO A PENAL COLONY ON MARS.
6-3
© 1993 United Feature Syndicate, Inc
THERE'S NO OXYGEN ON MARS.
OH, NOW YOU LEARN TO PLAN AHEAD.

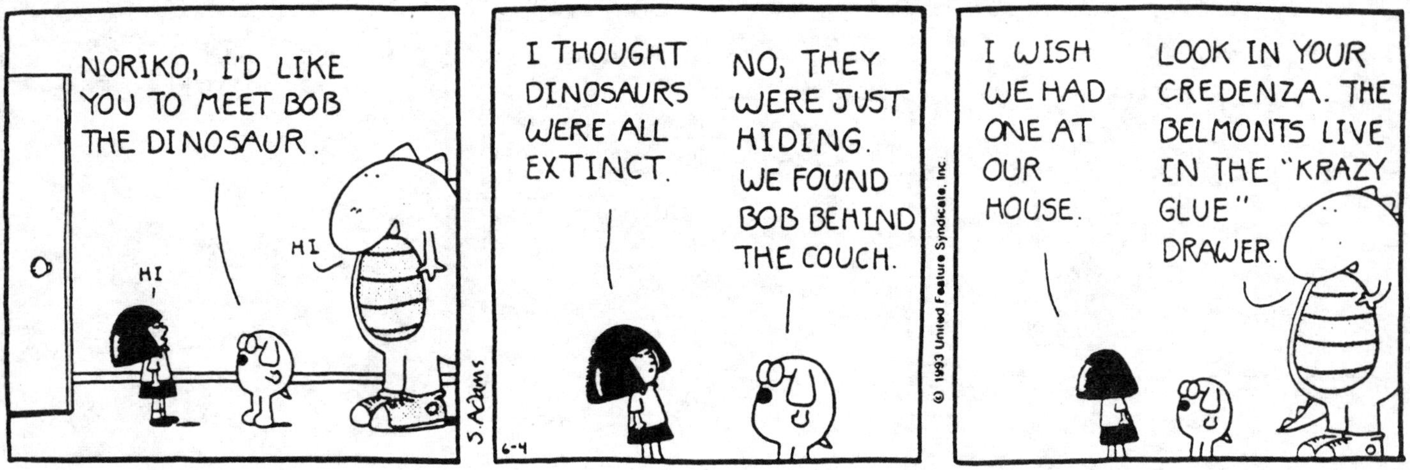
NORIKO, I'D LIKE YOU TO MEET BOB THE DINOSAUR.
HI
HI
S. Adams
6-4
I THOUGHT DINOSAURS WERE ALL EXTINCT.
NO, THEY WERE JUST HIDING. WE FOUND BOB BEHIND THE COUCH.
© 1993 United Feature Syndicate, Inc
I WISH WE HAD ONE AT OUR HOUSE.
LOOK IN YOUR CREDENZA. THE BELMONTS LIVE IN THE "KRAZY GLUE" DRAWER.

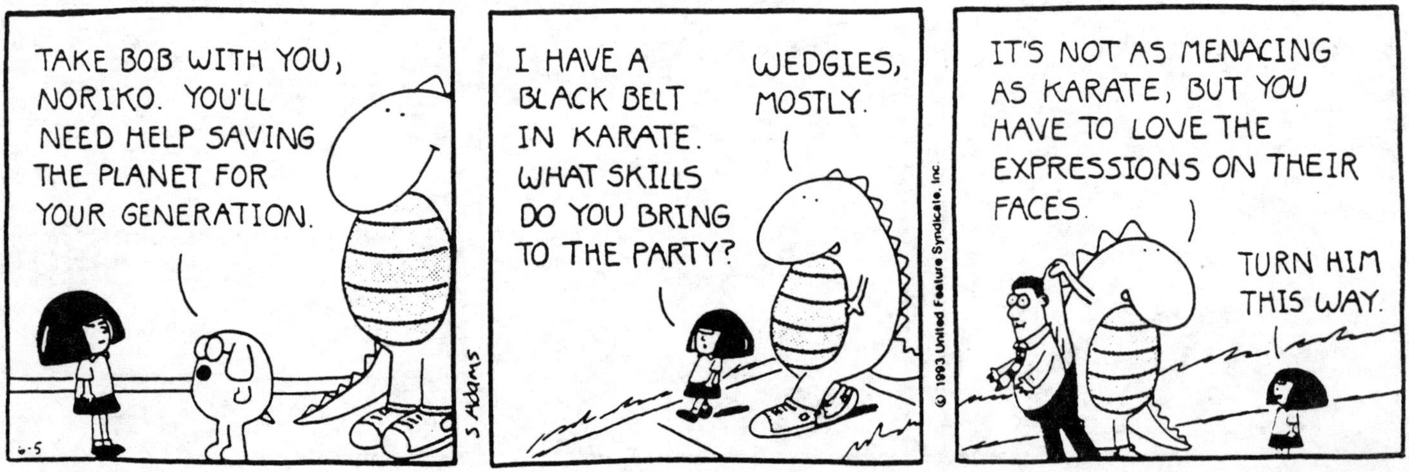
TAKE BOB WITH YOU, NORIKO. YOU'LL NEED HELP SAVING THE PLANET FOR YOUR GENERATION.
6-5
S. Adams
I HAVE A BLACK BELT IN KARATE. WHAT SKILLS DO YOU BRING TO THE PARTY?
WEDGIES, MOSTLY.
© 1993 United Feature Syndicate, Inc
IT'S NOT AS MENACING AS KARATE, BUT YOU HAVE TO LOVE THE EXPRESSIONS ON THEIR FACES.
TURN HIM THIS WAY.

IT'S TIME FOR YOUR ANNUAL PERFORMANCE REVIEW.
S. Adams
THE PROCESS IS THE SAME AS USUAL.
MAKE YOUR ACCOMPLISHMENTS FIT THE TRENDY CATEGORIES ON THIS FORM.
"1. ESTIMATE THE CASH VALUE OF THE EMPOWERMENT YOU DISPLAYED THIS YEAR. CITE EXAMPLES."
TRY TO MAKE YOUR ACCOMPLISHMENTS MATCH THE RAISE I'VE ALREADY DECIDED FOR YOU.
WHY DON'T YOU JUST TELL ME WHAT YOU'VE DECIDED?
WHAT--AND RUIN THE MOTIVATIONAL VALUE OF THE PROCESS??
HOW DID I GET STUCK WITH ALL THE CYNICAL EMPLOYEES?
6-6

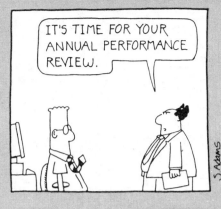

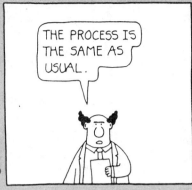

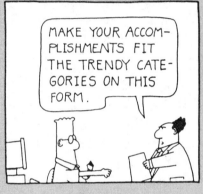

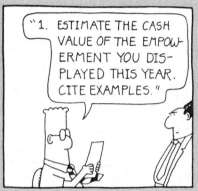

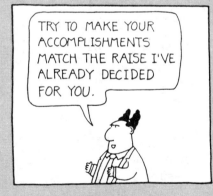

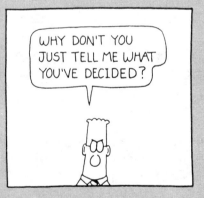

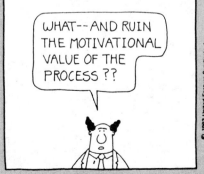

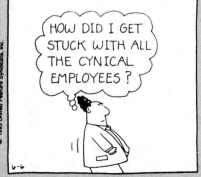

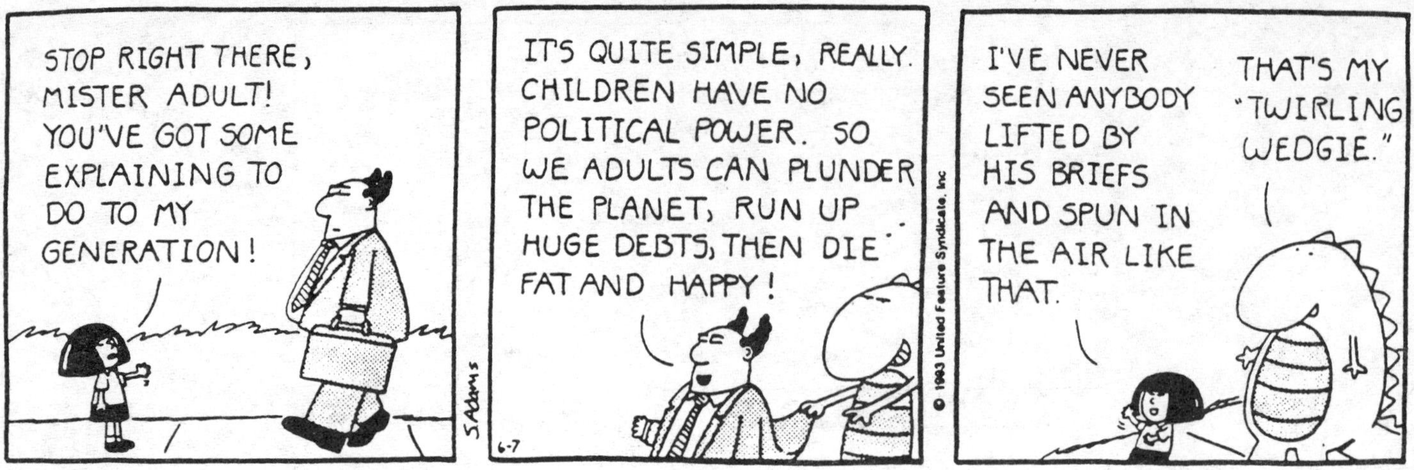
STOP RIGHT THERE, MISTER ADULT! YOU'VE GOT SOME EXPLAINING TO DO TO MY GENERATION!
S. Adams
6-7
IT'S QUITE SIMPLE, REALLY. CHILDREN HAVE NO POLITICAL POWER. SO WE ADULTS CAN PLUNDER THE PLANET, RUN UP HUGE DEBTS, THEN DIE FAT AND HAPPY!
© 1993 United Feature Syndicate, Inc
I'VE NEVER SEEN ANYBODY LIFTED BY HIS BRIEFS AND SPUN IN THE AIR LIKE THAT.
THAT'S MY "TWIRLING WEDGIE."

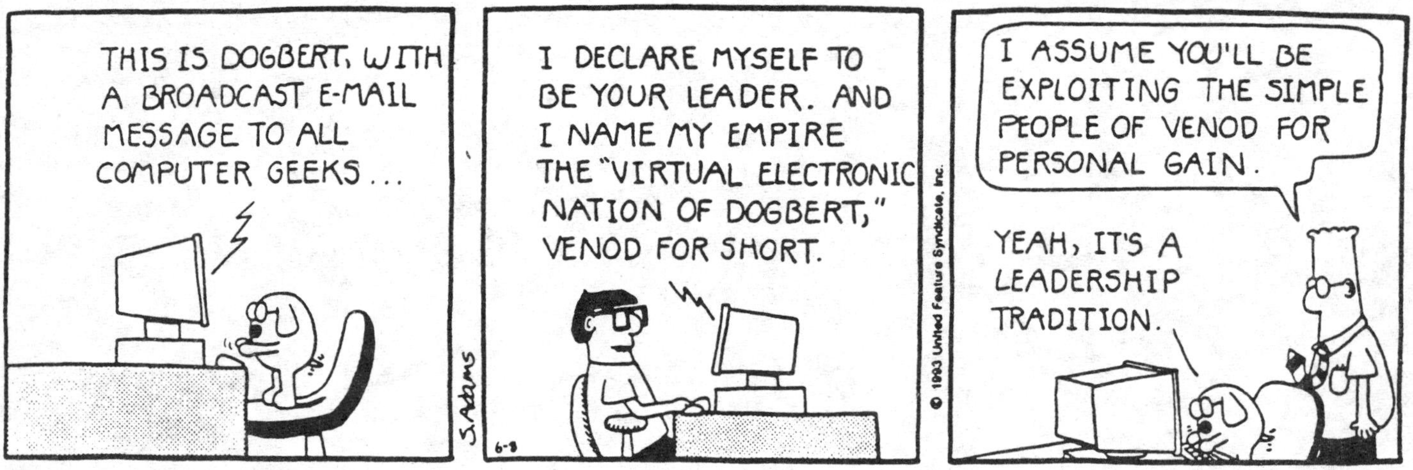
THIS IS DOGBERT, WITH A BROADCAST E-MAIL MESSAGE TO ALL COMPUTER GEEKS...
S. Adams
6-8
I DECLARE MYSELF TO BE YOUR LEADER. AND I NAME MY EMPIRE THE "VIRTUAL ELECTRONIC NATION OF DOGBERT," VENOD FOR SHORT.
© 1993 United Feature Syndicate, Inc.
I ASSUME YOU'LL BE EXPLOITING THE SIMPLE PEOPLE OF VENOD FOR PERSONAL GAIN.
YEAH, IT'S A LEADERSHIP TRADITION.

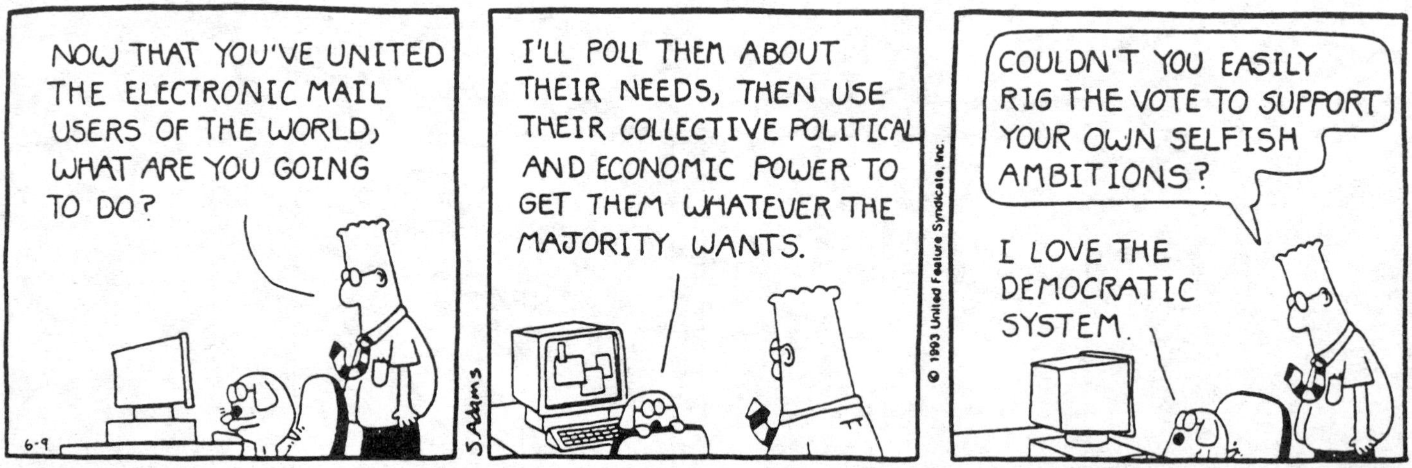
NOW THAT YOU'VE UNITED THE ELECTRONIC MAIL USERS OF THE WORLD, WHAT ARE YOU GOING TO DO?
6-9
S. Adams
I'LL POLL THEM ABOUT THEIR NEEDS, THEN USE THEIR COLLECTIVE POLITICAL AND ECONOMIC POWER TO GET THEM WHATEVER THE MAJORITY WANTS.
© 1993 United Feature Syndicate, Inc.
COULDN'T YOU EASILY RIG THE VOTE TO SUPPORT YOUR OWN SELFISH AMBITIONS?
I LOVE THE DEMOCRATIC SYSTEM.

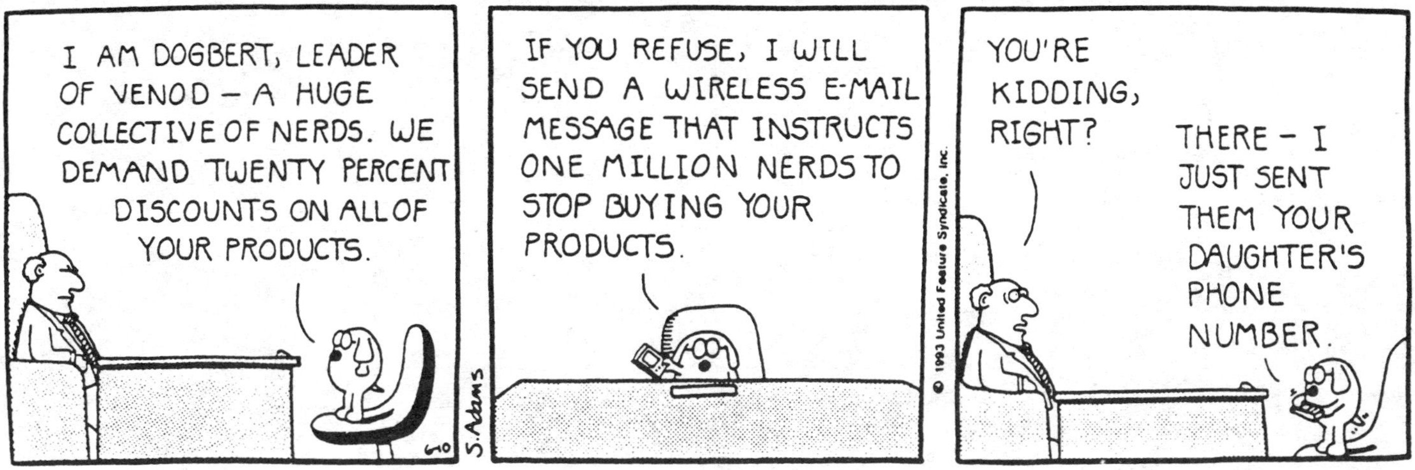
I AM DOGBERT, LEADER OF VENOD – A HUGE COLLECTIVE OF NERDS. WE DEMAND TWENTY PERCENT DISCOUNTS ON ALL OF YOUR PRODUCTS.
6-10
S. Adams
IF YOU REFUSE, I WILL SEND A WIRELESS E-MAIL MESSAGE THAT INSTRUCTS ONE MILLION NERDS TO STOP BUYING YOUR PRODUCTS.
© 1993 United Feature Syndicate, Inc.
YOU'RE KIDDING, RIGHT?
THERE – I JUST SENT THEM YOUR DAUGHTER'S PHONE NUMBER.

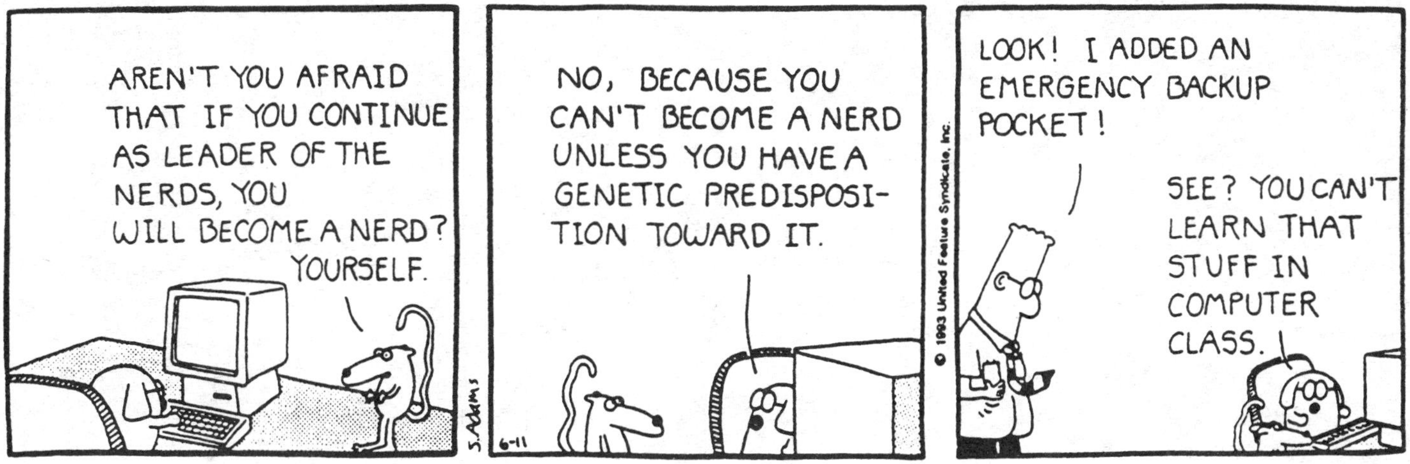
AREN'T YOU AFRAID THAT IF YOU CONTINUE AS LEADER OF THE NERDS, YOU WILL BECOME A NERD YOURSELF?
S. Adams
6-11
NO, BECAUSE YOU CAN'T BECOME A NERD UNLESS YOU HAVE A GENETIC PREDISPOSITION TOWARD IT.
© 1993 United Feature Syndicate, Inc.
LOOK! I ADDED AN EMERGENCY BACKUP POCKET!
SEE? YOU CAN'T LEARN THAT STUFF IN COMPUTER CLASS.

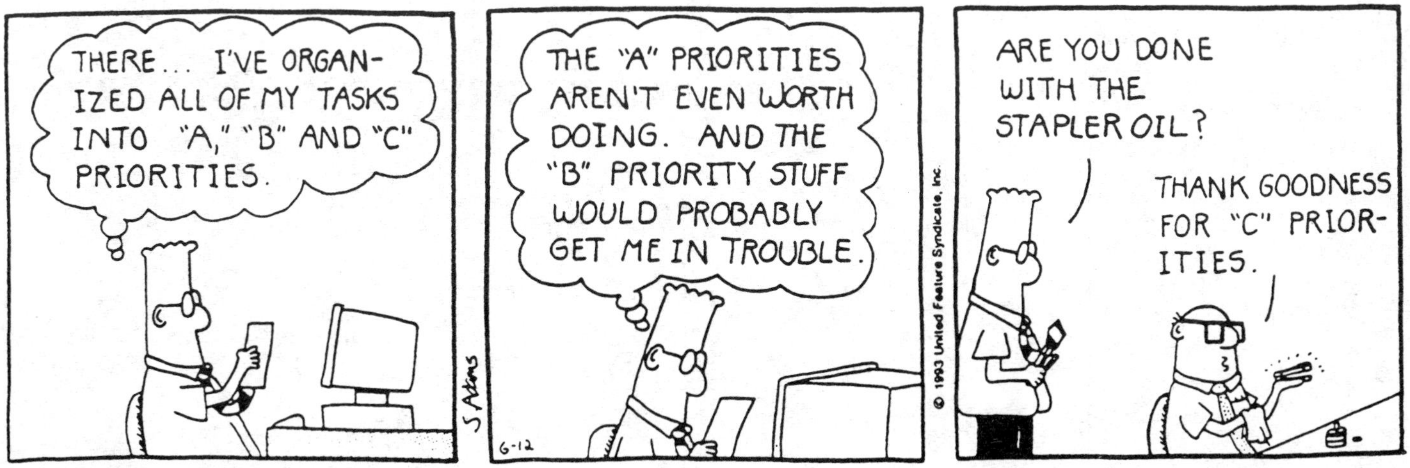
THERE... I'VE ORGANIZED ALL OF MY TASKS INTO "A," "B" AND "C" PRIORITIES.
S. Adams
6-12
THE "A" PRIORITIES AREN'T EVEN WORTH DOING. AND THE "B" PRIORITY STUFF WOULD PROBABLY GET ME IN TROUBLE.
© 1993 United Feature Syndicate, Inc.
ARE YOU DONE WITH THE STAPLER OIL?
THANK GOODNESS FOR "C" PRIORITIES.

CAN I HELP YOU?
SALE
S. Adams
I OPPOSE THE SLAUGHTER OF HELPLESS ANIMALS. DO YOU HAVE ANY SHOES THAT AREN'T MADE OF LEATHER?
YEAH, BUT THEY WOULD MAKE YOU LOOK LIKE A TWIT.
WELL, FORGET THAT.
DO YOU HAVE ANY SHOES MADE IN THIS COUNTRY?
YEAH, BUT THEY COST MORE.
OKAY, FORGET THAT.
JUST SHOW ME SOME SHOES THAT WEREN'T MADE WITH SLAVE LABOR.
6-13
WE CHARGE A PREMIUM FOR NO-SLAVE SHOES.
WELL, FORGET THAT.
© 1993 United Feature Syndicate, Inc.
HOW MUCH DID YOU SELL YOUR SOUL FOR?
FORTY BUCKS AND A LITTLE SHINE CLOTH.

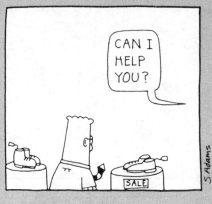

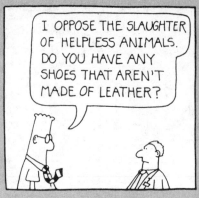

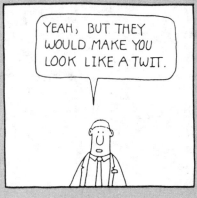

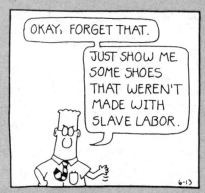

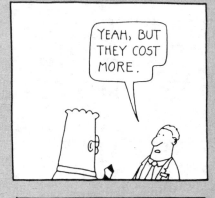

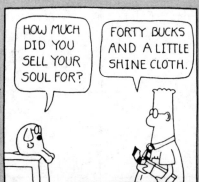

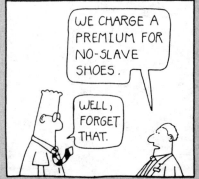

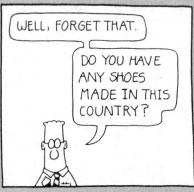

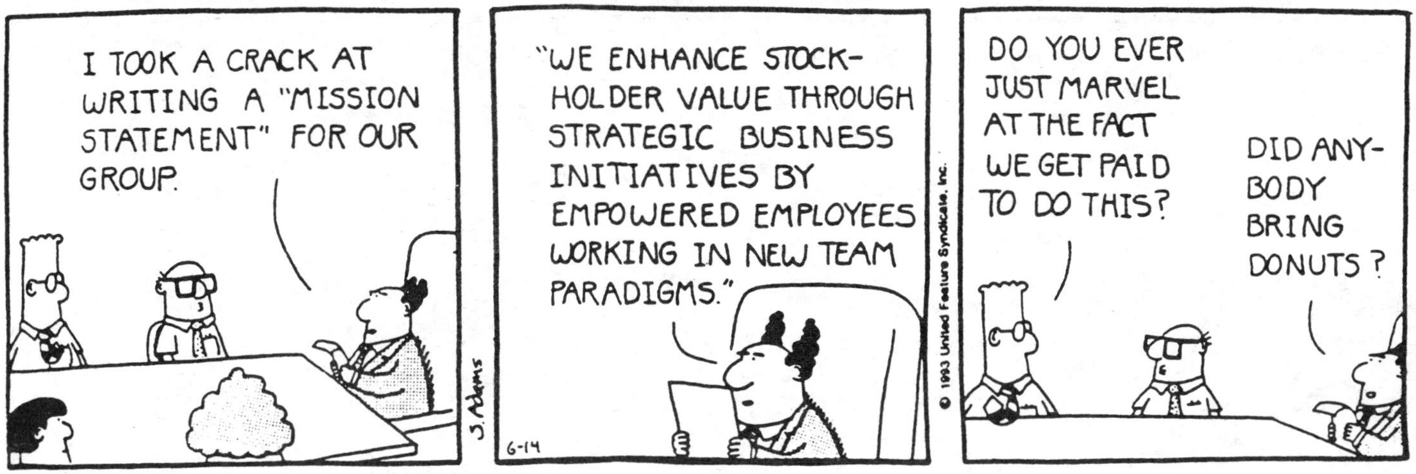
I TOOK A CRACK AT WRITING A "MISSION STATEMENT" FOR OUR GROUP.
"WE ENHANCE STOCK-HOLDER VALUE THROUGH STRATEGIC BUSINESS INITIATIVES BY EMPOWERED EMPLOYEES WORKING IN NEW TEAM PARADIGMS."
DO YOU EVER JUST MARVEL AT THE FACT WE GET PAID TO DO THIS?
DID ANY-BODY BRING DONUTS?
S. Adams
6-14
© 1993 United Feature Syndicate, Inc.

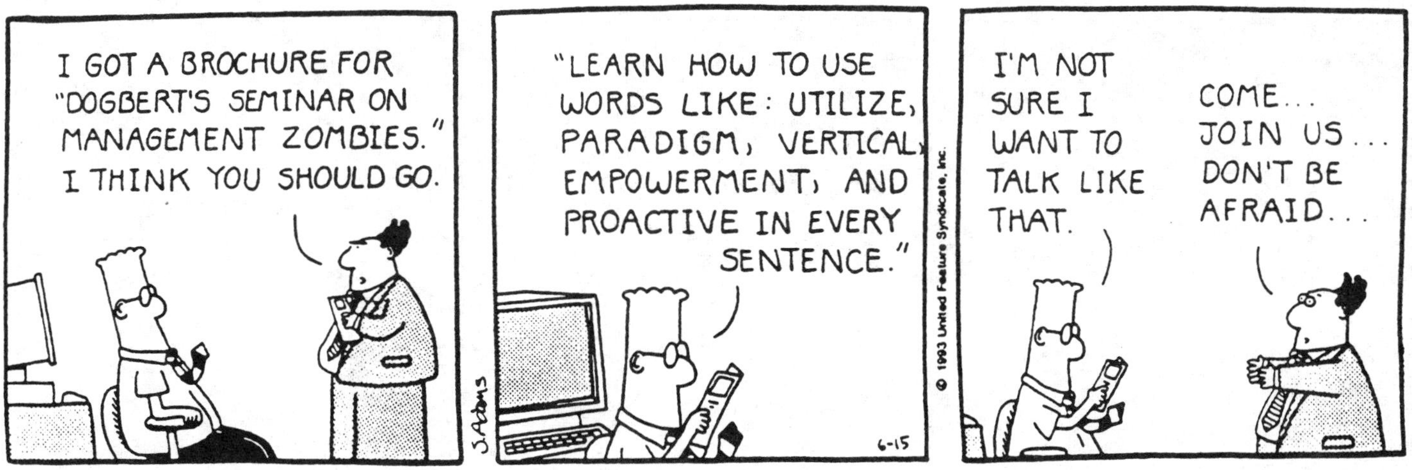
I GOT A BROCHURE FOR "DOGBERT'S SEMINAR ON MANAGEMENT ZOMBIES." I THINK YOU SHOULD GO.
"LEARN HOW TO USE WORDS LIKE: UTILIZE, PARADIGM, VERTICAL, EMPOWERMENT, AND PROACTIVE IN EVERY SENTENCE."
I'M NOT SURE I WANT TO TALK LIKE THAT.
COME... JOIN US... DON'T BE AFRAID...
S. Adams
6-15
© 1993 United Feature Syndicate, Inc.

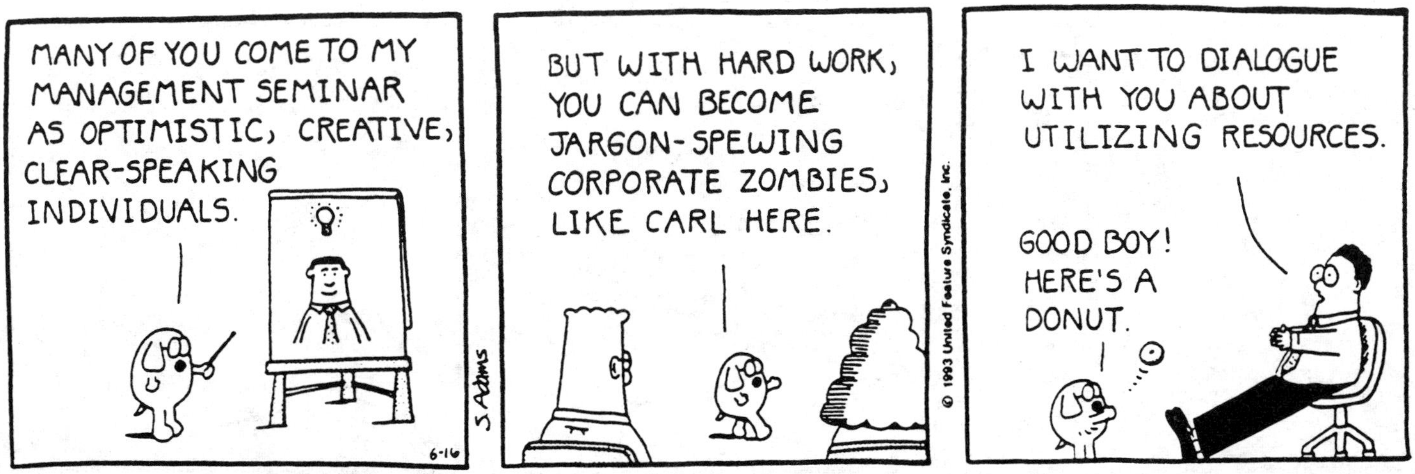
MANY OF YOU COME TO MY MANAGEMENT SEMINAR AS OPTIMISTIC, CREATIVE, CLEAR-SPEAKING INDIVIDUALS.
BUT WITH HARD WORK, YOU CAN BECOME JARGON-SPEWING CORPORATE ZOMBIES, LIKE CARL HERE.
I WANT TO DIALOGUE WITH YOU ABOUT UTILIZING RESOURCES.
GOOD BOY! HERE'S A DONUT.
S. Adams
6-16
© 1993 United Feature Syndicate, Inc.

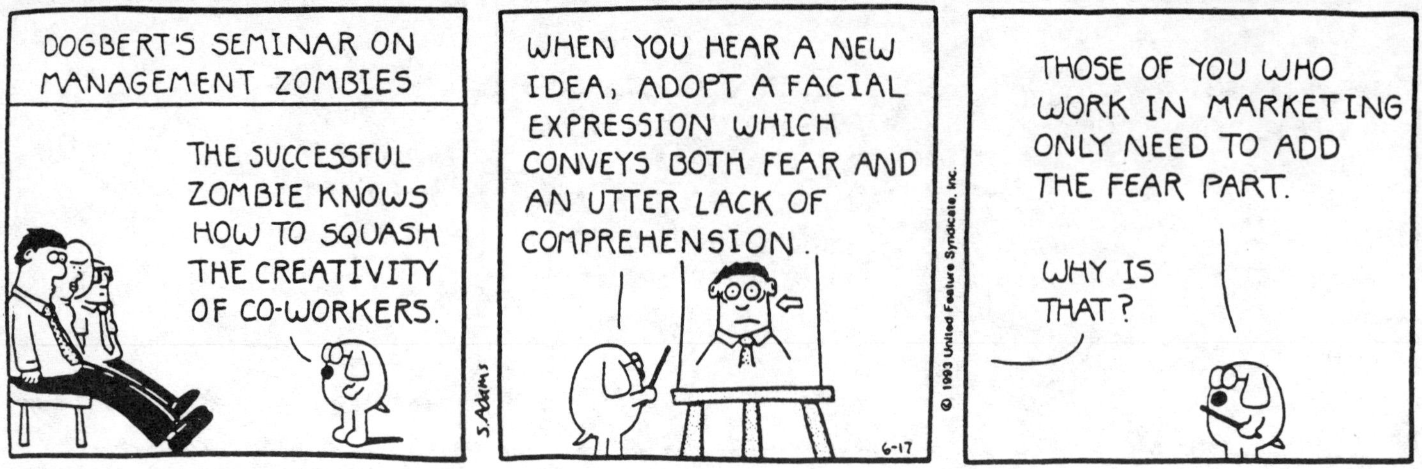
DOGBERT'S SEMINAR ON MANAGEMENT ZOMBIES
THE SUCCESSFUL ZOMBIE KNOWS HOW TO SQUASH THE CREATIVITY OF CO-WORKERS.
S. Adams
WHEN YOU HEAR A NEW IDEA, ADOPT A FACIAL EXPRESSION WHICH CONVEYS BOTH FEAR AND AN UTTER LACK OF COMPREHENSION.
6-17
© 1993 United Feature Syndicate, Inc.
THOSE OF YOU WHO WORK IN MARKETING ONLY NEED TO ADD THE FEAR PART.
WHY IS THAT?

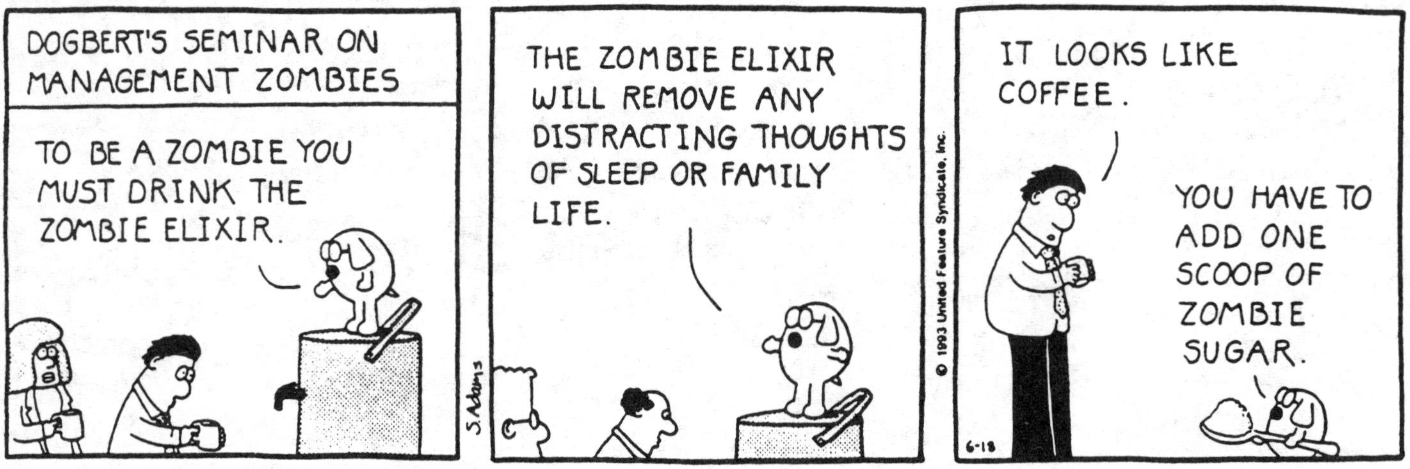
DOGBERT'S SEMINAR ON MANAGEMENT ZOMBIES
TO BE A ZOMBIE YOU MUST DRINK THE ZOMBIE ELIXIR.
S. Adams
THE ZOMBIE ELIXIR WILL REMOVE ANY DISTRACTING THOUGHTS OF SLEEP OR FAMILY LIFE.
© 1993 United Feature Syndicate, Inc.
IT LOOKS LIKE COFFEE.
YOU HAVE TO ADD ONE SCOOP OF ZOMBIE SUGAR.
6-18

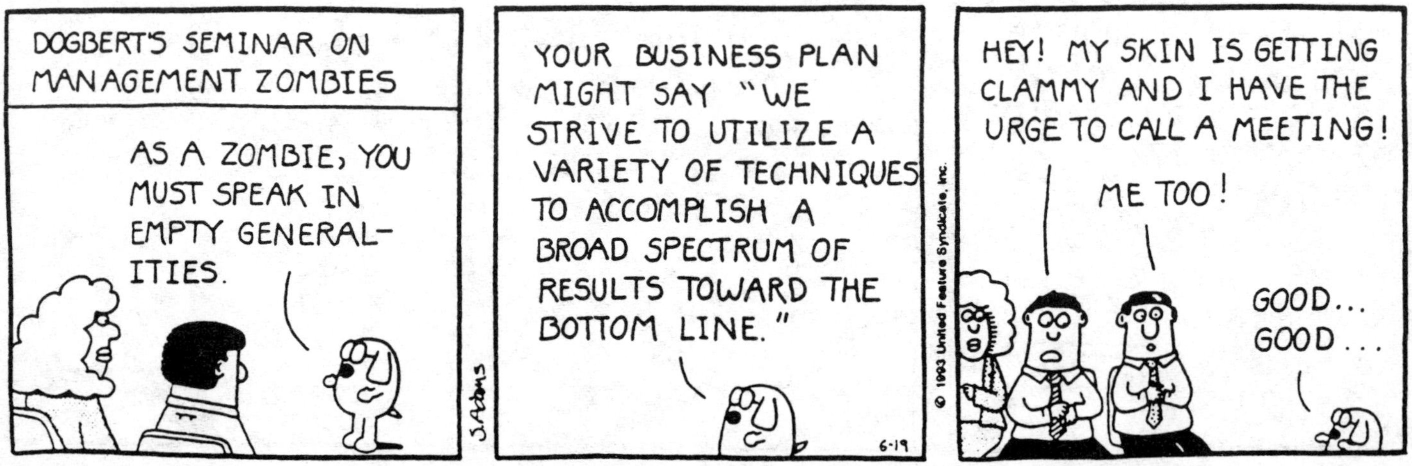
DOGBERT'S SEMINAR ON MANAGEMENT ZOMBIES
AS A ZOMBIE, YOU MUST SPEAK IN EMPTY GENERAL-ITIES.
S. Adams
YOUR BUSINESS PLAN MIGHT SAY "WE STRIVE TO UTILIZE A VARIETY OF TECHNIQUES TO ACCOMPLISH A BROAD SPECTRUM OF RESULTS TOWARD THE BOTTOM LINE."
6-19
© 1993 United Feature Syndicate, Inc.
HEY! MY SKIN IS GETTING CLAMMY AND I HAVE THE URGE TO CALL A MEETING!
ME TOO!
GOOD... GOOD...

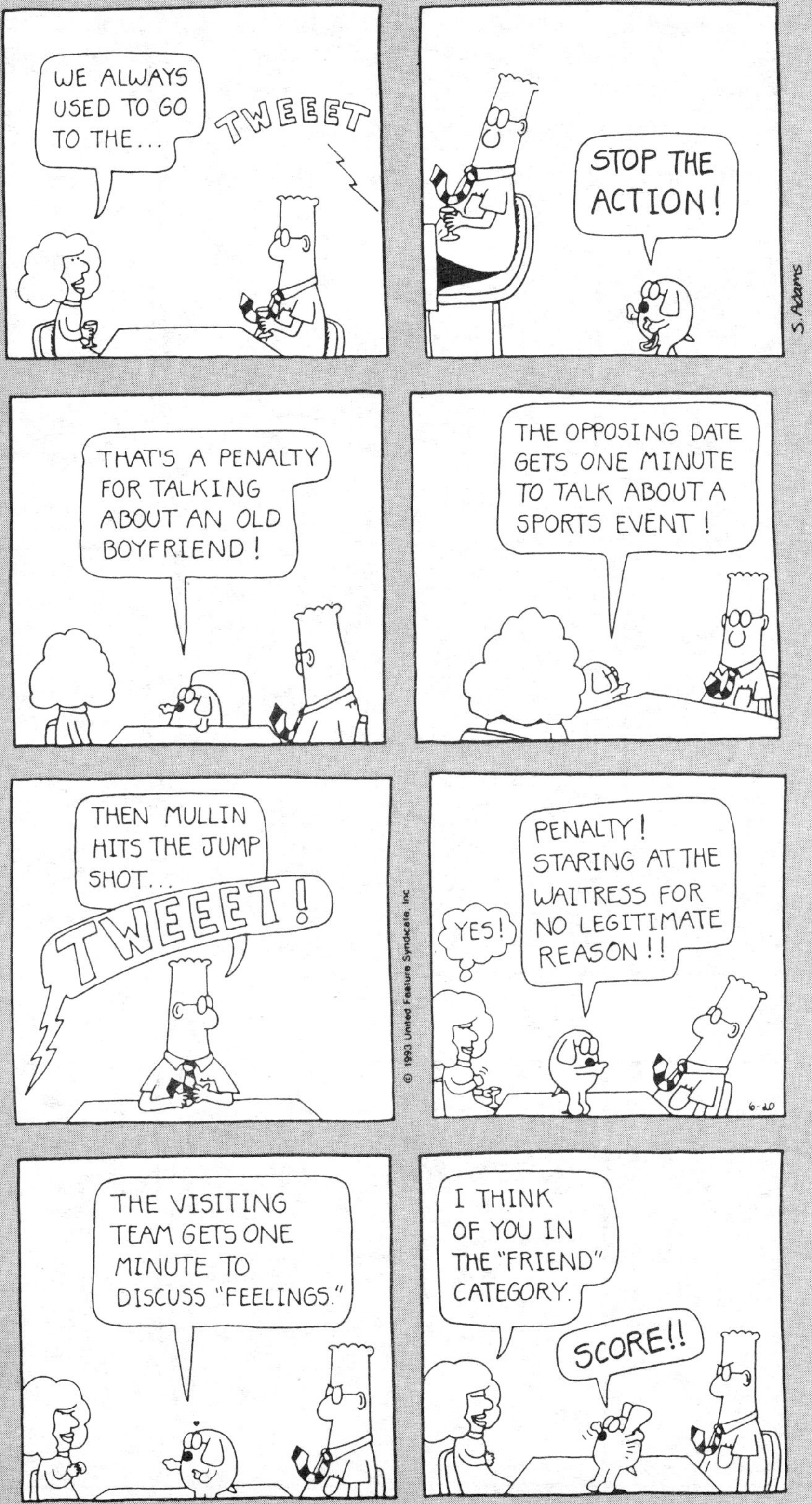
WE ALWAYS USED TO GO TO THE...
TWEEET
STOP THE ACTION!
S. Adams
THAT'S A PENALTY FOR TALKING ABOUT AN OLD BOYFRIEND!
THE OPPOSING DATE GETS ONE MINUTE TO TALK ABOUT A SPORTS EVENT!
THEN MULLIN HITS THE JUMP SHOT...
TWEEET!
© 1993 United Feature Syndicate, Inc
YES!
PENALTY! STARING AT THE WAITRESS FOR NO LEGITIMATE REASON!!
6-20
THE VISITING TEAM GETS ONE MINUTE TO DISCUSS "FEELINGS."
I THINK OF YOU IN THE "FRIEND" CATEGORY.
SCORE!!

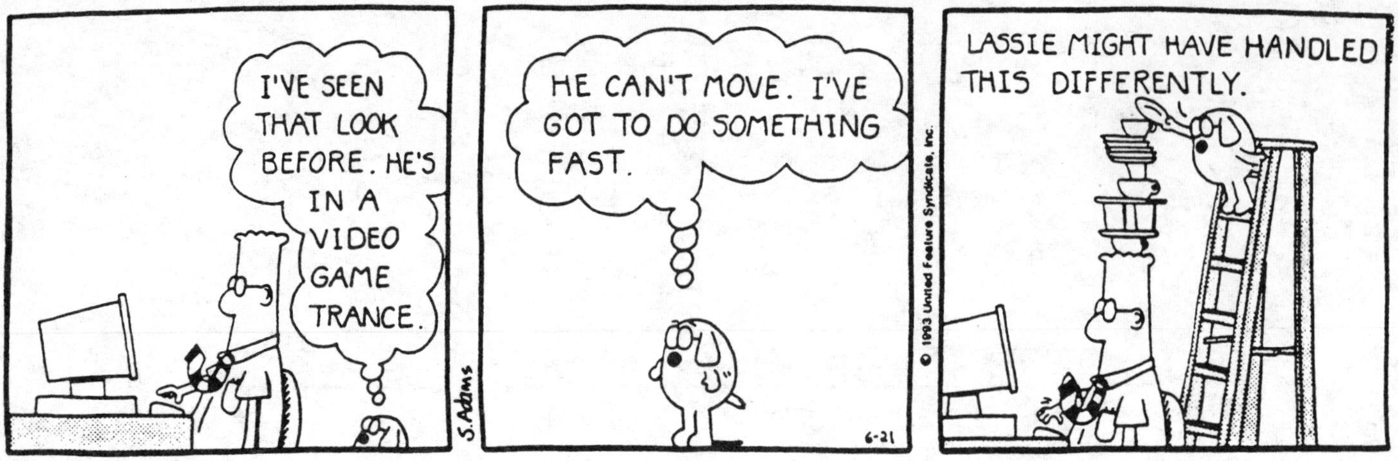
I'VE SEEN THAT LOOK BEFORE. HE'S IN A VIDEO GAME TRANCE.
S. Adams
HE CAN'T MOVE. I'VE GOT TO DO SOMETHING FAST.
6-21
© 1993 United Feature Syndicate, Inc.
LASSIE MIGHT HAVE HANDLED THIS DIFFERENTLY.

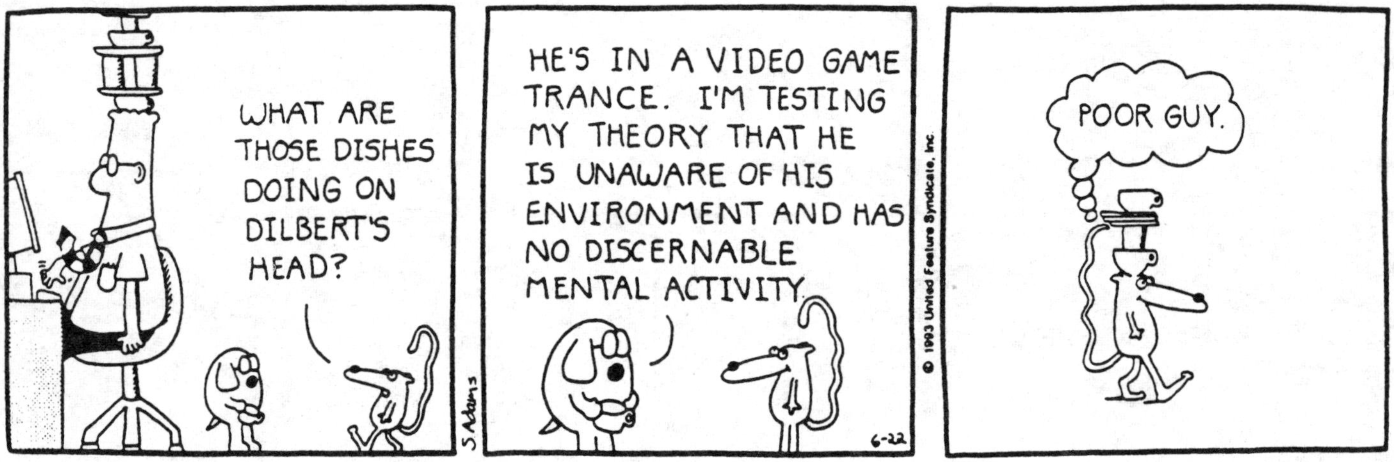
WHAT ARE THOSE DISHES DOING ON DILBERT'S HEAD?
S. Adams
HE'S IN A VIDEO GAME TRANCE. I'M TESTING MY THEORY THAT HE IS UNAWARE OF HIS ENVIRONMENT AND HAS NO DISCERNABLE MENTAL ACTIVITY.
6-22
© 1993 United Feature Syndicate, Inc.
POOR GUY.

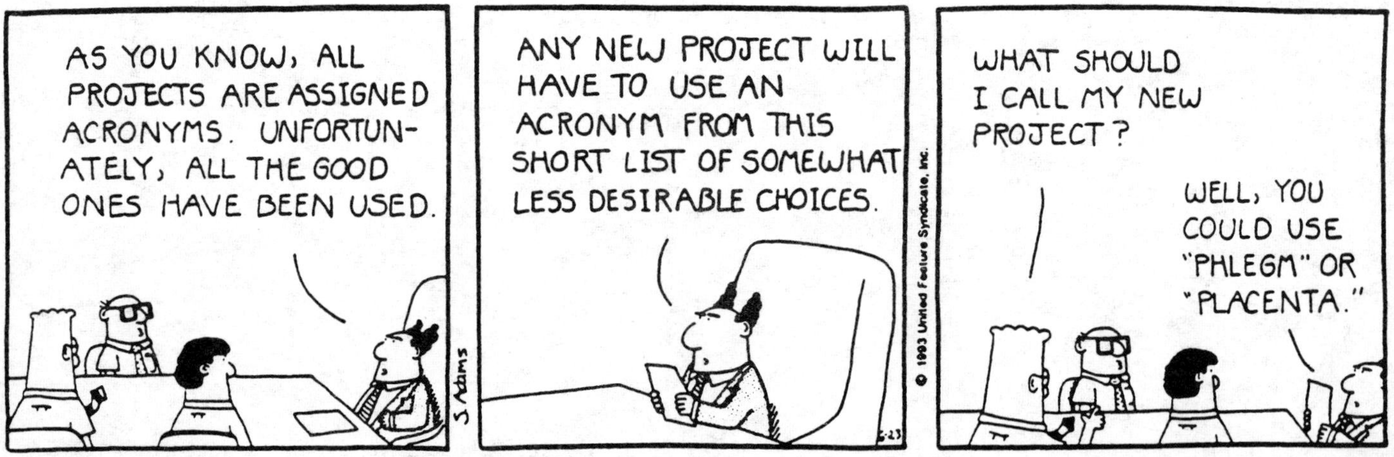
AS YOU KNOW, ALL PROJECTS ARE ASSIGNED ACRONYMS. UNFORTUN-ATELY, ALL THE GOOD ONES HAVE BEEN USED.
S. Adams
ANY NEW PROJECT WILL HAVE TO USE AN ACRONYM FROM THIS SHORT LIST OF SOMEWHAT LESS DESIRABLE CHOICES.
6-23
© 1993 United Feature Syndicate, Inc.
WHAT SHOULD I CALL MY NEW PROJECT?
WELL, YOU COULD USE "PHLEGM" OR "PLACENTA."

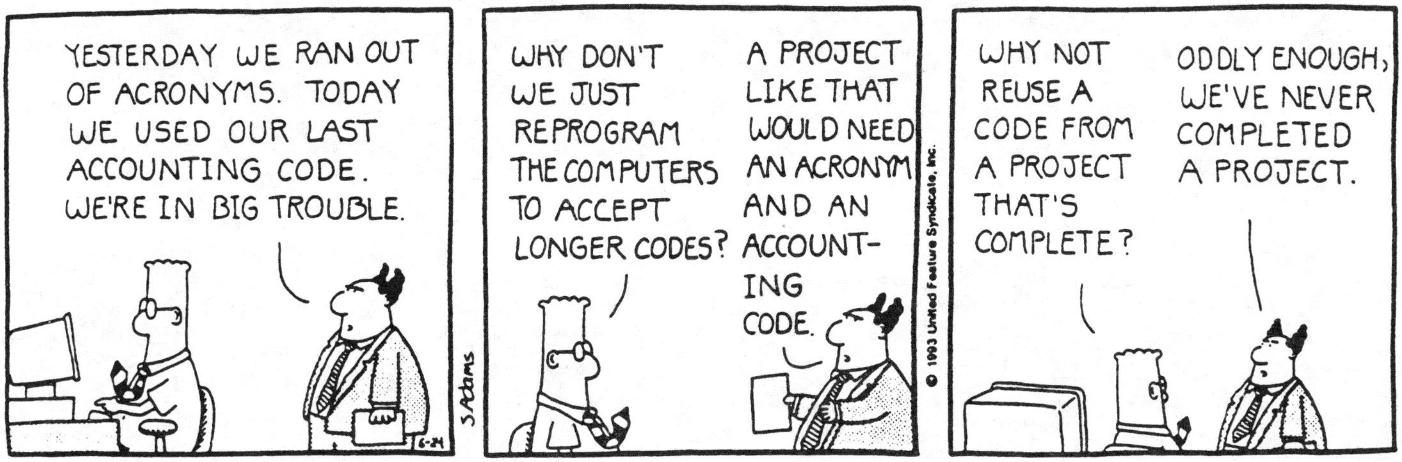
YESTERDAY WE RAN OUT OF ACRONYMS. TODAY WE USED OUR LAST ACCOUNTING CODE. WE'RE IN BIG TROUBLE.
WHY DON'T WE JUST REPROGRAM THE COMPUTERS TO ACCEPT LONGER CODES?
A PROJECT LIKE THAT WOULD NEED AN ACRONYM AND AN ACCOUNTING CODE.
WHY NOT REUSE A CODE FROM A PROJECT THAT'S COMPLETE?
ODDLY ENOUGH, WE'VE NEVER COMPLETED A PROJECT.
© 1993 United Feature Syndicate, Inc.

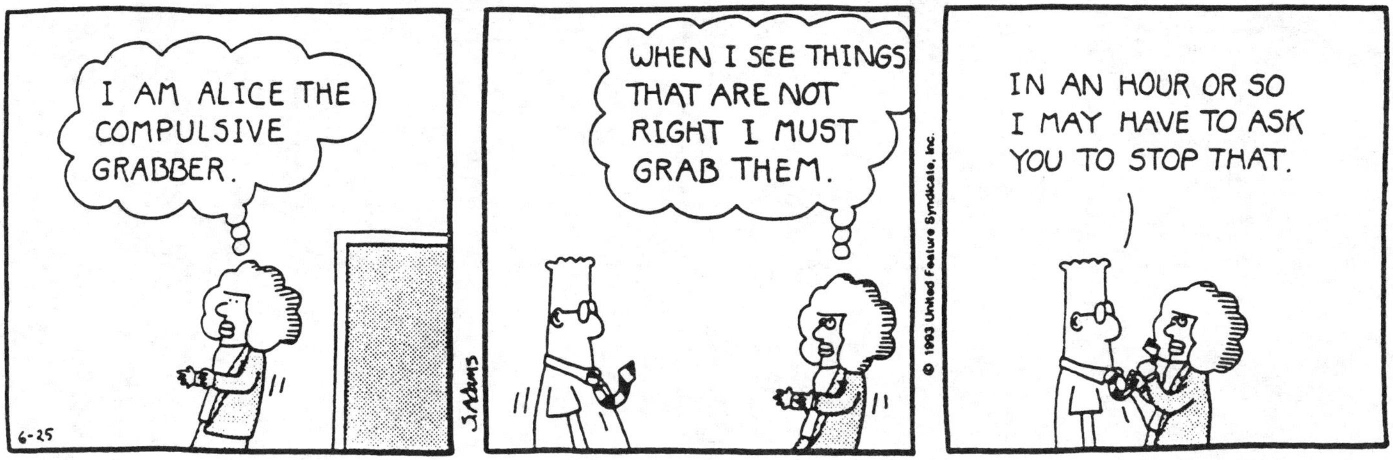
I AM ALICE THE COMPULSIVE GRABBER.
WHEN I SEE THINGS THAT ARE NOT RIGHT I MUST GRAB THEM.
IN AN HOUR OR SO I MAY HAVE TO ASK YOU TO STOP THAT.
© 1993 United Feature Syndicate, Inc.

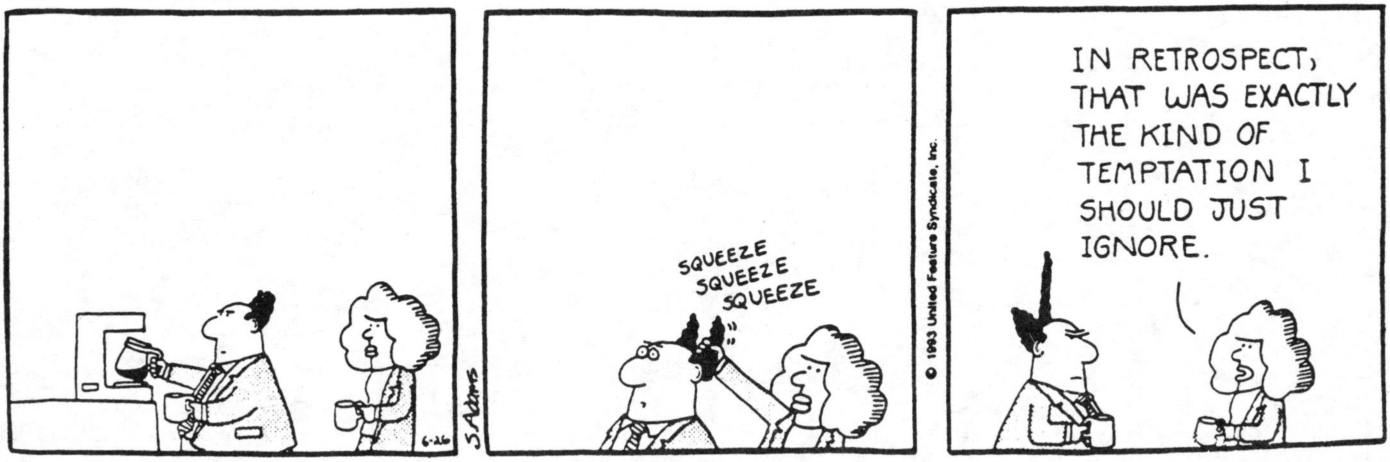
SQUEEZE SQUEEZE SQUEEZE
IN RETROSPECT, THAT WAS EXACTLY THE KIND OF TEMPTATION I SHOULD JUST IGNORE.
© 1993 United Feature Syndicate, Inc.

WE CAN SUCCEED IF EACH OF YOU WILL COMMIT TO GIVING 110%.
S Adams
THAT WOULD BE TEN PERCENT OVER THE THEORETICAL MAXIMUM.
CAN'T BE DONE.
PLUS YOU HAVE YOUR VACATION DAYS AND YOUR SICK DAYS . . .
HECK, THESE STAFF MEETINGS TAKE TEN PERCENT RIGHT OFF THE TOP . . .
AND WHAT ABOUT ALL THE TIMES SOMETHING UNEX-PECTED COMES UP ?
© 1993 United Feature Syndicate, Inc.
I THINK WE COULD GIVE YOU . . . WHAT ?
FORTY-THREE PERCENT.
6.27
AND THAT'S NOT A COMMITMENT.
IT'S AN ESTIMATE.
CAN WE CONTINUE THE MEETING NOW ?
I'M OVER MY ESTIMATE FOR TODAY.

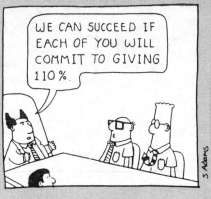

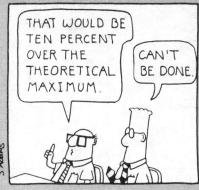

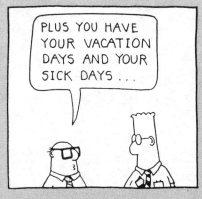

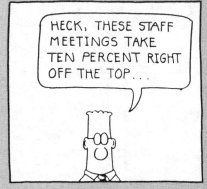

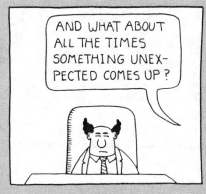

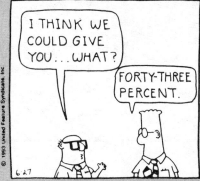

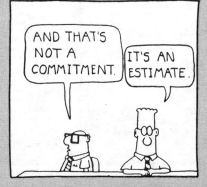

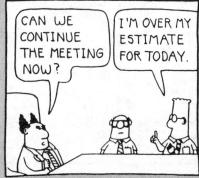

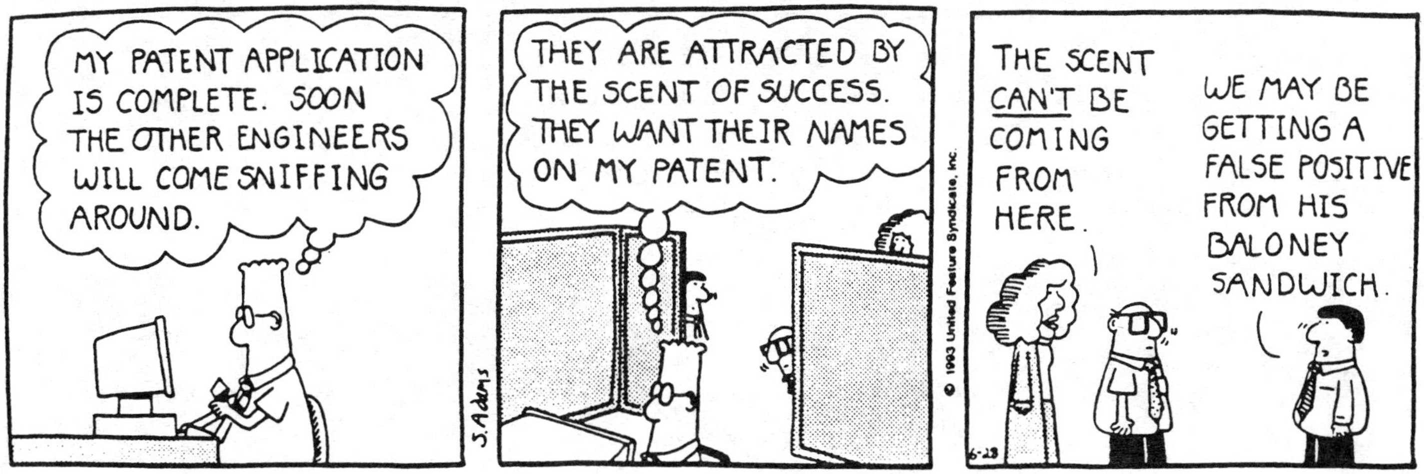
MY PATENT APPLICATION IS COMPLETE. SOON THE OTHER ENGINEERS WILL COME SNIFFING AROUND.
S.Adams
THEY ARE ATTRACTED BY THE SCENT OF SUCCESS. THEY WANT THEIR NAMES ON MY PATENT.
© 1993 United Feature Syndicate, Inc.
THE SCENT CAN'T BE COMING FROM HERE.
WE MAY BE GETTING A FALSE POSITIVE FROM HIS BALONEY SANDWICH.
6-28

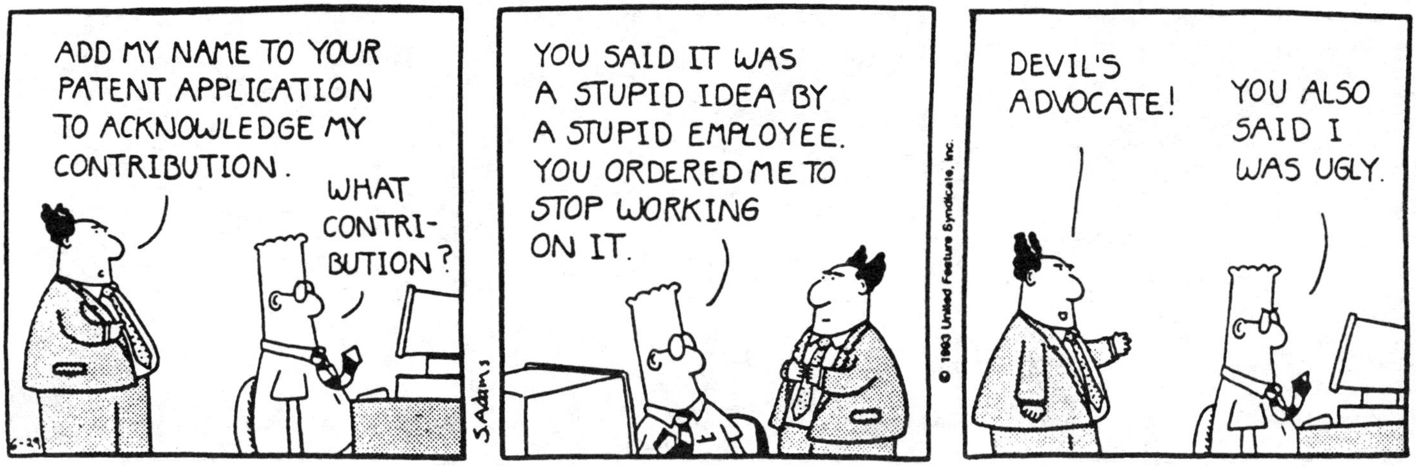
ADD MY NAME TO YOUR PATENT APPLICATION TO ACKNOWLEDGE MY CONTRIBUTION.
WHAT CONTRI-BUTION?
6-29
S.Adams
YOU SAID IT WAS A STUPID IDEA BY A STUPID EMPLOYEE. YOU ORDERED ME TO STOP WORKING ON IT.
© 1993 United Feature Syndicate, Inc.
DEVIL'S ADVOCATE!
YOU ALSO SAID I WAS UGLY.

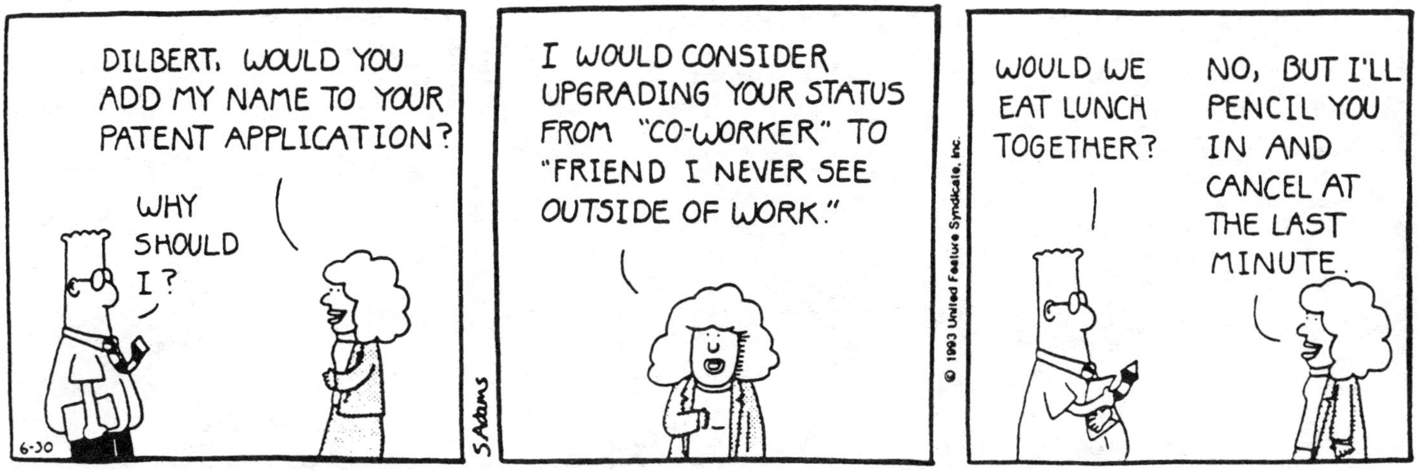
DILBERT, WOULD YOU ADD MY NAME TO YOUR PATENT APPLICATION?
WHY SHOULD I?
6-30
S.Adams
I WOULD CONSIDER UPGRADING YOUR STATUS FROM "CO-WORKER" TO "FRIEND I NEVER SEE OUTSIDE OF WORK."
© 1993 United Feature Syndicate, Inc.
WOULD WE EAT LUNCH TOGETHER?
NO, BUT I'LL PENCIL YOU IN AND CANCEL AT THE LAST MINUTE.

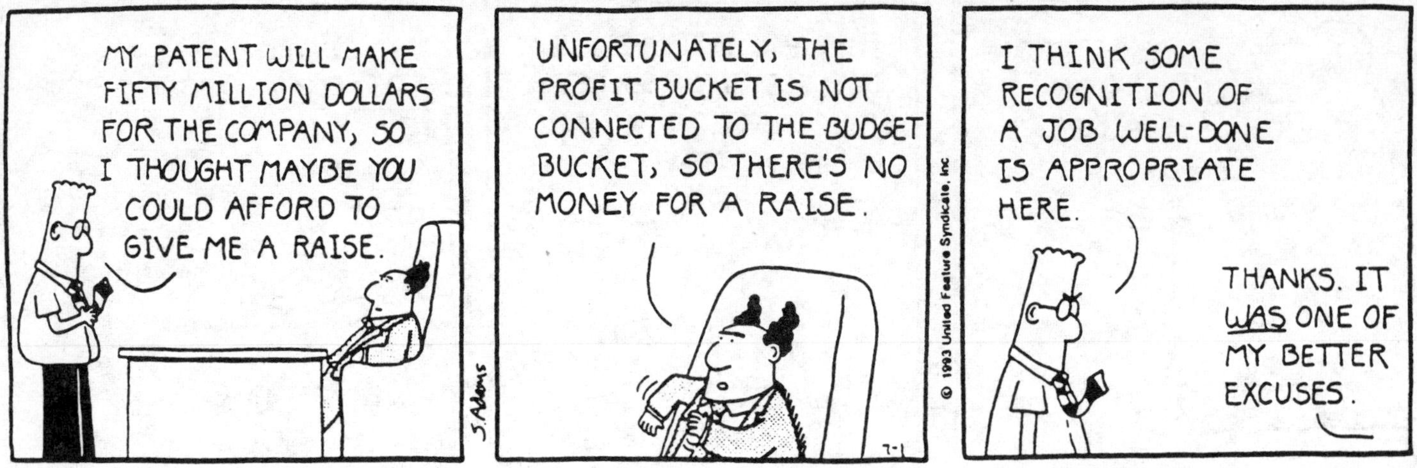
MY PATENT WILL MAKE FIFTY MILLION DOLLARS FOR THE COMPANY, SO I THOUGHT MAYBE YOU COULD AFFORD TO GIVE ME A RAISE.
S. Adams
UNFORTUNATELY, THE PROFIT BUCKET IS NOT CONNECTED TO THE BUDGET BUCKET, SO THERE'S NO MONEY FOR A RAISE.
7-1
© 1993 United Feature Syndicate, Inc
I THINK SOME RECOGNITION OF A JOB WELL-DONE IS APPROPRIATE HERE.
THANKS. IT WAS ONE OF MY BETTER EXCUSES.

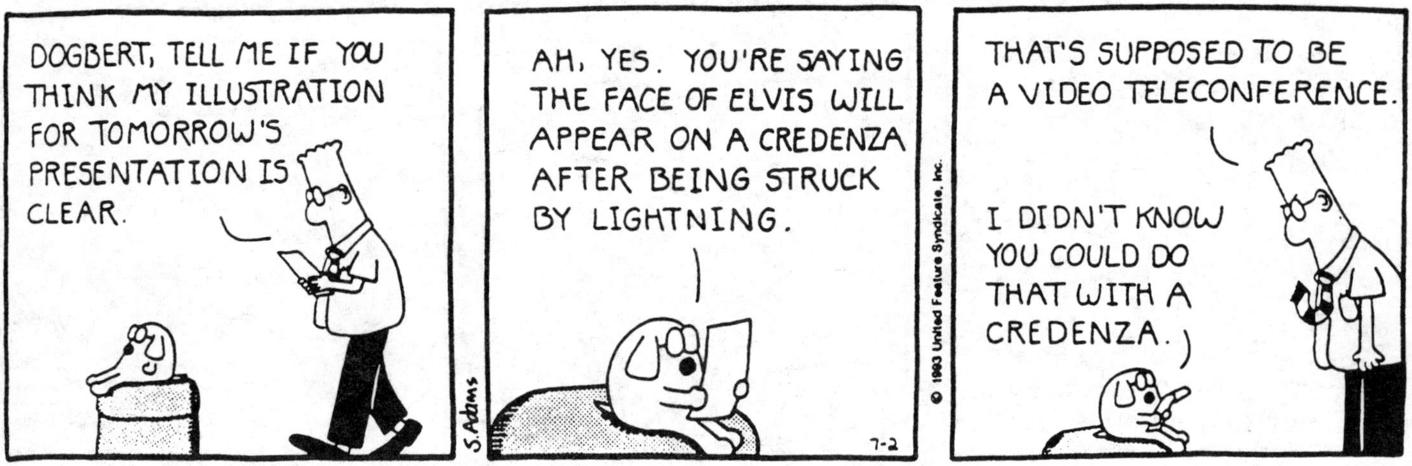
DOGBERT, TELL ME IF YOU THINK MY ILLUSTRATION FOR TOMORROW'S PRESENTATION IS CLEAR.
S. Adams
AH, YES. YOU'RE SAYING THE FACE OF ELVIS WILL APPEAR ON A CREDENZA AFTER BEING STRUCK BY LIGHTNING.
7-2
© 1993 United Feature Syndicate, Inc.
THAT'S SUPPOSED TO BE A VIDEO TELECONFERENCE.
I DIDN'T KNOW YOU COULD DO THAT WITH A CREDENZA.

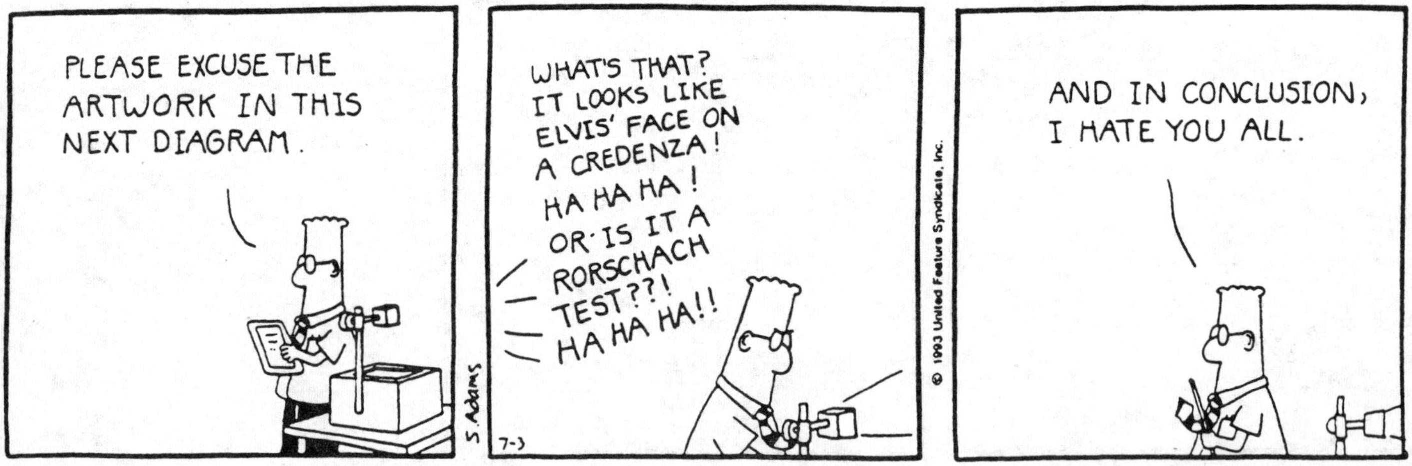
PLEASE EXCUSE THE ARTWORK IN THIS NEXT DIAGRAM.
S. Adams
WHAT'S THAT? IT LOOKS LIKE ELVIS' FACE ON A CREDENZA! HA HA HA! OR IS IT A RORSCHACH TEST??! HA HA HA!!
7-3
© 1993 United Feature Syndicate, Inc.
AND IN CONCLUSION, I HATE YOU ALL.

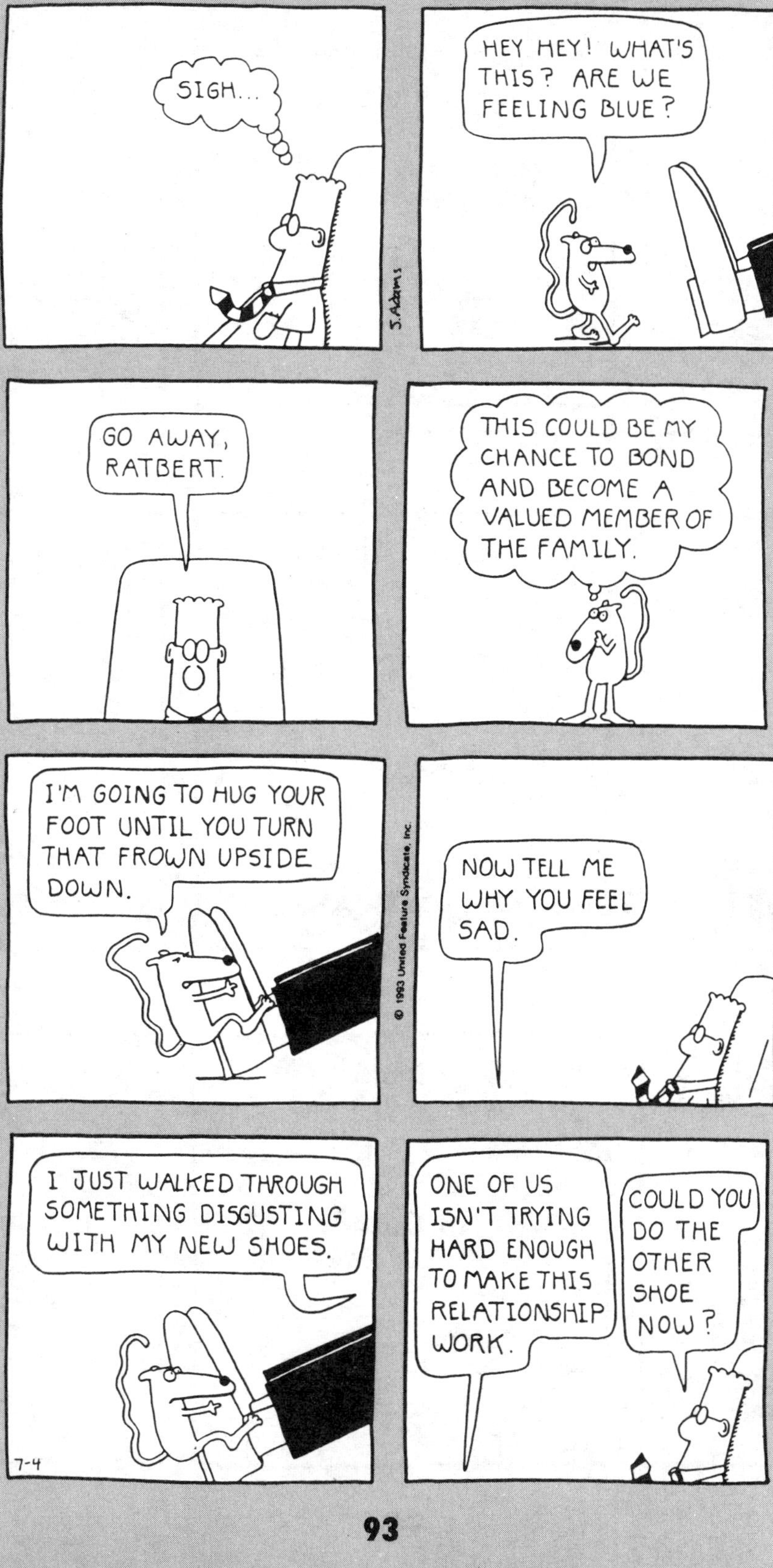
SIGH...
J. Adams
HEY HEY! WHAT'S THIS? ARE WE FEELING BLUE?
GO AWAY, RATBERT.
THIS COULD BE MY CHANCE TO BOND AND BECOME A VALUED MEMBER OF THE FAMILY.
I'M GOING TO HUG YOUR FOOT UNTIL YOU TURN THAT FROWN UPSIDE DOWN.
© 1993 United Feature Syndicate, Inc.
NOW TELL ME WHY YOU FEEL SAD.
I JUST WALKED THROUGH SOMETHING DISGUSTING WITH MY NEW SHOES.
7-4
ONE OF US ISN'T TRYING HARD ENOUGH TO MAKE THIS RELATIONSHIP WORK.
COULD YOU DO THE OTHER SHOE NOW?

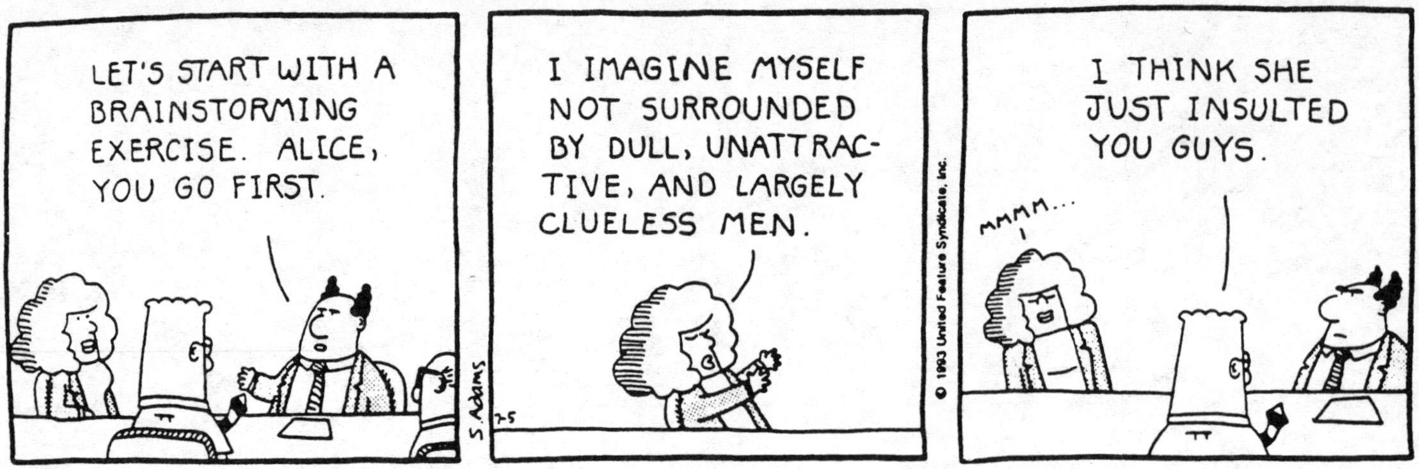
LET'S START WITH A BRAINSTORMING EXERCISE. ALICE, YOU GO FIRST.
S. Adams
7-5
I IMAGINE MYSELF NOT SURROUNDED BY DULL, UNATTRACTIVE, AND LARGELY CLUELESS MEN.
© 1993 United Feature Syndicate, Inc.
MMMM...
I THINK SHE JUST INSULTED YOU GUYS.

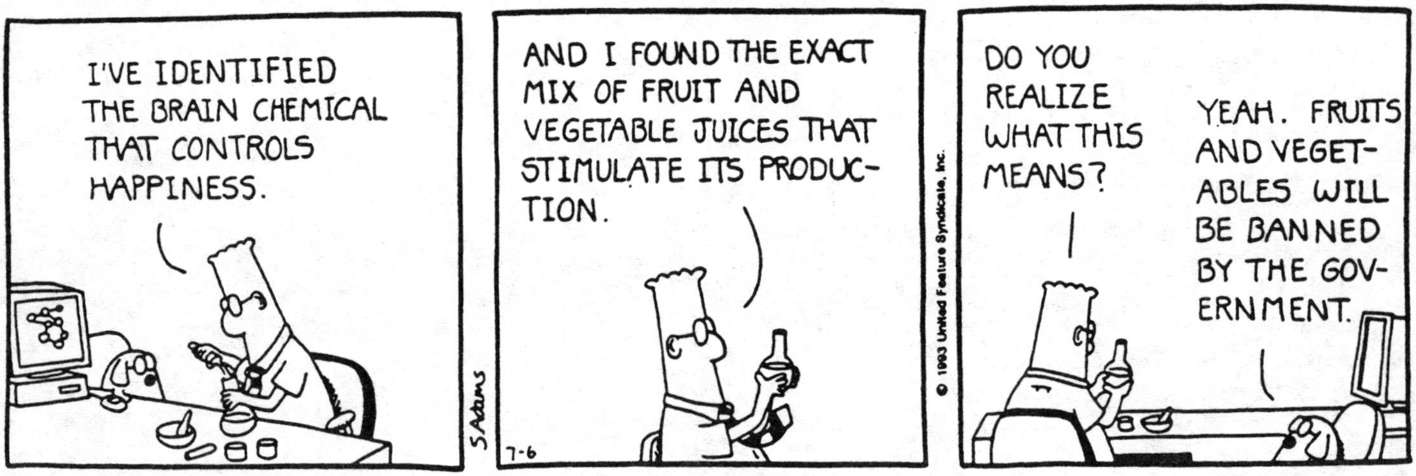
I'VE IDENTIFIED THE BRAIN CHEMICAL THAT CONTROLS HAPPINESS.
S. Adams
7-6
AND I FOUND THE EXACT MIX OF FRUIT AND VEGETABLE JUICES THAT STIMULATE ITS PRODUCTION.
© 1993 United Feature Syndicate, Inc.
DO YOU REALIZE WHAT THIS MEANS?
YEAH. FRUITS AND VEGETABLES WILL BE BANNED BY THE GOVERNMENT.

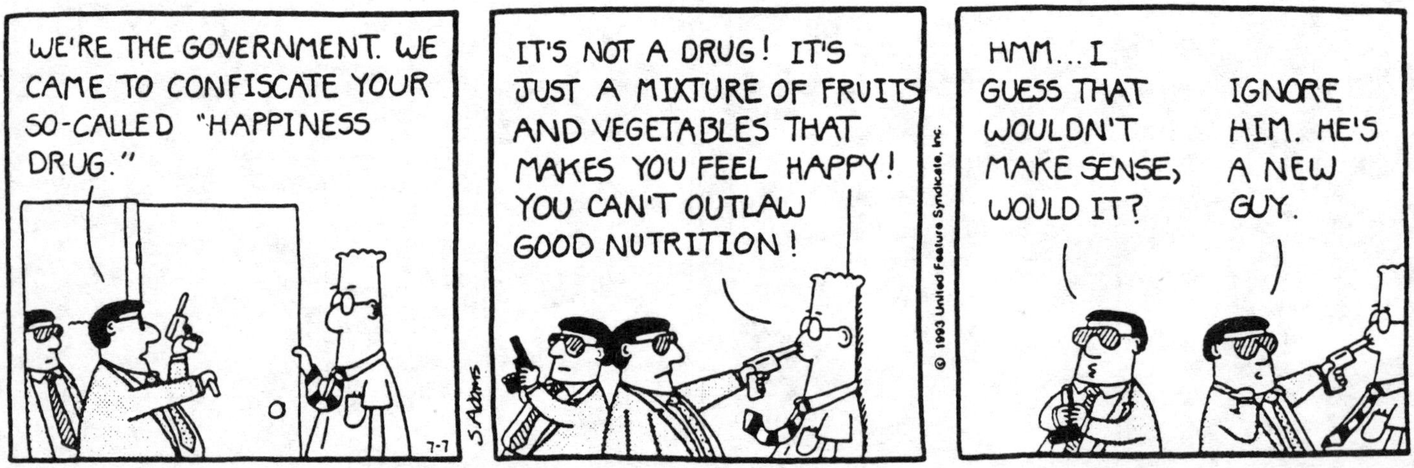
WE'RE THE GOVERNMENT. WE CAME TO CONFISCATE YOUR SO-CALLED "HAPPINESS DRUG."
7-7
S. Adams
IT'S NOT A DRUG! IT'S JUST A MIXTURE OF FRUITS AND VEGETABLES THAT MAKES YOU FEEL HAPPY! YOU CAN'T OUTLAW GOOD NUTRITION!
© 1993 United Feature Syndicate, Inc.
HMM... I GUESS THAT WOULDN'T MAKE SENSE, WOULD IT?
IGNORE HIM. HE'S A NEW GUY.

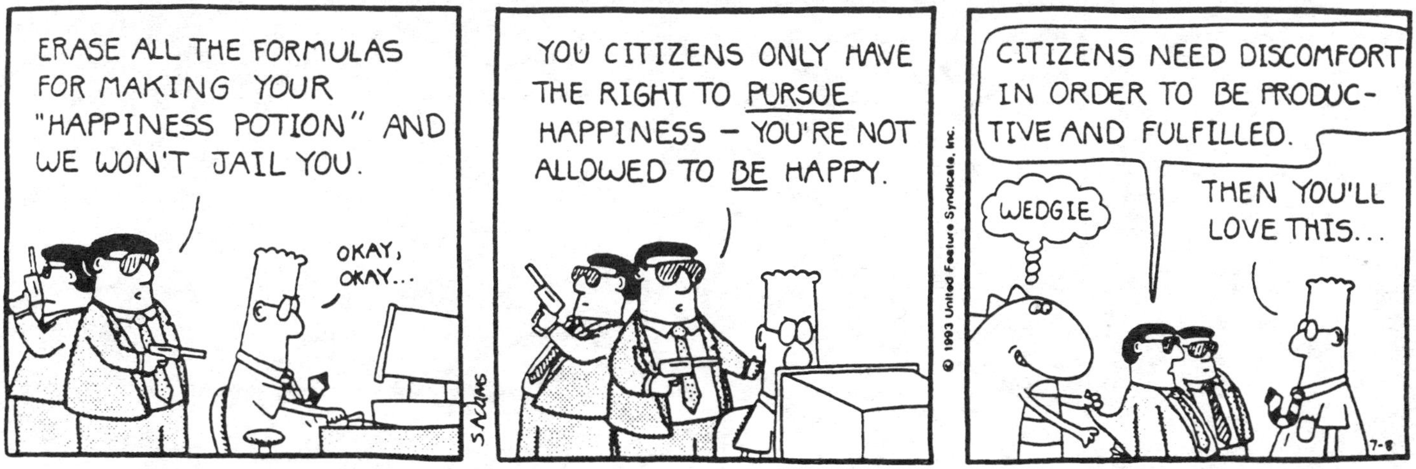
ERASE ALL THE FORMULAS FOR MAKING YOUR "HAPPINESS POTION" AND WE WON'T JAIL YOU.
OKAY, OKAY...
S. ADAMS
YOU CITIZENS ONLY HAVE THE RIGHT TO PURSUE HAPPINESS – YOU'RE NOT ALLOWED TO BE HAPPY.
© 1993 United Feature Syndicate, Inc.
CITIZENS NEED DISCOMFORT IN ORDER TO BE PRODUCTIVE AND FULFILLED.
WEDGIE
THEN YOU'LL LOVE THIS...
7-8

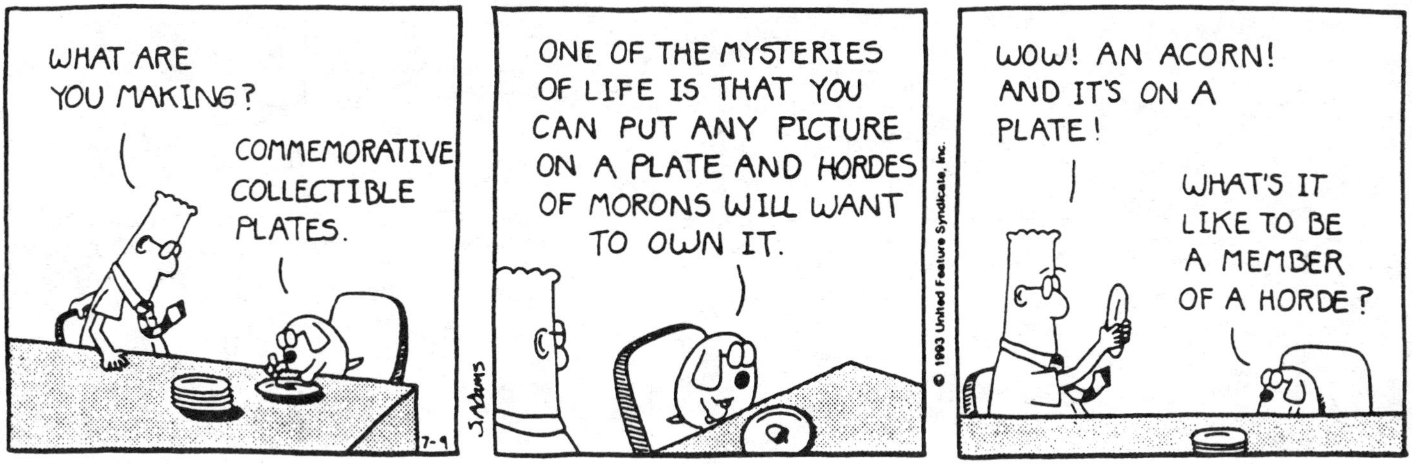
WHAT ARE YOU MAKING?
COMMEMORATIVE COLLECTIBLE PLATES.
7-9
S. Adams
ONE OF THE MYSTERIES OF LIFE IS THAT YOU CAN PUT ANY PICTURE ON A PLATE AND HORDES OF MORONS WILL WANT TO OWN IT.
© 1993 United Feature Syndicate, Inc.
WOW! AN ACORN! AND IT'S ON A PLATE!
WHAT'S IT LIKE TO BE A MEMBER OF A HORDE?

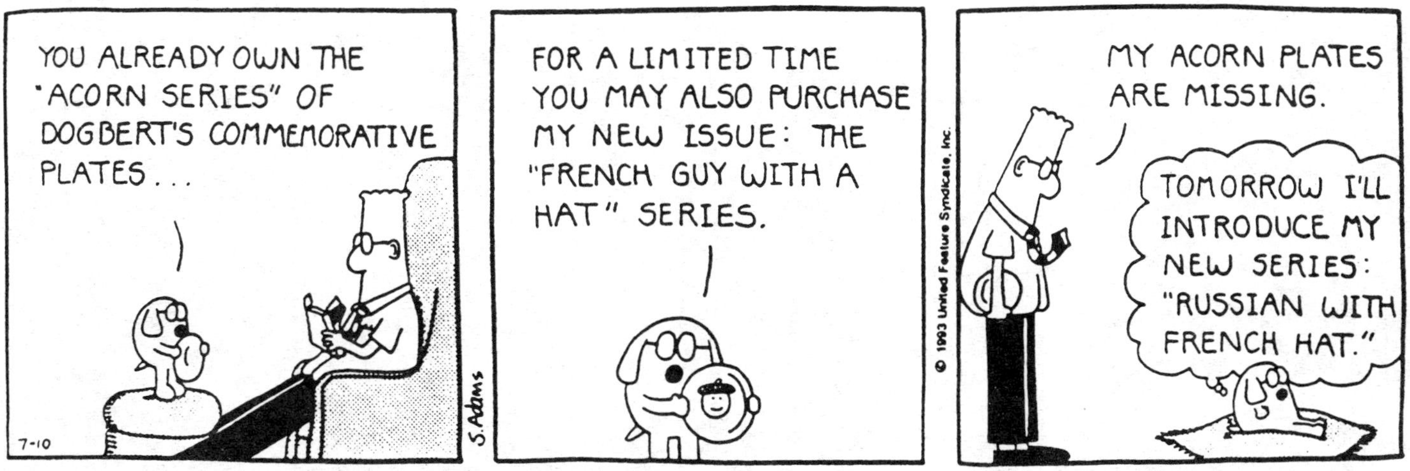
YOU ALREADY OWN THE "ACORN SERIES" OF DOGBERT'S COMMEMORATIVE PLATES...
7-10
S. Adams
FOR A LIMITED TIME YOU MAY ALSO PURCHASE MY NEW ISSUE: THE "FRENCH GUY WITH A HAT" SERIES.
© 1993 United Feature Syndicate, Inc.
MY ACORN PLATES ARE MISSING.
TOMORROW I'LL INTRODUCE MY NEW SERIES: "RUSSIAN WITH FRENCH HAT."

MAYBE I'M UNLUCKY IN LOVE BECAUSE I'M SO KNOWLEDGEABLE ABOUT SCIENCE THAT I INTIMIDATE PEOPLE.
THEIR INTIMIDATION BECOMES LOW SELF-ESTEEM, THEN THEY REJECT ME TO PROTECT THEIR EGOS.
OCCAM'S RAZOR.
WHAT IS "OCCAM'S RAZOR"?
A GUY NAMED OCCAM HAD A RULE ABOUT THE WORLD.
BASICALLY, HE SAID THAT WHEN THERE ARE MULTIPLE EXPLANATIONS FOR SOMETHING, THE SIMPLEST EXPLANATION IS USUALLY CORRECT.
THE SIMPLEST EXPLANATION FOR YOUR POOR LOVE LIFE IS THAT YOU'RE IMMENSELY UNATTRACTIVE.
© 1993 United Feature Syndicate, Inc.
MAYBE OCCAM HAD ANOTHER RULE THAT SPECIFICALLY EXEMPTED THIS SITUATION, BUT HIS HOUSE BURNED DOWN WITH ALL HIS NOTES.
THEN HE FORGOT.
7-11
OCCAM'S RAZOR.
I'M AN IDIOT?
I DON'T THINK WE CAN RULE IT OUT AT THIS POINT.

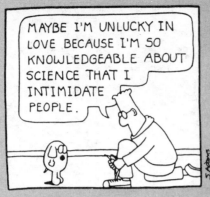

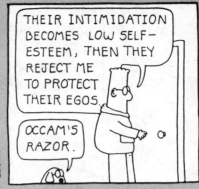

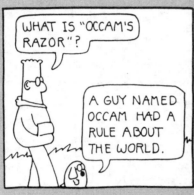

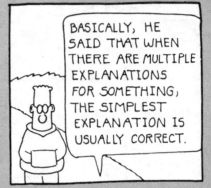

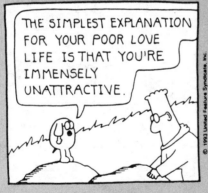

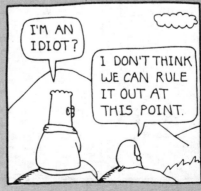

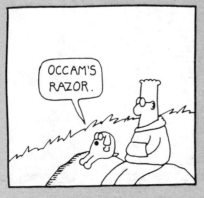

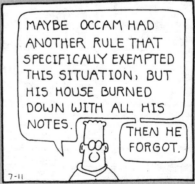

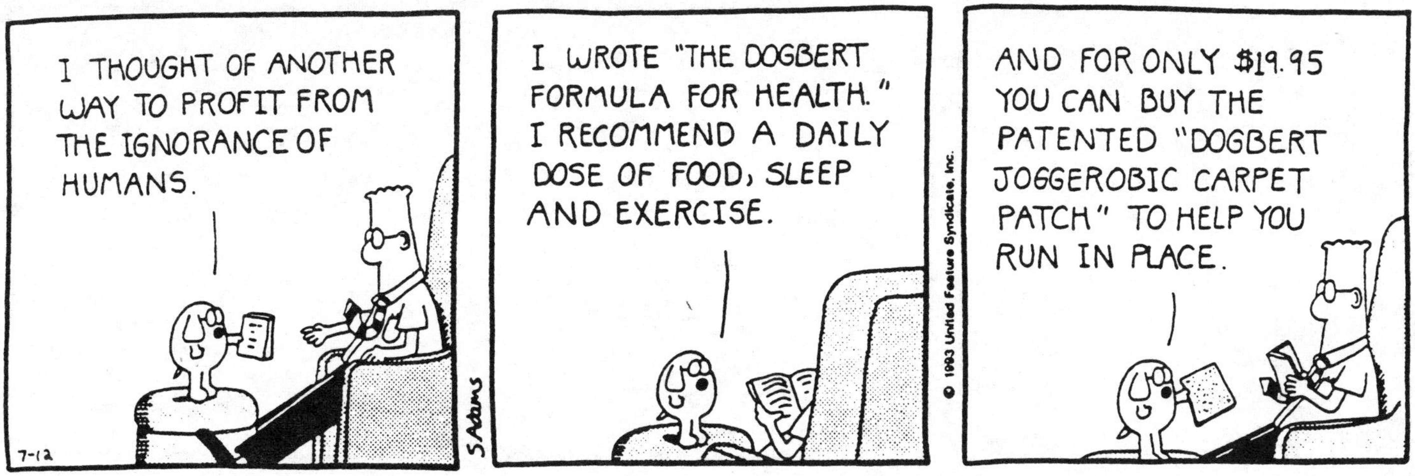
I THOUGHT OF ANOTHER WAY TO PROFIT FROM THE IGNORANCE OF HUMANS.
7-12
S. Adams
I WROTE "THE DOGBERT FORMULA FOR HEALTH." I RECOMMEND A DAILY DOSE OF FOOD, SLEEP AND EXERCISE.
© 1993 United Feature Syndicate, Inc.
AND FOR ONLY $19.95 YOU CAN BUY THE PATENTED "DOGBERT JOGGEROBIC CARPET PATCH" TO HELP YOU RUN IN PLACE.

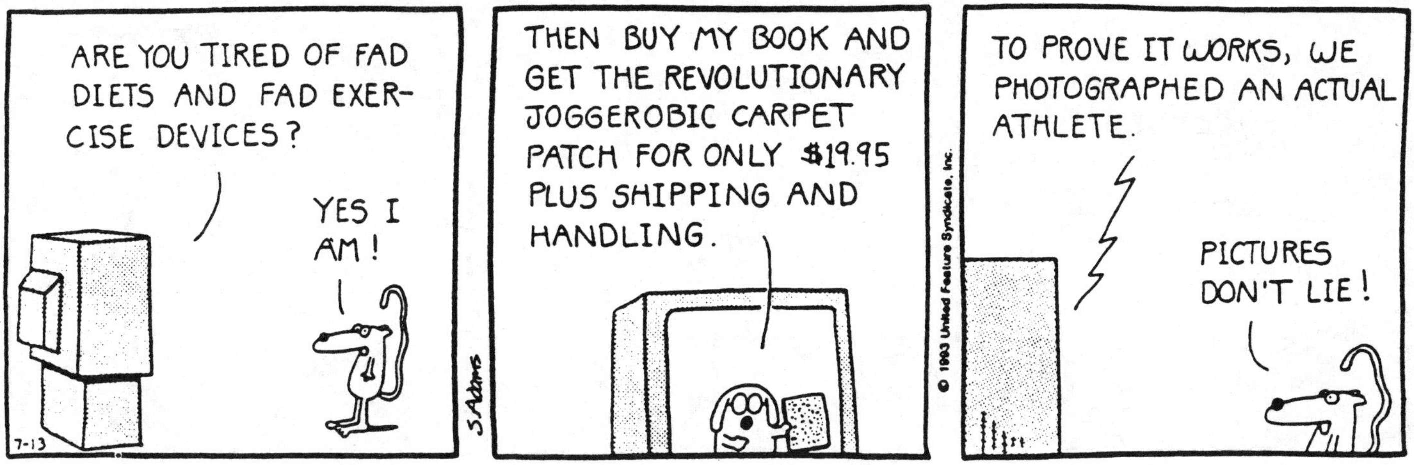
ARE YOU TIRED OF FAD DIETS AND FAD EXERCISE DEVICES?
YES I AM!
7-13
S. Adams
THEN BUY MY BOOK AND GET THE REVOLUTIONARY JOGGEROBIC CARPET PATCH FOR ONLY $19.95 PLUS SHIPPING AND HANDLING.
© 1993 United Feature Syndicate, Inc.
TO PROVE IT WORKS, WE PHOTOGRAPHED AN ACTUAL ATHLETE.
PICTURES DON'T LIE!

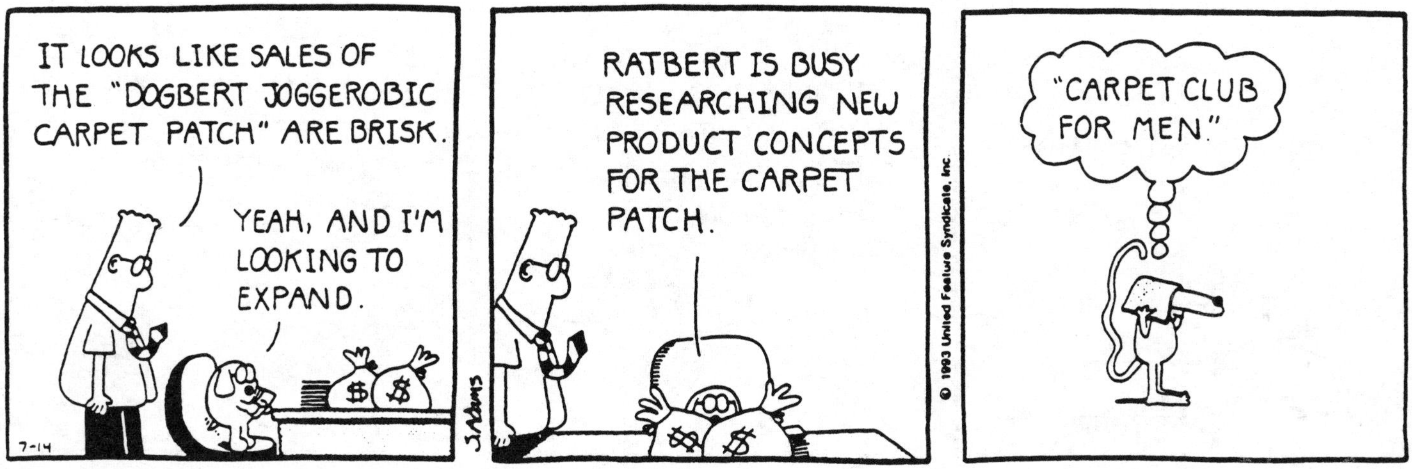
IT LOOKS LIKE SALES OF THE "DOGBERT JOGGEROBIC CARPET PATCH" ARE BRISK.
YEAH, AND I'M LOOKING TO EXPAND.
7-14
S. Adams
RATBERT IS BUSY RESEARCHING NEW PRODUCT CONCEPTS FOR THE CARPET PATCH.
© 1993 United Feature Syndicate, Inc.
"CARPET CLUB FOR MEN."

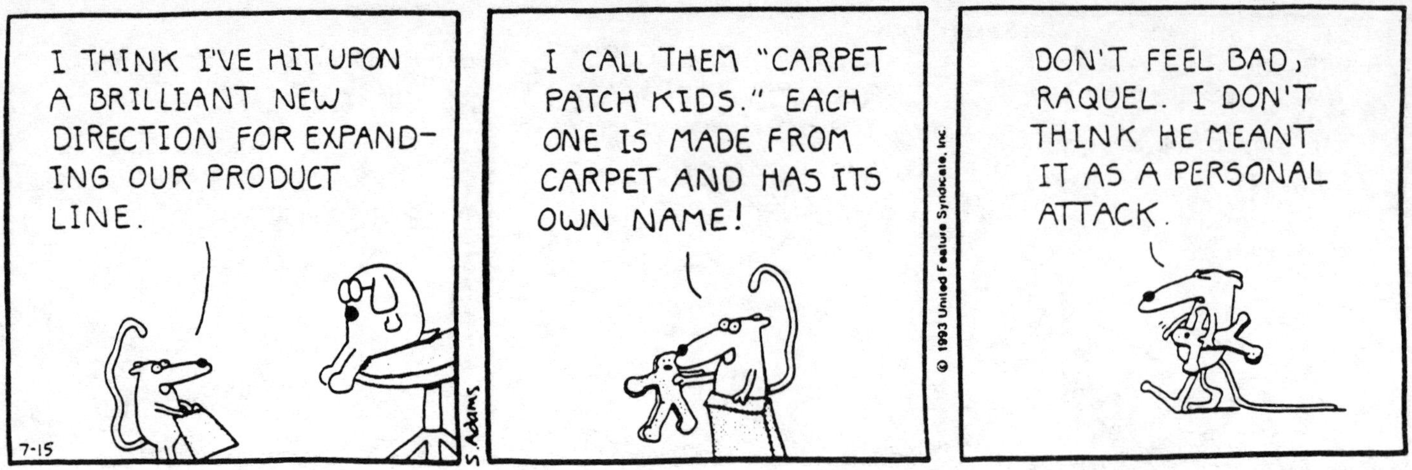
I THINK I'VE HIT UPON A BRILLIANT NEW DIRECTION FOR EXPANDING OUR PRODUCT LINE.
7-15
S. Adams
I CALL THEM "CARPET PATCH KIDS." EACH ONE IS MADE FROM CARPET AND HAS ITS OWN NAME!
© 1993 United Feature Syndicate, Inc.
DON'T FEEL BAD, RAQUEL. I DON'T THINK HE MEANT IT AS A PERSONAL ATTACK.

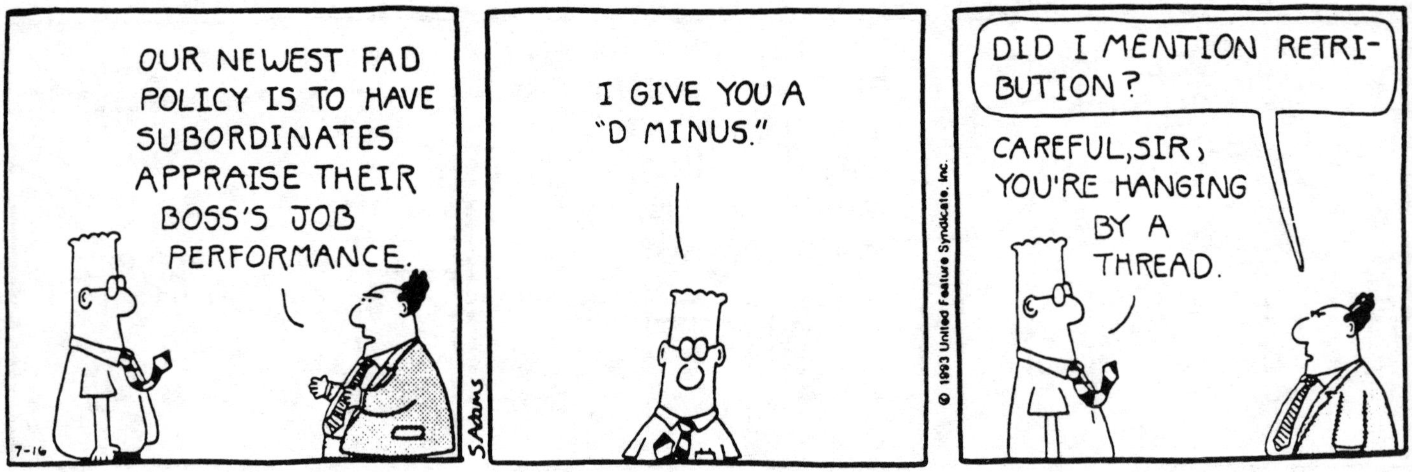
OUR NEWEST FAD POLICY IS TO HAVE SUBORDINATES APPRAISE THEIR BOSS'S JOB PERFORMANCE.
7-16
S. Adams
I GIVE YOU A "D MINUS."
© 1993 United Feature Syndicate, Inc.
DID I MENTION RETRIBUTION?
CAREFUL, SIR, YOU'RE HANGING BY A THREAD.

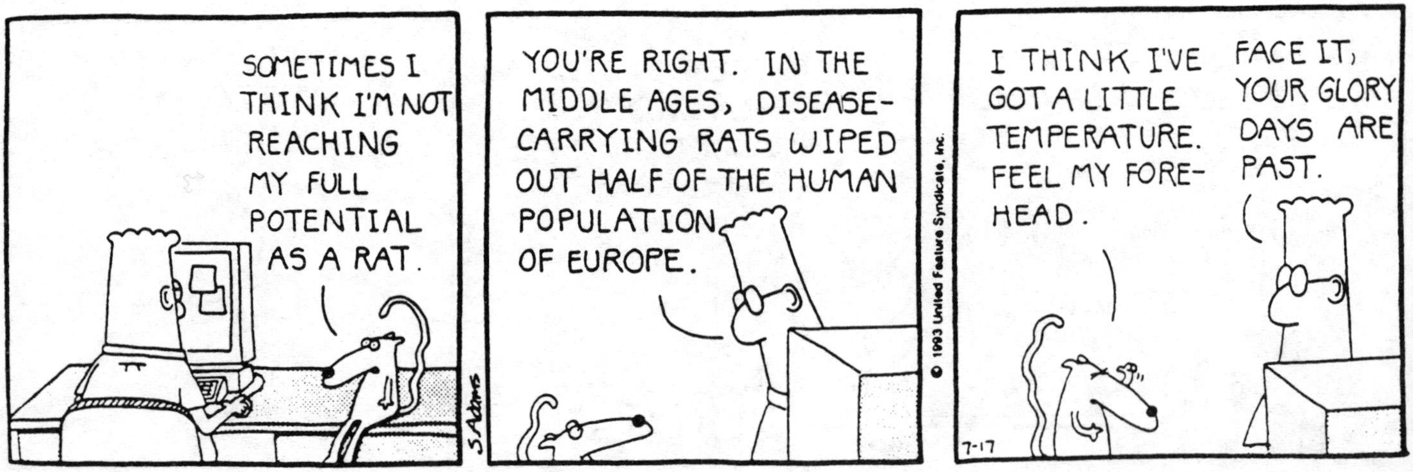
SOMETIMES I THINK I'M NOT REACHING MY FULL POTENTIAL AS A RAT.
S. Adams
YOU'RE RIGHT. IN THE MIDDLE AGES, DISEASE-CARRYING RATS WIPED OUT HALF OF THE HUMAN POPULATION OF EUROPE.
© 1993 United Feature Syndicate, Inc.
I THINK I'VE GOT A LITTLE TEMPERATURE. FEEL MY FOREHEAD.
FACE IT, YOUR GLORY DAYS ARE PAST.
7-17

THE AWARD FOR BEST ATTENDANCE GOES TO DILBERT.
S. ADAMS
I'D LIKE TO THANK THE PEOPLE WHO MADE THIS POSSIBLE.
FIRST, I'D LIKE TO THANK THE WOMEN IN THE COMPANY WHO HAVE REJECTED ME OVER THE YEARS...
BECAUSE OF THEM I HAVE NO GERM-RIDDLED CHILDREN TO INFECT ME.
AND THANKS TO MY CO-WORKERS FOR NEVER TELLING ME ABOUT IMPORTANT MEETINGS, THUS KEEPING MY GERM EXPOSURE TO A MINIMUM.
© 1993 United Feature Syndicate, Inc.
AND THANKS TO MY BOSS FOR NEVER ASSIGNING A PROJECT IMPORTANT ENOUGH TO INDUCE STRESS AND WEAKEN MY IMMUNE SYSTEM.
BUT WHAT MAKES THIS AWARD SPECIAL IS THAT EACH OF YOU HAD TO GET SICK IN ORDER FOR ME TO WIN.
7-18
WHEN YOU HAVE YOUR HEALTH, YOU HAVE EVERYTHING, DOGBERT.
NO, YOU ALSO HAVE TO GLOAT.

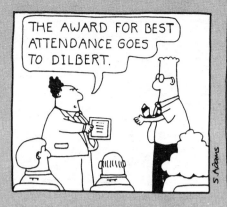

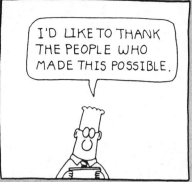

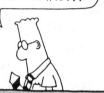

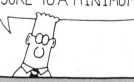

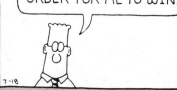

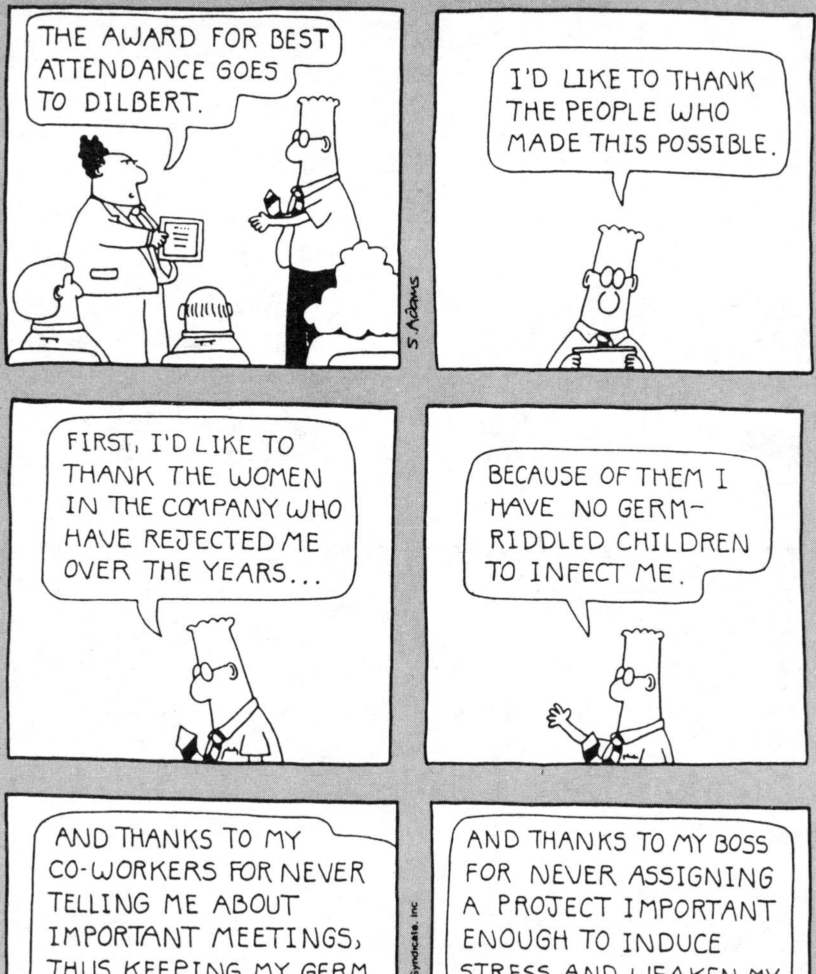

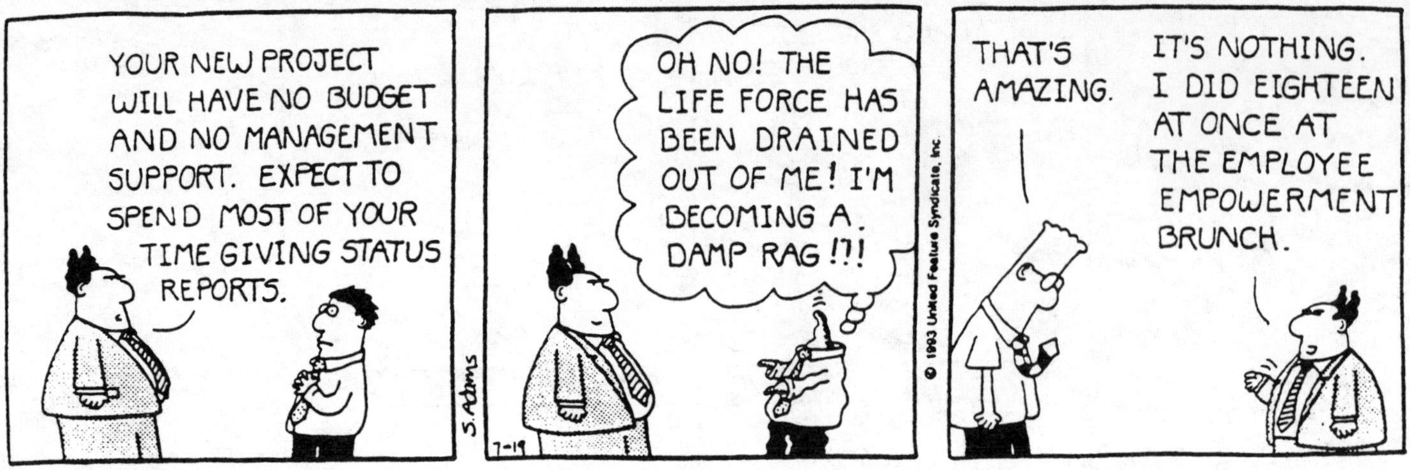
YOUR NEW PROJECT WILL HAVE NO BUDGET AND NO MANAGEMENT SUPPORT. EXPECT TO SPEND MOST OF YOUR TIME GIVING STATUS REPORTS.
S. Adams
7-19
OH NO! THE LIFE FORCE HAS BEEN DRAINED OUT OF ME! I'M BECOMING A DAMP RAG !?!
© 1993 United Feature Syndicate, Inc.
THAT'S AMAZING.
IT'S NOTHING. I DID EIGHTEEN AT ONCE AT THE EMPLOYEE EMPOWERMENT BRUNCH.

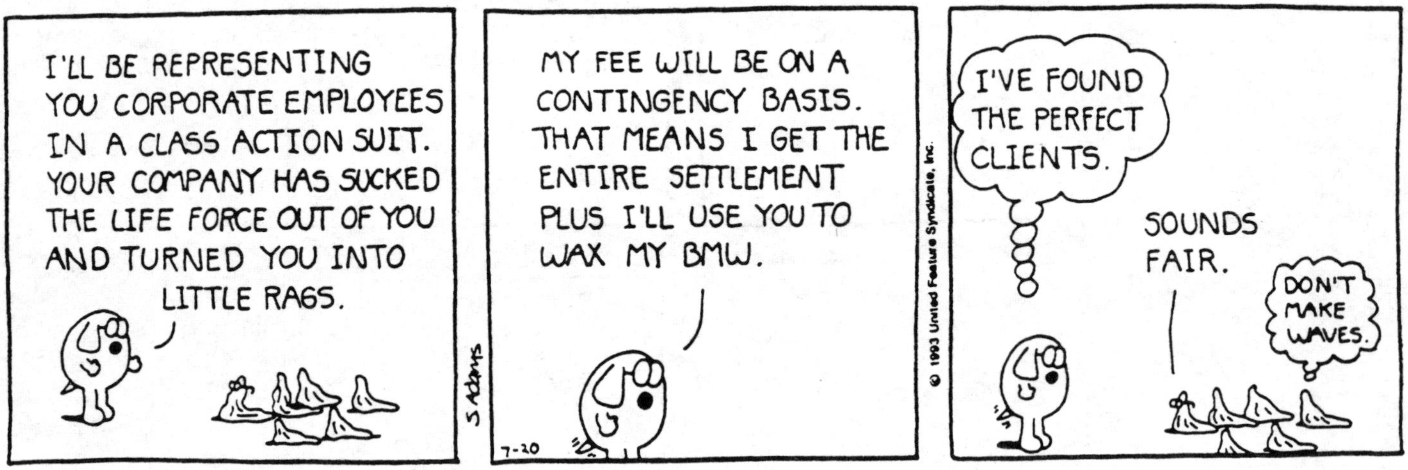
I'LL BE REPRESENTING YOU CORPORATE EMPLOYEES IN A CLASS ACTION SUIT. YOUR COMPANY HAS SUCKED THE LIFE FORCE OUT OF YOU AND TURNED YOU INTO LITTLE RAGS.
S. Adams
MY FEE WILL BE ON A CONTINGENCY BASIS. THAT MEANS I GET THE ENTIRE SETTLEMENT PLUS I'LL USE YOU TO WAX MY BMW.
7-20
© 1993 United Feature Syndicate, Inc.
I'VE FOUND THE PERFECT CLIENTS.
SOUNDS FAIR.
DON'T MAKE WAVES.

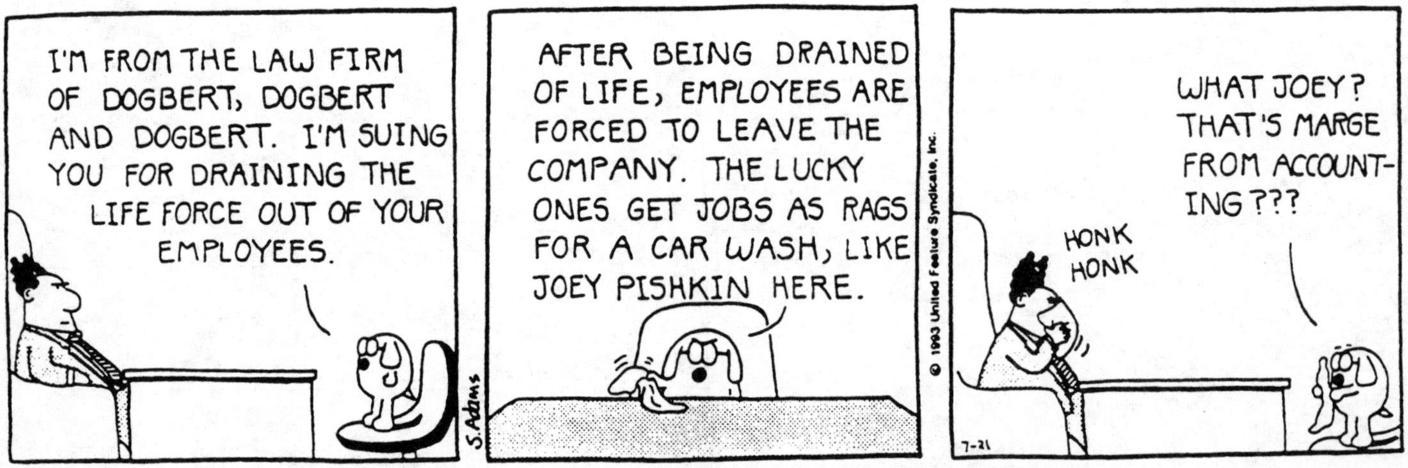
I'M FROM THE LAW FIRM OF DOGBERT, DOGBERT AND DOGBERT. I'M SUING YOU FOR DRAINING THE LIFE FORCE OUT OF YOUR EMPLOYEES.
S. Adams
AFTER BEING DRAINED OF LIFE, EMPLOYEES ARE FORCED TO LEAVE THE COMPANY. THE LUCKY ONES GET JOBS AS RAGS FOR A CAR WASH, LIKE JOEY PISHKIN HERE.
© 1993 United Feature Syndicate, Inc.
HONK HONK
WHAT JOEY? THAT'S MARGE FROM ACCOUNTING???
7-21

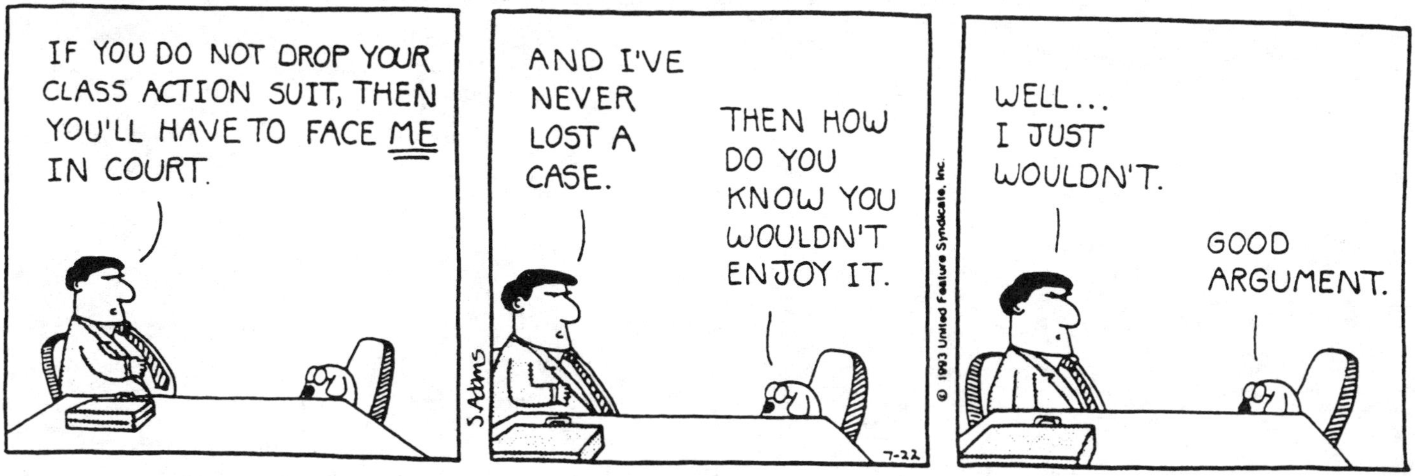

IF YOU DO NOT DROP YOUR CLASS ACTION SUIT, THEN YOU'LL HAVE TO FACE ME IN COURT.
AND I'VE NEVER LOST A CASE.
THEN HOW DO YOU KNOW YOU WOULDN'T ENJOY IT.
WELL... I JUST WOULDN'T.
GOOD ARGUMENT.
S. Adams
7-22
© 1993 United Feature Syndicate, Inc.

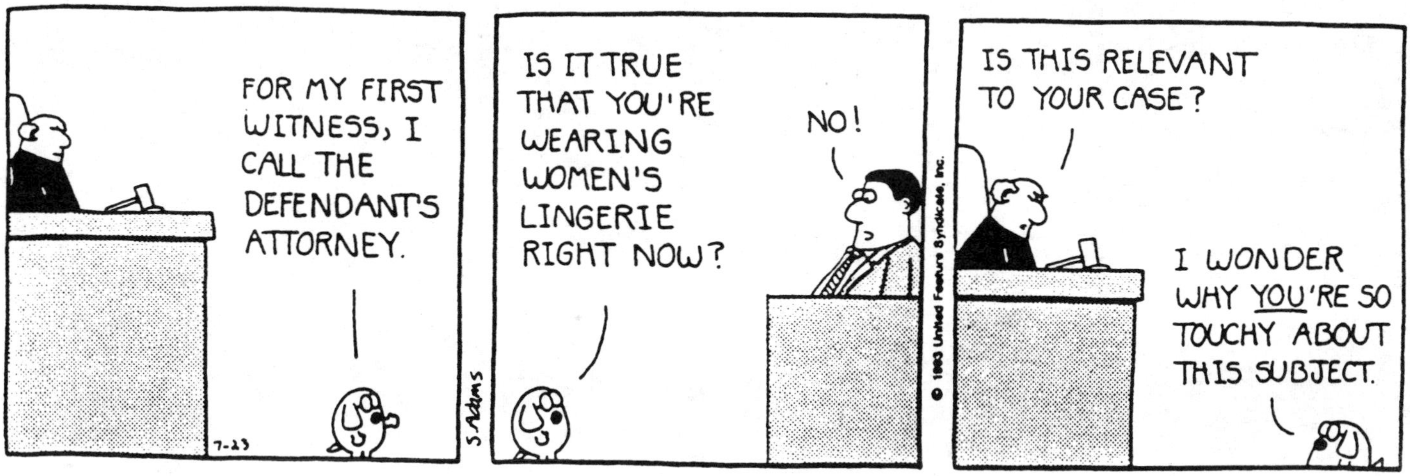

FOR MY FIRST WITNESS, I CALL THE DEFENDANT'S ATTORNEY.
7-23
IS IT TRUE THAT YOU'RE WEARING WOMEN'S LINGERIE RIGHT NOW?
NO!
S. Adams
IS THIS RELEVANT TO YOUR CASE?
I WONDER WHY YOU'RE SO TOUCHY ABOUT THIS SUBJECT.
© 1993 United Feature Syndicate, Inc.

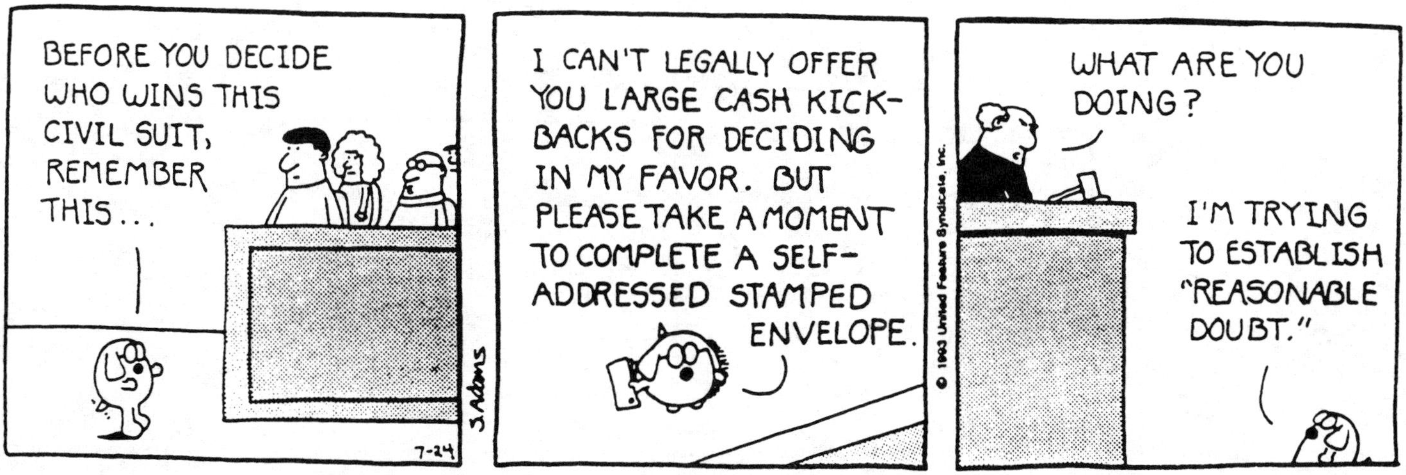

BEFORE YOU DECIDE WHO WINS THIS CIVIL SUIT, REMEMBER THIS...
7-24
I CAN'T LEGALLY OFFER YOU LARGE CASH KICK-BACKS FOR DECIDING IN MY FAVOR. BUT PLEASE TAKE A MOMENT TO COMPLETE A SELF-ADDRESSED STAMPED ENVELOPE.
S. Adams
WHAT ARE YOU DOING?
I'M TRYING TO ESTABLISH "REASONABLE DOUBT."
© 1993 United Feature Syndicate, Inc.

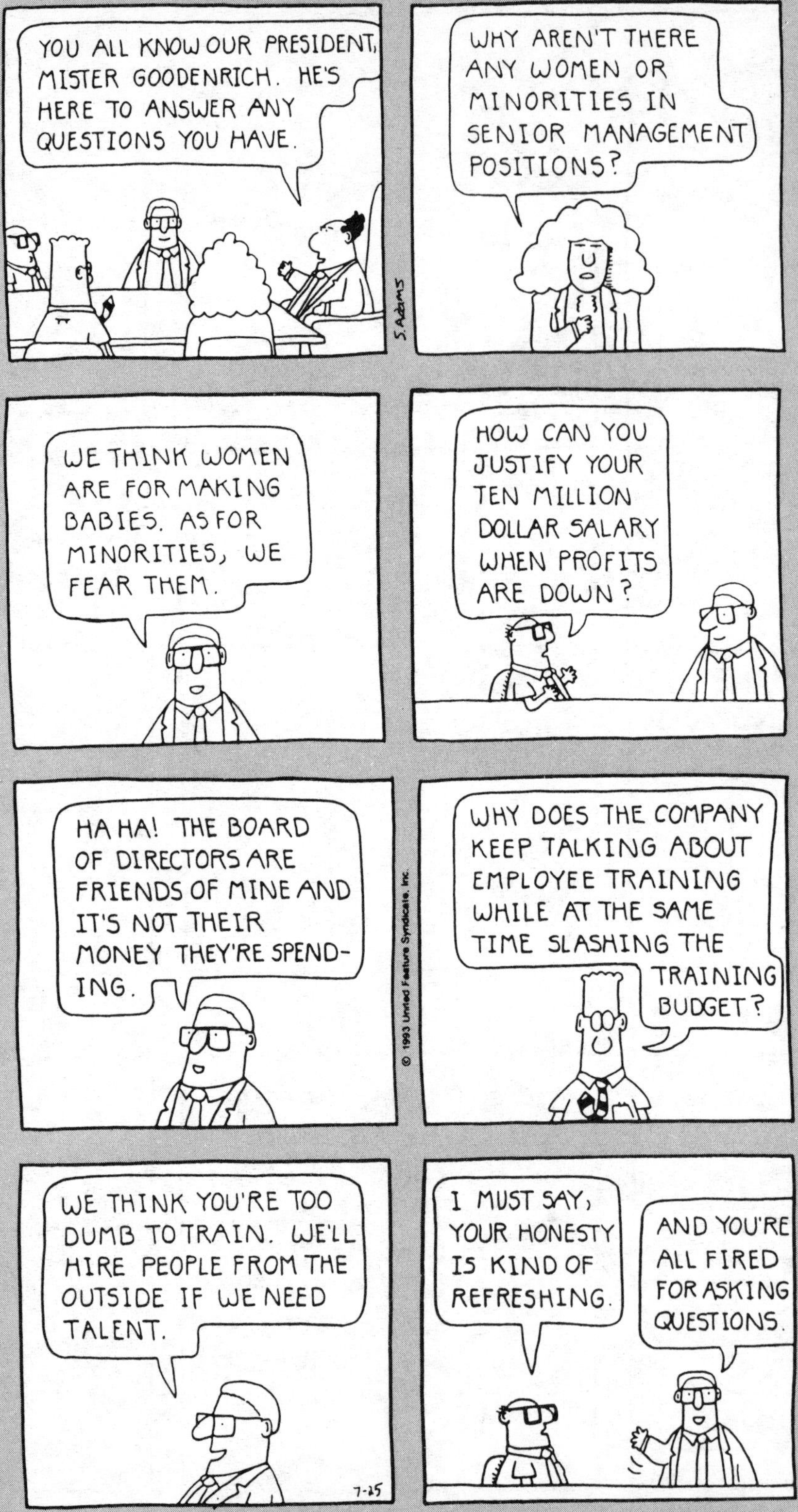
YOU ALL KNOW OUR PRESIDENT, MISTER GOODENRICH. HE'S HERE TO ANSWER ANY QUESTIONS YOU HAVE.
S. Adams
WHY AREN'T THERE ANY WOMEN OR MINORITIES IN SENIOR MANAGEMENT POSITIONS?
WE THINK WOMEN ARE FOR MAKING BABIES. AS FOR MINORITIES, WE FEAR THEM.
HOW CAN YOU JUSTIFY YOUR TEN MILLION DOLLAR SALARY WHEN PROFITS ARE DOWN?
HA HA! THE BOARD OF DIRECTORS ARE FRIENDS OF MINE AND IT'S NOT THEIR MONEY THEY'RE SPEND-ING.
© 1993 United Feature Syndicate, Inc.
WHY DOES THE COMPANY KEEP TALKING ABOUT EMPLOYEE TRAINING WHILE AT THE SAME TIME SLASHING THE TRAINING BUDGET?
WE THINK YOU'RE TOO DUMB TO TRAIN. WE'LL HIRE PEOPLE FROM THE OUTSIDE IF WE NEED TALENT.
7-25
I MUST SAY, YOUR HONESTY IS KIND OF REFRESHING.
AND YOU'RE ALL FIRED FOR ASKING QUESTIONS.

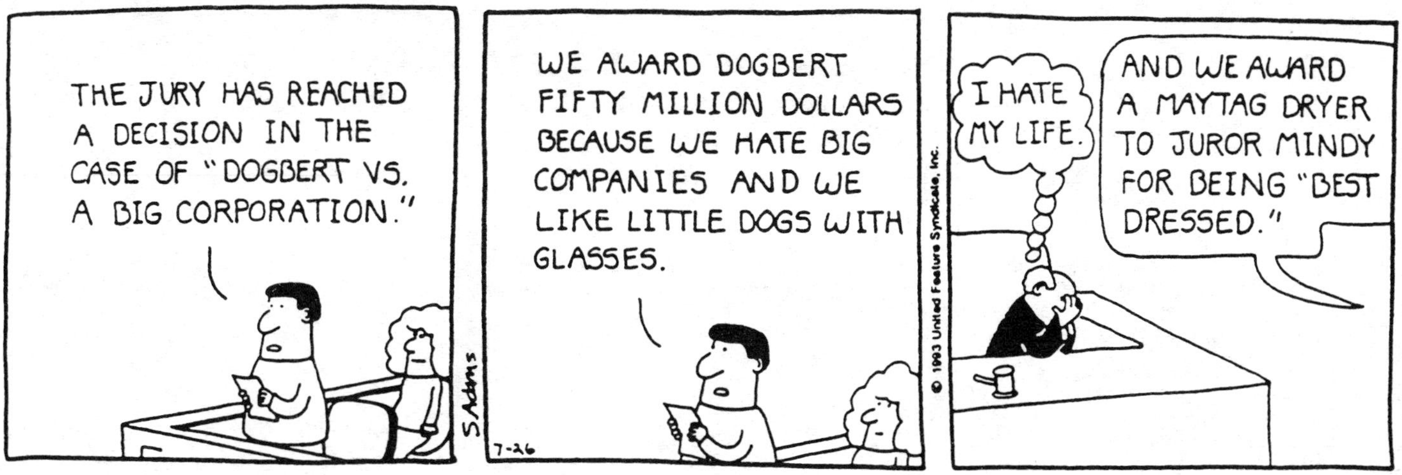
THE JURY HAS REACHED A DECISION IN THE CASE OF "DOGBERT VS. A BIG CORPORATION."
S. Adams
7-26
WE AWARD DOGBERT FIFTY MILLION DOLLARS BECAUSE WE HATE BIG COMPANIES AND WE LIKE LITTLE DOGS WITH GLASSES.
I HATE MY LIFE.
AND WE AWARD A MAYTAG DRYER TO JUROR MINDY FOR BEING "BEST DRESSED."
© 1993 United Feature Syndicate, Inc.

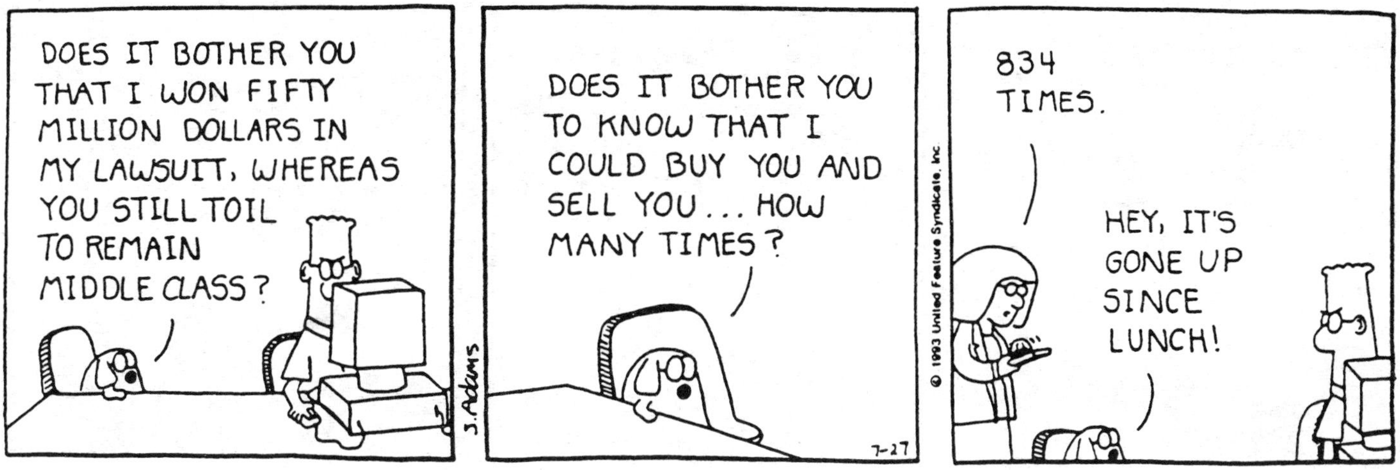
DOES IT BOTHER YOU THAT I WON FIFTY MILLION DOLLARS IN MY LAWSUIT, WHEREAS YOU STILL TOIL TO REMAIN MIDDLE CLASS?
S. Adams
DOES IT BOTHER YOU TO KNOW THAT I COULD BUY YOU AND SELL YOU ... HOW MANY TIMES?
7-27
834 TIMES.
HEY, IT'S GONE UP SINCE LUNCH!
© 1993 United Feature Syndicate, Inc.

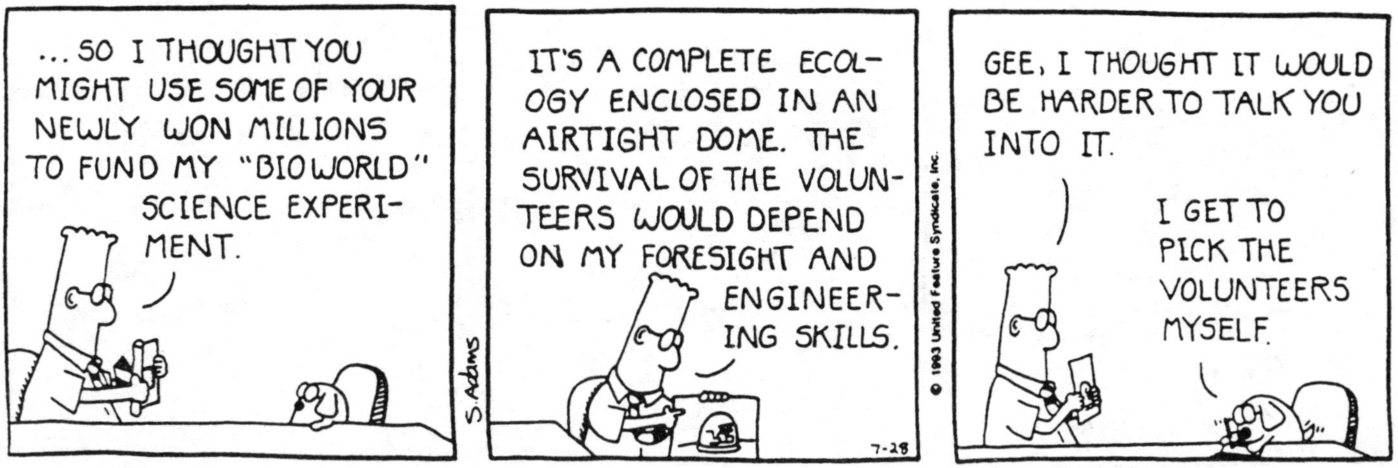
... SO I THOUGHT YOU MIGHT USE SOME OF YOUR NEWLY WON MILLIONS TO FUND MY "BIOWORLD" SCIENCE EXPERIMENT.
S. Adams
IT'S A COMPLETE ECOLOGY ENCLOSED IN AN AIRTIGHT DOME. THE SURVIVAL OF THE VOLUNTEERS WOULD DEPEND ON MY FORESIGHT AND ENGINEERING SKILLS.
7-28
GEE, I THOUGHT IT WOULD BE HARDER TO TALK YOU INTO IT.
I GET TO PICK THE VOLUNTEERS MYSELF.
© 1993 United Feature Syndicate, Inc.

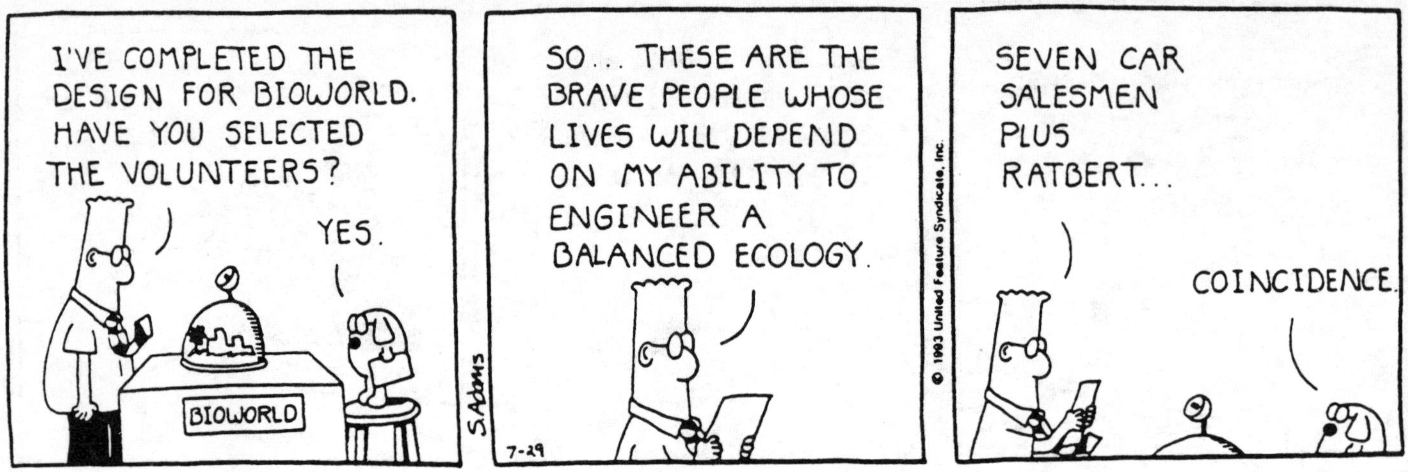
I'VE COMPLETED THE DESIGN FOR BIOWORLD. HAVE YOU SELECTED THE VOLUNTEERS?
YES.
BIOWORLD
S. Adams
7-29
SO... THESE ARE THE BRAVE PEOPLE WHOSE LIVES WILL DEPEND ON MY ABILITY TO ENGINEER A BALANCED ECOLOGY.
© 1993 United Feature Syndicate, Inc.
SEVEN CAR SALESMEN PLUS RATBERT...
COINCIDENCE.

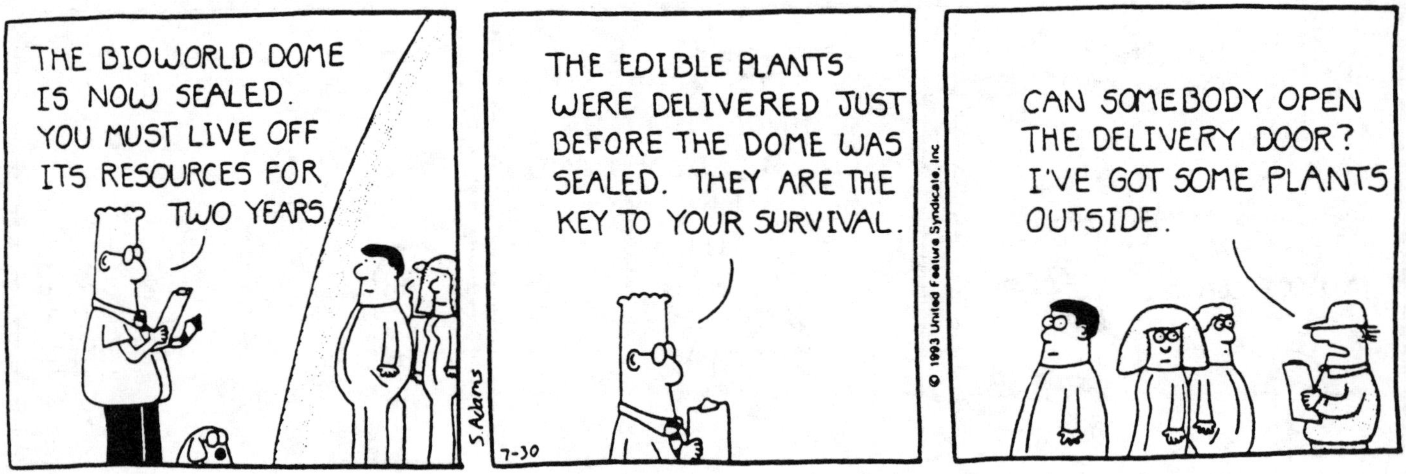
THE BIOWORLD DOME IS NOW SEALED. YOU MUST LIVE OFF ITS RESOURCES FOR TWO YEARS.
S. Adams
7-30
THE EDIBLE PLANTS WERE DELIVERED JUST BEFORE THE DOME WAS SEALED. THEY ARE THE KEY TO YOUR SURVIVAL.
© 1993 United Feature Syndicate, Inc.
CAN SOMEBODY OPEN THE DELIVERY DOOR? I'VE GOT SOME PLANTS OUTSIDE.

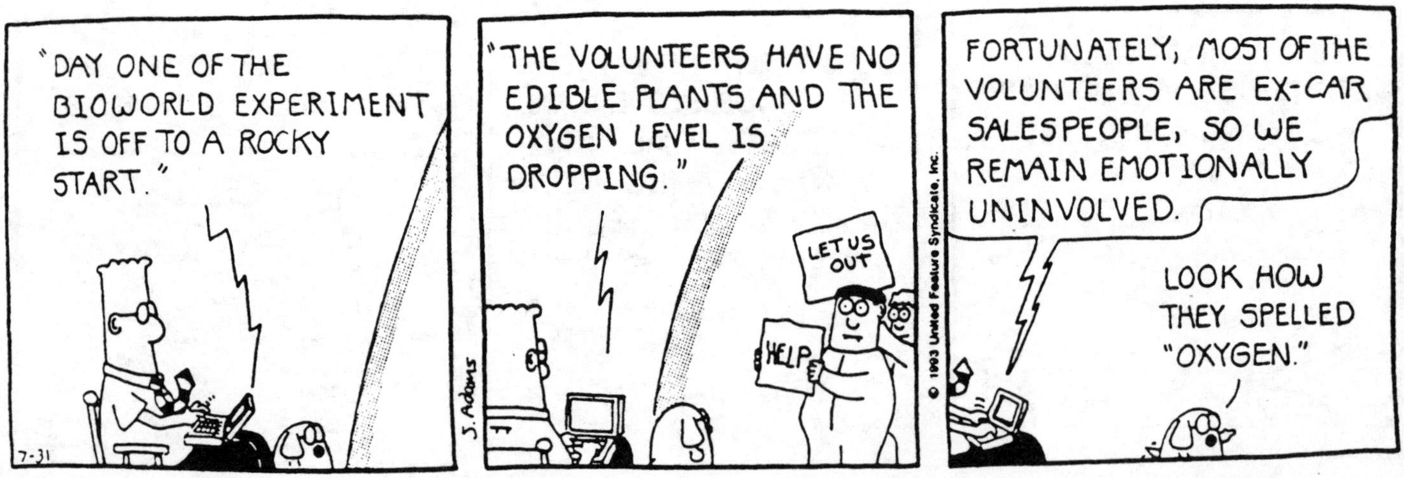
"DAY ONE OF THE BIOWORLD EXPERIMENT IS OFF TO A ROCKY START."
7-31
S. Adams
"THE VOLUNTEERS HAVE NO EDIBLE PLANTS AND THE OXYGEN LEVEL IS DROPPING."
LET US OUT
HELP
© 1993 United Feature Syndicate, Inc.
FORTUNATELY, MOST OF THE VOLUNTEERS ARE EX-CAR SALESPEOPLE, SO WE REMAIN EMOTIONALLY UNINVOLVED.
LOOK HOW THEY SPELLED "OXYGEN."

IS IT THE FLU ?
HMM...
S. Adams
I HAD THE COMPUTER RUN AN ECONOMIC REPORT ON THE MARKET VALUE OF YOUR ORGANS.
I COULD MAKE THOUSANDS OF DOLLARS BY SELLING YOUR PARTS FOR TRANSPLANTS.
OF COURSE, THIS IS ALL MOOT UNLESS YOU DIE IN MY OFFICE WHILE UNDER MY CARE.
BUT IF I LET YOU DIE FROM THE FLU THEN MY MALPRACTICE INSURANCE WILL GO UP AGAIN.
© 1993 United Feature Syndicate, Inc.
BUT IF YOU LIVE I CAN CONTINUE TO BILL YOU FOR UNNECESSARY TESTS.
THERE'S A SLIGHT ECONOMIC ADVANTAGE TO KEEPING YOU ALIVE... IF YOU LEAVE THREE PINTS OF BLOOD AND DO ME A LITTLE FAVOR.
8·1
THEN I HAD TO WAX HIS JEEP WITH MY CLOTHES.
APPARENTLY HE DIDN'T KNOW WHAT KIND OF FABRICS YOU WEAR.

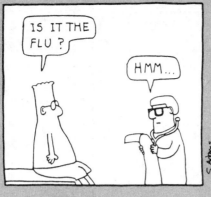

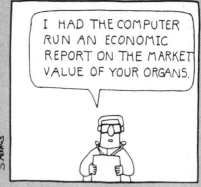

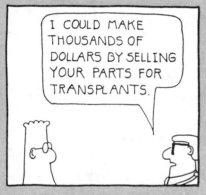

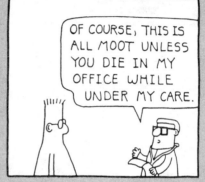

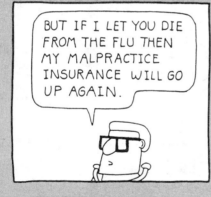

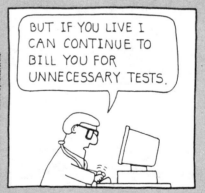

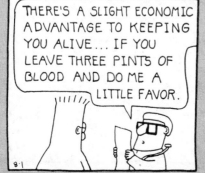

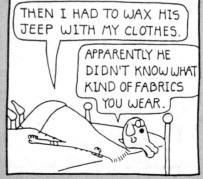

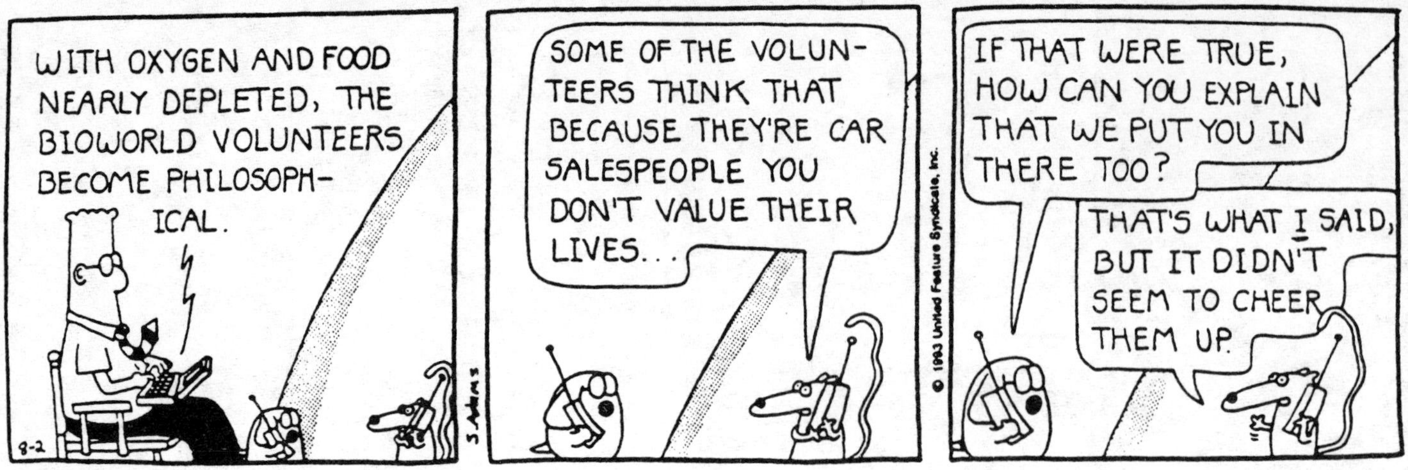
WITH OXYGEN AND FOOD NEARLY DEPLETED, THE BIOWORLD VOLUNTEERS BECOME PHILOSOPH-ICAL.
8-2
S. Adams
SOME OF THE VOLUNTEERS THINK THAT BECAUSE THEY'RE CAR SALESPEOPLE YOU DON'T VALUE THEIR LIVES...
© 1993 United Feature Syndicate, Inc.
IF THAT WERE TRUE, HOW CAN YOU EXPLAIN THAT WE PUT YOU IN THERE TOO?
THAT'S WHAT I SAID, BUT IT DIDN'T SEEM TO CHEER THEM UP.

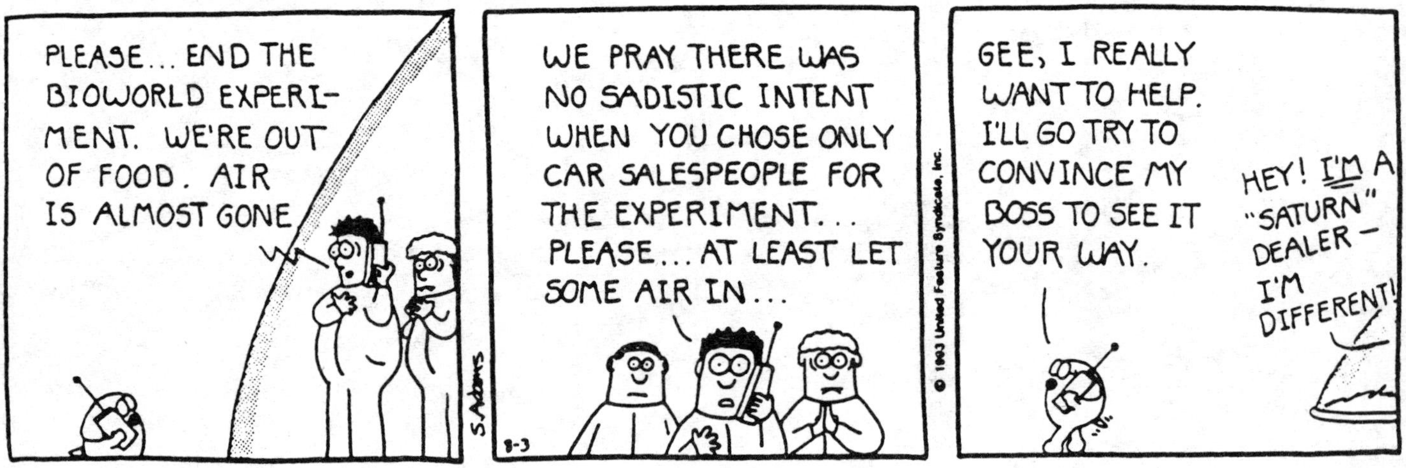
PLEASE... END THE BIOWORLD EXPERIMENT. WE'RE OUT OF FOOD. AIR IS ALMOST GONE
S. Adams
8-3
WE PRAY THERE WAS NO SADISTIC INTENT WHEN YOU CHOSE ONLY CAR SALESPEOPLE FOR THE EXPERIMENT... PLEASE... AT LEAST LET SOME AIR IN...
© 1993 United Feature Syndicate, Inc.
GEE, I REALLY WANT TO HELP. I'LL GO TRY TO CONVINCE MY BOSS TO SEE IT YOUR WAY.
HEY! I'M A "SATURN" DEALER – I'M DIFFERENT!

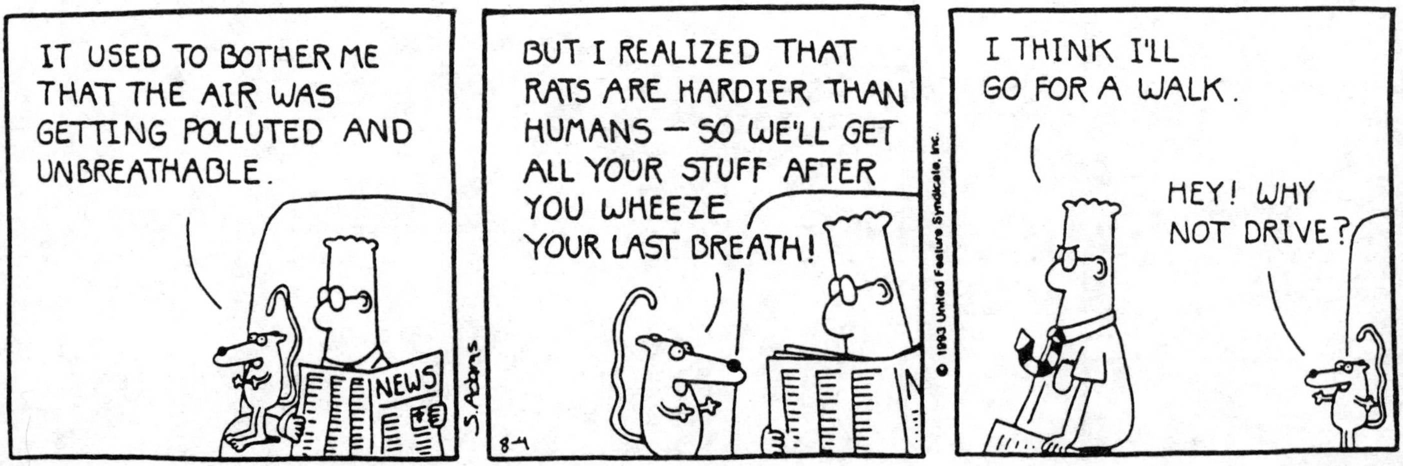
IT USED TO BOTHER ME THAT THE AIR WAS GETTING POLLUTED AND UNBREATHABLE.
NEWS
S. Adams
8-4
BUT I REALIZED THAT RATS ARE HARDIER THAN HUMANS – SO WE'LL GET ALL YOUR STUFF AFTER YOU WHEEZE YOUR LAST BREATH!
© 1993 United Feature Syndicate, Inc.
I THINK I'LL GO FOR A WALK.
HEY! WHY NOT DRIVE?

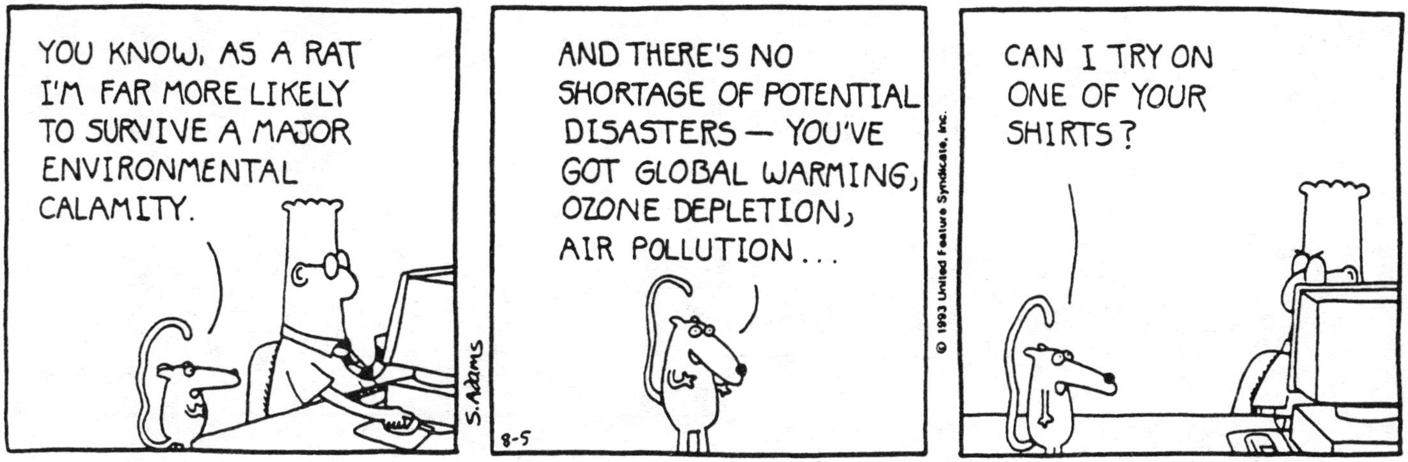
YOU KNOW, AS A RAT I'M FAR MORE LIKELY TO SURVIVE A MAJOR ENVIRONMENTAL CALAMITY.
S. Adams
AND THERE'S NO SHORTAGE OF POTENTIAL DISASTERS — YOU'VE GOT GLOBAL WARMING, OZONE DEPLETION, AIR POLLUTION...
8-5
© 1993 United Feature Syndicate, Inc.
CAN I TRY ON ONE OF YOUR SHIRTS?

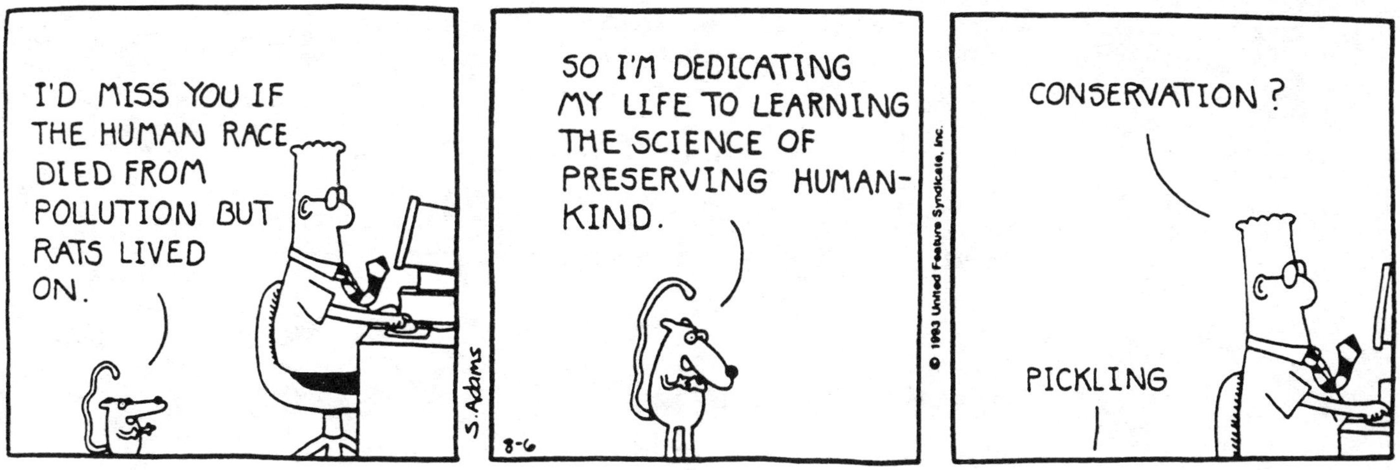
I'D MISS YOU IF THE HUMAN RACE DIED FROM POLLUTION BUT RATS LIVED ON.
S. Adams
SO I'M DEDICATING MY LIFE TO LEARNING THE SCIENCE OF PRESERVING HUMAN-KIND.
8-6
© 1993 United Feature Syndicate, Inc.
CONSERVATION?
PICKLING

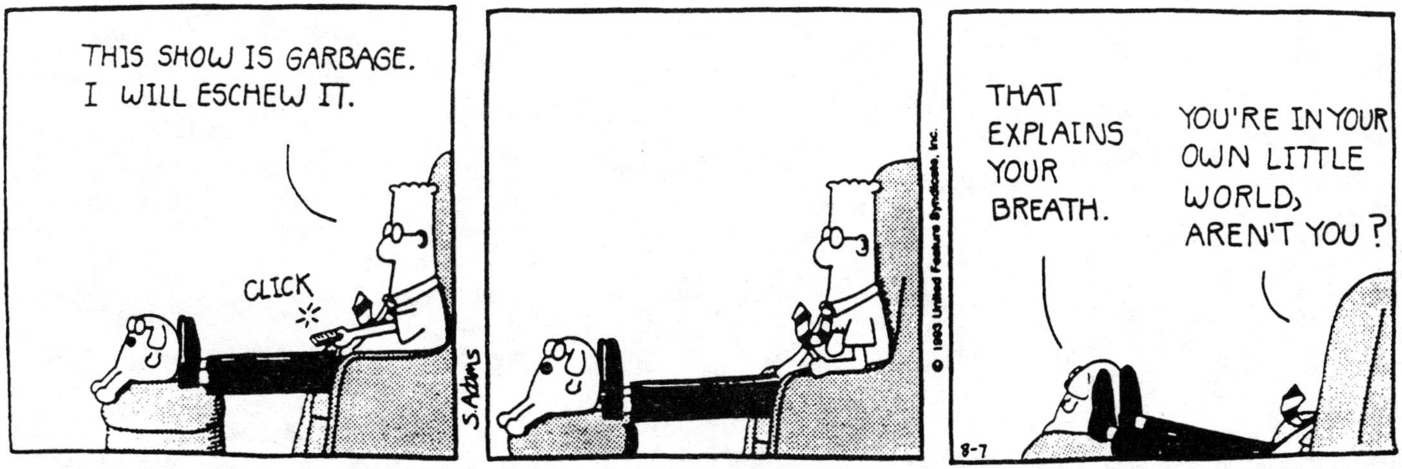
THIS SHOW IS GARBAGE. I WILL ESCHEW IT.
CLICK
S. Adams
© 1993 United Feature Syndicate, Inc.
THAT EXPLAINS YOUR BREATH.
YOU'RE IN YOUR OWN LITTLE WORLD, AREN'T YOU?
8-7

WHAT'S WRONG WITH YOU?
I HAVE A.W.S.
S. Adams
YOU HAVE "ATTRACTIVE WOMAN SYNDROME" HERE??
SHE WAS JUST HIRED.
RUN!
DILBERT, I'D LIKE YOU TO MEET LIZ.
UH-OH... MY METABOLISM IS INCREASING. MY BRAIN IS SUPPRESSING WHAT LITTLE SOCIAL SKILLS I HAVE.
HI
IT'S A PLEASURE TO MEET ME. I HOPE YOU NEVER FIND A LIVE TURTLE IN YOUR SOUP.
© 1993 United Feature Syndicate, Inc
AAAGH! WHAT WAS THAT SUPPOSED TO MEAN??
SLAP
8-8
OH GREAT... THE CORRECTION FLUID WASN'T DRY. IT'S STUCK TO MY EYEBROWS.
WHAT CAN I DO TO STOP FRIGHTENING ATTRACTIVE WOMEN?
THAT MASK IS A STEP IN THE RIGHT DIRECTION.

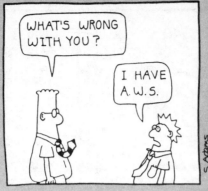

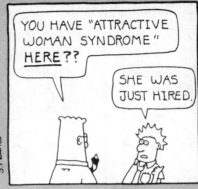

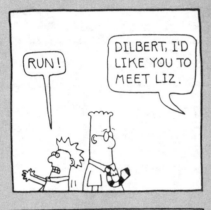

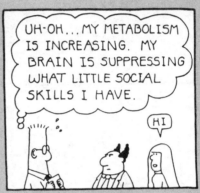

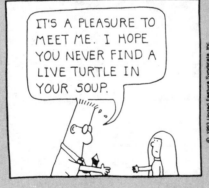

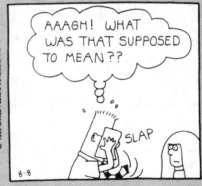

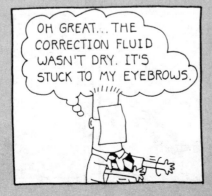

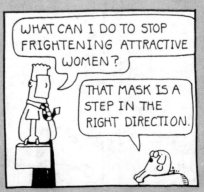

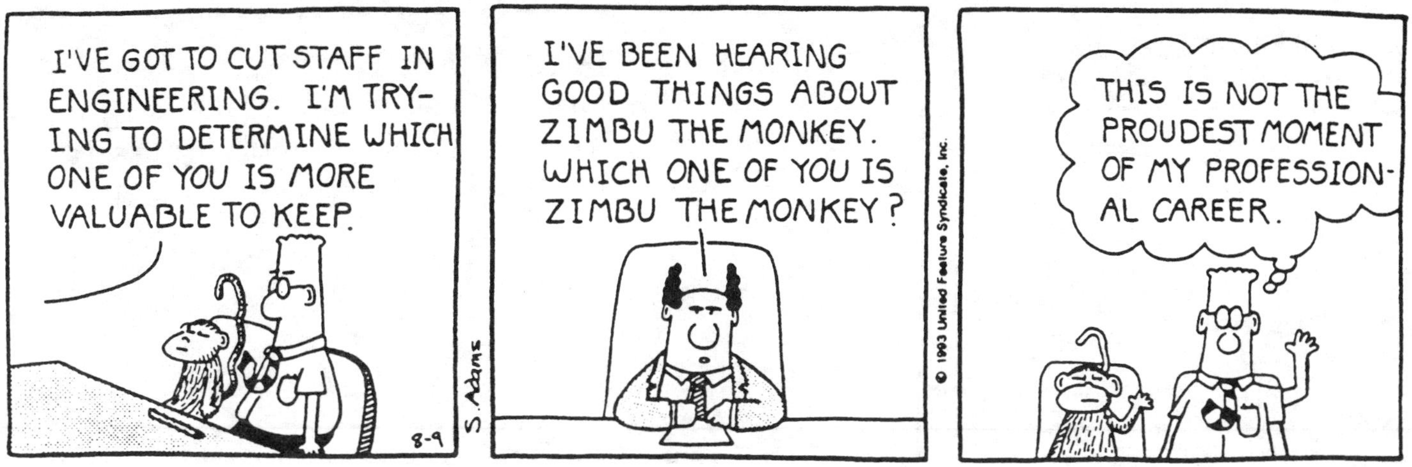
I'VE GOT TO CUT STAFF IN ENGINEERING. I'M TRYING TO DETERMINE WHICH ONE OF YOU IS MORE VALUABLE TO KEEP.
I'VE BEEN HEARING GOOD THINGS ABOUT ZIMBU THE MONKEY. WHICH ONE OF YOU IS ZIMBU THE MONKEY?
THIS IS NOT THE PROUDEST MOMENT OF MY PROFESSIONAL CAREER.
© 1993 United Feature Syndicate, Inc.

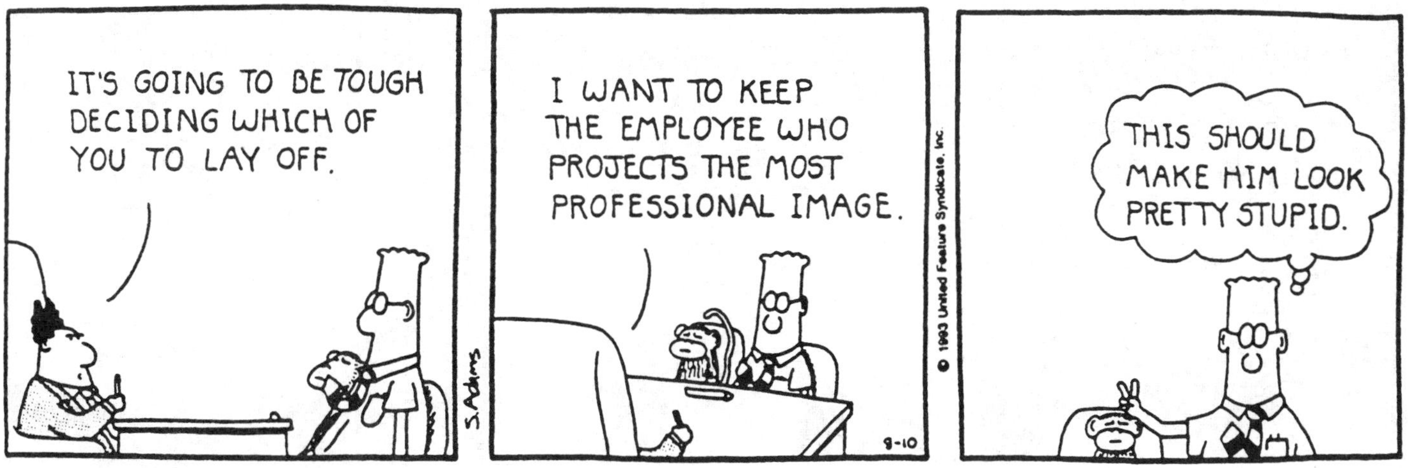
IT'S GOING TO BE TOUGH DECIDING WHICH OF YOU TO LAY OFF.
I WANT TO KEEP THE EMPLOYEE WHO PROJECTS THE MOST PROFESSIONAL IMAGE.
THIS SHOULD MAKE HIM LOOK PRETTY STUPID.
© 1993 United Feature Syndicate, Inc.

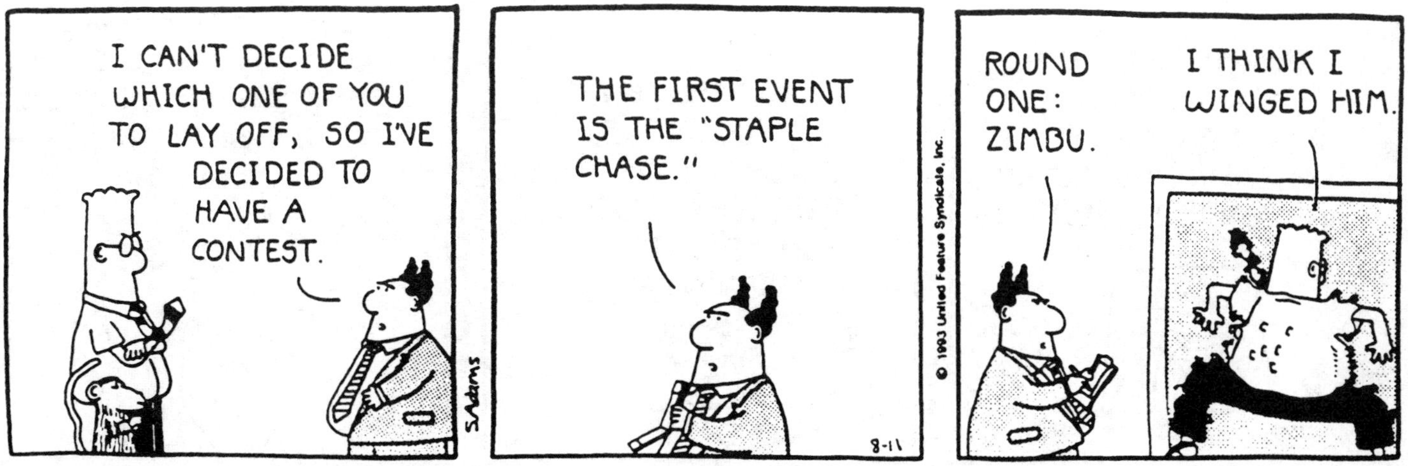
I CAN'T DECIDE WHICH ONE OF YOU TO LAY OFF, SO I'VE DECIDED TO HAVE A CONTEST.
THE FIRST EVENT IS THE "STAPLE CHASE."
ROUND ONE: ZIMBU.
I THINK I WINGED HIM.
© 1993 United Feature Syndicate, Inc.

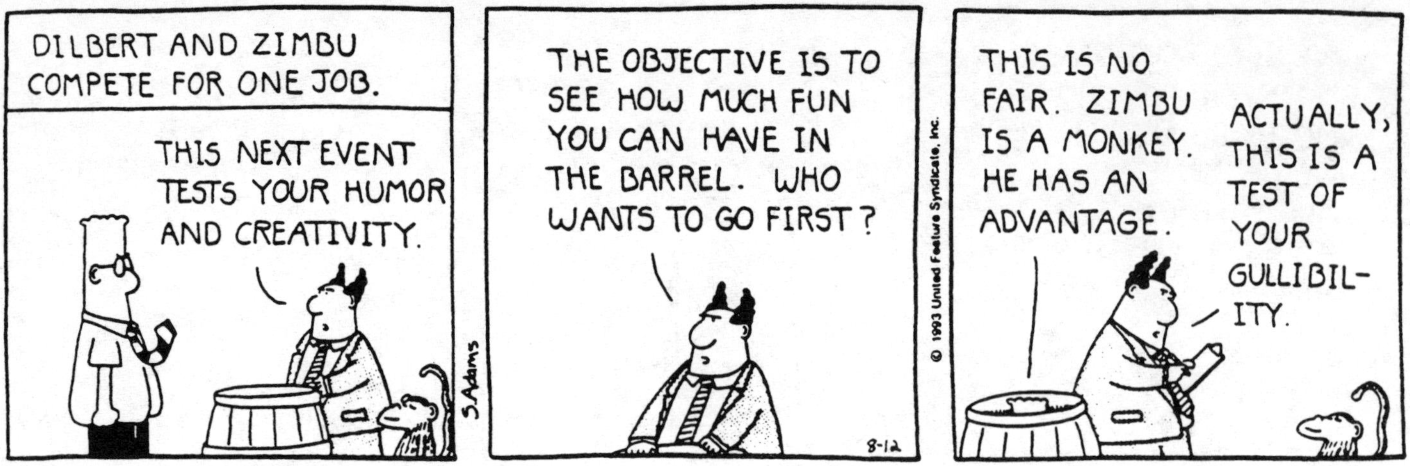
DILBERT AND ZIMBU COMPETE FOR ONE JOB.
THIS NEXT EVENT TESTS YOUR HUMOR AND CREATIVITY.
S.Adams
THE OBJECTIVE IS TO SEE HOW MUCH FUN YOU CAN HAVE IN THE BARREL. WHO WANTS TO GO FIRST?
8-12
© 1993 United Feature Syndicate, Inc.
THIS IS NO FAIR. ZIMBU IS A MONKEY. HE HAS AN ADVANTAGE.
ACTUALLY, THIS IS A TEST OF YOUR GULLIBIL-ITY.

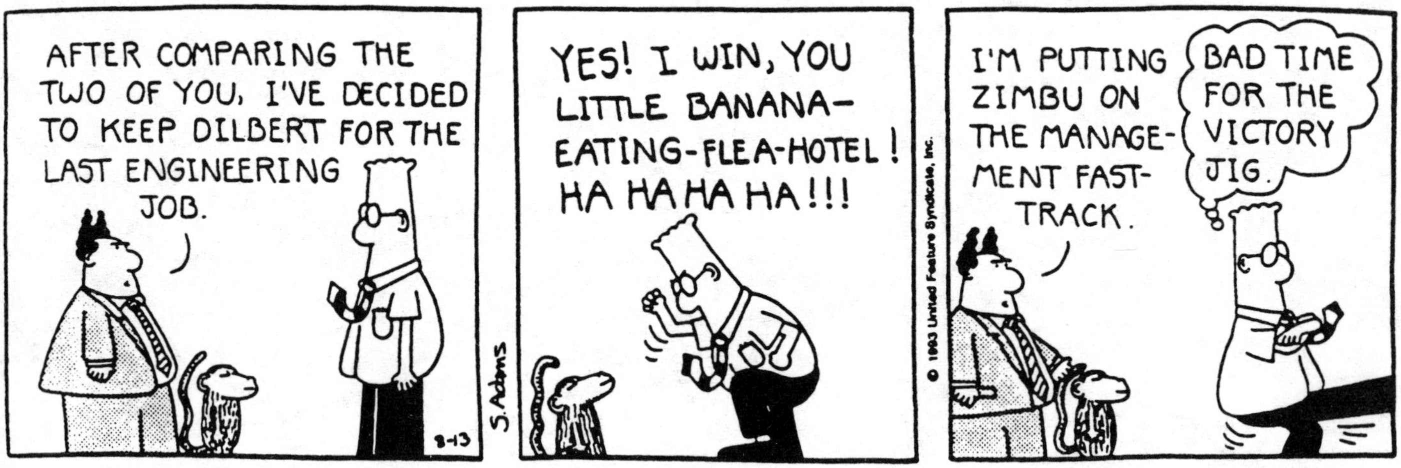
AFTER COMPARING THE TWO OF YOU, I'VE DECIDED TO KEEP DILBERT FOR THE LAST ENGINEERING JOB.
8-13
S.Adams
YES! I WIN, YOU LITTLE BANANA-EATING-FLEA-HOTEL! HA HA HA HA!!!
© 1993 United Feature Syndicate, Inc.
I'M PUTTING ZIMBU ON THE MANAGE-MENT FAST-TRACK.
BAD TIME FOR THE VICTORY JIG.

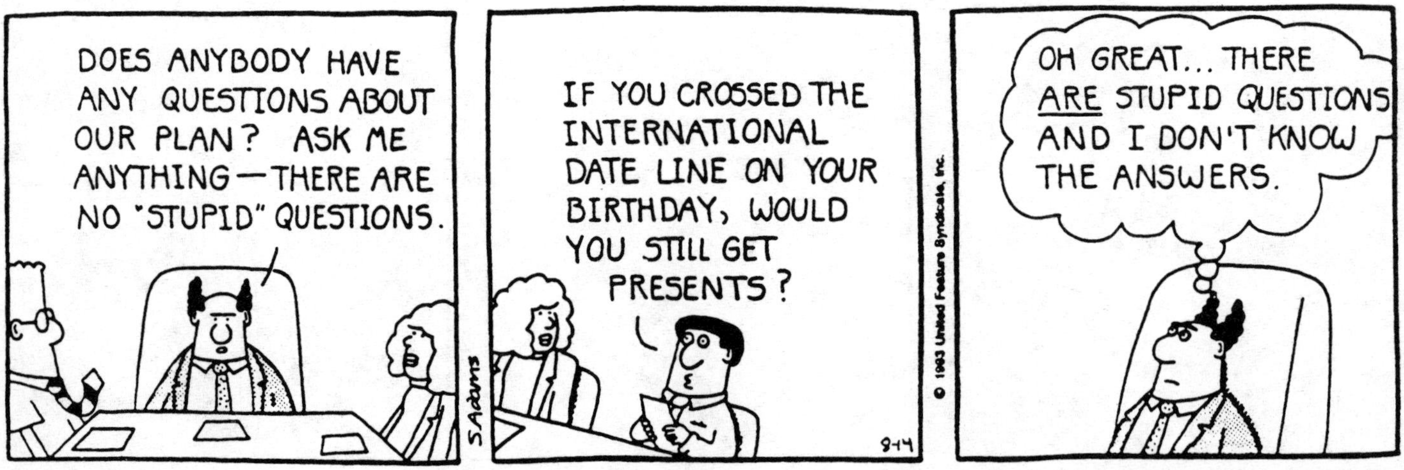
DOES ANYBODY HAVE ANY QUESTIONS ABOUT OUR PLAN? ASK ME ANYTHING—THERE ARE NO "STUPID" QUESTIONS.
S.Adams
IF YOU CROSSED THE INTERNATIONAL DATE LINE ON YOUR BIRTHDAY, WOULD YOU STILL GET PRESENTS?
8-14
© 1993 United Feature Syndicate, Inc.
OH GREAT... THERE ARE STUPID QUESTIONS AND I DON'T KNOW THE ANSWERS.

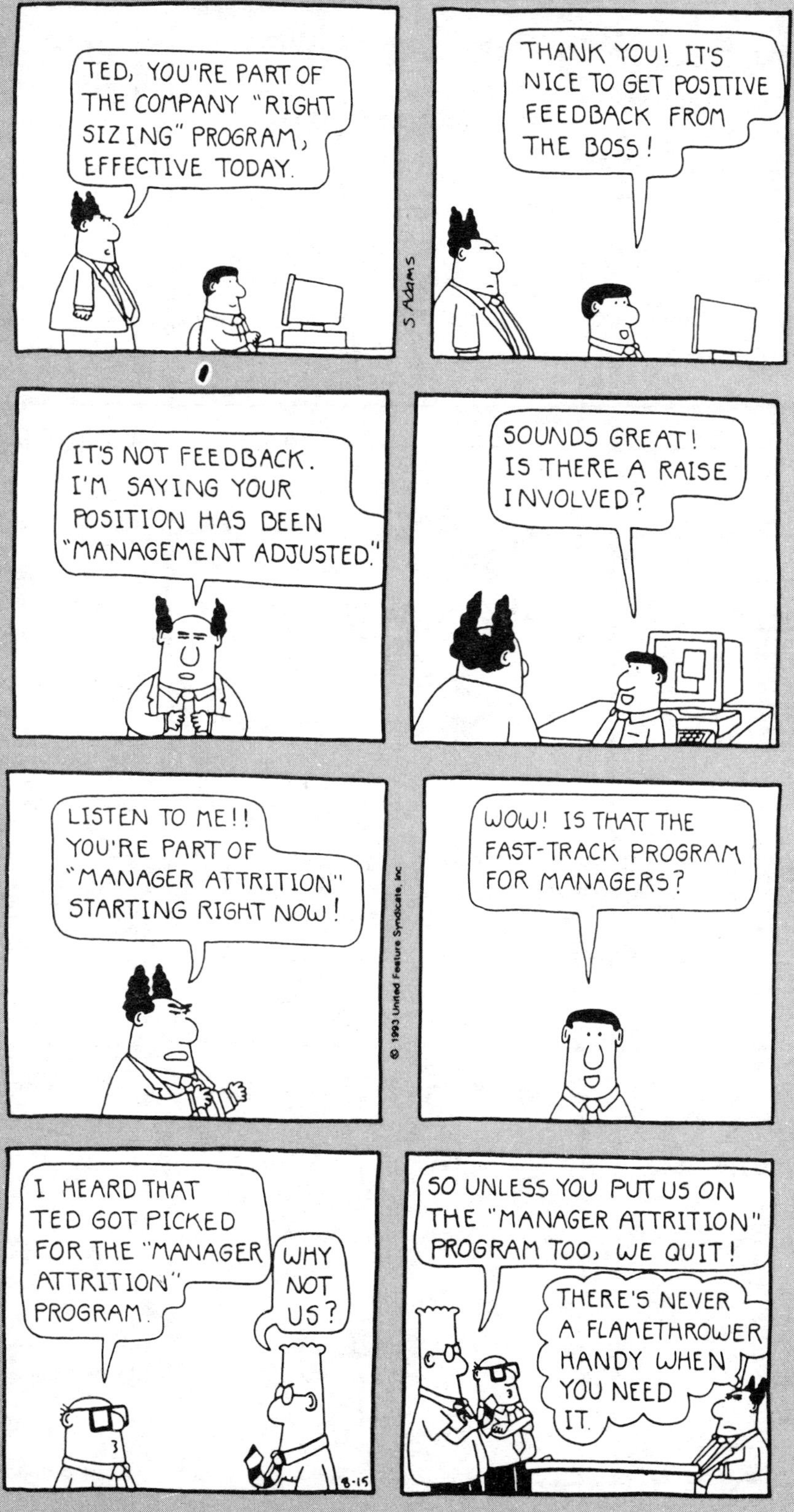
TED, YOU'RE PART OF THE COMPANY "RIGHT SIZING" PROGRAM, EFFECTIVE TODAY.
S Adams
THANK YOU! IT'S NICE TO GET POSITIVE FEEDBACK FROM THE BOSS!
IT'S NOT FEEDBACK. I'M SAYING YOUR POSITION HAS BEEN "MANAGEMENT ADJUSTED."
SOUNDS GREAT! IS THERE A RAISE INVOLVED?
LISTEN TO ME!! YOU'RE PART OF "MANAGER ATTRITION" STARTING RIGHT NOW!
© 1993 United Feature Syndicate, Inc
WOW! IS THAT THE FAST-TRACK PROGRAM FOR MANAGERS?
I HEARD THAT TED GOT PICKED FOR THE "MANAGER ATTRITION" PROGRAM.
WHY NOT US?
8-15
SO UNLESS YOU PUT US ON THE "MANAGER ATTRITION" PROGRAM TOO, WE QUIT!
THERE'S NEVER A FLAMETHROWER HANDY WHEN YOU NEED IT.

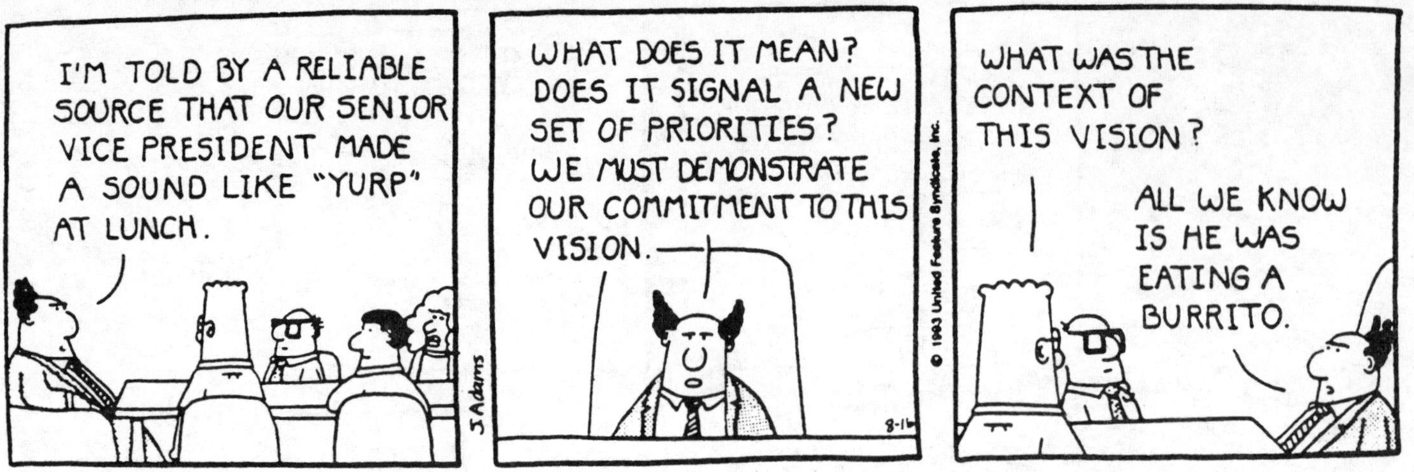
I'M TOLD BY A RELIABLE SOURCE THAT OUR SENIOR VICE PRESIDENT MADE A SOUND LIKE "YURP" AT LUNCH.
S. Adams
WHAT DOES IT MEAN? DOES IT SIGNAL A NEW SET OF PRIORITIES? WE MUST DEMONSTRATE OUR COMMITMENT TO THIS VISION.
8-16
© 1993 United Feature Syndicate, Inc.
WHAT WAS THE CONTEXT OF THIS VISION?
ALL WE KNOW IS HE WAS EATING A BURRITO.

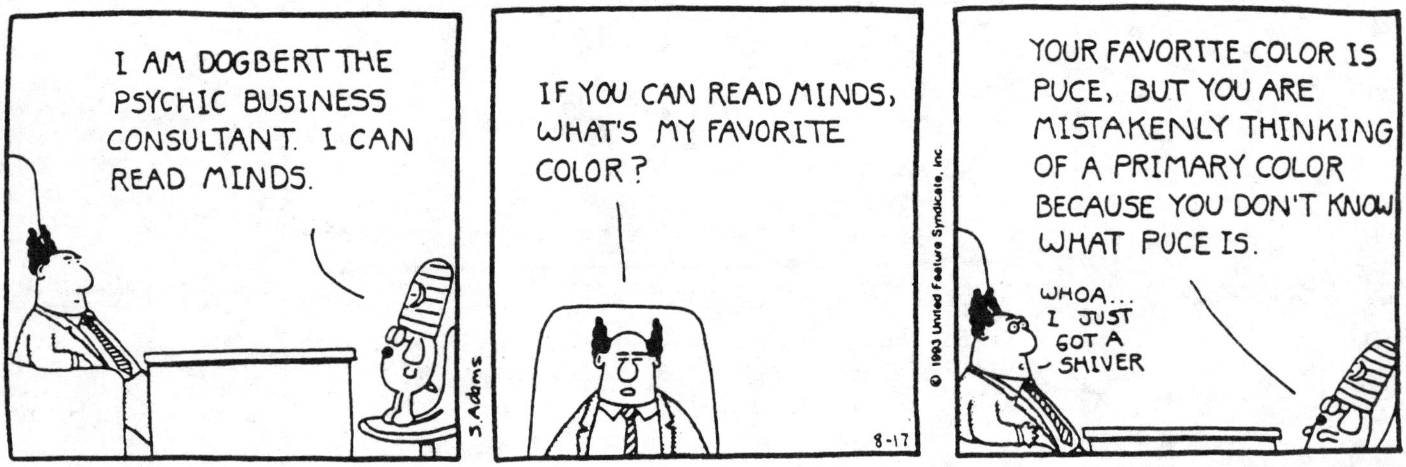
I AM DOGBERT THE PSYCHIC BUSINESS CONSULTANT. I CAN READ MINDS.
S. Adams
IF YOU CAN READ MINDS, WHAT'S MY FAVORITE COLOR?
8-17
© 1993 United Feature Syndicate, Inc.
YOUR FAVORITE COLOR IS PUCE, BUT YOU ARE MISTAKENLY THINKING OF A PRIMARY COLOR BECAUSE YOU DON'T KNOW WHAT PUCE IS.
WHOA... I JUST GOT A SHIVER

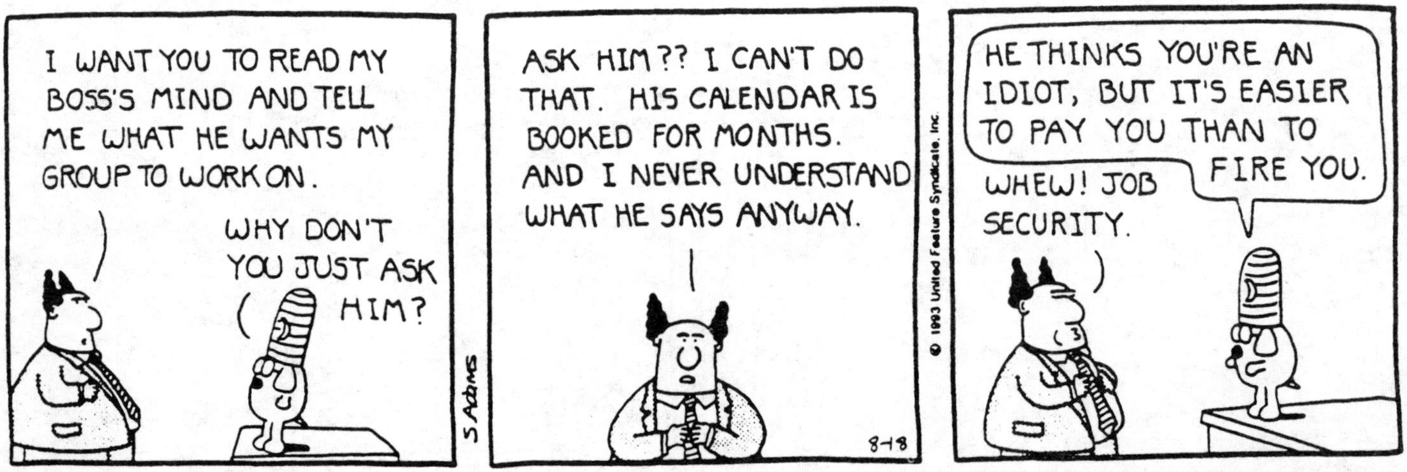
I WANT YOU TO READ MY BOSS'S MIND AND TELL ME WHAT HE WANTS MY GROUP TO WORK ON.
WHY DON'T YOU JUST ASK HIM?
S. Adams
ASK HIM?? I CAN'T DO THAT. HIS CALENDAR IS BOOKED FOR MONTHS. AND I NEVER UNDERSTAND WHAT HE SAYS ANYWAY.
8-18
© 1993 United Feature Syndicate, Inc.
HE THINKS YOU'RE AN IDIOT, BUT IT'S EASIER TO PAY YOU THAN TO FIRE YOU.
WHEW! JOB SECURITY.

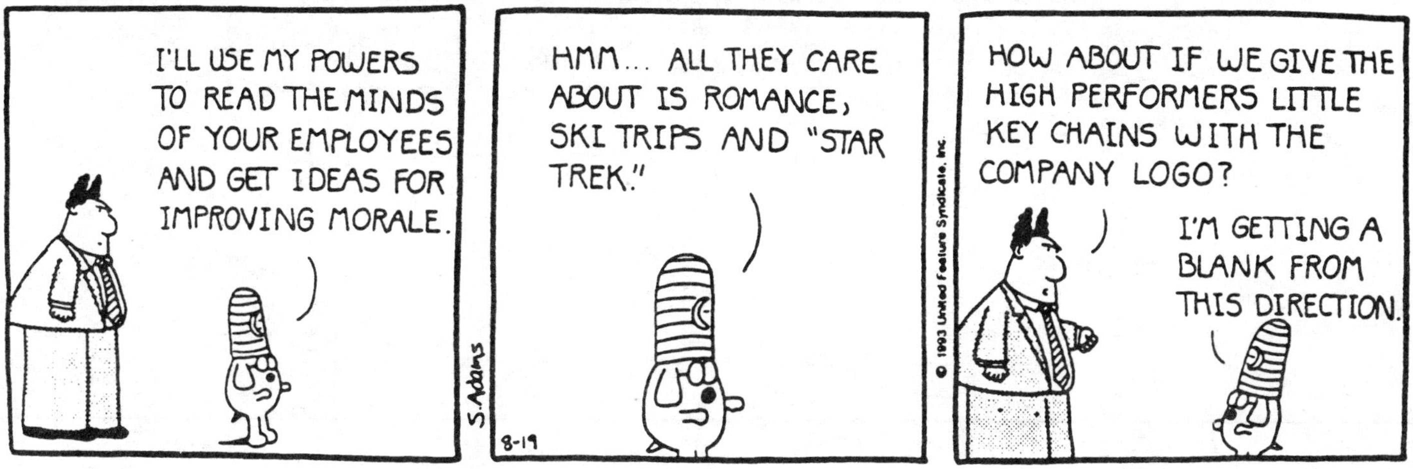
I'LL USE MY POWERS TO READ THE MINDS OF YOUR EMPLOYEES AND GET IDEAS FOR IMPROVING MORALE.
HMM... ALL THEY CARE ABOUT IS ROMANCE, SKI TRIPS AND "STAR TREK."
HOW ABOUT IF WE GIVE THE HIGH PERFORMERS LITTLE KEY CHAINS WITH THE COMPANY LOGO?
I'M GETTING A BLANK FROM THIS DIRECTION.

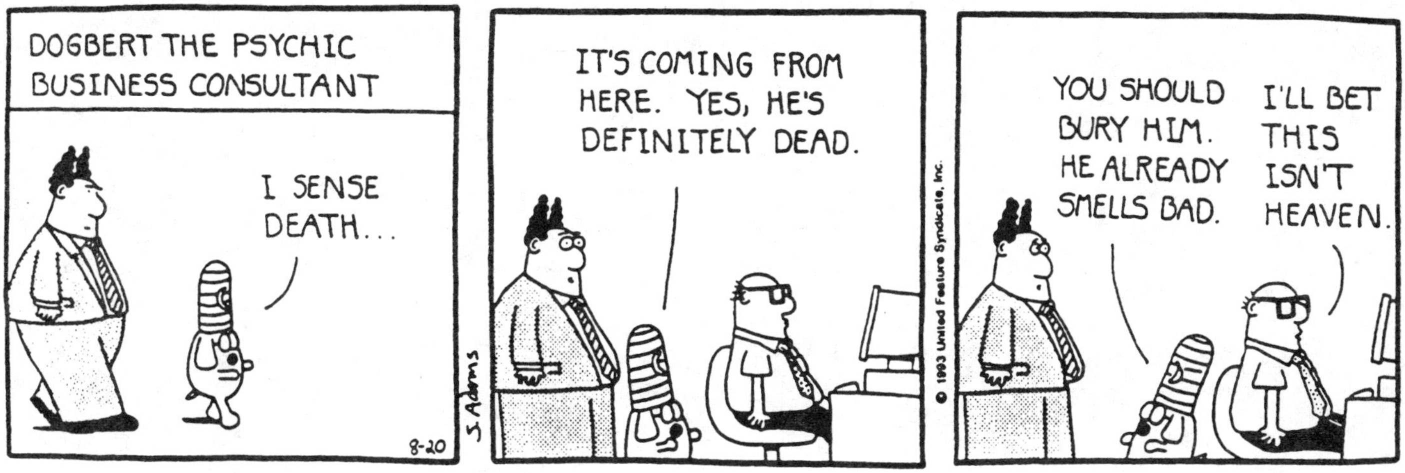
DOGBERT THE PSYCHIC BUSINESS CONSULTANT
I SENSE DEATH...
IT'S COMING FROM HERE. YES, HE'S DEFINITELY DEAD.
YOU SHOULD BURY HIM. HE ALREADY SMELLS BAD.
I'LL BET THIS ISN'T HEAVEN.

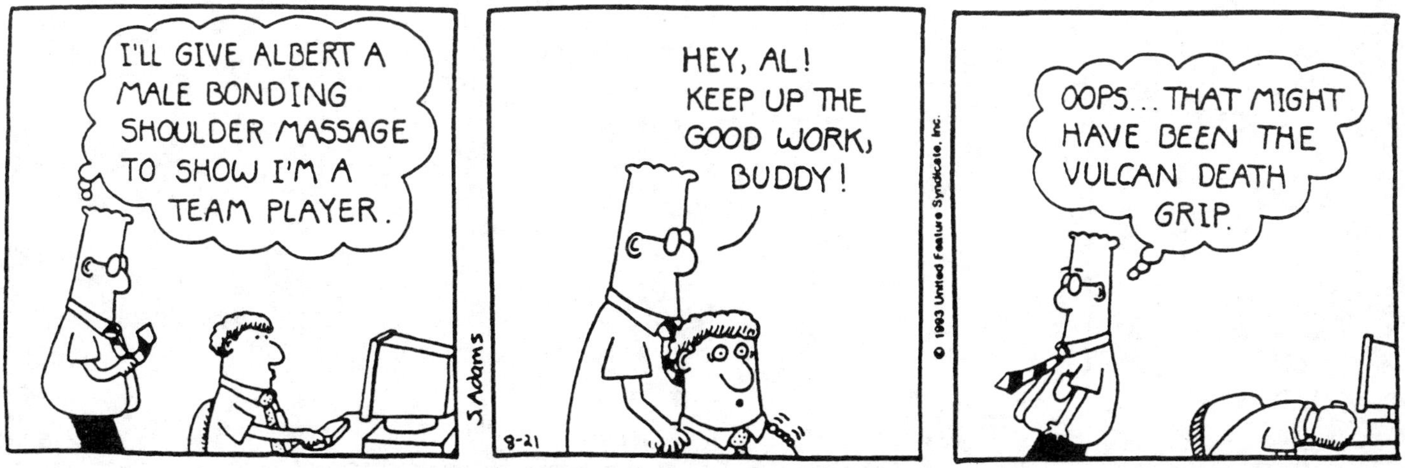
I'LL GIVE ALBERT A MALE BONDING SHOULDER MASSAGE TO SHOW I'M A TEAM PLAYER.
HEY, AL! KEEP UP THE GOOD WORK, BUDDY!
OOPS... THAT MIGHT HAVE BEEN THE VULCAN DEATH GRIP.

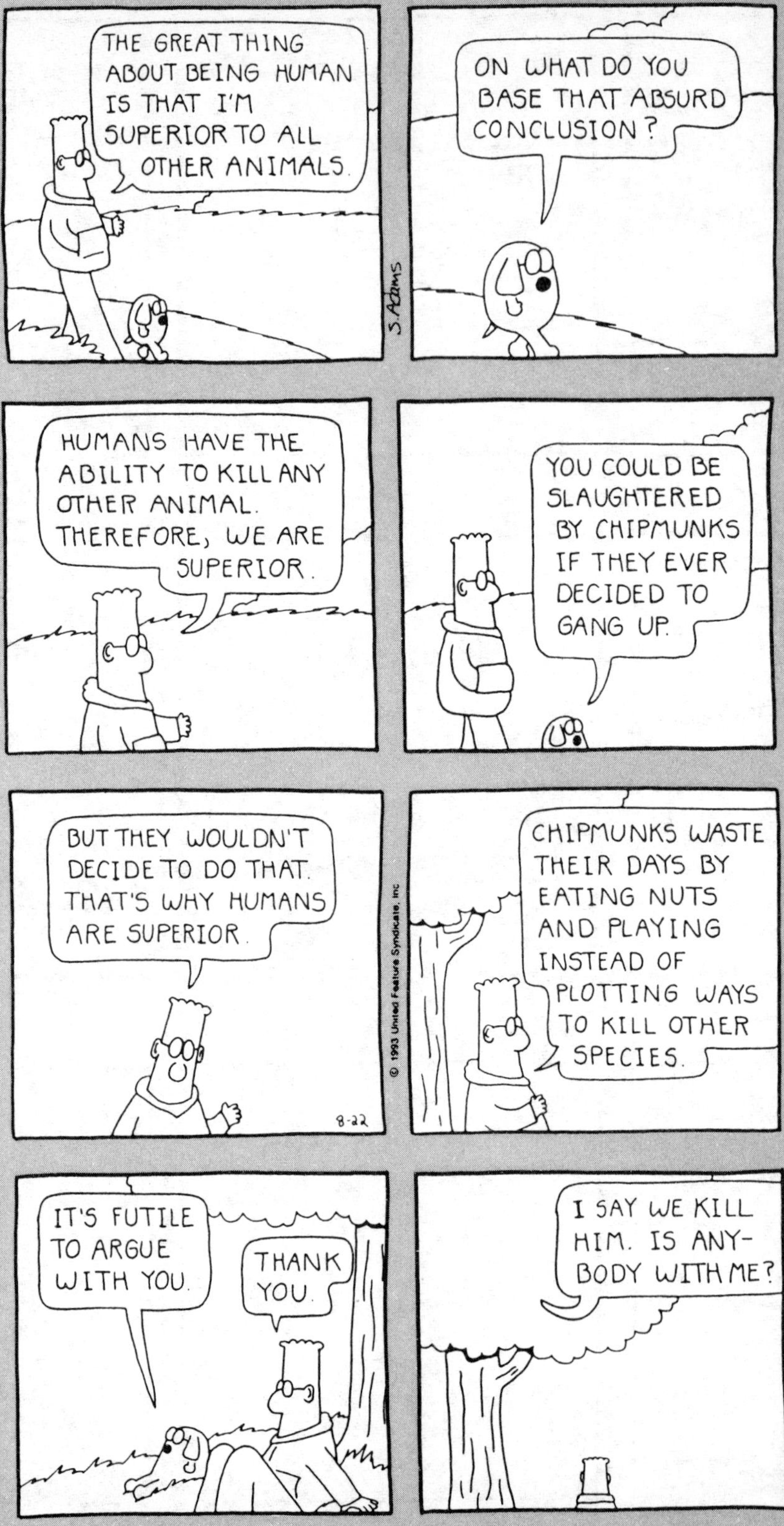
THE GREAT THING ABOUT BEING HUMAN IS THAT I'M SUPERIOR TO ALL OTHER ANIMALS.
S. Adams
ON WHAT DO YOU BASE THAT ABSURD CONCLUSION?
HUMANS HAVE THE ABILITY TO KILL ANY OTHER ANIMAL. THEREFORE, WE ARE SUPERIOR.
YOU COULD BE SLAUGHTERED BY CHIPMUNKS IF THEY EVER DECIDED TO GANG UP.
BUT THEY WOULDN'T DECIDE TO DO THAT. THAT'S WHY HUMANS ARE SUPERIOR.
8-22
© 1993 United Feature Syndicate, Inc
CHIPMUNKS WASTE THEIR DAYS BY EATING NUTS AND PLAYING INSTEAD OF PLOTTING WAYS TO KILL OTHER SPECIES.
IT'S FUTILE TO ARGUE WITH YOU.
THANK YOU.
I SAY WE KILL HIM. IS ANYBODY WITH ME?

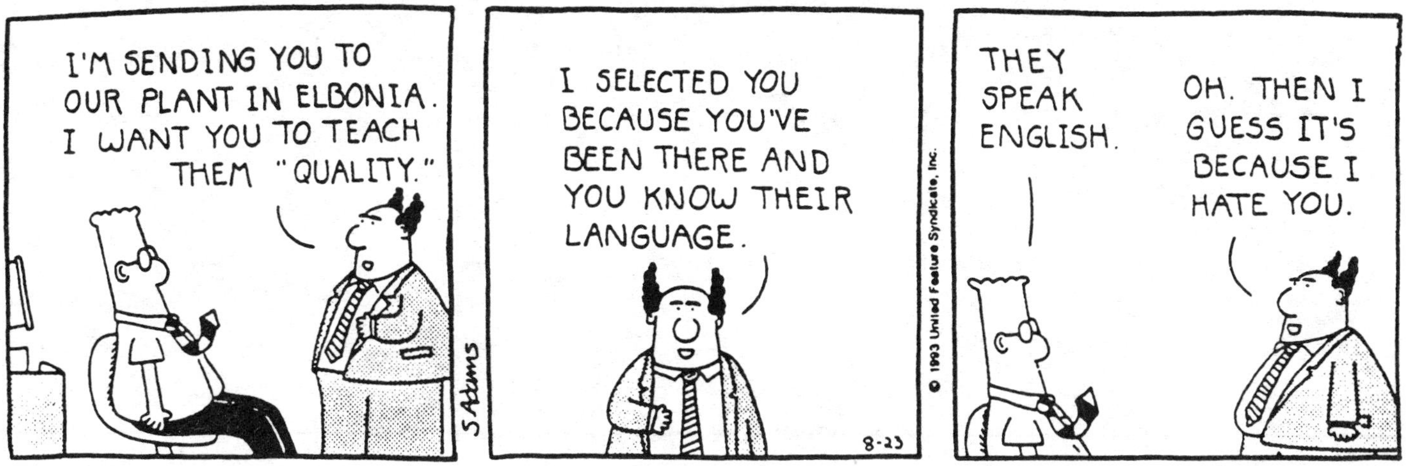
I'M SENDING YOU TO OUR PLANT IN ELBONIA. I WANT YOU TO TEACH THEM "QUALITY."
S. Adams
I SELECTED YOU BECAUSE YOU'VE BEEN THERE AND YOU KNOW THEIR LANGUAGE.
8-23
© 1993 United Feature Syndicate, Inc.
THEY SPEAK ENGLISH.
OH. THEN I GUESS IT'S BECAUSE I HATE YOU.

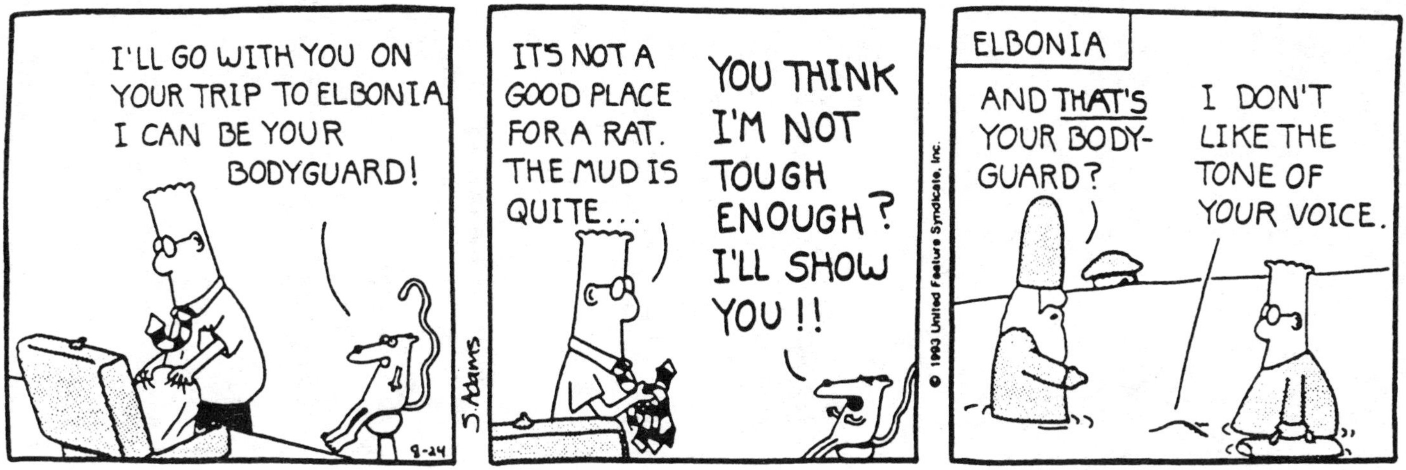
I'LL GO WITH YOU ON YOUR TRIP TO ELBONIA. I CAN BE YOUR BODYGUARD!
8-24
S. Adams
IT'S NOT A GOOD PLACE FOR A RAT. THE MUD IS QUITE...
YOU THINK I'M NOT TOUGH ENOUGH? I'LL SHOW YOU!!
© 1993 United Feature Syndicate, Inc.
ELBONIA
AND THAT'S YOUR BODY-GUARD?
I DON'T LIKE THE TONE OF YOUR VOICE.

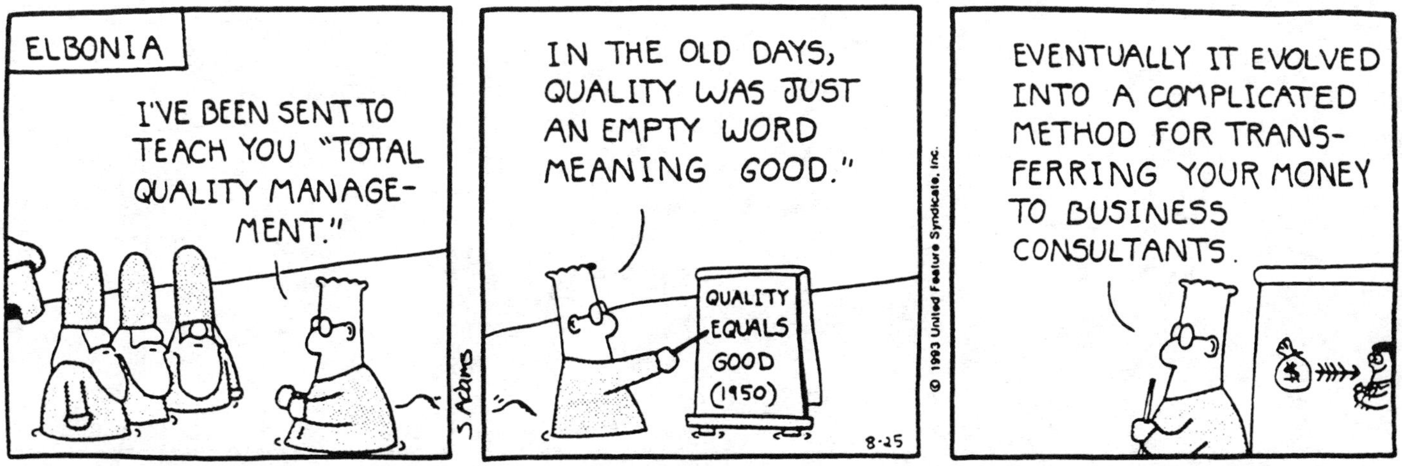
ELBONIA
I'VE BEEN SENT TO TEACH YOU "TOTAL QUALITY MANAGE-MENT."
S. Adams
IN THE OLD DAYS, QUALITY WAS JUST AN EMPTY WORD MEANING "GOOD."
QUALITY EQUALS GOOD (1950)
8-25
© 1993 United Feature Syndicate, Inc.
EVENTUALLY IT EVOLVED INTO A COMPLICATED METHOD FOR TRANS-FERRING YOUR MONEY TO BUSINESS CONSULTANTS.

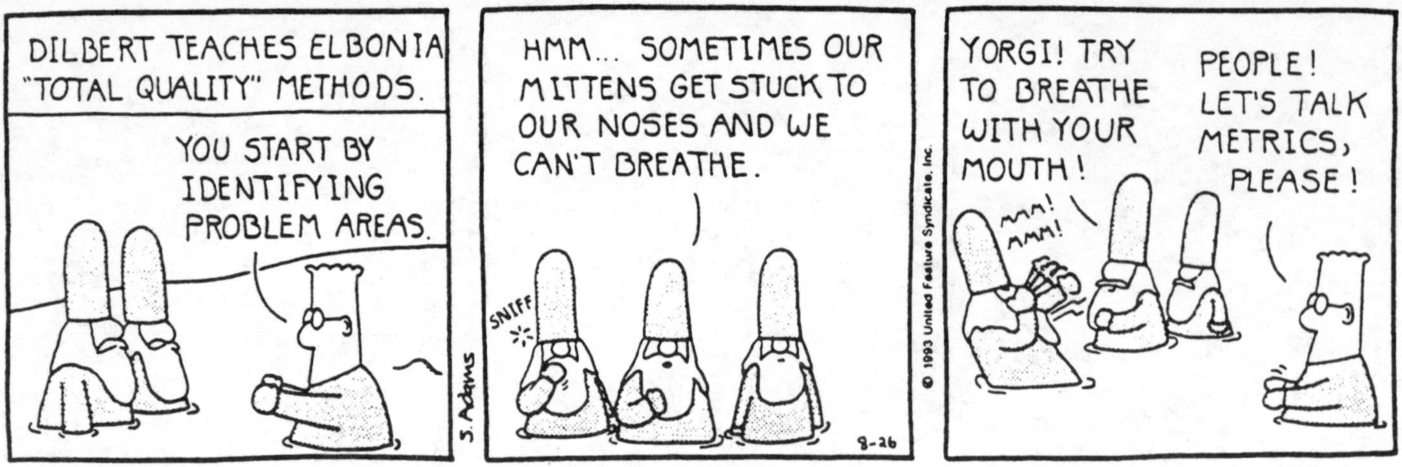
DILBERT TEACHES ELBONIA "TOTAL QUALITY" METHODS.
YOU START BY IDENTIFYING PROBLEM AREAS.
S. Adams
HMM... SOMETIMES OUR MITTENS GET STUCK TO OUR NOSES AND WE CAN'T BREATHE.
SNIFF
8-26
© 1993 United Feature Syndicate, Inc.
YORGI! TRY TO BREATHE WITH YOUR MOUTH!
MMM! MMM!
PEOPLE! LET'S TALK METRICS, PLEASE!

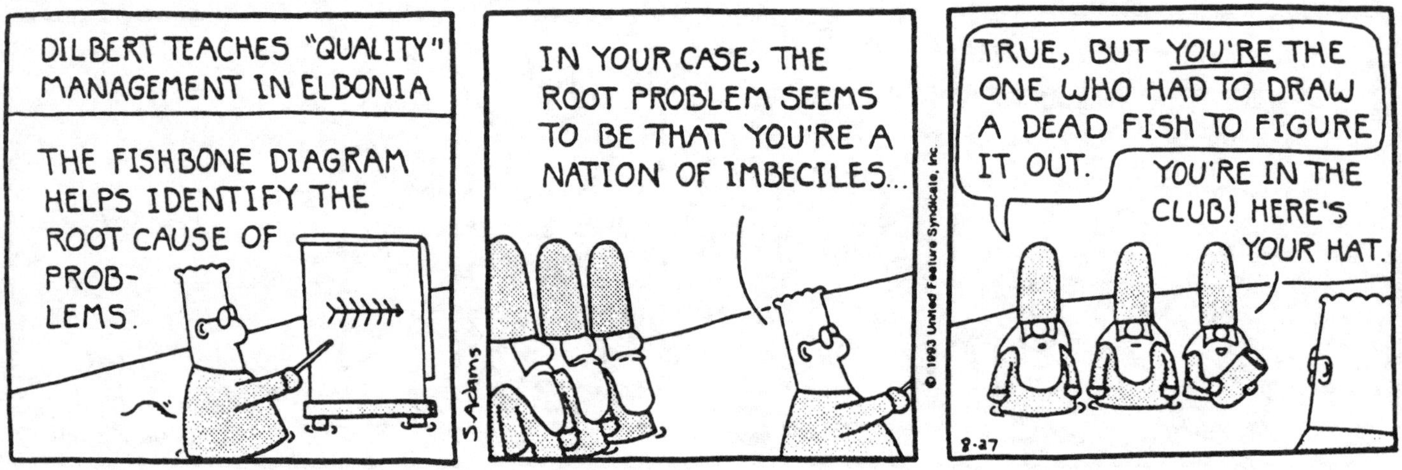
DILBERT TEACHES "QUALITY" MANAGEMENT IN ELBONIA
THE FISHBONE DIAGRAM HELPS IDENTIFY THE ROOT CAUSE OF PROB-LEMS.
S. Adams
IN YOUR CASE, THE ROOT PROBLEM SEEMS TO BE THAT YOU'RE A NATION OF IMBECILES...
© 1993 United Feature Syndicate, Inc.
TRUE, BUT YOU'RE THE ONE WHO HAD TO DRAW A DEAD FISH TO FIGURE IT OUT.
YOU'RE IN THE CLUB! HERE'S YOUR HAT.
8-27

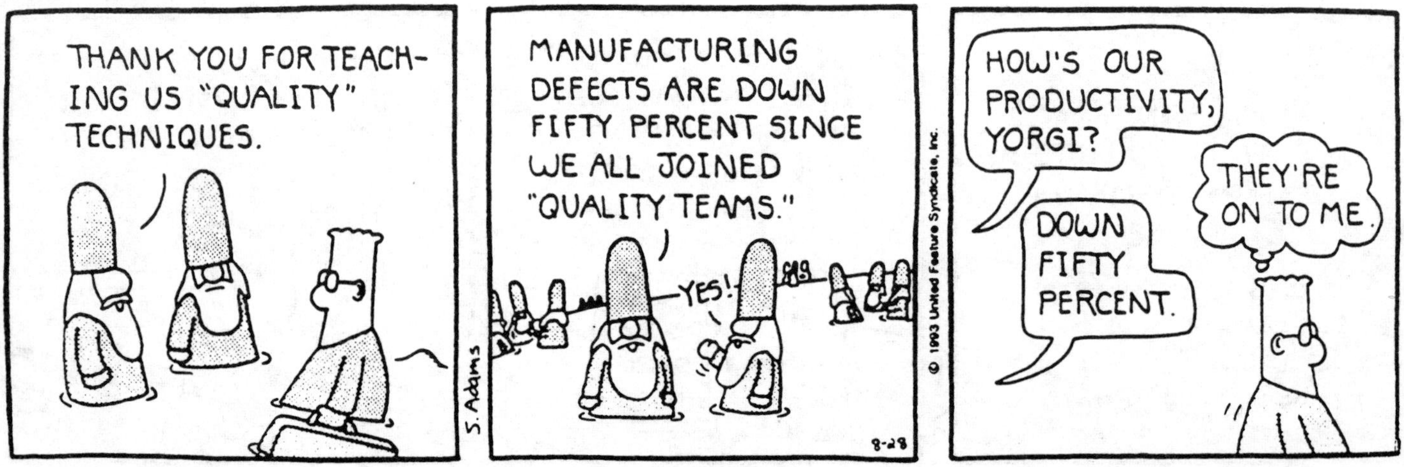
THANK YOU FOR TEACH-ING US "QUALITY" TECHNIQUES.
S. Adams
MANUFACTURING DEFECTS ARE DOWN FIFTY PERCENT SINCE WE ALL JOINED "QUALITY TEAMS."
YES!
8-28
© 1993 United Feature Syndicate, Inc.
HOW'S OUR PRODUCTIVITY, YORGI?
DOWN FIFTY PERCENT.
THEY'RE ON TO ME.

WHAT WE NEED IS MORE COMMUNICATION BETWEEN MANAGEMENT AND... WHATEVER YOU ARE.
S. Adams
SO, ONCE A MONTH I'LL HAVE "OPEN DOOR DAY."
YOU CAN DROP BY AND WHINE ABOUT ANYTHING YOU WANT.
I'LL LISTEN WITH A CONCERNED EXPRESSION LIKE THIS.
THEN I'LL EXPLAIN WHY EVERYTHING IS FINE JUST THE WAY IT IS.
© 1993 United Feature Syndicate, Inc
THEN, MORALE WILL IMPROVE, PROFITS WILL SKYROCKET AND MY STOCK OPTIONS WILL MAKE ME RICH!!
8-29
MAY I MAKE SOME OBSERVATIONS ABOUT YOUR PLAN?
UH... FORGET IT.
DO YOU NOTICE HOW CONCERNED I LOOK?

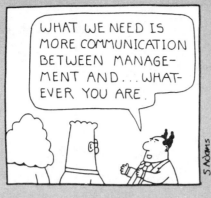

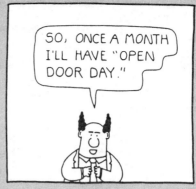

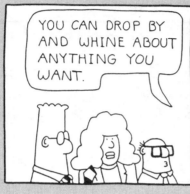

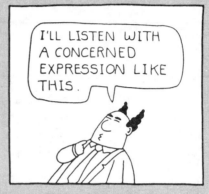

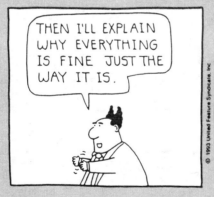

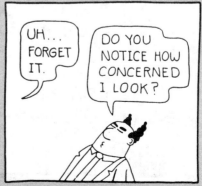

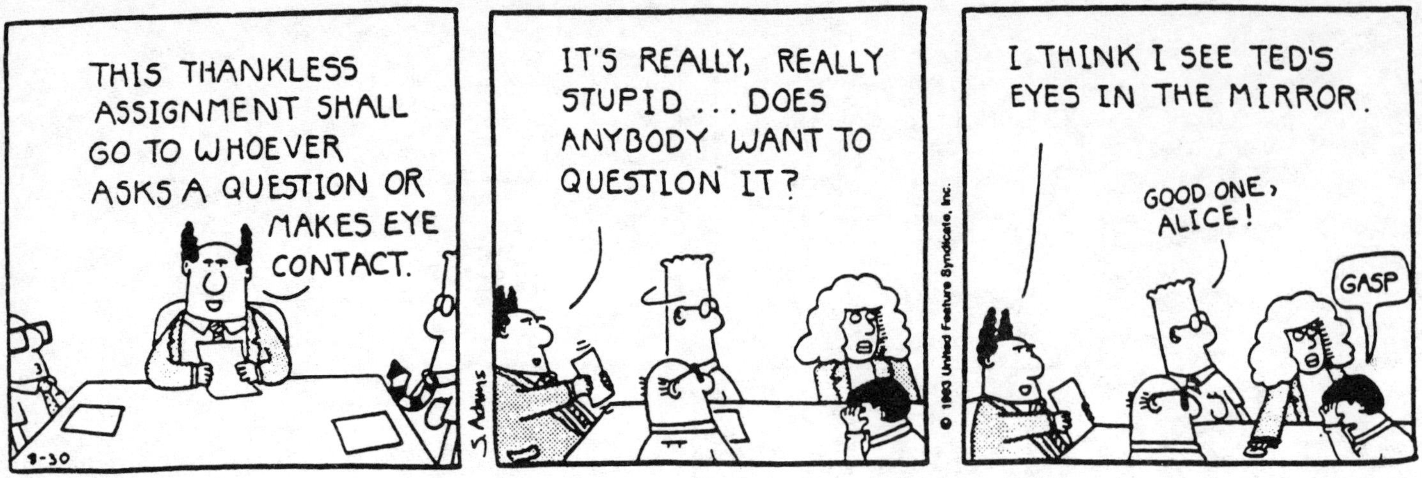
THIS THANKLESS ASSIGNMENT SHALL GO TO WHOEVER ASKS A QUESTION OR MAKES EYE CONTACT.
8-30
S. Adams
IT'S REALLY, REALLY STUPID ... DOES ANYBODY WANT TO QUESTION IT?
© 1993 United Feature Syndicate, Inc.
I THINK I SEE TED'S EYES IN THE MIRROR.
GOOD ONE, ALICE!
GASP

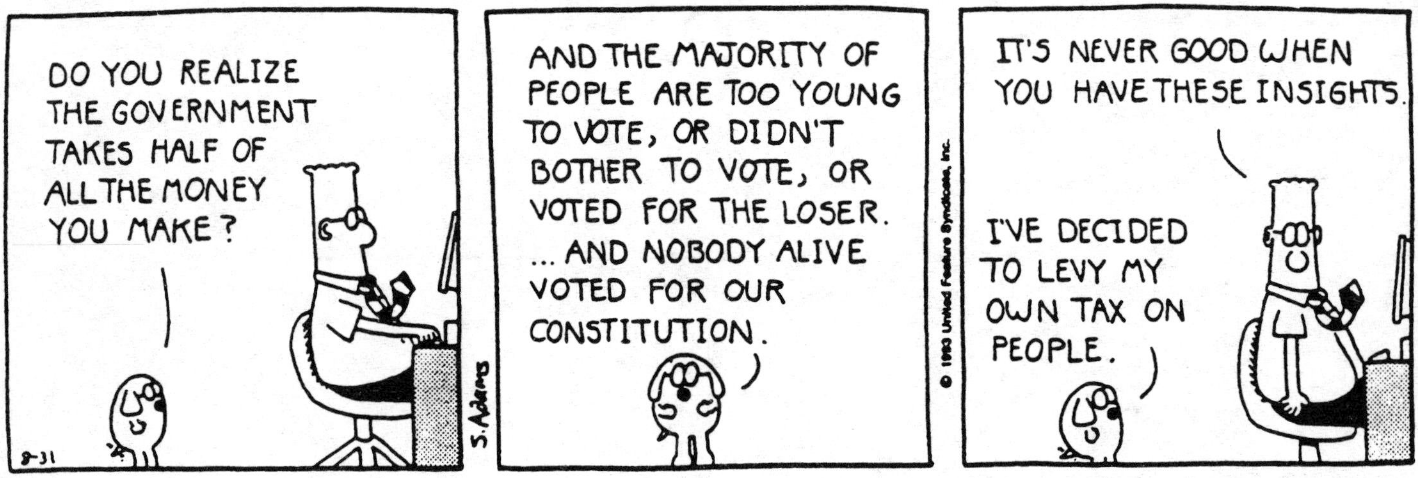
DO YOU REALIZE THE GOVERNMENT TAKES HALF OF ALL THE MONEY YOU MAKE?
8-31
S. Adams
AND THE MAJORITY OF PEOPLE ARE TOO YOUNG TO VOTE, OR DIDN'T BOTHER TO VOTE, OR VOTED FOR THE LOSER. ... AND NOBODY ALIVE VOTED FOR OUR CONSTITUTION.
© 1993 United Feature Syndicate, Inc.
IT'S NEVER GOOD WHEN YOU HAVE THESE INSIGHTS.
I'VE DECIDED TO LEVY MY OWN TAX ON PEOPLE.

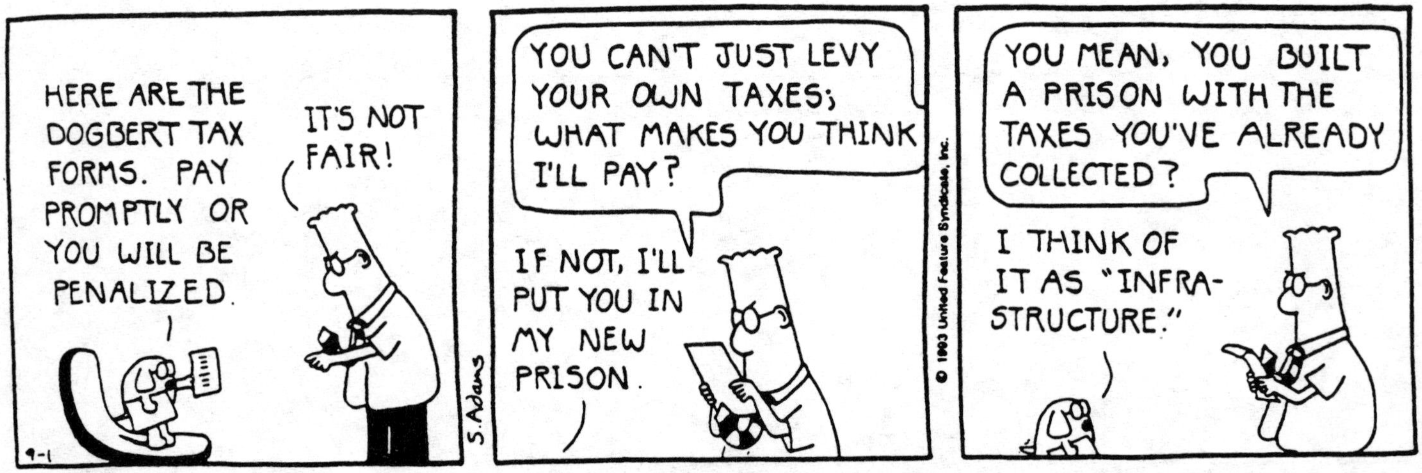
HERE ARE THE DOGBERT TAX FORMS. PAY PROMPTLY OR YOU WILL BE PENALIZED.
IT'S NOT FAIR!
9-1
S. Adams
YOU CAN'T JUST LEVY YOUR OWN TAXES; WHAT MAKES YOU THINK I'LL PAY?
IF NOT, I'LL PUT YOU IN MY NEW PRISON.
© 1993 United Feature Syndicate, Inc.
YOU MEAN, YOU BUILT A PRISON WITH THE TAXES YOU'VE ALREADY COLLECTED?
I THINK OF IT AS "INFRA-STRUCTURE."

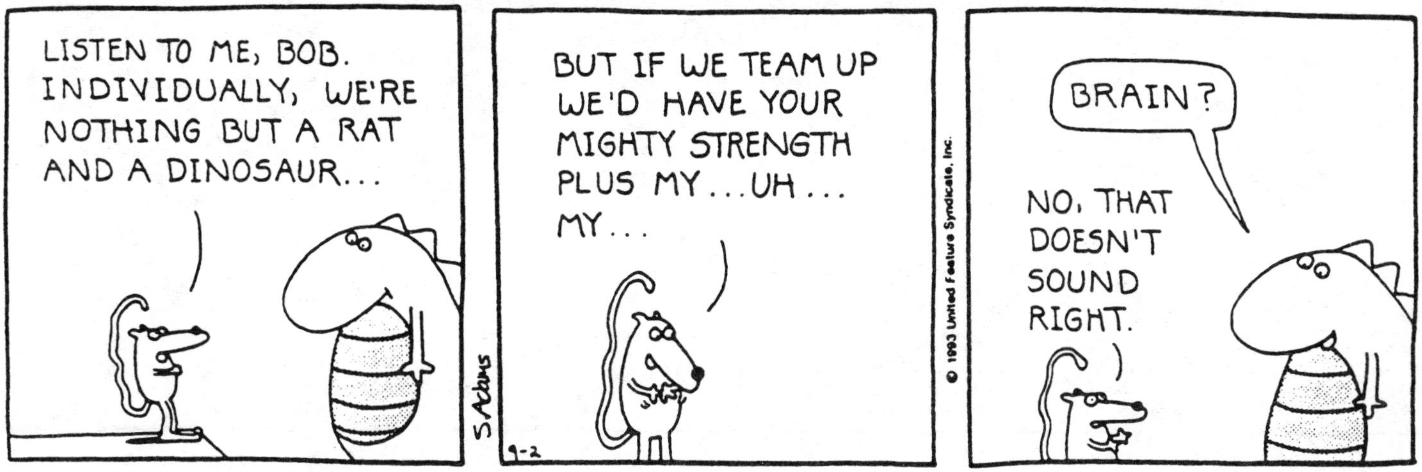
LISTEN TO ME, BOB. INDIVIDUALLY, WE'RE NOTHING BUT A RAT AND A DINOSAUR...
S. Adams
9-2
BUT IF WE TEAM UP WE'D HAVE YOUR MIGHTY STRENGTH PLUS MY...UH... MY...
© 1993 United Feature Syndicate, Inc.
BRAIN?
NO, THAT DOESN'T SOUND RIGHT.

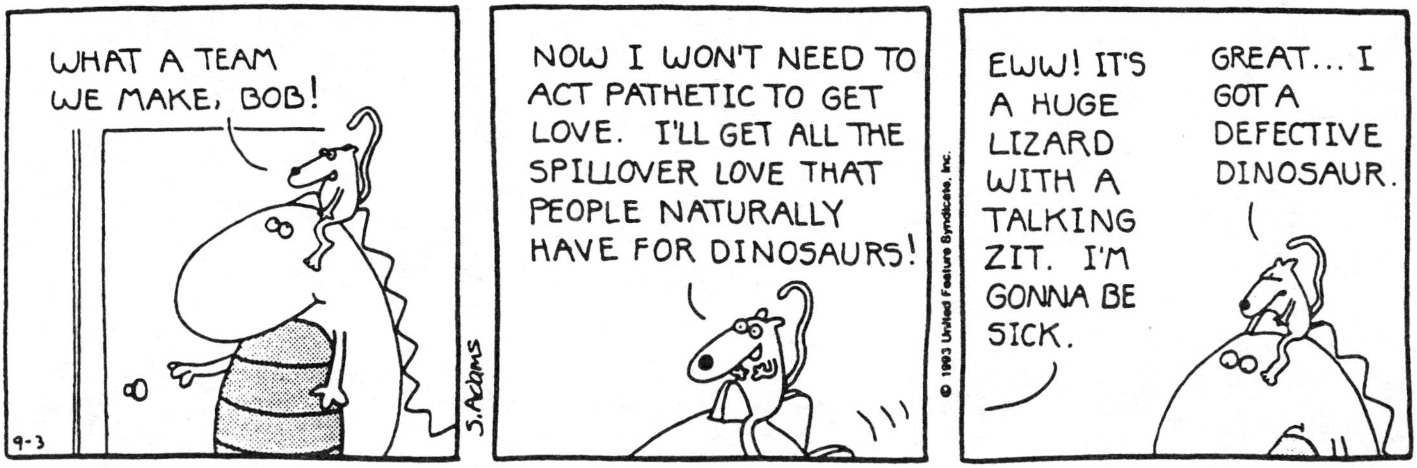
WHAT A TEAM WE MAKE, BOB!
9-3
S. Adams
NOW I WON'T NEED TO ACT PATHETIC TO GET LOVE. I'LL GET ALL THE SPILLOVER LOVE THAT PEOPLE NATURALLY HAVE FOR DINOSAURS!
© 1993 United Feature Syndicate, Inc.
EWW! IT'S A HUGE LIZARD WITH A TALKING ZIT. I'M GONNA BE SICK.
GREAT... I GOT A DEFECTIVE DINOSAUR.

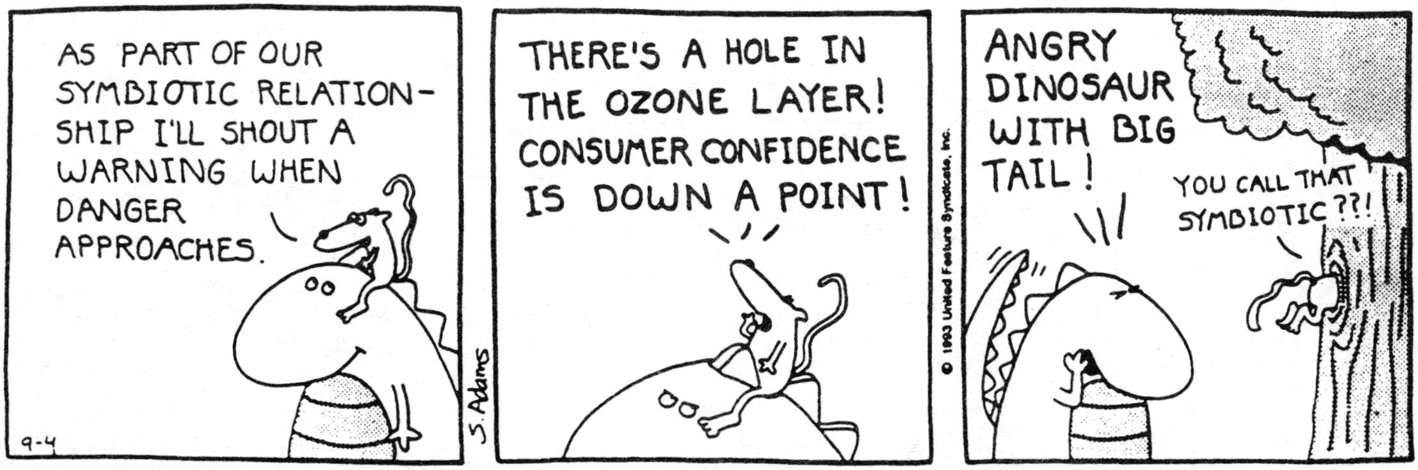
AS PART OF OUR SYMBIOTIC RELATIONSHIP I'LL SHOUT A WARNING WHEN DANGER APPROACHES.
9-4
S. Adams
THERE'S A HOLE IN THE OZONE LAYER! CONSUMER CONFIDENCE IS DOWN A POINT!
© 1993 United Feature Syndicate, Inc.
ANGRY DINOSAUR WITH BIG TAIL!
YOU CALL THAT SYMBIOTIC??!

I'M BUILDING A PERMANENT FILE OF ALL THE STUPID THINGS YOU SAY.
S Adams
AT LEAST IT'S ONLY A FEW PAGES LONG.
THIS IS JUST THE TABLE OF CONTENTS.
THE FULL DATABASE WILL BE COMPRESSED ON CD ROMS.
I HIRED JUAN AND HIS CREW TO DESIGN THE SYSTEM AND TYPE IN THE DATA.
WE'RE WORKING OVER-TIME.
© 1993 United Feature Syndicate, Inc.
THE NEW COMPUTER CENTER IS DONE... WE HAD TO LEVEL THE NEIGHBOR'S GARAGE.
9-5
BY ANY CHANCE, ARE YOU STILL UPSET THAT I ASKED YOU TO FETCH MY SLIPPERS?
DID YOU GET THAT ONE?
I'LL NEED TO HIRE MORE PEOPLE.

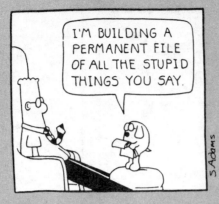

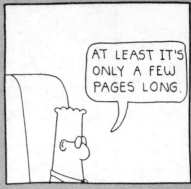

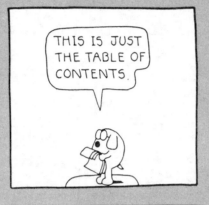

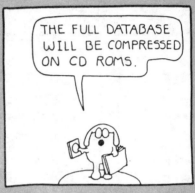

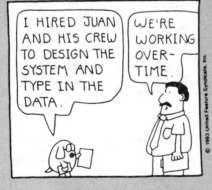

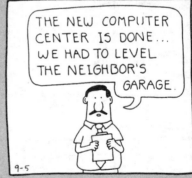

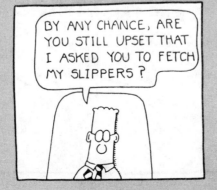

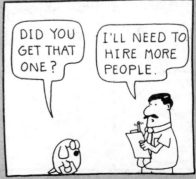

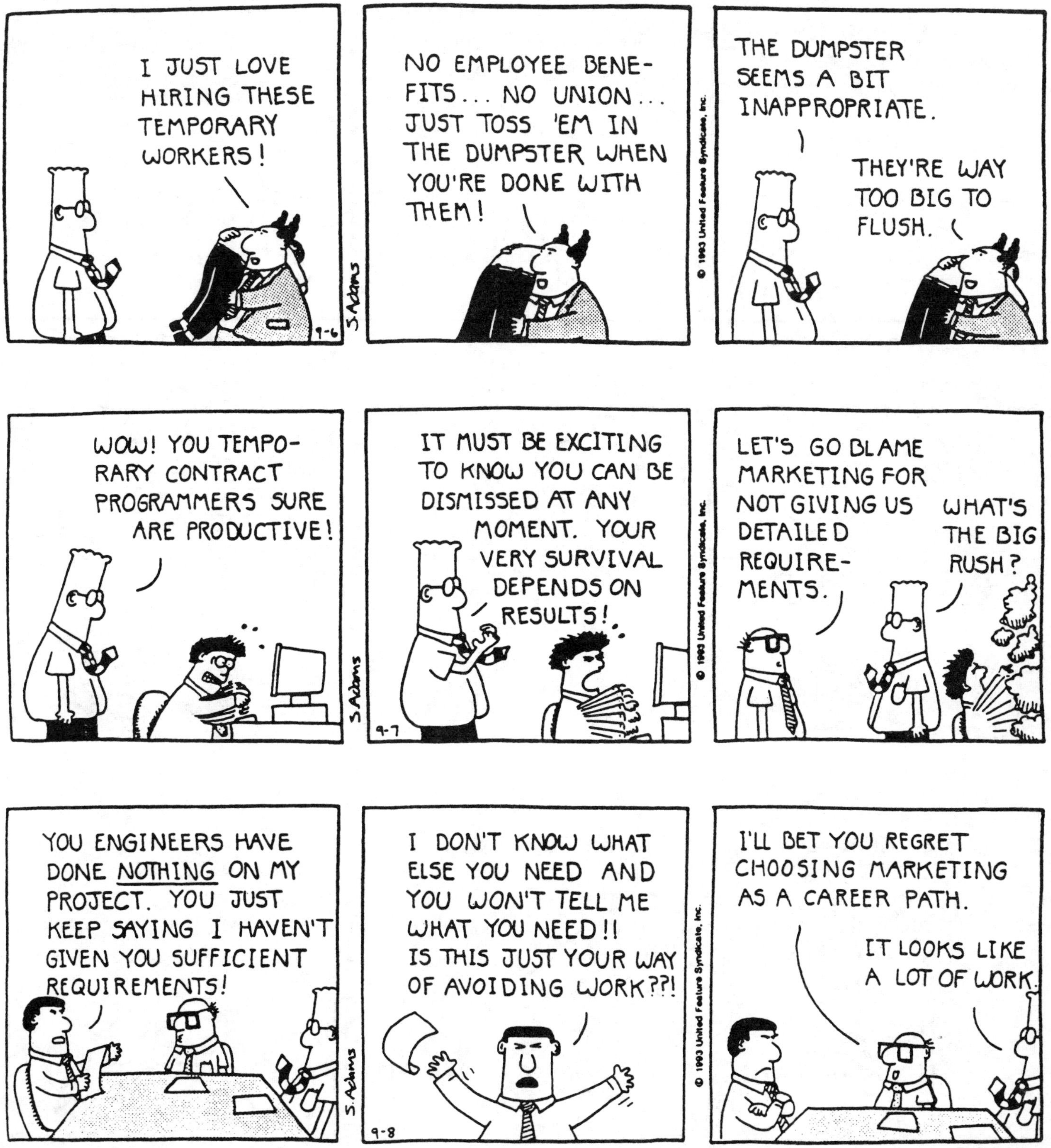
I JUST LOVE HIRING THESE TEMPORARY WORKERS!
9-6
S. Adams
NO EMPLOYEE BENEFITS... NO UNION... JUST TOSS 'EM IN THE DUMPSTER WHEN YOU'RE DONE WITH THEM!
© 1993 United Feature Syndicate, Inc.
THE DUMPSTER SEEMS A BIT INAPPROPRIATE.
THEY'RE WAY TOO BIG TO FLUSH.
WOW! YOU TEMPORARY CONTRACT PROGRAMMERS SURE ARE PRODUCTIVE!
S. Adams
9-7
IT MUST BE EXCITING TO KNOW YOU CAN BE DISMISSED AT ANY MOMENT. YOUR VERY SURVIVAL DEPENDS ON RESULTS!
© 1993 United Feature Syndicate, Inc.
LET'S GO BLAME MARKETING FOR NOT GIVING US DETAILED REQUIREMENTS.
WHAT'S THE BIG RUSH?
YOU ENGINEERS HAVE DONE NOTHING ON MY PROJECT. YOU JUST KEEP SAYING I HAVEN'T GIVEN YOU SUFFICIENT REQUIREMENTS!
S. Adams
9-8
I DON'T KNOW WHAT ELSE YOU NEED AND YOU WON'T TELL ME WHAT YOU NEED!! IS THIS JUST YOUR WAY OF AVOIDING WORK??!
© 1993 United Feature Syndicate, Inc.
I'LL BET YOU REGRET CHOOSING MARKETING AS A CAREER PATH.
IT LOOKS LIKE A LOT OF WORK.

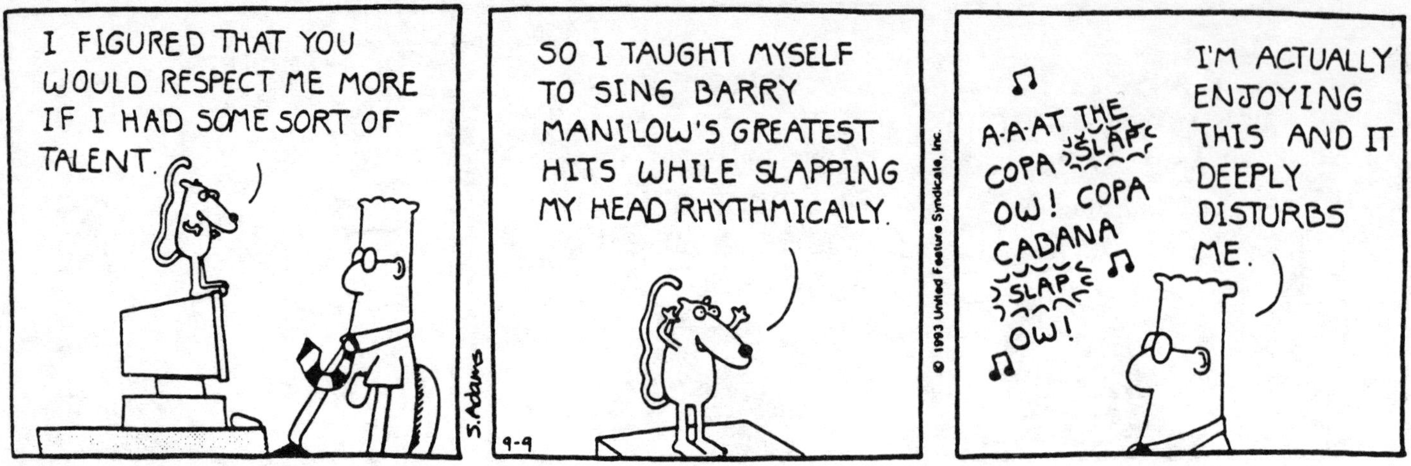
I FIGURED THAT YOU WOULD RESPECT ME MORE IF I HAD SOME SORT OF TALENT.
SO I TAUGHT MYSELF TO SING BARRY MANILOW'S GREATEST HITS WHILE SLAPPING MY HEAD RHYTHMICALLY.
A-A-AT THE COPA SLAP OW! COPA CABANA SLAP OW!
I'M ACTUALLY ENJOYING THIS AND IT DEEPLY DISTURBS ME.
S. Adams
9-9
© 1993 United Feature Syndicate, Inc.

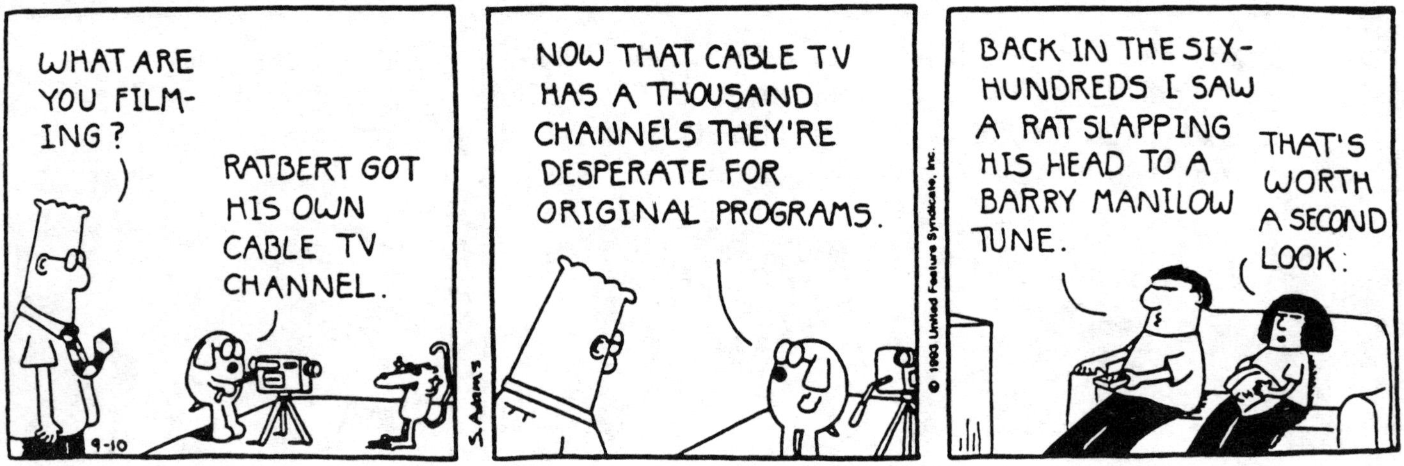
WHAT ARE YOU FILMING?
RATBERT GOT HIS OWN CABLE TV CHANNEL.
NOW THAT CABLE TV HAS A THOUSAND CHANNELS THEY'RE DESPERATE FOR ORIGINAL PROGRAMS.
BACK IN THE SIX-HUNDREDS I SAW A RAT SLAPPING HIS HEAD TO A BARRY MANILOW TUNE.
THAT'S WORTH A SECOND LOOK.
9-10
S. Adams
© 1993 United Feature Syndicate, Inc.

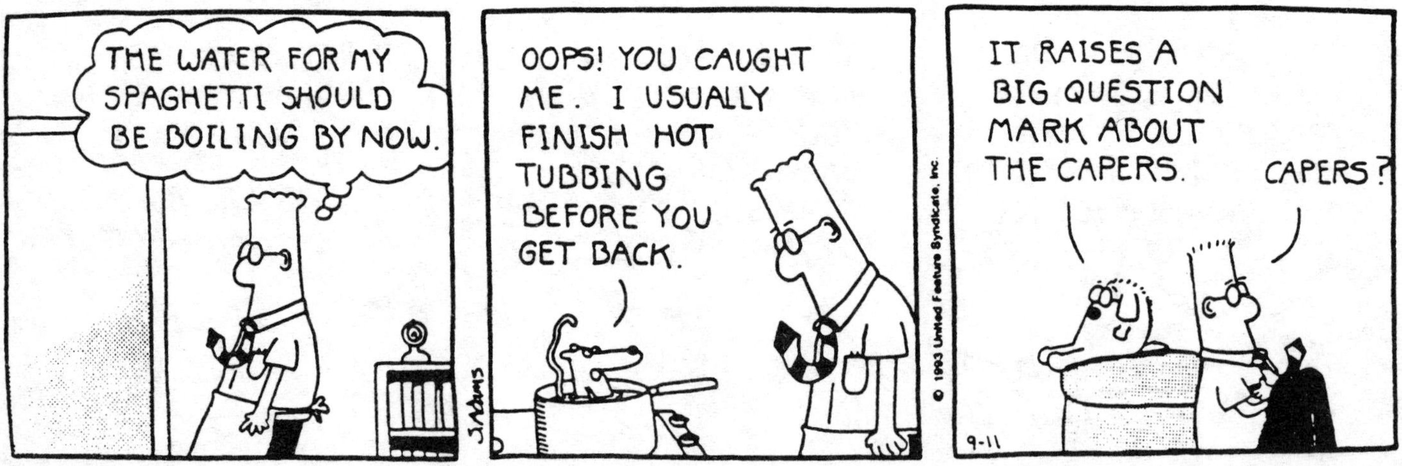
THE WATER FOR MY SPAGHETTI SHOULD BE BOILING BY NOW.
OOPS! YOU CAUGHT ME. I USUALLY FINISH HOT TUBBING BEFORE YOU GET BACK.
IT RAISES A BIG QUESTION MARK ABOUT THE CAPERS.
CAPERS?
S. Adams
9-11
© 1993 United Feature Syndicate, Inc.

NERVOUS ED, I'M ASSIGNING YOU TO A SPECIAL PROJECT.
S. Adams
SPECIAL ASSIGNMENT? THAT MEANS YOU DON'T HAVE ANY REAL WORK FOR ME.
EVERYBODY KNOWS THAT A SPECIAL ASSIGNMENT IS A KISS OF DEATH.
YOU'LL BE SHARING A CUBICLE WITH SIX OTHER EMPLOYEES WHO ARE ALSO ON SPECIAL ASSIGNMENT.
DON'T PANIC YET... MAYBE IT'S SOMETHING IMPORTANT... MAYBE IT'S SOMETHING THAT COULD MAKE AN IMPACT.
© 1993 United Feature Syndicate, Inc
YOUR ASSIGNMENT IS TO IMPROVE EMPLOYEE EMPOWERMENT.
9-12

THANKS FOR LETTING US WATCH.
DID YOU LIKE THE PART ABOUT SIX IN THE CUBICLE?

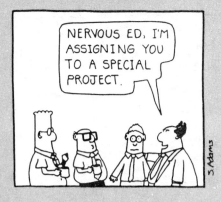

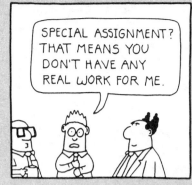

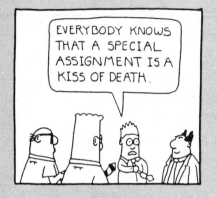

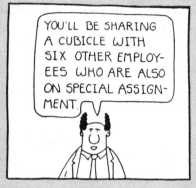

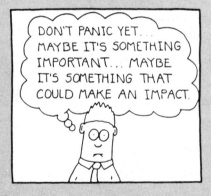

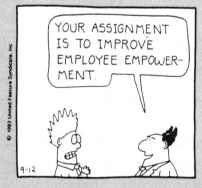

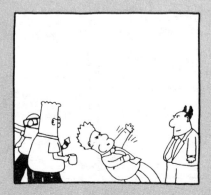

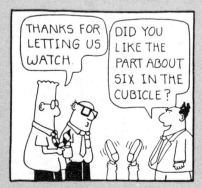

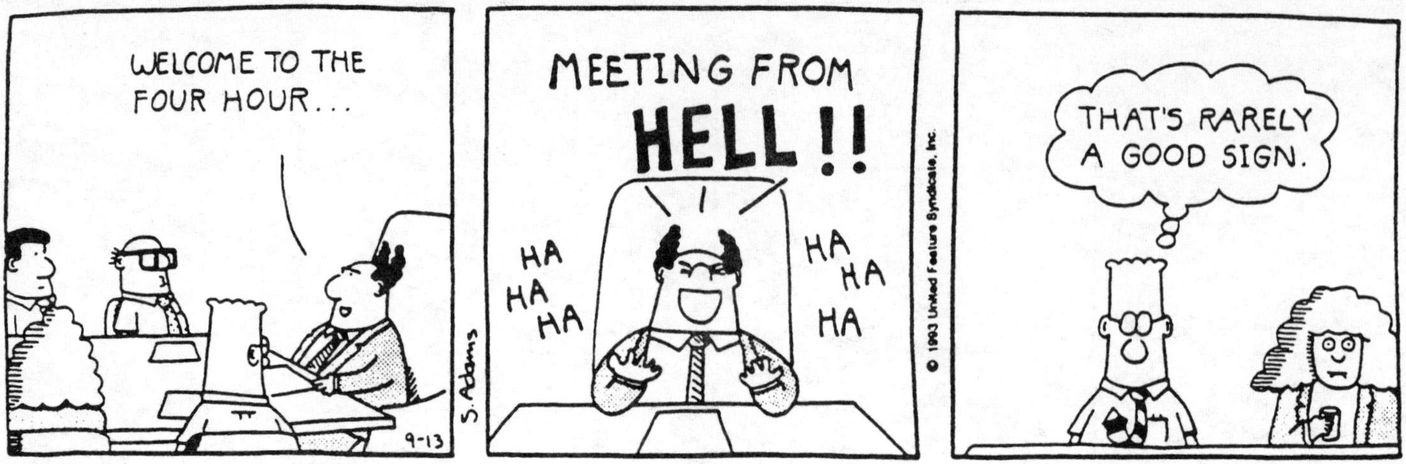
WELCOME TO THE FOUR HOUR...
MEETING FROM HELL!!
HA HA HA
HA HA HA
THAT'S RARELY A GOOD SIGN.
S. Adams 9-13
© 1993 United Feature Syndicate, Inc.

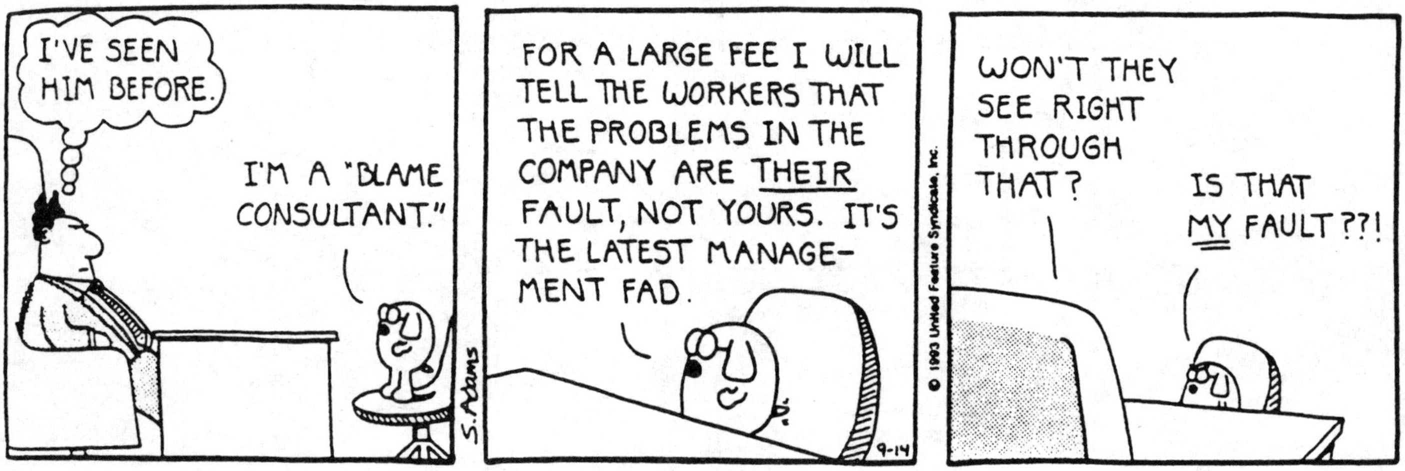
I'VE SEEN HIM BEFORE.
I'M A "BLAME CONSULTANT."
FOR A LARGE FEE I WILL TELL THE WORKERS THAT THE PROBLEMS IN THE COMPANY ARE THEIR FAULT, NOT YOURS. IT'S THE LATEST MANAGEMENT FAD.
WON'T THEY SEE RIGHT THROUGH THAT?
IS THAT MY FAULT??!
S. Adams 9-14
© 1993 United Feature Syndicate, Inc.

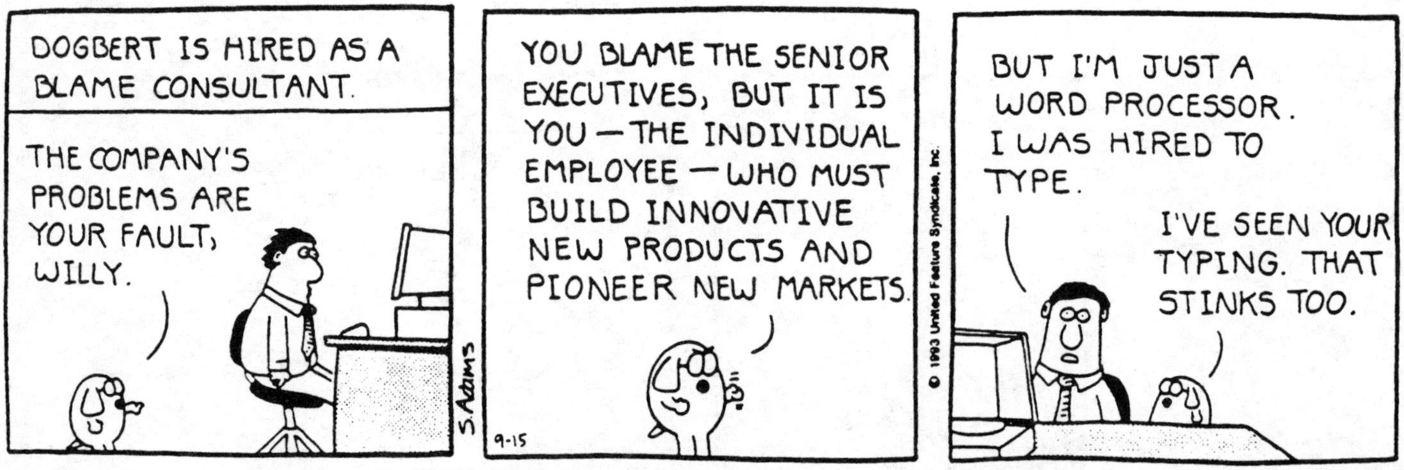
DOGBERT IS HIRED AS A BLAME CONSULTANT.
THE COMPANY'S PROBLEMS ARE YOUR FAULT, WILLY.
YOU BLAME THE SENIOR EXECUTIVES, BUT IT IS YOU — THE INDIVIDUAL EMPLOYEE — WHO MUST BUILD INNOVATIVE NEW PRODUCTS AND PIONEER NEW MARKETS.
BUT I'M JUST A WORD PROCESSOR. I WAS HIRED TO TYPE.
I'VE SEEN YOUR TYPING. THAT STINKS TOO.
S. Adams 9-15
© 1993 United Feature Syndicate, Inc.

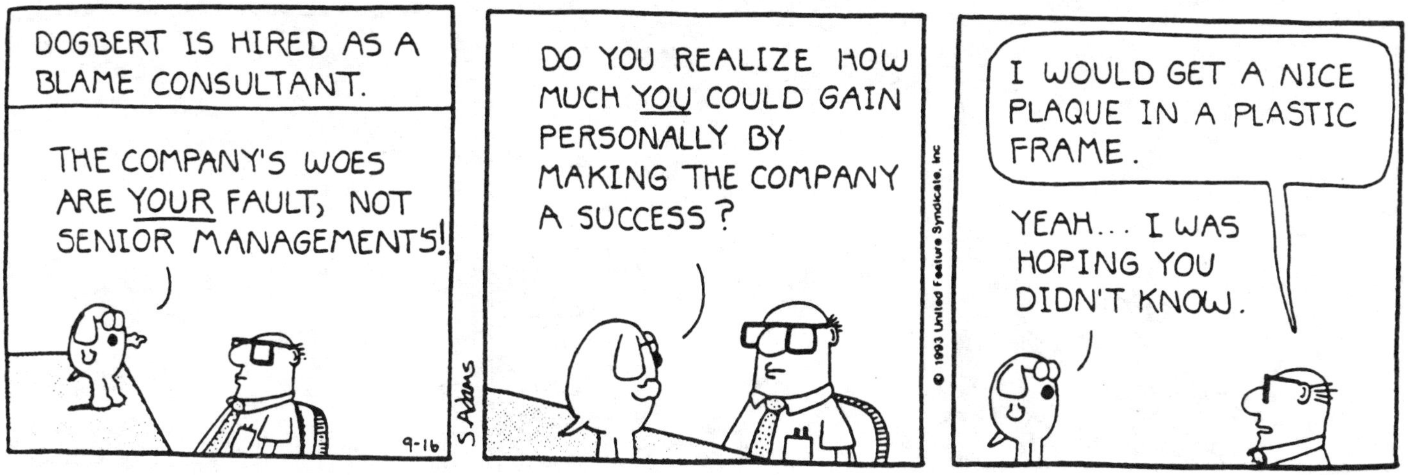
DOGBERT IS HIRED AS A BLAME CONSULTANT.
THE COMPANY'S WOES ARE YOUR FAULT, NOT SENIOR MANAGEMENT'S!
9-16
S. Adams
DO YOU REALIZE HOW MUCH YOU COULD GAIN PERSONALLY BY MAKING THE COMPANY A SUCCESS?
© 1993 United Feature Syndicate, Inc
I WOULD GET A NICE PLAQUE IN A PLASTIC FRAME.
YEAH... I WAS HOPING YOU DIDN'T KNOW.

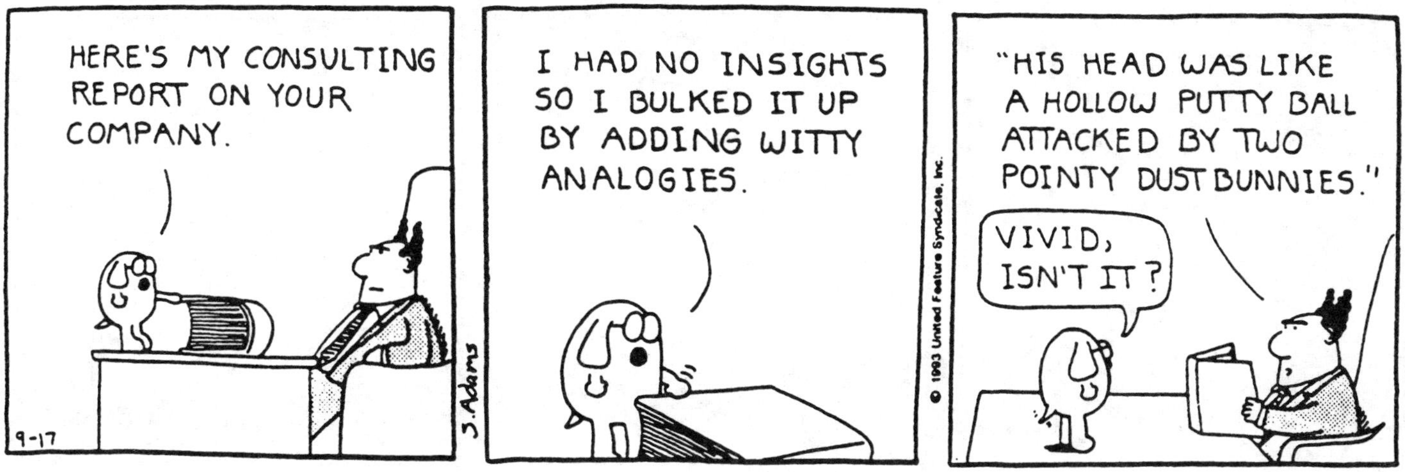
HERE'S MY CONSULTING REPORT ON YOUR COMPANY.
9-17
S. Adams
I HAD NO INSIGHTS SO I BULKED IT UP BY ADDING WITTY ANALOGIES.
© 1993 United Feature Syndicate, Inc.
"HIS HEAD WAS LIKE A HOLLOW PUTTY BALL ATTACKED BY TWO POINTY DUST BUNNIES."
VIVID, ISN'T IT?

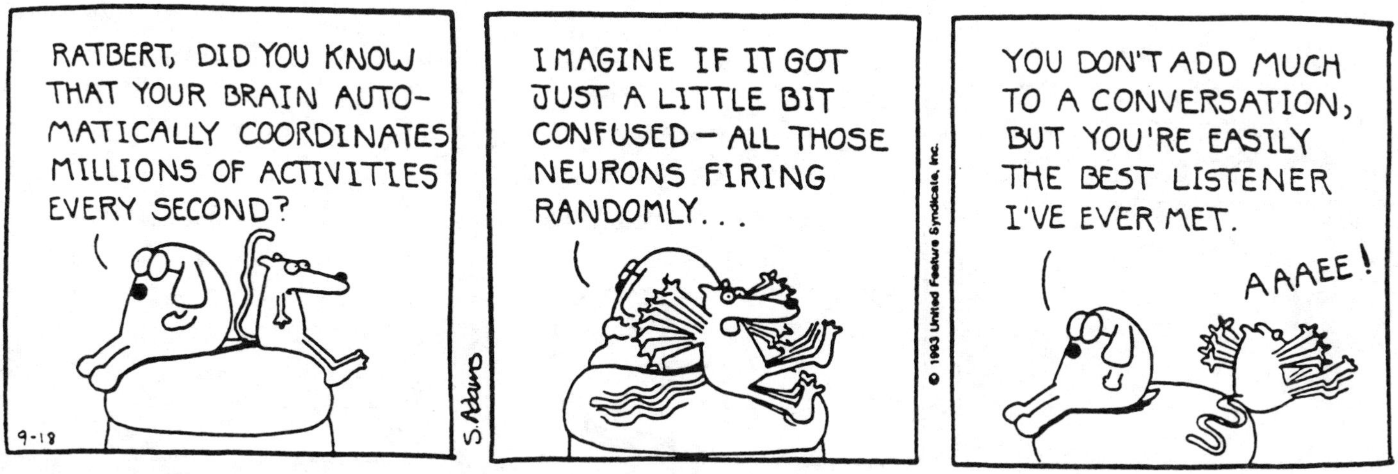
RATBERT, DID YOU KNOW THAT YOUR BRAIN AUTOMATICALLY COORDINATES MILLIONS OF ACTIVITIES EVERY SECOND?
9-18
S. Adams
IMAGINE IF IT GOT JUST A LITTLE BIT CONFUSED — ALL THOSE NEURONS FIRING RANDOMLY...
© 1993 United Feature Syndicate, Inc.
YOU DON'T ADD MUCH TO A CONVERSATION, BUT YOU'RE EASILY THE BEST LISTENER I'VE EVER MET.
AAAEE!

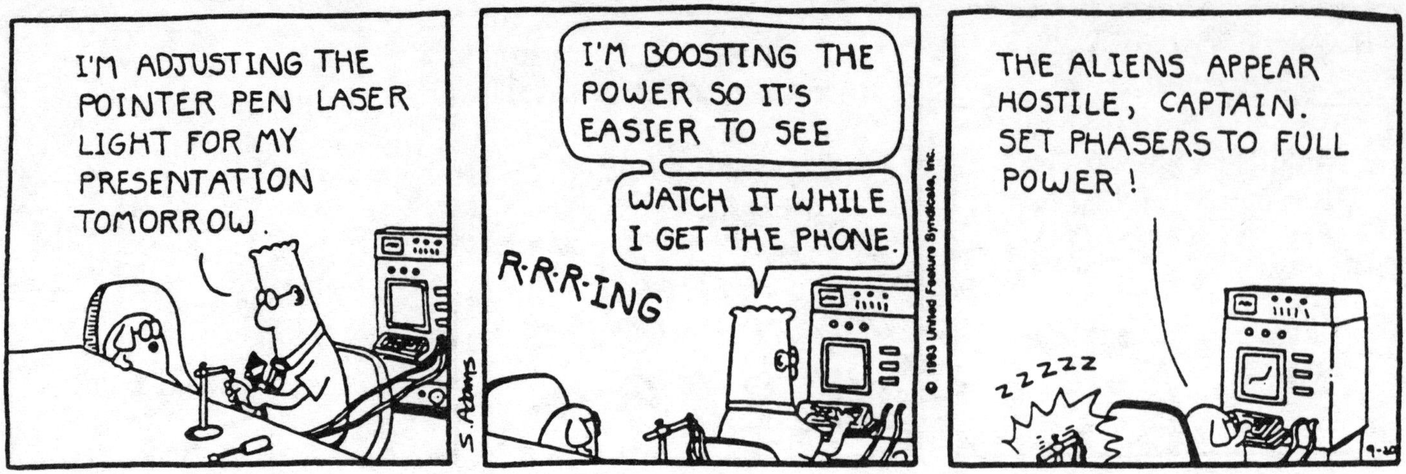
I'M ADJUSTING THE POINTER PEN LASER LIGHT FOR MY PRESENTATION TOMORROW.
S. Adams
I'M BOOSTING THE POWER SO IT'S EASIER TO SEE
WATCH IT WHILE I GET THE PHONE.
R-R-R-ING
© 1993 United Feature Syndicate, Inc.
THE ALIENS APPEAR HOSTILE, CAPTAIN. SET PHASERS TO FULL POWER!
ZZZZZ

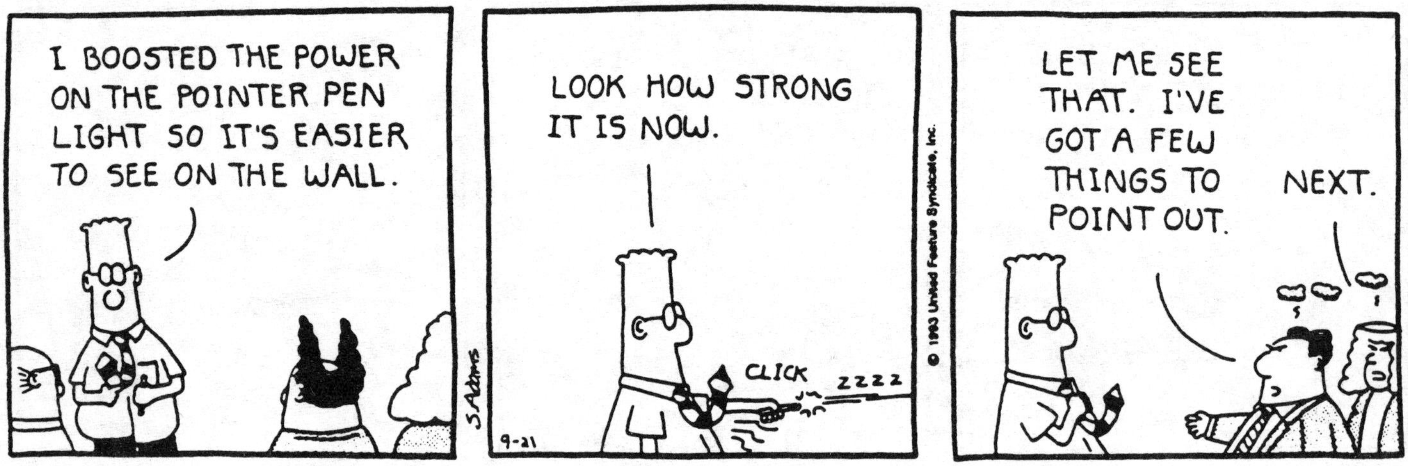
I BOOSTED THE POWER ON THE POINTER PEN LIGHT SO IT'S EASIER TO SEE ON THE WALL.
S. Adams
LOOK HOW STRONG IT IS NOW.
CLICK
ZZZZ
9-21
© 1993 United Feature Syndicate, Inc.
LET ME SEE THAT. I'VE GOT A FEW THINGS TO POINT OUT.
NEXT.

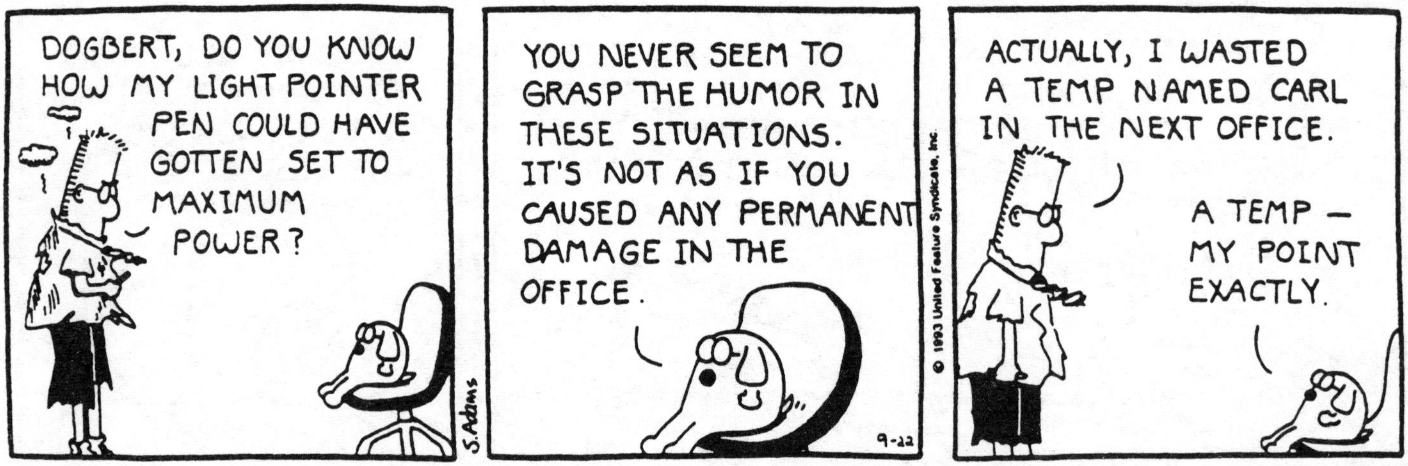
DOGBERT, DO YOU KNOW HOW MY LIGHT POINTER PEN COULD HAVE GOTTEN SET TO MAXIMUM POWER?
S. Adams
YOU NEVER SEEM TO GRASP THE HUMOR IN THESE SITUATIONS. IT'S NOT AS IF YOU CAUSED ANY PERMANENT DAMAGE IN THE OFFICE.
9-22
© 1993 United Feature Syndicate, Inc.
ACTUALLY, I WASTED A TEMP NAMED CARL IN THE NEXT OFFICE.
A TEMP — MY POINT EXACTLY.

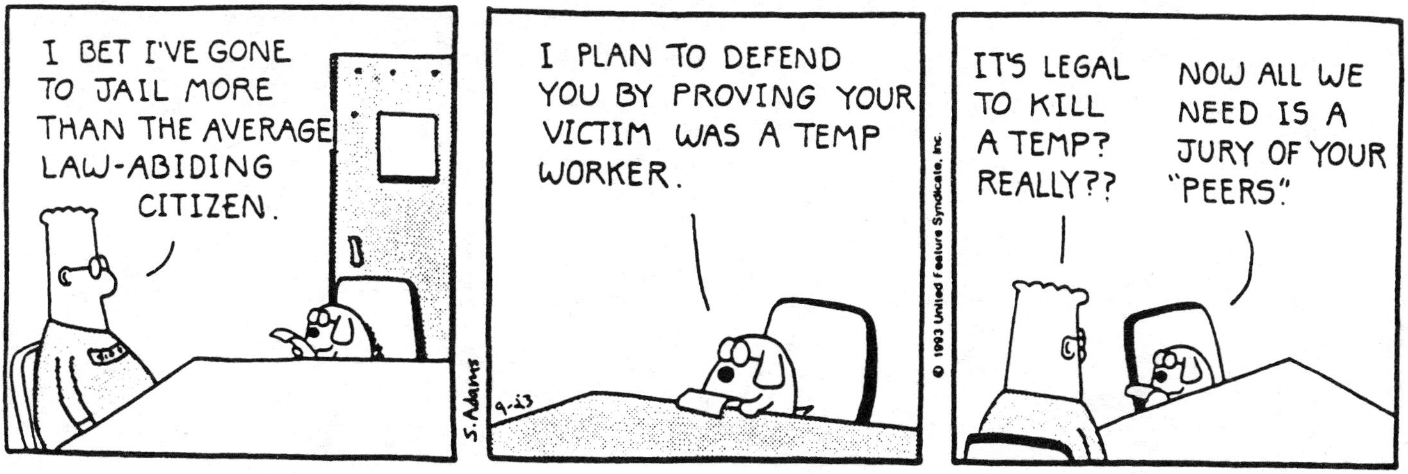
I BET I'VE GONE TO JAIL MORE THAN THE AVERAGE LAW-ABIDING CITIZEN.
S. Adams
9-23
I PLAN TO DEFEND YOU BY PROVING YOUR VICTIM WAS A TEMP WORKER.
© 1993 United Feature Syndicate, Inc.
IT'S LEGAL TO KILL A TEMP? REALLY??
NOW ALL WE NEED IS A JURY OF YOUR "PEERS."

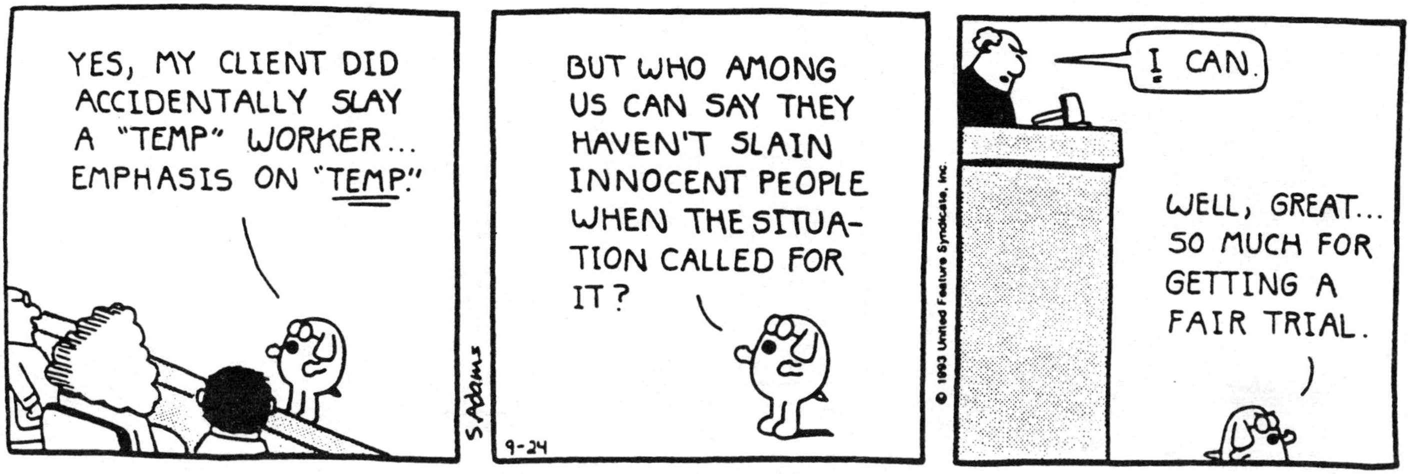
YES, MY CLIENT DID ACCIDENTALLY SLAY A "TEMP" WORKER... EMPHASIS ON "TEMP."
S. Adams
9-24
BUT WHO AMONG US CAN SAY THEY HAVEN'T SLAIN INNOCENT PEOPLE WHEN THE SITUATION CALLED FOR IT?
© 1993 United Feature Syndicate, Inc.
I CAN.
WELL, GREAT... SO MUCH FOR GETTING A FAIR TRIAL.

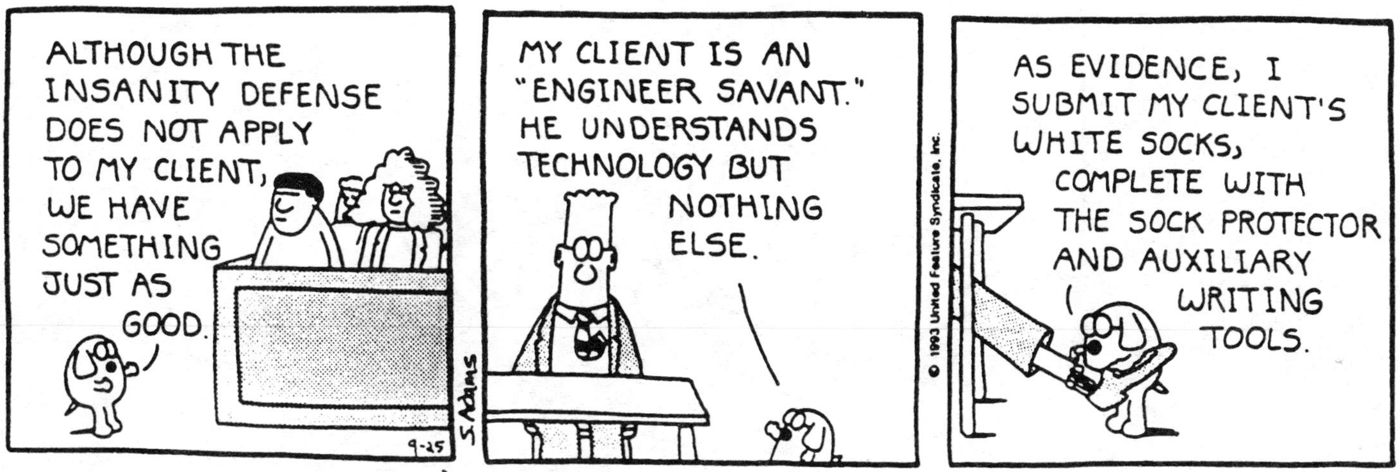
ALTHOUGH THE INSANITY DEFENSE DOES NOT APPLY TO MY CLIENT, WE HAVE SOMETHING JUST AS GOOD.
9-25
S. Adams
MY CLIENT IS AN "ENGINEER SAVANT." HE UNDERSTANDS TECHNOLOGY BUT NOTHING ELSE.
© 1993 United Feature Syndicate, Inc.
AS EVIDENCE, I SUBMIT MY CLIENT'S WHITE SOCKS, COMPLETE WITH THE SOCK PROTECTOR AND AUXILIARY WRITING TOOLS.

WE FIND THE DEFENDANT INNOCENT BY REASON OF BEING GENERALLY CLUELESS.
9-27
S. Adams
I KNOW I SHOULD BE HAPPY, BUT IT'S SO INSULTING... WHAT WILL ALL MY FRIENDS THINK?
© 1993 United Feature Syndicate, Inc.
I CALL THAT A WIN-WIN SCENARIO.
...NOT THAT I HAVE ANY.

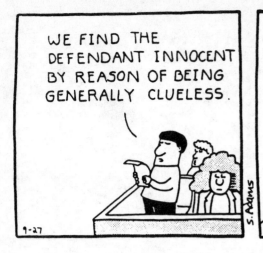

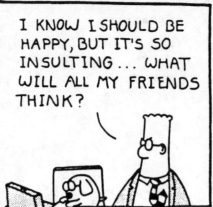

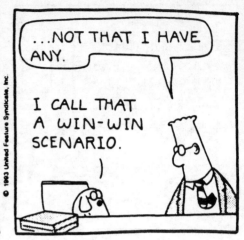

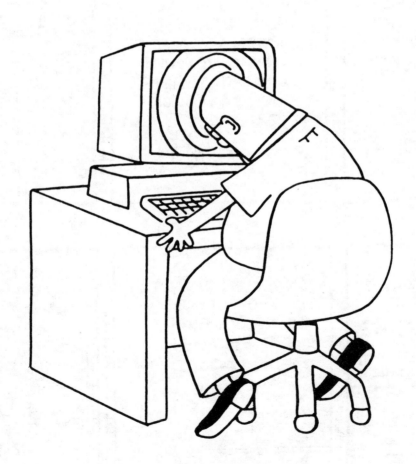